East Granby

the evolution of a Connecticut town

East Granby

the evolution of a Connecticut town

by
Mary Jane Springman
and
Betty Finnell Guinan

Published for the
EAST GRANBY HISTORICAL COMMITTEE
by
PHOENIX PUBLISHING
Canaan, New Hampshire

Springman, Mary Jane.
East Granby
Bibliography: p. 316
Includes index.
1. East Granby (Conn.)—History. I. Guinan, Betty Finnell. II. East Granby Historical Committee. III. Title.
F104.E1S67 1983 974.6'2 83-6325
ISBN 0-914016-95-4

Printed in the United States of America
by Courier Printing Company
Binding by New Hampshire Bindery
Design by A. L. Morris

CONTENTS

ACKNOWLEDGMENTS

The members of the East Granby Historical Committee would like to join the authors in thanking those who contributed their time and skills that this book might be written and published. The majority of the volunteers were residents of East Granby and many were committee members, but quite a few were residents of other towns. In addition, the committee would like to thank the staffs of the Connecticut State Library and the Connecticut Historical Society for their invaluable assistance with research.

Researchers and interviewers

David H. Baldwin, Robert Barry, Jeanne Daggett, Ruth Gledhill, Elsie S. Granger, Lawrence W. Lang, Betty Micheli, Alice F. Newman, Thomas F. Newman, Jeffrey E. Phillips, Bonney E. Prout, Eugene J. Riccio, Helen K. Root, Evelyn M. Samsel, Kathryn A. Samsel, Lawrence E. Scanlon, Roger H. Stowell, Patricia Thayer, L. Mazie Viets, Gail Westfall, Virginia Wileikis, Ethel H. Wilson.

Interviewees

Norman I. Adams, Hattie T. Barber, Edward A. Bartkus, John G. Bazyk, Rollin W. Cowles, Stewart C. Cowles, Mae S. Eames, Gertrude M. Fletcher, Arthur Fox, Douglas M. Gay, H. Clifford Goslee, Rebecca P. Holcomb, Hazel G. Lampson, Warren E. Lampson, Peter J. May, Mildred McKinnie, Joseph L. McKinnie, Adelaide M. Millea, Helen G. Moody, Florence G. Porter, Helen K. Root, Edgar H. Seymour, R. Dudley Seymour, Kenneth M. Seymour, Maida G. Seymour, Louise J. Sharp, Marie C. Sheldon, Roger H. Stowell, Olin C. Turner, Dan W. Viets, L. Mazie Viets, Miriam W. Viets, Rushia S. West, Ina C. Wilcox.

Advisors

James W. Bingham, Geology; Edward P. Hogan, the Cowles Manufacturing Company; Raymond A. Horn, Ruth S. Hummel, and Melvin J. Schneidermeyer, the Farmington Canal; Thomas F. Newman, the Civil War; Lyman G. Potter, architecture of the 1830 Congregational meetinghouse; John W. Shannahan, Newgate prison and copper mine; William M. Vibert, the Revolutionary War.

Photographers and illustrators

Joyce Bennett, Dan Damer, Harold C. Hansen, Barbara Marks, Edward F. Phillips, Ralph Shepherd, Lester Smith, Alan B. Viets, Walter Wick.

Editors

Charles E. Funk, literary editor and indexer of the text/Mary Newman, copy editor.

Indexers and typists

Marlene K. Alexander, Jeannette D. DaMotta, Sandra Graves, Lynn F. Lockwood, Carole McLellan, Arthur M. Micheli, Carol Price, Evelyn M. Samsel, Ruth S. Westervelt.

Publication consultant

Robert R. Patterson.

Publication committee

William S. Mayer, chairman; William O. Newman, treasurer and present treasurer to the East Granby Historical Committee; Amy M. Hunderlach, Gordon F. Granger, George L. Guinan.

COMMITTEE MEMBERS

RECOGNIZING that the style of life in East Granby had changed markedly since they were children, H. Clifford Goslee and several other longtime residents of the town decided that they would like a book to serve as a record of how they and preceeding generations had lived. In January 1971, at the suggestion of Mr. Goslee, First Selectman William S. Mayer approved the formation of a non-profit committee to collect information and illustrative material.

The enthusiasm generated by the project soon swelled the group to an unwieldy number. Consequently, when the East Granby Historical Committee became an official town body by a vote at a town meeting in 1973, the committee was limited to seven members appointed by the board of selectmen. The number was increased to eight at a later town meeting.

The members of the original committee and those appointed to the official town committee are:

Original Committee

Ann C. Cahill
H. Clifford Goslee, past chairman
Betty Guinan, secretary
Charles R. Kingsbury
Helen K. Root
Walter Wileikis
Ethel H. Wilson, past chairman

Official Town Committee

Betty Guinan, secretary 1973-83
Helen K. Root, past treasurer 1973-83
Lawrence E. Scanlon 1973-74
Mary Jane Springman 1973-80
Roger H. Stowell 1973-83
Walter Wileikis, chairman 1973-83
Ethel H. Wilson, past chairman 1973-75
Edward F. Phillips 1974-79
Alice F. Newman 1975-77
Marlene K. Alexander 1977-78
Ralph H. Viets 1979-83
Charles E. Funk 1980-83
Amy M. Hunderlach 1980-83
Thomas F. Howard 1982-83

PREFACE

THE TOWN of East Granby has undergone an evolutionary process similar to that of many Connecticut towns that began as sections of older towns. In years past, events which took place in the geographic area that is now East Granby were interwoven with the history of its parent towns—Windsor, Simsbury, and Granby. By fortuitously placing his house where he did when he left Windsor, John Griffin became the first settler, not of one town, but three. Likewise, the mining on Copper Hill and Newgate Prison are as much a part of the history of Simsbury and Granby as they are of East Granby.

Studying the histories of the parent towns and disentangling the people who lived in and the events that took place in the region now East Granby were the first challenges we faced when undertaking this history. The voluminous history of Windsor by Henry R. Stiles; Simsbury's three comprehensive histories by Lucius I. Barber, John E. Ellsworth, and William M. Vibert; and the collection of essays published by the Salmon Brook Historical Society of Granby were invaluable for this exercise.

The most helpful published sources by far, however, were the pamphlets written by Albert Carlos Bates (1865-1954), an East Granby native who served for many years as librarian of the Connecticut Historical Society. This book would have been far less than it is without his carefully researched texts about the Turkey Hills Ecclesiastical Society, the predecessor of the Town of East Granby, and his collection of manuscripts such as diaries, account books, letters, and town, church, and school records.

Using the primary sources collected by Mr. Bates and many more graciously provided by interested people along with tape-recorded interviews with longtime residents, we addressed our final and most rewarding challenge: trying to enlarge upon what had already been published about the town. As expected, we did not uncover any major personage or event hitherto totally unknown, but we and our zealous researchers unearthed a wealth of details that we hope will make the town of generations past more understandable and vivid to the townspeople of today. We also hope that as our readers follow the evolution of East Granby from a lonely outpost to the community it is now that they will gain a new perspective on the many state and national events that affected the town and its people.

In closing we wish to extend personal thanks to those already mentioned in the list of acknowledgments who have worked with us through the years. For the last two years of the project, our literary editor, Charles E. Funk, met with us weekly to review our work and help with revisions. Mary Newman called on her long experience as a professional copy editor for several major New York publishing houses and spent countless hours keeping the text's style consistent with her high standards. We are also grateful for the approval and support we received from A. L. Morris, Publisher, and Adrian A. Paradis, Editor, of Phoenix Publishing, the members of the East Granby Historical Committee, and our understanding families.

The study of this town's history has intrigued us and enhanced our lives for more than a decade. We have looked forward to this day when you, the reader, would pick up our book and begin to share our discoveries and enthusiasm about East Granby.

Mary Jane Springman
Betty Guinan

March 31, 1983

East Granby

the evolution of a Connecticut town

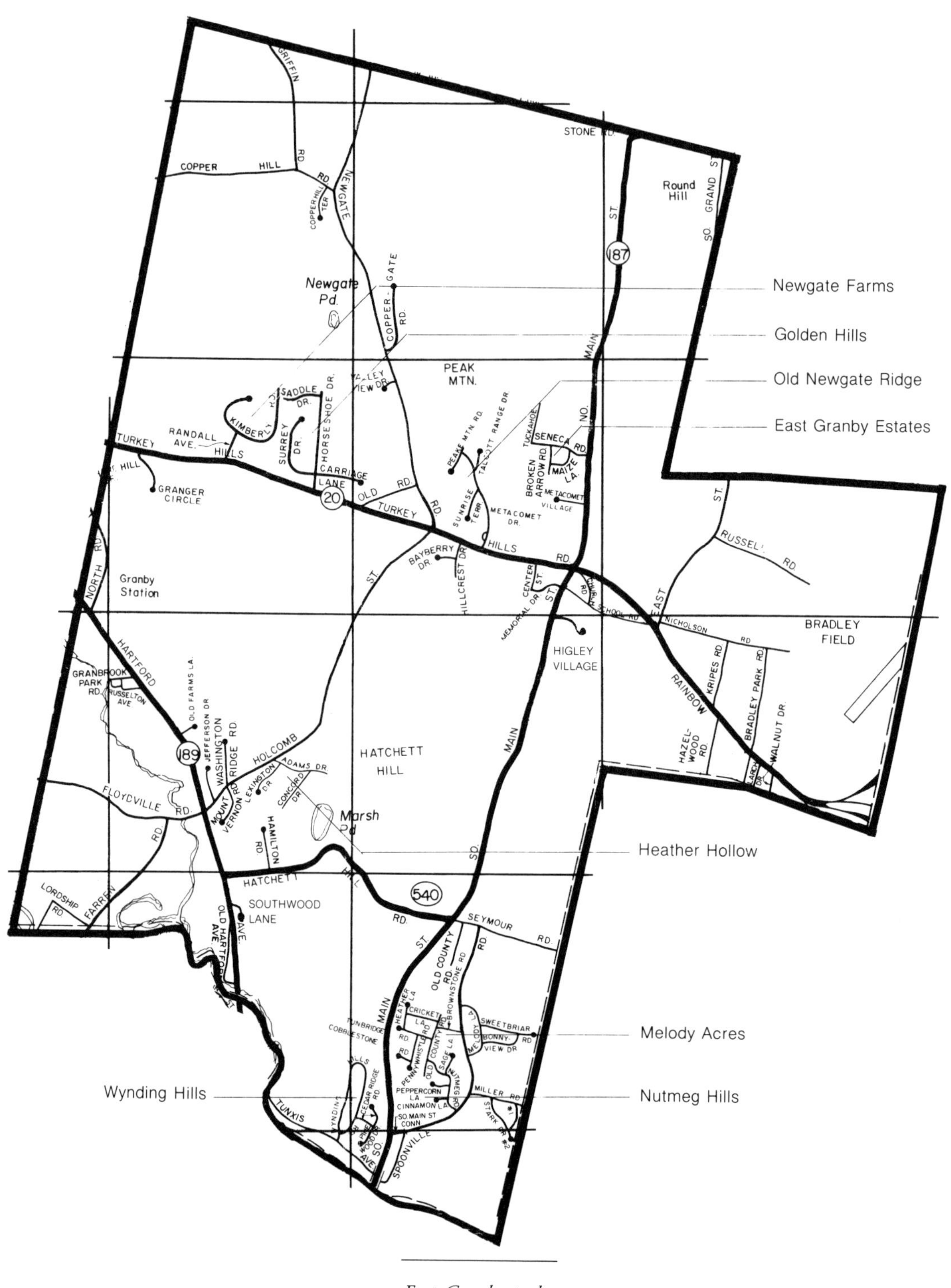

East Granby today

Prologue

Origins and Antecedents

The townspeople of East Granby, Connecticut, formerly the Turkey Hills Ecclesiastical Society, share a community experience that stretches back almost to the beginning of the English colonies in America. The land they have since inherited was then a vast, forested wilderness challenging the endurance and ingenuity of all who came here. How the first settlers and their successors tamed the wilderness and built the town is a more-than-300-year adventure.

THE EARLIEST SETTLERS of the East Granby area came from the town of Windsor. Windsor was founded in 1633 by a company of fur traders from the thirteen-year-old Plymouth Colony (later absorbed into Massachusetts Colony). The men set up a trading post where the Farmington River enters the Connecticut River about 53 miles upstream from Long Island Sound.

The area's River Indians had encouraged the English to come to the Windsor site, which they called Matianuck. These scattered and relatively peaceful tribes hoped that alliance with the English would protect them from the aggressive Pequot tribe who lived along Long Island Sound. The Pequots were allied with the Dutch, who had just built a fort about 6 miles downriver where the City of Hartford stands today.

For a while the fur trade was brisk. The natives brought the traders beaver pelts by the thousands as well as raccoon, otter, muskrat, mink, and fox which they trapped all over the surrounding territory. A few years after the traders arrived, however, settlers surged into the area and the Indians and animals alike began a slow retreat.

The first settlers to arrive were a group of Puritan families who had journeyed from England on the ship *Mary and John* and had founded the town of Dorchester in the Massachusetts Bay Colony in 1630. About five years later some of these families migrated to the trading post to build the town that they named Windsor.

The settlers had in their ranks persons with all the skills and attributes deemed necessary in those times to form a proper British settlement. They included farmers, craftsmen, minor government officials, military officers, ministers, able single men, and growing families. Some may have been sons other than the eldest, who were excluded from inheriting their fathers' estates under the English law of primogeniture. Many settlers, moreover, had been persecuted in England because of their religious beliefs.

This group and a similar one, a contingent from the company known as "the Lords and Gentlemen" headed by John Winthrop, Jr., set straightaway to tame their wilderness and bring a measure of order and security to Windsor and the young Connecticut Colony. Windsor men fought in 1637 in the brief but bloody offensive action known as the Pequot War. In 1639 delegates from Windsor, Hartford, and Wethersfield adopted the Fundamental Orders of Connecticut, the expression of their unique plan for self-government which is celebrated as the first written constitution of any government, anywhere.

As emigration from England increased, Windsor grew in size and importance. It became a thriving port which supplied oceangoing vessels with cargoes of native raw materials to be used by manufacturers abroad. As a result of the growth in population, the most desirable land in Windsor was soon claimed. Sons and daughters of the original settlers and new arrivals to the colonies had to look elsewhere for land.

In their search for new resources for trade and new land to homestead, many settlers setting out from Windsor followed the course of the Farmington River west toward the Massaco Indian territory. The Massaco land, which included much of present-day Simsbury and Canton and parts of Barkhamsted and the Granbys, later formed the bulk of the far-reaching colonial Town of Simsbury. The portion of this town bordering Windsor eventually became the Town of East Granby. White men had scouted this land as early as 1643 and found it good. About 1664 one of these men brought his family from Windsor to settle. His name was John Griffin.

The Lay of The Land

Virgin forest covered the East Granby area when John Griffin first saw it. The mountain ridge that runs like a spine down the length of today's town dominated all. This ridge is valued today for its scenic lookouts and hiking trails, but the colonials viewed it as an unfortunate impediment to their travel. The difficulty they had crossing it influenced the development of the town.

The mountain ridge is part of the Talcott Range, which extends from the Mount Tom Range in Massachusetts to East Rock in New Haven, Connecticut. The part of the ridge that reaches an elevation of 730 feet northwest of the town's center is called Peak Mountain. The early settlers sometimes called it Greenstone Mountain and referred to its eastern slope as Turkey Hills. A precipitous face of exposed rock on the mountain's west side has become known as Newgate Cliffs. Lying west of the cliffs is a smaller ridge, later called the Copper Hill.

At Hatchet Hill to the south, the ridge rises to its second highest elevation in town. Curiously, the earliest known map of the area gives the name Hatchet Hill to the 450-foot rise south of Hatchet Hill Road, while modern maps apply the name to the 490-foot elevation north of the road. Tradition holds that an Indian traded the land that includes the rises for a hatchet. The name can be traced back to the 18th century.

In its entirety, the section of the Talcott Range within East Granby has traditionally been called, simply, "the Mountain."

In prehistoric times, great mountains rose on the eastern and western perimeters of what is now Connecticut. Debris from these eroding mountains formed layers of sediment across the floor of the valley between them. The sediment hardened into rock, forming the typical local sandstone that was used in the brownstone buildings popular in past decades.

The top layer of sedimentary rock contains the fossilized records of prehistoric

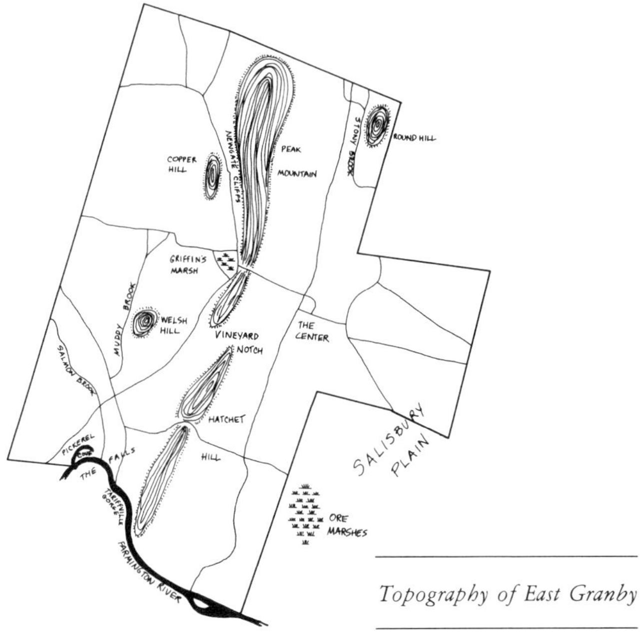

Topography of East Granby

life in the area. Dinosaur footprints have been found in sandstone in East Granby Estates (a housing area off North Main Street) and along the Farmington River.

Between the layers of sedimentary rock are three layers of igneous rock formed from lava flows during ancient volcanic eruptions. These layers are mined for traprock used widely in modern road construction. The middle and greatest of these layers is up to 300 feet thick.

About 170 million years ago, during the phenomenon known as the Palisade disturbance, the sediment-lava beds of the valley floor tilted along faults. Erosion over millions of years emphasized the igneous rocks as ridges. Thus, the Talcott Mountain ridge came into being, and with it, East Granby's Mountain.

Like the many ridges from Nova Scotia to Virginia which have the same origin, the Mountain stretches north and south and has a gentle slope on its eastern side and a sharp drop on its western. Erosion created breaks on the ridge line, which became natural sites of east-west passages. Among these are the Tariffville Gorge, Vineyard Notch, and the pass through which Hatchet Hill Road runs. There are also smaller ridges made of thinner lava flows paralleling the main one, such as the ridge that runs under the East Granby High School.

At the end of the Ice Age, some 20,000 to 30,000 years ago, the Talcott Mountain ridge divided the water melting from the glaciers that covered the area. From the eastern side of the ridge, the water ran into ancient Lake Hitchcock that formed in what is now the Connecticut River Valley. Before the river broke through and drained its water into Long Island Sound, glacial Lake Hitchcock was held back by a great dam of glacial debris where the towns of Rocky Hill and Glastonbury are now. The lake, which varied from 3 to 10 miles wide, extended as far as northern Massachusetts.

On the western side of the ridge, the glacial runoff flowed south along the Farm-

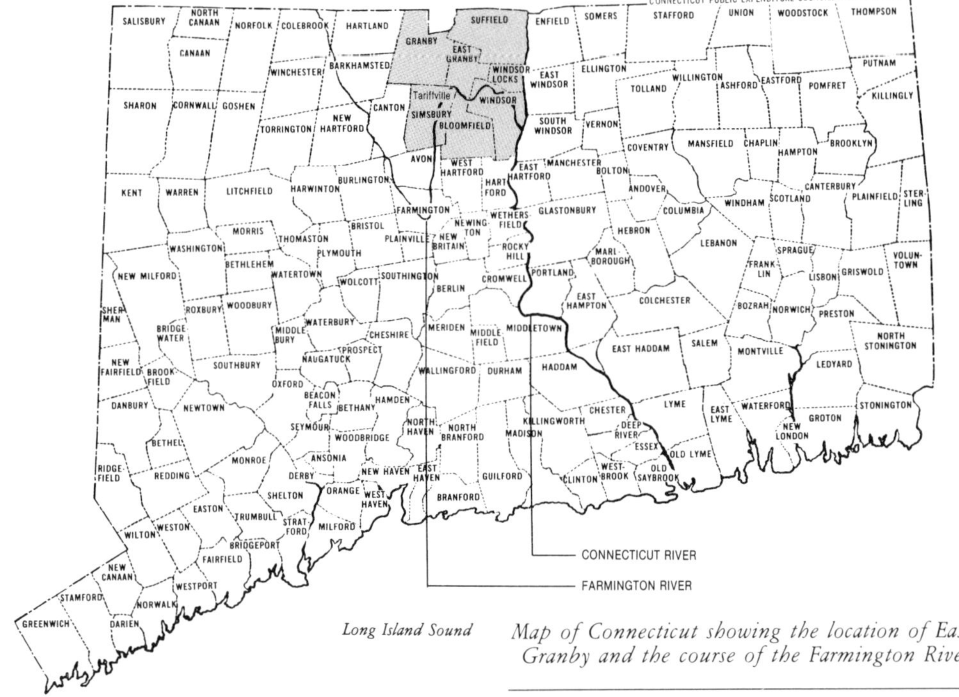

Map of Connecticut showing the location of East Granby and the course of the Farmington River

ington Valley and the present Quinnipiac River and emptied into Long Island Sound. In time, glacial deposits formed a dam near the present Town of Plainville, and the water backed up to the north to form another lake. As the glacial ice melted, the trapped water found a new outlet through the ridge's fault between present-day East Granby and the Village of Tariffville in the northeast corner of present-day Simsbury.

After the lake emptied, the new course of the Farmington River became apparent. It flowed south to where its course had been blocked, then switched back in Farmington and wound north, then east through the Tariffville Gorge and into Lake Hitchcock. As the river entered the lake, it left deposits of sand that formed a delta. Bradley International Airport and the easternmost portion of East Granby are on this sandy delta land, named Salisbury Plain by the first white settlers. The runoff from melting glaciers left deposits of sand, gravel, and rock called eskers and kames on both sides of the Mountain. Round Hill, in the northeast part of town, is a drumlin—a composite of compacted glacial material ranging in size from silt to boulders—which rises more that 50 feet above its bedrock base.

The Farmington River, which forms the town's southern boundary, was alternately called "Windsor Ferry River" or "the Rivulet" by the colonials and "Tunxis-sepos," the turning place of the little river, by the Indians. This river was the avenue along which the first white men came from Windsor and a source of power for the mills that eventually were built.

In the 1640s the Farmington River flowed through a primeval wilderness that was part of the virgin forest that stretched almost uniformly from New England to the Mississippi River. This forest nurtured trees as tall as twenty-story buildings. Many were

15 feet in circumference. What is more, these giants grew so densely in places that the summer sun did not reach below their canopy. The accumulated humus of centuries, a spongy, water-laden layer of decaying vegetation and moss, carpeted the forest floor.

The area's first settlers plunged into the cool, quiet solemnity of the forest. Those strong enough to cope with the isolation, the lack of civilization's refinements, the unfamiliar ways of the Indians, and the fickleness of nature reaped a bountiful harvest of timber. Some prospered by exporting ships' masts, tar, potash, barrel staves, planks, and other wood products which England needed because her forests had become all but exhausted.

The forest also provided the colonists with lumber for homes and meetinghouses, mills and tools, docks and bridges. It was a seemingly inexhaustible source of fuel for home and industry. And most important, after the timber was felled, the forest floor became rich cropland. In addition to the rivers and forests, the many local marshes proved valuable to the colonists. Waterfowl and a variety of game inhabited them. Marsh bottoms sometimes yielded iron in the form of bog ore. When drained, marshland made rich farm soil.

The Indians

Artifacts that the Indians left behind indicate that no tribe ever had a permanent winter village within the area that is now East Granby, but at least three had hunting camps here. The Congregational Church centennial address given by the Reverend Charles Chamberlain in 1876 mentions two traditionally known camp locations. One is on the south side of Round Hill west of South Grand Street and the other is to the south of Russell Road.

The Massaco Indians, whose main village was in the present-day Weatogue section of Simsbury, hunted in the western part of the town. Experts consider this group a branch of the larger Tunxis tribe based in the area that is now the Town of Farmington.

The Poquonock Indians held the eastern portion of East Granby. Their main settlement was near the Farmington River at the site of the present Village of Poquonock. Both the Massacoes and the Poquonocks were part of a group known as River Indians. Because of similarities in their dialects, some scientists classify them as part of the Wappinger Confederacy. When the first settlers arrived, this confederacy numbered about 5000 persons living in the southern Connecticut River Valley and west to the Hudson River.*

The Agawam Indians claimed the northern segment of the town. They were a sub-tribe of the Pocomtock Confederacy in Massachusetts whose headquarters were in the Springfield-Deerfield vicinity. They had several villages and numerous campsites; one was near the Congamond Lakes. Their hunting territory in Connecticut included Enfield, Suffield, Hartland, and Somers, as well as the Granbys.

Although the Indians spent the winter elsewhere, the spring spawning run of shad and salmon up the Farmington River brought the men to a fishing camp at the rapids along the town's southern boundary. Here and along Salmon Brook they caught fish and eels with nets, hooks, and spears. Lamprey eels congregated on rocks above and

*Modern authorities claim the Indian population was rather sparse. Only 15,000 to 18,000 Indians lived in all of New England after the great 1616-17 epidemic which killed about a third of their former number. Another epidemic, among the local Indians in 1633-34, was recorded by the first Windsor settlers.

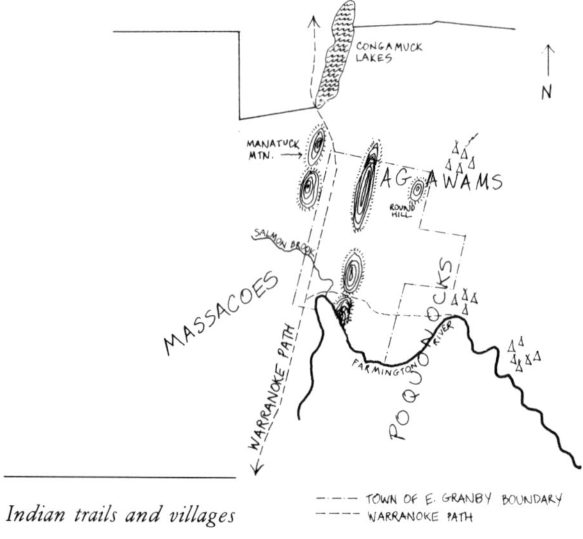

Indian trails and villages

below the rapids in the Tariffville Gorge.

For centuries local streams and marshes drew Indian hunters dressed in breechclouts and moccasins and smeared head to toe with bear grease to ward off mosquitos. Here they bagged the swamp creatures: waterfowl, turtles, frogs, snakes, beaver, otter, and muskrat. They also tracked deer, bear, fox, wolves, and the occasional panther and moose. Hundreds of species of birds, including wild turkeys, lived in or migrated through the hunting grounds. The Indians of southern New England prized cloaks woven with wild turkey feathers.

The Indians did some hunting with bows and arrows, but more often trapped their game. Hunting parties would drive their prey into narrowing, funnel-shaped corridors fashioned from the undergrowth. Some of the hunters waited behind blinds at the outlet for the kill. At times the hunting parties were made up of visiting Indians who came to share the area's bounty. New Haven Colony records show that Indians in the Windsor vicinity had a pact with those in Milford to visit one another to hunt and fish.

While the men hunted, the women cultivated vegetables, mostly native corn, beans, and squash. They planted their crops on the fertile flood plains along the rivers. The men might help with farming when the need arose, and only men tended the tobacco crop. All work was done with stone, wood, bone, or shell implements, as the Indians had no iron. All food to be stored for winter was dried or smoked, for the Indians had neither salt nor vinegar.

Indians of this region built dome-shaped wigwams in their permanent villages. They embedded sapling trees in the ground to form the round perimeter of the wigwam and bent the treetops together and tied them. Then they fastened bark and grass mats on this framework. Since the Indians used indoor fires on occasion, they left a hole at the top of the structure to allow smoke to escape. Although they were sometimes smoky, the wigwams were snug and warm. For their seasonal farming and hunting settlements, the Indians used small, easily dismantled, portable wigwams or huts.

A map drafted by an authority on Connecticut Indians, the late Mathias Spiess of Manchester, shows two major Indian trails in the East Granby area in the 1600s. According to Spiess, these thoroughfares were for messengers and the seasonal migration of tribes going between villages and campgrounds. The north-south trail, called the Warranoke or Hampton-Westfield Path, passed through the extreme western portion of East Granby. It was a branch of the Quinnipiac Trail, which led from New Haven to Canada. The east-west trail led from the Warranoke Path through the fault in the mountain ridge at Hatchet Hill and on to the Poquonock village.

Local residents have found Indian relics west of the Mountain along what is believed to be an Indian hunting path. The trail of reported artifacts extends from the Farmington River north through the Copper Hill section of town. However, the Metacomet Trail, which runs along the top of the Mountain and bears King Philip's Indian name, Metacom, was neither created nor used by the Indians. It was blazed in the 1930s by Boy Scouts. Indian trails generally went through lowlands.

Each local tribe or clan was led by a sachem, or chief—a position acquired by birthright. Members of the tribe could choose a sachem from among siblings, however, and occasionally one would be a woman if she were the only suitable member of the established royal family. The sachem was aided by a group of men called sagamores. Although the sachem exercised leadership, tribal decisions were made by general agreement.

In some areas of New England there was great rivalry and distrust among tribes, and the Indians frequently fought with one another and the colonists. The natives of this area, though they vied with other tribes, were relatively peaceful and friendly toward the English. On every occasion when the local Indians disputed the English settlers' right to parcels of land, the claim was settled by negotiation. When the local colonists worried about an Indian attack, they worried most about raiding parties from distant tribes.

About 1660 some of the Indian leaders in New England became alarmed at the encroachment of the swelling English population. The alcohol introduced by the English debauched many Indians. European firearms made intertribal warfare much more deadly. The white man, who used domesticated animals as well as game for meat, had attitudes about the use of the land that were foreign to the Indians. The Indians also found themselves subjected to the white man's code of laws. Some of their own number even espoused the white man's religion. The Indian leaders felt their influence ebbing and their way of life threatened.

A general uprising occurred in 1675. It was called King Philip's War, because it was precipitated by Philip of the Wampanoag tribe in Massachusetts. For the next two years, roving bands of Indians terrorized much of New England. They killed the settlers and destroyed houses and crops. Connecticut, Massachusetts, and Rhode Island raised armies and tried to eliminate the hostile Indians.

During the latter part of King Philip's War, the settlement of Simsbury was burned after the settlers had fled to Windsor. Though it was never proven, Indians from the Springfield area were blamed.

Intertribal dissension and poor organization brought an end to the Indian raids, but unrest and racial distrust continued. About the time the war ended, most Indians left this region and eventually joined a tribe near Stockbridge, Massachusetts. As far as is known, they lived there until evacuated by the United States government to a reservation on Lake Winnebago in Wisconsin in 1834.

Even though few Indians were left in this area after King Philip's War, the threat of violence was not over. To the north, the French began organizing Indians to fight and to terrorize British settlements in hopes of attaining political and economic dominance in the new world. In 1708 the General Assembly ordered Simsbury to establish two garrisons. These were built in the area that is now Granby.

As late as 1724 an alarm was spread warning that a band of hostile Indians was again heading toward Connecticut. Patrols were sent out and more garrisons established throughout the settled areas. In case of attack, citizens were to be ready to gather in these fortified dwellings, which were stocked with arms and supplies.

In his *Historical Sketch of Turkey Hills and East Granby, Connecticut,* written in 1949, Albert Carlos Bates mentions "a brick building near the north end of East Granby Street . . . called 'the old fort.'" (East Granby Street was another name for North Main Street.) Bates' contemporary, Elizabeth Newberry Parsons, in her pamphlet *A Brief History of East Granby,* states that the 1724 alarm "brought out forty-one soldiers from Windsor and twenty-six from Hartford to a garrison built on land owned by Clarence Case." Case lived at 195-197 North Main Street. Early records confirm that there was a house on this property in 1726. Because of its strategic northern location and early origin, it seems quite possible that the house was fortified. Whether or not it was the same brick house Bates mentions cannot be determined, though it is unlikely in this area that a house of such early origin would be constructed of anything but wood. Land records do show a brick house on the property by 1810.

Another house that stood near 2 Washington Ridge Road may have been fortified as a garrison. Also, Edward Thompson's will, dated 1806, mentions a "house called the block fort" near 74 South Main Street.

The need for garrisons in this area ended about 1726. Tensions had subsided, the few Indians who remained hunted freely again in the forests, and the settlers lived and worked without fear of attack.

I

The Simsbury Years

from the settling of Simsbury to the separation of Granby

c. 1664 - 1786

Chronological Highlights

1633	*Windsor founded thirteen years after landing of Pilgrims at Plymouth.*
c. 1645	*Tar works established on Farmington River in present North Bloomfield by John Griffin and Michael Humphrey.*
c. 1664	*John Griffin and family settled west of the Mountain on land within the present East Granby.*
1670	*Simsbury incorporated.*
1675-76	*King Philip's War*
1705	*Copper discovered at Copper Hill.*
c. 1707	*First settlement east of the Mountain in Turkey Hills.*
1725	*First steel made in the English colonies produced by Samuel Higley.*
c. 1735	*First copper coins made in the English colonies produced by Samuel Higley.*
1736	*Turkey Hills Ecclesiastical Society established.*
1738	*First Congregational meetinghouse erected.*
1773	*Newgate Prison established.*
1775-83	*Revolutionary War.*

1

Sergeant John Griffin and the Settling of Simsbury

ABOUT TEN YEARS after the founding of Windsor, John Griffin began harvesting the local forests. He and his business associate, Michael Humphrey, cut down pine trees in a swath along the Farmington River. They progressed from Windsor, where they lived, through what was to become North Bloomfield and the Tariffville section of Simsbury. In this search for pine, John Griffin crossed the river at "the Falls"* and established his place in the history of East Granby. Griffin was the first European to settle within what are now the town's boundaries.

In 1662, after John Griffin had been working at making tar almost twenty years, the governor of Connecticut, John Winthrop, Jr., delivered a paper on the subject to the Royal Society in London. He stated that in all New England "most tar is made about Connecticut above 50 miles up the river, where there be great plains of those pines on both sides [of] the river something up into the land from the riverside."

Winthrop was under the impression that most of the tar made at this time was from pine knots found on the floor of the pine barrens. These knots were resin-rich limb joints, all that remained of trees that had fallen many years before; whole trees were cut down only for candlewood, resinous splints used as substitutes for candles, he says. At this time, according to Winthrop, colonial tar makers were trying to develop a method for extracting resinous sap from living trees by girdling them, slashing the trunk so that the sap would ooze out. They would like to know if anyone in Norway, Sweden, or elsewhere had found a way to do this successfully, he stated.

Winthrop gave a description of the process then in use to manufacture tar from pine knots: After bringing several cartloads to a convenient spot, the tar maker would construct a raised hearth from stones gathered in the vicinity and paved with clay or loam. He sloped the hearth to the middle and ran a gutter from the middle out one side. This was to channel the hot tar into a vessel placed beside the hearth.

*"The Falls" is the name given by the early settlers to the stretch of the Farmington River between present-day Tariffville and East Granby. It was a shallow near the northernmost bend of the river in the days before the river was dammed. An ancient fording place for the Indians, it was the only spot for miles where the river could be forded with any safety when the river was swollen during the spring thaws. The settlements on both sides of the river were later called "the Falls," a name that is no longer used.

Then the tar maker piled the knots on the hearth in the same manner used by charcoal makers and completed the kiln by covering the heap with a coating of clay or loam. He left a hole at the top through which he introduced fire and allowed smoke to escape. He also opened or closed at will smaller holes in the sides of the earthen kiln to regulate the amount of oxygen that got to the fire. As the knots slowly burned, their sap, transformed into tar, dripped down to the hearth and out to the waiting pot.

Pitch, Winthrop says, was made from tar in three ways. Tar could be boiled down into pitch, or second, tar could be boiled with rosin added to reduce the boiling time needed. Pitch made this way differed somewhat in quality from the first, he says. Third, a pot of tar could be set afire and allowed to burn until it was the consistency of pitch. Colonial ship carpenters generally employed this method, he says. The English navy and merchant marine, as well as colonial shipbuilders, used tar and pitch to waterproof and preserve ships' hulls and lines.

Some time after this paper was written, the colonials began to cut down the yellow "pitch" pines and manufacture tar from the whole tree. No one knows exactly what methods John Griffin used in his manufacturing, but according to the text of a grant of land made to him by the General Assembly in 1663, John Griffin "was the first [to perfect]* the art of making pitch and tar in these parts."

Griffin tended his outlying tar works for a number of years from his home, known as "the old Stiles place," in Windsor. He had come to Windsor, a man in his thirties, during the first decade of the town's existence. There he married Anna Bancroft on May 13, 1647. Six or seven of their ten children were born while they lived in Windsor.

Griffin moved his family to territory now in East Granby about 1664. He moved, most likely, as a natural step in the pursuit of his pitch and tar business. His "commute" from Windsor to his tar works probably became too wearing as he went farther and farther afield for new stands of pine.

The prevailing tradition holds that Griffin built his house on the western slope of a hill that lies north of Holcomb Street almost across from the entrance to Heather Hollow. This elevation has been called Welsh Hill from the 1700s. According to the Griffin genealogy, John Griffin was a Welshman, and the hill, which in his day rose out of a sweep of pine forest, might have been named for him.

Perhaps, too, Griffin felt it was at last relatively safe to bring his family to this distant outpost. Other Windsor residents were beginning to build a new community on the fertile flood plains along both sides of the Farmington River in the Massaco Indian lands. They were thus beginning the settlement forming the eventual center of Simsbury. Some were grown sons of the first Windsor settlers who were looking for a good place to establish their own families, since the better farmland in Windsor itself was already taken. Four of this group of pioneers, including Michael Humphrey, were Anglicans who left Windsor shortly after complaining to the General Assembly about the strictness of the "ancient" Reverend John Warham, Windsor's Congregational minister.

Griffin himself had a vital interest in the Massaco lands, which stemmed from

*The original record, housed in the Connecticut State Archives, is so worn that the words in this space are missing. Richard H. Phelps, who quoted the record in the mid-19th century, used the words "to perfect." Phelps' contemporary, Lucius I. Barber, indicated the words were missing when he read the record, but he also inserted "to perfect."

an incident many years before. In September 1646 John Griffin and other men from Windsor presented petitions to the commissioners of the United Colonies of New England. (This inter-colony agency was formed in 1643 to promote solidarity among the English plantations and to deal with their common enemies—the Dutch, French, and Indians.) The men informed the commission that an Indian had willfully and maliciously set fire to quantities of their pitch and tar, bedding, and a cart loaded with candlewood, tools, and other articles, causing damage valued at £100. They stated they could prove that the arsonist was Manahannoose, a Warranoke Indian.

Connecticut magistrates had issued a warrant for the Indian's arrest and he had been seized by the English, but rescued by a company of Indians led by Chickwallop, sachem of the Nonatuck tribe of Connecticut River Indians based near Northhampton, Massachusetts. The Indians had "jeered and abused" the Connecticut men and had spirited Manahannoose into Massachusetts and out of their jurisdiction.

The commissioners sent John Griffin and Jonathan Gilbert, a Hartford resident, to ask Chickwallop to deliver Manahannoose for an impartial trial with assurance that the Indian would have safe conduct to and from the New Haven Colony where the commission was currently in session. The commissioners also instructed Griffin, Gilbert, and the men accompanying them to use force if that seemed necessary and prudent to bring in Manahannoose.

Griffin and Gilbert returned to the commissioners with a disturbing report. They had not been able to locate either Chickwallop or Manahannoose. Furthermore, when they went to Warranoke, the sagamores and other Indians there confronted them fully armed with arrows, hatchets, swords, and cocked guns. The Indians, however, had offered the Englishmen eight fathom of wampum and promised more in restitution.

Hearing this, the commissioners decided it would set a bad precedent if the Indians were allowed to rescue and protect the accused man. They declared that thereafter a colony could send its forces into another colony to apprehend an Indian suspect. Being very practical, they also declared that the plaintiff in the case should pay the cost of the mission. Likewise, because it would be an expense to a colony to keep a convicted Indian in prison and there was danger that he might escape and cause more trouble, the Indian, if found guilty, was to be turned over to the plaintiff. As his punishment, the Indian was to serve as a slave or be shipped to the West Indies and exchanged for a Negro slave. It was under this ruling that Indians later captured during King Philip's War (1675-76) were condemned to slavery, if not executed.

Apparently Manahannoose was eventually brought to trial. A copy of a deposition made in court by John Griffin in 1662, and now in the Simsbury town records, tells the outcome of the case. The court delivered Manahannoose to Griffin, but luckily for the old Indian, three of his friends interceded in his behalf. Since they could not raise the 500 fathom of wampum set as the price for Manahannoose's release, they signed over to Griffin all their holdings in Massaco.

Griffin was not destined to exercise his claim in Massaco. A colonial law prohibited individuals from making land deals with Indians. In 1661 Griffin surrendered his claim in Massaco "for the use and benefit of the plantation of Windsor."

However, stating the purpose to be a reward for his perfection of the tar-making process, two years later the General Assembly awarded Griffin a grant of 200 acres in the Falls area. Both Pickerel Cove and the island within it were part of this grant. After

Massaco became Simsbury, the town granted him additional property running from Pickerel Cove northward 1½ miles, plus scattered outlying lots. The greater part of Griffin's land is now within East Granby, with some also in Granby. The earliest records refer to Griffin's land as his "Homestead." Later it became known as "Griffin's Lordship." With more than a thousand acres, Griffin was by far the largest landowner in the area.

About twenty households, scattered over a 10-mile stretch along both sides of the Farmington River, made up the frontier settlement of Massaco in 1668. That May the Massaco settlers petitioned the General Assembly to be allowed to form their own ecclesiastical society. The Assembly answered by ruling at its October session that Massaco "may be improved for the making of a plantation." It appointed a committee from its members to oversee the settlement's progress. The following year the Assembly excused the Massaco plantation from colonial taxes for three years, probably to induce more families to settle there.

Also in 1669 the General Assembly appointed John Case to the office of constable of Massaco. Case, one of the first settlers, was to keep the peace and to serve as a representative from the Assembly to the plantation. The Massaco Plantation elected two representatives, Constable Case and Joshua Holcomb, whom it sent to the next session of the Assembly. During this session (May 1670) the Assembly incorporated the plantation, granting it the privileges of a town and recognizing the settlers' choice of the name Simsbury.

As soon as Simsbury became a town, John Griffin began a career of public service. He and Michael Humphrey went to the General Assembly as Simsbury's representatives in the fall of 1670. In 1674 Griffin and Simon Wolcott became Simsbury's first townsmen of record.* These officials are now called selectmen. Griffin was reelected in 1677 to serve with Joshua Holcomb and Samuel Wilcoxson, and apparently he held this position until he died four years later. At the time, a selectman's responsibilities included managing town affairs and settling disputes over trespass and debts.

The General Assembly called on Griffin numerous times to help distinguished colony leaders settle disputes with the Indians. Simsbury had a particular problem with the title to its land stemming from the fact that the town's area, as described in its charter, far exceeded the land Griffin or any other local citizen had secured from the Indians. The town stretched 10 miles northerly from Farmington and 10 miles westerly from Windsor, a total of 64,000 acres. Recognizing that challenges would arise, the General Assembly had stated in the charter that it granted Simsbury this area, "providing it does not prejudice any former grant, and be in the power of this Court so to dispose." Finally, in 1680, the nine Indians who felt Simsbury had encroached on land belonging to them agreed to sell their claims. They reserved the right to hunt, fish, and take food on the land.

Griffin also played a part in repeated attempts to establish a boundary between Windsor and Simsbury. In 1675 he was one of the perambulators chosen to negotiate and pace off a line acceptable to both towns. (The present boundary between East Granby and its neighboring towns to the east was not set until long after Griffin's time.)

*Town records for the years 1670-80 are incomplete as they had to be reconstructed from memory and the remains of "the original and some other copies coming to my view," as the town clerk noted after the original records had burned.

The town government of Simsbury began with a minimum of officials and only added more of the offices required of towns by the General Assembly as the town grew. Besides its constable, representatives, and selectmen, the town Griffin knew had a commissioner, who was similar to a modern justice of the peace, and a collector of rates, or tax collector.

In 1675 the town added two assessors, called listers, who compiled the Grand List from records of real and personal property each man in town furnished once a year. The items listed were evaluated according to assessments set by the General Assembly. Both the colony and the town based their taxes on the Grand List. In addition, a poll tax was levied on males over the age of eighteen. Taxes could be paid in grain, for which the colony—and sometimes the town—set a value per bushel. Simsbury at times gave a discount for cash.

Wild and domestic animals constantly threatened fields of grain which were the mainstay of life for the early Simsbury settlers. Good fences were imperative. Simsbury, like most colonial towns short of labor and time, wanted to encompass as much land with as little fence as possible. The community financed the building of a five-rail fence around the perimeter of all its cultivated land rather than around each separate field. The town assigned each householder a portion of the fence to maintain. Then it elected officials called fence viewers to inspect the fence regularly and to call to task anyone who neglected his duty.

The town also had a town clerk who doubled as a surveyor. Aside from keeping the records, the first known clerk, John Slater, went on location to reckon property lines, using a surveyor's chain and landmarks like trees and boulders. He also set off necessary roads which ran as directly as possible from house to house.

Way wardens, forerunners of the Highway Department, had the power to "call out" the men of the town between the ages of fourteen and sixty to contribute their carts and labor to keep the roads in good repair. In 1679 the General Assembly notified all towns that the main roads between towns must be made at least one rod wide. The earliest record of a roadway in Simsbury names "Goodman Griffin's Path." ("Goodman," like "Mister," was a designation of social rank.) This path came from Windsor, crossed the Farmington River at the Falls, and then branched west around Pickerel Cove toward the center of Simsbury and northeast toward Griffin's home.

Colonial law required each town to elect an innkeeper "to provide for strangers and travelers and also such of the inhabitants as live remote . . . on the Sabbath, training days, etc." The town also had a number of minor offices such as inspectors of pork and corn, of measures, and of leather.

Perhaps the most controversial town issue during John Griffin's tenure was the selection of a site for the meetinghouse. While the inhabitants considered and then rejected one location after another, the traveling minister from Hartford, Mr. Samuel Stone, held services and the town officials held town meetings in private homes. The dispute raged for about twelve years, interrupted by King Philip's War. The main question was whether the meetinghouse should be on the west side of the Farmington River, somewhere along what is now Hopmeadow Street, or on the east side of the river near Terry's Plain Road. Because there was no bridge across the river, getting to the meetinghouse would be a hardship on those settlers who lived on the opposite bank.

Finally it was decided to draw lots, the preferred Old Testament method for settling disputes. The west side won, and the meetinghouse was built in 1683 at what is now the front gate of the cemetery in the center of Simsbury. Consequently, to get to church and town meetings, John Griffin's family and later residents in his locale had only to cross Salmon Brook, which was relatively easy to bridge. Simsbury's first bridge over the Farmington River near the center of Simsbury was built at Weatogue, but not until 1734.

Connecticut felt in constant threat of attack from the Dutch in New York, the French in Canada, and the Indians on all sides, so the colony required each settlement to man and maintain a military unit. By law, almost every able man over the age of sixteen bore arms and drilled regularly. In 1673 the General Assembly's Grand Committee for ordering of the militia appointed "Mr. Simon Wolcott and John Griffin to those that shall command the Trainband of Simsbury."

That same year the Grand Committee raised a troop of 163 dragoons. Simsbury, the colony's smallest town, was to supply seven men, compared to the forty-four required of Hartford. These foot soldiers were to be provided with "a good sword and belt, a serviceable musket or carbine, with a shot pouch and powder and bullets . . . and a horse to expedite their march." The dragoons could be called to aid any town.

When the Indian threat escalated into King Philip's War two years later, a contingent of soldiers, whether raised by the colony or the town is not known, was housed in a garrison in Simsbury. Also in 1675 the General Assembly made John Griffin sergeant of the trainband, the highest rank possible in a troop as small as Simsbury's. That title has been linked with his name forever after.

The Town of Simsbury waited with apprehension as reports of Indian attacks and massacres showed the action to be spreading. In the fall of 1675, with "a deep sense of eminent danger," the General Assembly gave the people of Simsbury one week to evacuate, getting "their women and children, corn and the best of their estate to places of most hopeful security." The Assembly also ordered that the Simsbury garrison be abandoned. Many of the Simsbury townsfolk retreated to Windsor.

When no attack materialized, some of the people returned to their homes. The General Assembly again ordered them out on March 3, 1676, and they fled in haste, hiding what they could of their possessions. On Sunday, March 26, the deserted town was sacked and burned by a band of Indians. Simsbury historian Lucius I. Barber states: "About forty dwelling houses, together with a large number of barns and other buildings, were thus consumed. During all the Indian Wars before or since, no English settlement suffered such a total and complete destruction as in this conflagration."

Griffin was an aging man when the rebuilding of Simsbury began. He died in 1681 at about the age of seventy-three. His burial site is not known. His widow and ten children, ranging in age from eight to thirty-two, survived him.

The records of his personal property show a man typical of his time. He left a wealth of land, a few simple household effects, and none of the accouterments of ease or luxury.

John Griffin was the first permanent European settler of Massaco and of the original Town of Simsbury, which then stretched far beyond the boundaries of that town today. Griffin obviously never knew that he would later also be acclaimed as the first settler of the Town of East Granby. In fact, he never knew about the settlement of Turkey Hills, the forerunner of today's town, which would encompass most of his property in less than fifty years after his passing.

2

Minerals, Mines, and Miners

Had a piece of marcasite which seemed to contain copper. An Indian brought [it] *from up in the country, but there have been such wars among the heathen in these parts that there could be no travelling that way upon such discoveries, but time, I hope, will give better opportunities.*

THUS wrote the governor of the Connecticut Colony, John Winthrop, Jr., in 1661, to Sir Robert Moray, a fellow member of the Royal Society in London. Winthrop was destined not to make the great discovery he anticipated. He died in 1676, just as King Philip's War was ending. Some years later, in 1702, the General Assembly revived interest in mineral deposits when it passed an act "For the encouragement of such as shall lay out themselves upon the discovery of mines or minerals for the public good."

The Simsbury Mines on Copper Hill

The townspeople of Simsbury had the exciting privilege of being the first in Connecticut to report the discovery of what was either silver or copper in their town. Two townsmen were sent out from the town meeting held December 18, 1705, to locate and determine the nature of the find. The ore deposit was just west of Peak Mountain on the small ridge that came to be called Copper Hill.

Copper had been found in many other colonies, including neighboring Massachusetts and New York. It had been mined unproductively about 1642 by Governor John Endicott of Massachusetts, who had imported Swedish workmen to refine his ore. Copper would soon be discovered as close as the towns of Farmington and Wallingford. However, this was the first strike in Connecticut, and the townspeople of Simsbury were undoubtedly jubilant with hopes of a new undertaking and potential wealth.

Simsbury's first move was to reserve all mine and mineral rights to the town. Similar action had been taken previously by the town when a deposit of rocks suitable for millstones was found. Copper Hill was still common land then, never having been granted to individuals.

Early in 1707 sixty-four inhabitants formed a Company of Proprietors to develop and manage the proposed mines. Proprietorship was limited to those who had been on the tax list in 1706. A few eligible townspeople declined to participate.

The town gave the proprietors the franchise to all the copper ore they could dig. In return the proprietors agreed that they would pay the town 10 shillings for every ton of ore, would pay master workman Lamrock Flowers to supervise the digging of mines, would pay the Reverend Dudley Woodbridge for his services as town minister, and would see to the construction of a "copper works." Since the townspeople feared the town might be attacked again, the agreement with the proprietors also provided for the possible interruption of mining and the burning of the works during war. As no one in town knew how to refine copper, the proprietors selected a Company of Undertakers (i.e., operators) who were to devise a refining method and to supervise the construction and operation of a dam, mill, and forge for the work. The undertakers were town minister Dudley Woodbridge and his relatives: John Woodbridge of Springfield; the Timothy Woodbridges, Senior and Junior; and Hezekiah Willis of Hartford. All the Woodbridges were ministers and Willis later became Secretary of the General Assembly. These five were not chosen because of any particular knowledge of metallurgy but because, as the best educated men in the community, they might be able to come up with the necessary process.

The agreement with the undertakers designated "for pious uses one-tenth of all the copper readied for market by the undertakers." The profit from two-thirds of this amount was to be used to maintain the schoolmaster in Simsbury and the other third to aid the Collegiate School (now Yale University), which had opened several years before.

Construction of a mine proceeded slowly while numerous disputes over its management arose among the townspeople. The future of the mines was so unsure that by 1709 there was deliberation at a town meeting whether or not to shut down operations. As a result, the town voted to enlist the aid of three arbitrators, William Pitkin and John Haynes of Hartford and John Hooker of Farmington.

The General Assembly had always assumed the role of guardian of the people's welfare. Noting that the mines constituted "a public benefit," it appointed the same men chosen by Simsbury to be its own commissioners for the mines. This act of the Assembly on May 12, 1709, is stated by many historians to be the first mining charter granted in America.

Despite the enhanced standing of the proprietors and the mediation of the commissioners, dissatisfaction with mine operations continued to plague the town and the proprietors. Finally, in 1712, the proprietors became suspicious of the undertakers, who could not account for ore that the proprietors had sent to them. The controversy that ensued clearly shook the proprietors' confidence in their own ability to develop the mines. It was time to embark on a new plan.

In October of 1712, having disbanded the Company of Undertakers, fifty-two proprietors signed new articles governing the mines. This agreement, which stood for the next forty-one years, gave the power of attorney to a committee of six. These men handled most of the mine transactions from that time forward.

The committee immediately granted a thirty-year lease to William Partridge, Jonathan Belcher, and Timothy Woodbridge, Jr. Woodbridge was now the minister at Simsbury. Partridge and his son-in-law Belcher were Boston merchants. Belcher would become governor of Massachusetts and New Hampshire (1730-41) and of New Jersey (1747-57).

The lease gave the lessees the right to mine and refine any mineral except iron that might be found in Simsbury. It relieved the town of responsibility should anyone be injured in the mines and required that the lessees turn over to the King and Queen of England one-fifth of any gold or silver they might find. This stipulation had its origin in the Charter of Connecticut.

The townspeople apparently approved of the lease the committee had made because the next year they voted to give the proprietors total control of the mines. In return, the proprietors turned over to the town most of the £80 payment Partridge had given them as his first year's rent. The town used this revenue not for a schoolmaster but for a supply of ammunition.

Of the three new lessees, Belcher was to take the most active part in the operation of the mines. By 1717 he had bought out Partridge, and thus he controlled two-thirds of the mining interests. By the same date Elias Boudinot and Charles Crommeline, New York City merchants, and Jaheel Brenton of Rhode Island owned the Woodbridge one-third interest. These three formed a loose partnership.

Preparations for mining got underway as soon as the 1712 lease was signed. The town instructed the town clerk and surveyor, John Slater, to survey and set the boundaries of the mining land on Copper Hill. He marked off a rectangle 140 rods east and west and about 360 rods north and south, using a pine tree and a black oak to set the boundaries. The total area was about 315 acres.

Partridge immediately ordered a house built on Copper Hill, probably to lodge his miners. Stables and other outbuildings were put up later. The lessees also leased and bought large tracts of land in the area surrounding the mines. They used this land for pastures and gardens. It also gave them a supply of wood for smelting and access to streams which supplied the power they needed for stamping mills. Stamping mills crushed boulders so that copper-rich ore could be separated by hand from ordinary rock.

An early map of Simsbury, drawn about 1732, shows a stamping mill on Muddy Brook. This mill is thought to be one owned by Belcher, although at least two other lessees owned stamping mills in town. In 1842 Richard Bacon, then overseer of the mine, wrote that since he had found slag at this site, he believed there had been a smelter there, too.

Actual mining did not begin under the lessees until 1714, and it is doubtful that the Woodbridges mined at all. In 1715 Belcher went to England and brought back a dozen miners and a skilled refiner. He set up a refinery in Boston and proceeded to have his ore transported overland to Windsor and Hartford from where it was shipped on coastal sloops to his refinery. It seems that not enough ore came out of his mines, which by now included those in Wallingford and Farmington, to make it feasible to keep his own refinery open. So, from about 1720, Belcher shipped his ore from Boston to refineries in Bristol, England.

Boudinot, Crommeline, and Brenton, on the other hand, elected to set up a refinery in Simsbury. They purchased a mill from the estate of Thomas Barber in 1717 and Boudinot brought in a refiner from Philadelphia, John Casper Hoofman. This company also imported skilled workmen from Germany. The area surrounding their furnaces on Hop Brook in West Simsbury was long known as Hanover, after these workmen's native city.

The copper mines attracted investors from both England and Holland as well as those from the colonies. Through sale and inheritance, about forty persons shared in the mining leases for varying amounts of time.

None of the interested parties appear to have achieved significant financial success. Jonathan Belcher spent the equivalent of about $100,000 (as calculated by Creel Richardson in 1928) during his thirty-year association with the mines. The investments made by the other companies probably totaled another $100,000. Belcher complained bitterly of his "continual loss." He often reprimanded his Hartford agent, William Pitkin, for not paying closer attention to his affairs. (Belcher himself never visited the mines.) He also railed at the refineries in England, which he felt undervalued his ore. The other absentee investors also had their share of agents who lacked interest and maybe a few who were dishonest.

The overriding problem with the mining operations, though, seems to have been the primitive state of mining and refining technology in those early times. Most of the work was done slowly and tediously by hand. It took Belcher's men more than four years to complete a 250-foot "level," or horizontal shaft, to drain the seeping water that constantly flooded the underground caverns and had to be pumped out by hand.

The miners removed rock and ore with hand tools and explosives. They bored holes with an instrument like the modern star drill, alternately turning its bit and pounding it with a sledge hammer. The sledge hammer occasionally broke the arm of the man holding the drill. When enough holes had been drilled in the mine wall, the miners filled them with black powder and ran a fine trail of powder from them—safety fuse had not yet been invented. The ignited powder sometimes blew up the miners as well as the mine wall.

The ore itself was a problem, too. It apparently was not of consistently high grade and it was of a type that was very difficult to refine. A report by Charles U. Shepard commissioned by the state in 1837 describes the ore as vitreous copper, "highly prized as an ore of copper," but the Francfort report in 1857 indicates that even at that later date, the ore that was being dug then was not yielding a fraction of the copper that it should because of the inadequate methods being used to refine it.

A 1976 geological report states that the ore now present in the mine contains from 0.2 to 6.4 percent copper. This study, done by John D. Perrin under the supervision of Dr. Norman Gray of the Geology Department at the University of Connecticut, also determined that approximately 4200 metric tons of ore-bearing gray sandstone had been removed from the mine up to that time. At an estimated ore grade of 2 percent, that would be equivalent to a mere 85 metric tons of copper. Considering the fact that this total includes ore dug in the 19th century as well as that dug by the colonials, it is understandable that the early lessees became disenchanted with their venture.

Both the proprietors and the General Assembly responded to the difficulties encountered by the lessees, because a successful mine would have benefited the entire colony. The proprietors reduced the rent on the mines. Belcher's share fell from £80 annually to £6 3s 4d, and many years no rent at all was paid. The General Assembly sent commissioners to settle disputes between companies and, when the joint venture became untenable, authorized the division of the mine property. It even exempted the mining employees from military duty for a time.

The English Parliament noticed the infant American copper industry in 1721.

It passed an act to include copper ore in the list of colonial goods that could not be shipped anywhere but to England.

With alternating good and bad fortunes, the mining operations continued. The miners excavated two main shafts and numerous exploratory pits. Months sometimes passed with very little good quality ore being dug and the complement of workmen dwindling. Then someone would strike a rich lens or pocket of ore, and the hill would come alive with activity until the new supply was exhausted. Belcher employed as many as twenty men to mine one strike.

But lucky strikes were not enough. By 1742, when the original lease ended, the mines had failed to develop into the steady source of income the investors had envisioned. None of them renewed. The mines reverted to the proprietors, who chose not to mine them.

In 1753 the remaining forty-seven proprietors appointed a committee of five to distribute the mines and land holdings. Captain John Viets, Jonathan Humphrey, and Abel Forward bought the other proprietors' shares. In 1770 Copper Hill resident John Viets, whose parental family had been the third to settle in the area now East Granby, controlled almost all of the mine land.

In 1772 James Holmes, an Englishman living in Salisbury, Connecticut, leased the mines for twenty years. After about a year of mining, he sold his lease to the Colony of Connecticut, which turned the main shafts into its first prison.

In retrospect, although they were a losing venture for many investors, the mines benefited the town of Simsbury. They brought outside capital into its primarily agricultural economy. The construction of mills and buildings provided a new market for some local suppliers of timber and building materials. They provided additional jobs for townsmen who were willing to mine. They drew an influx of workers from other colonies and abroad who settled and founded new families.

The West Iron Works at Stony Brook

A ready supply of iron ore must have attracted some settlers to the area. Marshes contained bog ore, a mixture of limonite and other hydrated oxides of iron intermingled with clay, sand, and organic compounds. An iridescent film on stagnant water indicated the presence of this type of iron ore.

In 1701 the inhabitants of Windsor voted that residents of Suffield and Windsor might take iron ore from Windsor commons to an iron works on Stony Brook in Suffield as long as inhabitants of both towns were employed to cut wood on common land in Suffield and to make and haul charcoal for use at the mill. Within the next twenty-five years, three iron works were established on Stony Brook. The third, called the West Iron Works, was just over colonial Simsbury's eastern border in Suffield.

Men with oxen carted some of the iron ore processed at these mills from marshes south of Rainbow Road and west of Stone Road at Simsbury's southeastern border with Windsor. (This Rainbow Road in Windsor is the continuation of East Granby's Seymour Road.) Until 1729 this land was commons with the exception of Tilton's Marsh, a 10-acre bog the Town of Windsor had given to James Eno and John Moses in 1669 in exchange for land along the Farmington River that the two men had bought from the Indians.

In an article in the *Connecticut Antiquarian* entitled "Iron in the Woods of Suffield," Delphina L. H. Clark describes these works as bloomeries where wrought iron was made directly from iron ore without any form of casting. A bloomery had a large, deep forge—a blacksmith's oversized forge—with a leather bellows run by a water wheel. Charcoal was put into the forge and ignited. When it reached a sufficiently high temperature, iron ore and limestone were added. Then the bellows pumped air over the fire to raise the temperature gradually to a very high heat, but not to the melting point of the iron.

The iron eventually fell to the bottom of the forge in a doughy mass called a loop. Bloomers took the loop from the forge and beat it with a tilt hammer to remove as many impurities as possible. The result was comparatively soft wrought iron that blacksmiths could hammer into articles such as hinges, door pulls, latches, bolts, foot scrapers, nails, and shoes for horses and oxen.

The West Iron Works may have been a slitting mill where wrought iron from the bloomery was made into rods for nails. It was in operation by 1724 and continued for perhaps twenty years, becoming defunct by 1749. The men who settled nearby provided wood, ore, charcoal, and labor for this manufactory, and John Lewis of North Main Street was one of its owners.

Samuel Higley, Early Metallurgist, Mine Owner, and Minter

Of all the settlers who came to the northeast corner of Simsbury during the onset of copper mining and iron making, the most remarkable by far was Samuel Higley. Higley was a Simsbury native born about 1687 in his parents' two-story home, which stood beside the road that ran from the center of Simsbury to Copper Hill. Long called Higley Town, the area is now the site of the Simsbury Airport, along the southwest boundary of East Granby.

Samuel Higley's father, Captain John Higley, had been a glovemaker's apprentice in Surrey, England. At the age of seventeen, he ran away and shipped out to the new world. For payment of his passage, the captain of the ship that brought him to Windsor indentured him to John Drake, a prosperous merchant. John Higley was like many young men in his day who accepted a term of indenture as the first step toward finding their fortunes in the colonies.

Higley prospered in his adopted land. When he was twenty-five he married Drake's daughter Hannah, and together they amassed a great deal of property in both Windsor and Simsbury. From his warehouses on the Connecticut River in Windsor, Higley carried on extensive trade with the Barbados Islands, importing sugar, molasses, and rum. In Simsbury he manufactured pitch and tar as had John Griffin before him. He also procured ships' masts, each fashioned from a single native pine, for the Royal Navy.

In 1684 John Higley and his family moved from Windsor to Simsbury. Along with seven other men with established reputations for service to the town, the General Assembly named John Higley in the 1687 Patent of Simsbury. The patent confirmed that the land reserved for the town in its 1670 charter was at last free and clear of Indian claims against the title. It also gave the town proprietors, all landowners in town though not necessarily residents, joint ownership of all the town commons and natural resources.

John Higley served Simsbury as a deputy to the General Assembly, a selectman, and a captain in the trainband. For a time he was the resident with the largest tax assessment.

He must also have had one of the largest families in town. John and Hannah had nine children. After she died, he married a young widow, Sarah Strong Bissel of Windsor, who had two children, and together they had seven more. Higley was quite able to assure all his children a secure foothold in the world. When he died, he bequeathed to them extensive real estate and a collection of books that was remarkably large for his time.

Samuel Higley, John and Hannah's eighth child, eventually settled in the area now making up East Granby. When Samuel was about seventeen, his father provided him with funds for room and board and sent him to live with the family's eldest daughter, Hannah Higley Trumbull, in Lebanon, Connecticut. One of Samuel's young nephews in this household, Jonathan Trumbull, later served as governor of Connecticut during the Revolutionary War.

According to Higley family tradition, Samuel Higley attended the Collegiate School in Saybrook for about two years. As a young bachelor, he was the schoolmaster in Woodbridge, New Jersey. Here, it seems, he acquired an interest in medicine.

In those days of limited medical knowledge, it was the custom for a man to observe and consult with practicing physicians until he had acquired enough knowledge and experience to practice alone. In 1717 Thomas Hooker and Samuel Mather, both doctors and ministers in Hartford, certified: "Considering the great want of learned and faithful physicians among us, and knowing Mr. Samuel Higley's abilities and the theory and practice in the art of physic and surgery, we the subscribers do hereby recommend him to the General Assembly now sitting as one qualified for a licentiate."

The Reverend Timothy Woodbridge, Sr., added that Samuel Higley had practiced medicine successfully the preceding winter at Woodbridge in the Jerseys. So schoolmaster Higley was licensed a doctor by the General Assembly and began his Connecticut practice, tending the sick and compounding medicines.

Two years later Dr. Higley married Abigail Beman at Westfield, Massachusetts. They settled in Simsbury's northeast corner in a house on the Mountain in Vineyard Notch between Hatchet Hill and Turkey Hills roads. From their elevation they had a picturesque view of both the Farmington River and Connecticut River valleys. Traces of their access road, spring, apple trees, and stones from their home's foundation could still be seen in the latter part of the 19th century.

Higley owned a considerable amount of land in Simsbury. He inherited acreage from his mother and his home lot from his father. The Town of Simsbury granted him part of the common lands that were distributed in 1723. In 1728 he purchased 143 acres adjoining his home lot to the west where he eventually built another home and began mining for copper.

The Simsbury town records disclose a story about the Higley family and property Samuel Higley claimed in his son's name. Higley's eldest brother Jonathan died in 1716 without a son. In his will he left his home lot and house to the first boy his brothers would name after him. Brewster, whose son Joseph was born just before his brother's death, added two girls to his family, one in 1717 and one in 1719. Nathaniel, another brother, married in 1720, but his first child, a daughter, was not born until 1723. The day Samuel's first child was born, he brought the midwife to witness his jubilant entry into the town records:

This may certify that my first born son whom I call Jonathan was born of Abigail, my wife, in Simsbury on Wednesday, June the twenty-first, at ten of the clock in the morning in the 7th year of the reign of George of Great Britain, King, etc., anno que Domini 1721.
Attest
Abigail Hays, *midwife* Samuel Higley

Samuel and Abigail Higley had two other children, Ann and Abigail.

After he moved to Turkey Hills, Samuel Higley continued practicing as a physician and embarked on several more endeavors. Multiple occupations were quite common in an area such as this, which did not have the population to provide many customers for a single trade. The scope of Higley's interests was remarkable, though, even for his time.

According to Higley genealogist Mary Coffin Johnson, Higley worked as a blacksmith. A blacksmith was perhaps the most skilled of the 18th century artisans. He wrought tools, utensils, and other functional and decorative hardware, as well as shoeing horses and oxen.

The scope of Samuel Higley's work with metals shows that he was more than a typical blacksmith. He was, in fact, the first man on record to make steel in America. For this accomplishment, Higley is considered one of the founders of American metallurgy.

In June 1725, according to the account in the General Assembly's records, Higley procured a few pieces of iron, weighing a pound or two in total, from two other local blacksmiths, Timothy Phelps and John Drake. A few days later he returned the same pieces to them with a significant difference. Phelps and Drake testified: "And we proved them and found them good steel, which was the first steel that ever was made in this country, that ever we saw or heard of."

Higley testified that it was with "great pains and costs [*that he*] found out and obtained a curious art, by which to convert, change, or transmute iron into good steel." The steelmaking process had once been a closely guarded skill passed on from father to son. Perhaps Higley pursuaded one of the German copper miners to teach him the technology or perhaps he arrived at his method through his own experimentation. One modern authority, Douglas Alan Fisher in *The Epic of Steel,* asserts that Higley and all the colonial steelmakers after him used the ancient cementation process.

To make steel by this method,

alternate layers of iron bars and charcoal were placed in two long cementation pots inside a furnace. After being sealed and kept at a cherry-red heat for about ten days, the bars absorbed enough carbon from the charcoal to form steel. Only scant quantities of steel were produced in this way and it was often uneven in quality.

In 1728 the General Assembly granted Higley and his business partner, Joseph Dewey of Hebron, Connecticut, exclusive rights for ten years to make steel in the colony. Higley was to bring his process to reasonable perfection in two years' time. Since his process was still in an experimental stage, Higley probably produced very little steel. He died, according to tradition, in 1737, just as his patent was running out.

While he held his steel patent, Samuel Higley worked briefly for Jonathan Belcher at the Simsbury Copper Mines. At first Belcher seemed to value Higley both as a miner and an assayer. Belcher mentioned in a letter in 1732 that he was glad Higley had begun excavating a shaft on North Hill. Shortly afterward Belcher began to complain about the quality of the ore shipped to him in Boston. "I am fully persuaded the men have stolen and conveyed away the richest and best of the ore," he wrote. Belcher called for Higley and John Christian Miller, a miner from Germany, to assay his ore in Boston in order to compare it with an assay of it as it came out of the mine. Belcher was pleased initially with the report Higley wrote him, but then his opinion soured. He wrote his Hartford agent, adding to his many complaints about the mine operations, that Higley was "acting the part of a vile cheat." This seems to have marked the end of Higley's association with Belcher.

By the spring of 1733 Higley had begun mining copper on his own property, now the farm at 79 Holcomb Street, about a mile and a half south of Belcher's mines. He built a new house close to his mine, which Mary Coffin Johnson visited in 1892. She remarks that its handwrought iron nails, hinges, and other hardware were probably fashioned by its blacksmith owner. The house and hardware are now gone.

Whether Higley was the first to operate his mine is not known, but Higley's mine definitely was worked at various times after his death. In 1825 Simsbury historian Lucius I. Barber talked with Theodore Hillyer, who remembered the Revolutionary War. Hillyer said: "When the war broke out the mining works were in progress there, and it was currently reported that the workmen had just struck a vein of pure native copper as large as a man's thigh, and that the works were broken off, through fear that it might fall into the hands of the enemy." The company of miners he refers to may have been one backed by Josiah Quincy of Boston.

Out of the Higley mine came the raw material for one of Samuel Higley's finest achievements. In addition to being America's first steelmaker, Higley was the first minter of copper coins in the English Americas.

The few existing Higley coppers, which are about the size of a half-dollar, bear clever and clear designs. Higley most likely made the dies for his coins from his own steel. In fact, from the number of designs he made, it seems he was at least as interested in making dies as he was in making coins. He made numerous dies, some for the obverse sides of the coins and some for the reverse sides.

Roughly five varieties of Higley Coppers are shown in the displays at the Connecticut State Library, Connecticut Historical Society, and Simsbury Historical Society. All are quite similar. They picture either an antlered deer, a broad ax, a trio of sledge hammers with a crown above each, a pointing hand, or a combination of these. The coins have various inscriptions: I CUT MY WAY THROUGH, I AM GOOD COPPER, THE VALUE OF THREE PENCE, VALUE ME AS YOU PLEASE, THE WHEELE GOES ROUND, and CONNECTICUT. Two bear the date 1737, thought to be the year of Higley's death.

Although they were never sanctioned by the colonial government, the Higley coppers circulated for years. It is impossible to determine how many were made. Some apparently were struck from the dies, which have since been lost, by other local men,

Higley coppers

principally his brother John, after Higley's death. A few of these bear the date 1739. Some of the coppers traveled abroad and some were melted down by 18th century goldsmiths. Since they were almost pure copper, the coins were highly valued as an alloy in gold jewelry.

Tradition among Higley's descendants holds that Samuel Higley died at sea, at the age of fifty. He was aboard a ship carrying a load of his copper ore when it sank during a storm en route to England. When it lost Samuel Higley, the little settlement of Turkey Hills in the northeast corner of Simsbury lost an educated townsman, once a schoolmaster, and a practicing physician, blacksmith, steelmaker, miner, and minter.

3

Turkey Hills: The Pattern and Progress of Settlement

WHEN John Griffin settled on or near Welsh Hill about 1664, he built the first homestead within the present boundaries of East Granby. Later his children built their homes west of the Mountain between the Falls and the path now called Hatchet Hill Road. The Thomas Holcomb family moved from Windsor and became the Griffins' first neighbors when they settled west of Salmon Brook near Pickerel Cove.

In 1711, six years after copper was discovered on Copper Hill, John Viets, a German doctor who had immigrated to New York, bought an 11-acre homesite from the Griffins. It was near Salmon Brook, a little south of Floydville Bridge.

After the town leased the mines to outside investors in 1712, skilled miners immigrated to Copper Hill. Thomas Stevens of Great Britain and John Christian Miller of Germany married local girls and built homes there. Thomas Stevens settled where the Copper Hill Country Club is today. John Christian Miller lived just south of the Suffield border near 245 Newgate Road. Eventually Dr. Viets' sons, John and Henry, also moved to Copper Hill.

Settlement began east of the Mountain sometime between 1707 and 1712 in the area north of Hatchet Hill and Seymour roads. Simsbury had attempted to distribute some of this common land as early as 1688 by dividing the area into twenty-three parcels and allotting them to certain of the proprietors and other inhabitants. The grantees, in turn, agreed to contribute to the support of the Reverend Edward Thompson, who was then preaching in Simsbury. These first grants were annulled, however, because they were not "laid out" within the six months required by law.

The lots were regranted, in many cases to the same men, in 1693. However, years passed and parcels of land sometimes changed hands before families actually moved onto them.

A boundary dispute with Suffield may have discouraged people from settling the northern grants. Simsbury frequently went to the General Assembly to complain about encroachment by Suffield on what Simsbury felt was its land. Simsbury said Suffield men were clearing, mowing, improving, and levying taxes on the land. At least one Simsbury man was arrested by a group of Suffield men. The record states that they confiscated "several barrels of his turpentine and twenty barrels of turpentine belong-

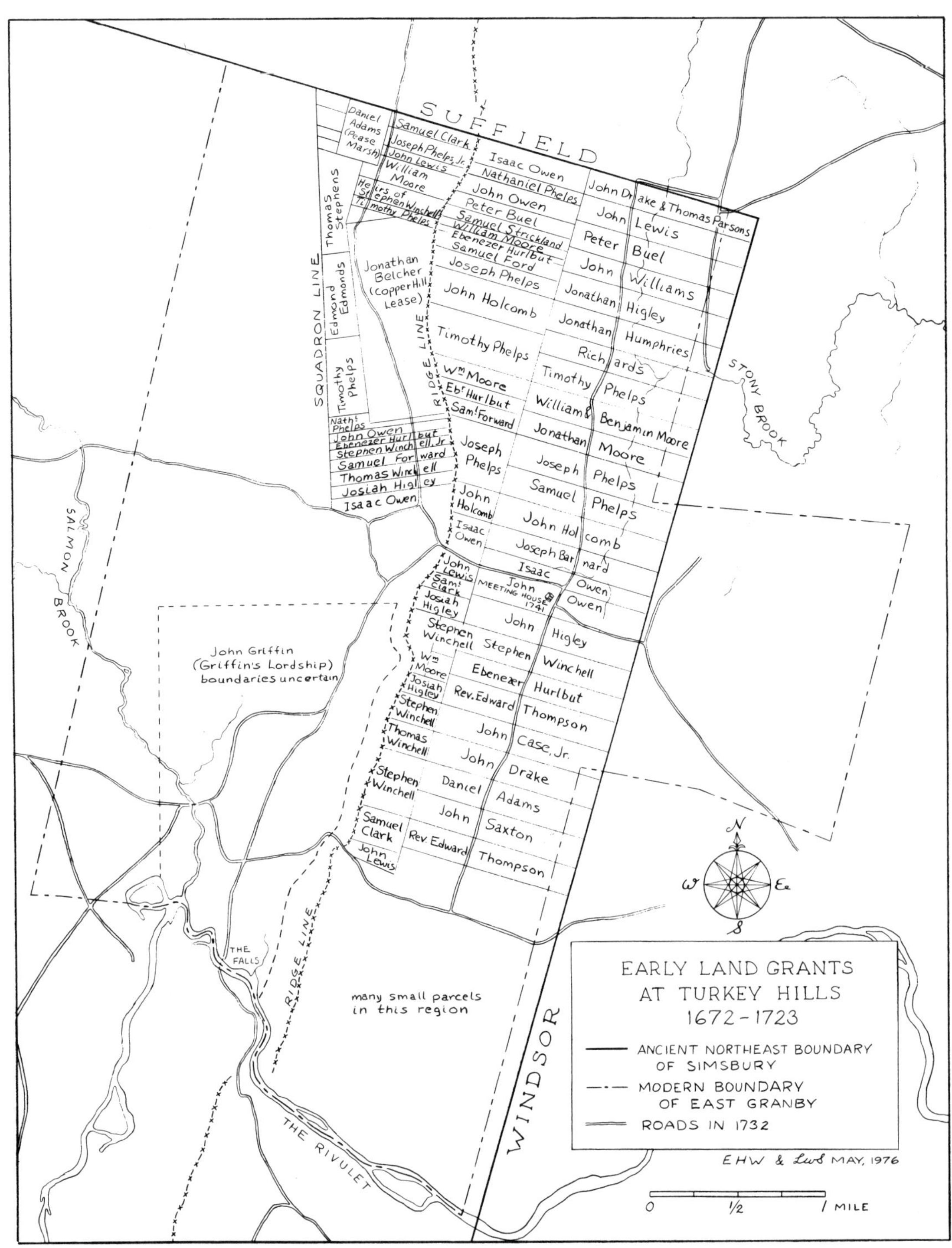
EARLY LAND GRANTS
AT TURKEY HILLS
1672-1723
ANCIENT NORTHEAST BOUNDARY OF SIMSBURY
MODERN BOUNDARY OF EAST GRANBY
ROADS IN 1732
EHW & LwS MAY, 1976
0
1/2
1 MILE
SUFFIELD
WINDSOR
SQUADRON LINE
RIDGE LINE
SALMON BROOK
STONY BROOK
THE RIVULET
THE FALLS
MEETING HOUSE 1741
John Griffin (Griffin's Lordship) boundaries uncertain
many small parcels in this region
Jonathan Belcher (Copper Hill Lease)
Daniel Adams (Pease Marsh)
Samuel Clark
Joseph Phelps Jr.
John Lewis
William Moore
Heirs of Stephen Winchell
Timothy Phelps
Thomas Stephens
Edmond Edmonds
Isaac Owen
Nathaniel Phelps
John Owen
Peter Buel
Samuel Strickland
William Moore
Ebenezer Hurlbut
Samuel Ford
Joseph Phelps
John Holcomb
John Drake & Thomas Parsons
John Lewis
Peter Buel
John Williams
Jonathan Higley
Jonathan Humphries
Richards
Timothy Phelps
William & Benjamin Moore
Jonathan Moore
Joseph Phelps
Samuel Phelps
John Holcomb
Joseph Barnard
Isaac Owen
John Owen
Wm Moore
Ebr Hurlbut
Saml Forward
Joseph Phelps
John Holcomb
Isaac Owen
Nathl Phelps
John Owen
Ebenezer Hurlbut
Stephen Winchell, Jr
Samuel Forward
Thomas Winchell
Josiah Higley
Isaac Owen
John Lewis
Saml Clark
Josiah Higley
John Higley
Stephen Winchell
Stephen Winchell
Wm Moore
Ebenezer Hurlbut
Josiah Higley
Rev. Edward Thompson
Stephen Winchell
John Case, Jr.
Thomas Winchell
John Drake
Stephen Winchell
Daniel Adams
John Saxton
Samuel Clark
Rev. Edward Thompson
John Lewis
N
S
W
E

ing to divers other persons of said Simsbury." At a town meeting in March 1711, Simsbury invested a townsman "with full power to seize any Suffield man trespassing within Simsbury bounds by taking timber, wood, hay, stone or impressing any lands in Simsbury and to prosecute them according to law."

Since the town of Suffield belonged to Massachusetts at this time, settling the boundary dispute meant setting the boundary between two colonies. When this was accomplished in 1713, Simsbury's claim to the land in dispute was upheld. Consequently, when the land was officially surveyed in 1716, a lot was added north of those granted in 1688.

In all there were twenty-four lots. In land records they are numbered from north to south with the second lot being called lot 1 to correspond to the 1688 grants. Lot 19 and about 160 acres south of lot 23, extending almost to Hatchet Hill and Seymour roads, were given to the Reverend Edward Thompson.

The 1716 survey established property lines for the grants. The size of the lots ranged from 60 to 100 acres each. They stretched approximately a mile from the foot of the Mountain eastward to Simsbury's boundary with Suffield and Windsor. They were approximately 30 to 50 rods wide.

Research indicates that the first settler east of the Mountain was Stephen Winchell. Winchell was living in Windsor in 1707 when he bought one of the Simsbury grants from Samuel Wilcockson "for a valuable sum of silver money to the quantity of 10 pounds." His land formed lot 17 and was about a third of a mile south of where School Street runs today. Winchell built a house and barn just west of the present Rainbow Road and moved his wife and six children into the wilderness. Exactly when he moved is not known, but his family and four others were living on the east side of the Mountain by 1712.

Once settlement began on the east side of the Mountain it continued steadily. In 1717 Joseph Alderman, then only twenty years old, cleared land for a homesite along the Farmington River near the present house at 38 Tunxis Avenue. In doing so, he took advantage of the Simsbury policy, adopted as early as 1710, that gave common land remote from the center of town to any person who improved it for four years. A few other early settlers also obtained land in this manner.

Not just anyone could move into town and take up residence, however. The early New England town was similar to a business corporation. All the original property owners, like stockholders, owned the town's ungranted land in common. All had a share in its use as meadow or woodland. And all had a right to participate in the decision on who might settle there.

Before he could settle permanently in any town, a man had to qualify as an "admitted inhabitant." At one time this entailed swearing that he was loyal to the government and that he was not a Jew, a Quaker, nor an atheist. He also had to convince enough of the inhabitants that he would be an asset to the town in order to receive a vote of approval from the majority at a town meeting. No town wanted to become responsible for supporting paupers. A bachelor was subjected to particularly close scrutiny, as the family was considered the foundation of a stable society. At one time Connecticut law forbade a single man to live alone if he was not a public official and had no servant.

Once a man was admitted as an inhabitant, he could vote in all elections for town officials and hold town offices. Until 1663 he could also elect town deputies to the General Assembly, though he could not serve as one unless he had been made a freeman, a more privileged class of citizen.

As of 1663 a man also had to be a freeman to vote for any official in the government of the Colony of Connecticut. Just as the legal definition of inhabitant changed with the years, so did that of freeman. When Simsbury became a town in 1670, a freeman was an admitted inhabitant who had been certified by the majority of his fellow townsmen to be "a person of civil, peaceable, and honest conversation," twenty-one years old, and with an estate of £20 besides his personal estate, and who had been approved by the General Assembly.

A Connecticut man did not have to be a member of the Congregational Church in order to vote or hold any civil office except governor. In this respect, the early government of the Connecticut colony differed from those in the New Haven and Massachusetts colonies, which would not grant suffrage to anyone who was not affiliated with the church.

A great deal of acreage in the northeast section of Simsbury was still owned in common in 1723. At a town meeting that lasted three days, 172 town proprietors and inhabitants divided 16,500 acres of the common land throughout Simsbury among themselves in quantities varying from 20 to 300 acres. The larger the grantee's taxable estate, the larger the grant he received.*

Among the grants of 1723 was an area west of the Mountain between the Suffield border and Turkey Hills Road (with the exception of land on Copper Hill that was leased for mining), the land on the eastern slope of the Mountain adjoining the 1693 grants, and much of the land south of them to the Farmington River. Most of the parcels of land between the 1693 grants and the river were less than 40 acres.

This 1723 division of land did not bring an influx of new settlers to the area partly because most if not all the men who received grants lived here already. Men who disposed of their grants usually sold them to other residents or gave them to their children. This large distribution of land marked the close of the opportunity to obtain free land through grant or homesteading in this area.

The first recorded communal effort by the settlers on the east side of the Mountain was a petition read at a Simsbury town meeting in 1712. It asks that the five families resident there be freed from taxes for two years because of the problems they faced:

The considerations are firstly — The difficulties that attend a new place — 2dly — It being out exposed to many difficulties as enemies — 2d [sic] *Remote from meeting and mill — 3ly The controversies attending the place about the fee simple of the land.*

Your humble servants
Stephen Winchel, Jonathan Moore,
Timo Phelps, William Moore, Barnard Bartlett

*Whether the common land should be divided among all the current residents of the town or among the original proprietors and their heirs, some of whom were nonresidents, caused considerable dispute among the townspeople. Samuel Higley, whose father had undeniably been a proprietor as he was named in the town's patent, wrote several petitions to the General Assembly on behalf of the proprietors. The General Assembly upheld the 1723 division but stipulated that all future distributions of common land should be made to proprietors and their heirs only.

The petition was denied. The families must have persisted, however, for nine months later the town reversed its negative vote.

In their petition, the townsmen had called themselves "inhabitants of the north-east part of the township of Simsbury." When setting down the reversed decision, the town clerk added that the northeast corner of the township was "commonly called *Turkey Hills*" (italics added). This is the name the new settlement would bear until it became a town in its own right 146 years later.

Turkey Hill was the original name for Peak Mountain. Large flocks of wild turkeys gathered on its slope to the east to feed on nuts in the fall. Eventually the name Turkey Hills applied to the land both east and west of Peak Mountain. Still later this land and more on both sides of the Mountain fell within the bounds of the Turkey Hills Ecclesiastical Society.

The Turkey Hills Ecclesiastical Society

As the number of settlers east of the Mountain increased and Turkey Hills began to prosper, a restive spirit grew in the people living there. The Simsbury meetinghouse, the sanctuary of their church and the seat of their government, was nine miles distant from some of their homes. Because horses were scarce and oxcarts slow, most walked to daylong church services and town meetings in all seasons. They crossed the Mountain,* bridged Salmon Brook, skirted Pickerel Cove, and followed the paths that have become Wolcott Road and Hopmeadow Street until they reached the meetinghouse. The trip was too arduous to be easily tolerated.** Their dissatisfaction led the people of Turkey Hills, in due course, to petition to have their own minister and to form their own ecclesiastical society.

Turkey Hills families could not elect to stay away from church. In those days Connecticut law required every citizen, whether he was a member of a church or not, to attend religious services each Sunday and fast day. Anyone who neglected to attend was brought before a magistrate and fined.

Until the Toleration Act of 1669, people of the Colony of Connecticut had been required to attend the Congregational Church, the established church of the colony. Connecticut's founding fathers had left England and come to the New England wilderness to establish a society in which they could practice their own religion without persecution. The idea that all other people should have the same religious freedom evolved only with time.

By the time the settlement began in Turkey Hills, people of other religions had increased in number throughout the colony and had begun to organize. But until St. Andrew's parish of the Anglican Church was founded in Simsbury's Scotland section (now North Bloomfield) about 1740, the Congregational Church was the only denomination available to the local townspeople.

For those who wished to join the Congregational Church (and many did not),

*At the time Turkey Hills Road over the Mountain was steeper than it is today. A work crew with steam drills reduced its grade just west of the Center during the fall and winter of 1900-01.

**A few of the families who settled on North Main Street went to the Suffield Congregational church, as the law mandating church attendance never stipulated which parish's services people had to attend. However, they did have to pay their church taxes for the support of the parish within which they lived.

there were two types of membership.* Adults joined as full members if they testified to a personal religious experience that included an overwhelming sense of guilt followed by a sense of forgiveness. Others, who had been baptized as children and had led respectable lives but who had not had a unique religious experience, joined as members under the "half-way covenant." All members could have their children baptized, but usually only full members were allowed to take communion.

Until 1727 by law all Connecticut citizens, whether church members or not, had to pay taxes to support the Congregational Church. All inhabitants of an ecclesiastical society voted on church doctrine. All participated in setting the local rates or taxes, choosing the minister, fixing his salary, and building and maintaining the meetinghouse.

By 1712 the congregation of the Simsbury church was fast becoming too large for the little meetinghouse on Hopmeadow Street. Another lengthy debate, reminiscent of the twelve-year controversy over the first building site, began. Should the old meetinghouse be enlarged or should a new one be built? Again, the old question, if the voters should decide on a new meetinghouse, where would it be located?

Finally, after thirteen years of discussion, with the vote at one meeting invariably rescinded at the next and the meetinghouse fast falling into a state of disrepair, the townspeople turned in desperation to the General Assembly. At one point a committee of the General Assembly proposed that the town be divided north and south into two ecclesiastical societies and that the northern society's meetinghouse be built near 90 Holcomb Street. The town rejected this plan, too.

In May 1729 the Turkey Hills settlers asked to be allowed to hire their own minister who would hold services in various homes. At that time the settlement had about thirty families, the minimum number the General Assembly usually recognized as sufficient to support a new parish. The Turkey Hills petition states that the settlers were

> *remote from public worship of God at the south part of the town* ... [so that] *we can't without difficulty give our attendance there.* ... *The greatest part of our families are under almost an impossibility to attend by reason of the distance and their tender years, so that religion and the interest in it seems to be in a languishing condition amongst us. We and our children* [are] *perishing for lack of vision. Whereas our numbers and abilities are at present but small, and we are not so able as we desire to bear the charge of preaching among us* ... *inasmuch as we are compelled to pay to the minister of the town of Simsbury and have little or no benefit,* ... *we humbly propose to the honorable court* ... *that we may be free from paying the minister's rate during the time that we have* ... *preaching among us.*

Many of the rest of Simsbury's townspeople objected to Turkey Hills' request. Its success would mean a loss of members and revenue for the existing congregation. Some people probably felt, quite rightly, that gaining the right to hire their own minister would be the first step toward complete independence for Turkey Hills.

The General Assembly decided in January 1730 that Turkey Hills could use its

*Apparently only one of John Griffin's children ever became a member of the Simsbury church, though all would have been obliged to attend it. This was his second son, Thomas, whose name appears on a list of forty-two members in 1710. Griffin's son-in-law Samuel Wilcockson was also a church member, but his daughter Mindwell Wilcockson was not. Thomas and Elizabeth Holcomb, the Griffins' only neighbors, were also listed as church members.

portion of the minister's rate to hire a Mr. Collins. He was almost certainly the Reverend Nathaniel Collins who had been the second minister in Enfield.

In 1732, with the site of a new meetinghouse still undecided, the Assembly repeated its permission for Turkey Hills to hire its own minister during the six coldest months each year, November through April. This ruling was in response to two documents. One, a map drawn by Samuel Higley,* clearly showed that the Simsbury meetinghouse was not in the center of the parish and that it could only be reached from Turkey Hills by a long trip over rough terrain. The other, a petition by William Moore and Timothy Phelps, estimated that Turkey Hills had forty-one families. It further stated that Turkey Hills had about 8000 acres of good land, especially on the east side of the Mountain.

Before the meetinghouse dispute was settled, the area around Copper Hill and the plain on the west side of the Mountain would be claimed by differing factions without much regard for the wishes of the residents of these areas. Also, these residents probably did not agree among themselves as to where they would like to attend church.

Encouraged by the previous support given them by the General Assembly, Turkey Hills residents petitioned in 1733 to be made a separate ecclesiastical society. The same year the majority of Simsbury's inhabitants indicated that they were at last sympathetic to Turkey Hills' cause. In March they voted that Turkey Hills and also Salmon Brook (now Granby) should "have liberty to be distinct ministerial societies or parishes," but the General Assembly was not yet ready to agree.

In 1735 Turkey Hills again petitioned to be allowed to form a separate church society for "the good of our own souls and the souls of our children." The next year, when the Assembly was again considering splitting Simsbury into a northern and southern society with Turkey Hills and Salmon Brook united and their meetinghouse on the west side of the Mountain, Turkey Hills protested. They pointed out that should that plan be adopted they would still have to travel two or three miles every Sunday, saying: "Our young children would be exposed to perishing circumstances; if they go to meeting, their bodies, and if they stay at home, their souls must be in perishing circumstances."

Finally in 1736, after twenty-four years of protesting that the Simsbury meetinghouse was too far away, the settlers of Turkey Hills were permitted by the General Assembly to become a separate ecclesiastical society within the Town of Simsbury. At this time Salmon Brook also became a separate society within the Town of Simsbury, and the Scotland section of town joined with parts of Windsor and Farmington to form the Wintonbury Ecclesiastical Society. Thereafter the southwest section of town that included the center of Simsbury was called the First Society.

The Turkey Hills Ecclesiastical Society was officially bounded "south by the little river *[the Farmington River]*, east by Windsor and Suffield bounds, north by Suffield, west by the last mentioned society *[Salmon Brook]*." A year later the Windsor families who lived along Simsbury's eastern border received permission to become part of the Turkey Hills Society while remaining part of the Town of Windsor. This area became known as the Windsor Half Mile because the lots the town granted there were half a mile wide from east to west.

Building a meetinghouse was the first major project for the people of Turkey Hills

*In 1973 an examiner of questioned documents of the Connecticut State Police verified that Samuel Higley was the author of this map by comparing the writing on the map with extant samples of Higley's handwriting.

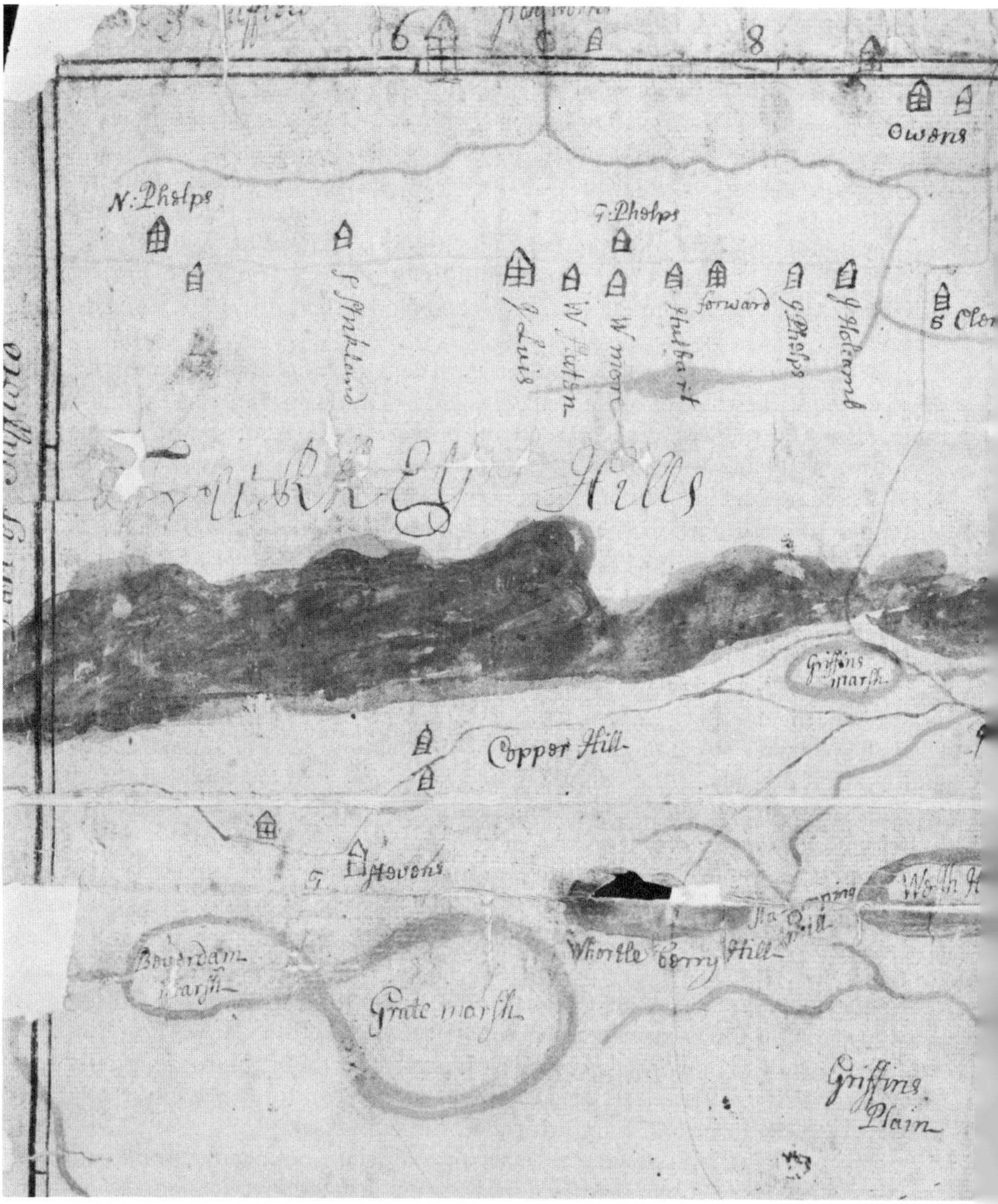

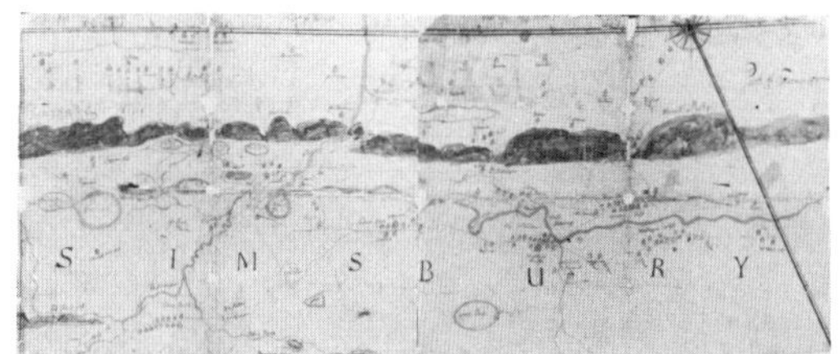

1732 Map of Simsbury in its entirety

Turkey Hills section of Simsbury.

Dr. Samuel Higley is believed to have made the map from which this portion is taken while Turkey Hills was petitioning to become a separate Ecclesiastical Society within the Town of Simsbury. He apparently presented the handsome, multicolored document to the General Assembly as evidence of the distance and difficulty of the trek Turkey Hills residents frequently were required to make to the Simsbury meetinghouse. The location of each Turkey Hills settler's house about 1732 is shown clearly, making the map an invaluable source for the study of local history. It is preserved in the Connecticut State Library Archives in Hartford.

Sketch of the Congregational meetinghouse, built 1738.

after they became a separate ecclesiastical society. Colonial law required each society to provide one.

Again the all-too-familiar question: Where should the meetinghouse be located? Turkey Hills applied for guidance to the General Assembly, whose committee chose a central site "in or against Samuel Clark's land." The site was just south of the present Combustion Engineering offices on South Main Street.

Samuel Clark objected strongly to having the meetinghouse built so close to his new house. Clark probably had visions of the townspeople's horses, oxen, carts, and sleighs all over his front yard during church services, because the society had no plans to build horse sheds. Also, the building proposed was to be of rougher construction than his house.

At a town meeting Samuel Clark was accused of getting Turkey Hills' deed of highways from the clerk by "some unjust means" before it could be recorded. Because the meetinghouse was to sit halfway on Clark's land and halfway on the highway, this was probably an attempt on Clark's part to foil building plans. However, it did not deter the society.

In October 1738 the society raised the frame of the meetinghouse. It shingled the roof and bought clapboards and nails during the following year. Clark still staunchly refused to sell to the society the land on which they were building. By October 1739 Clark had built a fence around the construction site. Though the society sent committee after committee to appeal to Clark and paid him £20 in damages, the fence remained until after his death. The society appointed a committee in 1771 to arrange for its removal. Clark's son Joel finally granted the land to the society in 1773.

The unpainted wooden meetinghouse had a cut stone foundation. Society records describe it as "40 feet in length and 35 feet in breadth; and 20 feet between joints." Its two gables were on the north and south ends of the building, which stood broadside to the road. A drawing done in 1793 and long accepted as a representation of this first meetinghouse shows "the great door" in one of the long sides.

The building had no chimney, thus no means of heat until 1828 when a stove was installed with the stovepipe run out a window. Its steeple was not added until 1798; however no bell ever hung in it. Customarily, when a meetinghouse had no bell, a drum or a raised flag summoned the townspeople.

Just when the structure was sufficiently complete to be used for church services is uncertain, but society meetings were being held in it by 1744. The parishioners voted to finish the interior walls "up to the girts," probably with wood sheathing, in 1748. They also voted to build a pulpit with a canopy to help to project the speaker's voice.

A year later the seats in the meetinghouse were "dignified" (that is, assigned precedence), the choicest being nearest the pulpit. Isaac Gillet, Joseph Forward, and Thomas Winchell were chosen to assign people to places in the nine "pews" and four "long seats." The pews were probably the stall-like seating enclosures common in churches of the day and the long seats what are now called pews.

The committee was instructed to assign seats according to a man's age and the amount of taxes he paid. Those who paid no taxes and were sixteen years or older were to be seated according to age alone. Thus the poor and the young were consigned to seats under the stairs and to the gallery. The gallery probably went along three sides of the church under an open ceiling.

In several years, those who sat in the long seats replaced them at their own expense with pews, which most likely cut down on drafts and helped contain the heat from the foot warmers and other paraphernalia the people brought along in winter to drive away the chill. By 1775 the society had grown until there were people regularly standing in the gallery during church services and society meetings. That year the society gave them permission to build seats if they wished, and it voted to have seats built for the black parishioners.

The ecclesiastical society also owned and cared for the parish's first cemetery. In 1722 a town meeting voted that Turkey Hills people "shall have liberty of a burying place to bury their dead if they purchase a place for the same." The site chosen was John Owen's sheep pasture, now the south half of the old cemetery at the center of town. The location was important, for men carried the coffin on their shoulders to the grave, however great the distance. Although the earliest gravestones are from the year 1737, there may be earlier, unmarked graves. Then, too, families sometimes buried their dead near their homes. Gravestones from these solitary graves have been used as doorsteps and in walkways by later generations.

The Congregational Church in the Society

Although the church records before 1776 are missing, it appears that the Saybrook Platform of 1708 influenced Turkey Hills church members as they organized their church government. The platform, which had been adopted by a convention of church leaders, had moved the Connecticut church away from the traditional Congregational practice of having autonomous congregations under strong ministers toward the Presbyterian practice of interaction among parishes in districts. Under the Saybrook Platform, a Congregational church belonged to an "association" of pastors.

These associations examined and licensed ministers before their ordination into the ministry. Consociations arbitrated disputes between pastors and their congregations, aided parishes without pastors to find candidates to fill the postions, and participated in the ordinations, installations, and dismissions of pastors.*

In Turkey Hills, the church members and all the other inhabitants of the ecclesiastical society participated in defining church doctrine and choosing and dismissing minsters. Church members were responsible for each parishioner's moral conduct, or "the sniffing out of sin." They also kept records of births, deaths, marriages, baptisms, and church covenants.

Each Sunday and fast day church services began by midmorning and ended at dusk. They included sermons and prayers, often an hour or more in duration, readings from scripture, and psalms chanted in an unmelodic drone.

Despite the obvious rigors of church attendance and the fact that some of the non-members might have preferred to spend their day of rest elsewhere, most Turkey Hills parishioners probably looked forward to Sunday. During the week the people, especially the women, were rather isolated on their farms. On Sunday they gathered together with their relatives and friends.

The midday intermission between services was a pleasant social hour. Groups gathered in homes near the meetinghouse to eat the noon meal they had brought with them. Some of the homes were inns with taprooms like Samuel Clark's next to the meetinghouse. Asahel Holcomb, who was a deacon of the church for over fifty years, was an innkeeper at the center of the parish. His first home was on the west half of lot 14, just north of Turkey Hills Road. An old foundation about a half-mile west of North Main Street may be the remains of this house. When he moved to 27-29 North Main Street around 1765, he opened that house to the public. In the pre-Revolutionary era before temperance movements appeared, tavernkeepers served their Sunday customers cider, beer, brandy, rum, flip (a drink made by sweetening hard cider and mixing it with spirits), and metheglin (made of honey and water fermented with yeast).

What to do about the minister must have been a frequent topic of conversation at the convivial gatherings in the taverns. The Turkey Hills Ecclesiastical Society dismissed its ministers with remarkable regularity. During the 108 years between 1742 and 1850 most of the parishes north of Hartford had about half-a-dozen ministers while Turkey Hills had fourteen. Five of these were temporary ministers who only stayed a few months. The parish was without a minister a total of thirty-nine years during this period. In contrast, the Suffield Congregational church enjoyed the uninterrupted ministry of the Reverend Ebenezer Gay and his son, Ebenezer, Jr., for ninety-five years.

Since ministers were better educated, owned larger libraries, and had a larger circle of associates than most of their parishioners, they were the cultural leaders in their communities. In their sermons, addresses, classes, and daily contact with the people, they influenced and educated them. A community left without an established minister, as Turkey Hills was so often, was deprived of both spiritual and practical leadership.

The Reverend Ebenezer Mills of Windsor was Turkey Hills' first settled minister,

*A licensed Congregational minister was "ordained" at a service in his first parish when he accepted the congregation's invitation to settle among them. He was "installed" in all subsequent parishes. He was "dismissed" when he and the congregation agreed to part. The term "dismission" or "dismissal" had about the same connotation as "honorable discharge." However, a congregation sometimes expressed disapproval of a minister by dismissing him without a recommendation.

100 South Main Street

though Mr. Collins and a Mr. Wolcott preached there occasionally before him. Mr. Mills, a Yale graduate, came to Turkey Hills in 1742 when he was only twenty-two. He married a Simsbury girl, Mary Drake, and built the house at 100 South Main Street called "the parsonage" in old records. (This house was greatly altered in the 19th century, so it is now quite different in appearance from the original.) Unlike better established and funded parishes, Turkey Hills did not provide a residence for its minister at that time.

Mr. Mills had agreed to a fixed salary but within two years he regretted the decision because inflation had depreciated its value. In 1745 the society appointed a committee to adjust Mr. Mills' salary but when nothing came of it by 1747, he complained to the local church consociation. A prolonged controversy followed during which the society offered Mr. Mills more than triple his original salary but attempts to settle with him were finally discontinued.

After Mr. Mills' dismissal in 1755, the society invited several ministers to settle and in 1760 finally secured the Reverend Nehemiah Strong. At first it seemed Mr. Strong would go the way of Mr. Mills, as arguments over money resumed. Society records say that "some that call themselves churchmen" were not paying their taxes. At one point the society resorted to the common practice of paying half Mr. Strong's salary in provisions. They gave him wheat, rye, corn, pork, and beef.

On May 13, 1766, a scandal surfaced from beneath the recorded financial difficulties. The settlers of Turkey Hills went before the North Consociation of Hartford County with seven charges against Mr. Strong.

They stated first that Mr. Strong had deceived the society by marrying a divorced woman shortly before his ordination and that his marriage had caused such great uneasiness and dissatisfaction among his parishioners that some of them had left the

Congregational Church and joined the Church of England. They would have gone either to St. Andrew's church just across the Farmington River in North Bloomfield or St. Ann's in Salmon Brook.*

As it happened, just before he left his tutoring post at Yale to come to Turkey Hills, Mr. Strong married Mrs. Lydia Smith Burr. Her first husband, Captain Andrew Burr, Jr., of New Haven, had gone to the West Indies. When he failed to return in four years, she divorced him on grounds of desertion and immediately married Mr. Strong. Burr returned and wanted her back. Mr. Strong resisted, so Burr petitioned the General Assembly, which annulled the divorce in May 1761, four months after Mr. Strong's ordination in Turkey Hills. Mrs. Strong went back to Burr.

The second charge against Mr. Strong was that his lawsuits with Burr and Darius Pinney, a local man, had hindered the pastor in his ministerial duties. Third, the complaints accused Mr. Strong of not trying to stop or reclaim those who left his church for the Church of England. Fourth, they said that Mr. Strong was guilty of equivocation and false representation while trying to evade a court action Darius Pinney wished to bring against him. Fifth, they said that Mr. Strong had agreed at the time of his ordination to accept part of his salary in provisions but later refused. Sixth, they said he refused to take the advice of his congregation and imprudently got into debt, then pressed the people so hard for money that they felt "a great uneasiness." Seventh, they claimed Mr. Strong preached unorthodox doctrine, *viz.:* "That God has made promises in His Word to the unregenerate to bestow saving and sanctifying grace by, or for, their endeavor or performance."

All charges were dismissed by the consociation, but first they were read in every church in the northern part of Hartford County. Mr. Strong wrote the weekly *Connecticut Courant* (predecessor to the *Hartford Courant*) requesting that the paper publish his side of the case. Editor Thomas Green devoted one and one-half pages of his four-page publication to the defense Mr. Strong had presented to the consociation.

Mr. Strong admitted that he had been involved in lawsuits with Burr and Pinney. He had bought a farm on North Main Street from Pinney but apparently had not been able to pay him when payment of his salary from the society was slow. So, he had asked the society for cash to pay the debt. Mr. Strong said he did not consider that he had dealt fraudulently with the society and he denied teaching unorthodox doctrine.

The consociation attempted to reconcile the minister and his parishioners but in February 1767 the society voted to dismiss him. The society petitioned the General Assembly to try to recover the £200 which they had initially given Mr. Strong in the expectation that he would settle in Turkey Hills. The petition was unanimously denied by the upper house and with only two dissenting votes in the lower. In addition, the Assembly allowed him £2 13s 8d in expenses.

Turkey Hills had a series of probationary ministers during the nine years following Mr. Strong's dismissal. Then, in the midst of the Revolutionary War, Turkey Hills celebrated the ordination of its third minister, the Reverend Aaron Jordan Booge. The affair, held November 26 and 27, 1776, must have been one to remember for a lifetime. Preparations had begun two weeks in advance with a day of fasting. Seventeen men

*The Reverend Roger Viets, grandson of Dr. John Viets, was the rector of St. Andrew's. His youthful vigor and dedication, shown by the many miles he traveled in his ministerial circuit, probably had as much to do as anything in influencing Turkey Hills residents to join the Church of England.

58 South Main Street

were appointed temporary tavernkeepers to house out-of-town guests and provide hospitality for all.*

On the appointed date an ecclesiastical council of pastors from eleven towns and a like number of deacons and other laymen gathered in John Thrall's house at 56 East Street. They questioned Mr. Booge, a Yale graduate from the section of Farmington that is now Avon, and examined his credentials. The next morning at eleven, the dignitaries officiated at a service in the meetinghouse which marked "the solemn setting apart *[of the]* said Mr. Booge *[to]* the sacred work of the Christian ministry and pastoral office in this place." Historian Albert Carlos Bates remarks that Mr. Booge's ordination ball was the most brilliant ever held in the community.

Schools in the Society

Most of the settlers of Turkey Hills were American colonists of the second and third generation. Their English born and educated fathers and grandfathers had helped

*Seven of these men lived in houses that are still standing in 1983: Elisha Winchell, 58 South Main Street; Daniel Halladay, 27 Hatchet Hill Road; Lemuel Bates, 116 North Main Street; Asahel Holcomb, 27-29 North Main Street; Nathaniel Mather, 62 Rainbow Road; Martin Winchell, 33 East Street. Elijah Owen lived in the back ell of the house at 23 East Street. Seven of them lived in houses that stood on or near the sites of newer houses that are still standing: Abel Forward, 43 Newgate Road; Elijah Alderman, 44 Hatchet Hill Road; Joseph Forward, 195-197 North Main Street; Benjamin Thrall, 88 South Main Street; Josiah Alford, 2 Washington Ridge Road; Daniel Willcox, 4 North Main Street; and Andrew Hillyer, south of 19 North Main Street. Joel Clark lived in the Samuel Clark house at the center of town and Zaccheus Gillet, on South Main Street.

To the Honoured Generall Assembly now sitting in Hartford.

Honoured ffathers.

Wee whose names are underwritten the present Inhabitants of Simsberry having bin formerly burthened by the inequallity of levying of rates (as the case is circumstanced with us) & now through the late afflictive dispensation of Gods providence having bin greater sufferers than other plantations in this collony & thereby allso in some measure at the present incapacitated to rayse rates in the common way that is stated in the country law: in this our infant state do humbly request & desire of this Honoured Assembly that they would be pleased to graunt us at the present that priviledge (which wee understand hath bin formerly & of late graunted to other plantations in their beginnings) viz: that all rates that shall be raysed for the defraying of publicke charges may be levyed only upon lands the farther grounds & reasons of this our request wee have desired Samuell Willcockson & Benajah Holcomb to represent to your Honours as our agents in this case: who are your very

Humble Servants.

May: 1th: 77

Samuell Stone.
Thomas Barber
John Petybone
Joseph Phelps
Peter Buell
John Drake
John Griffin
Josiah Clark
Nichall Humphrey
John Humphrey

…y Petition —

Letter to the General Assembly showing John Griffin's signature

write the 1639 Fundamental Orders of Connecticut and had served from the first in the General Assembly. Some settlers were descendants of William Phelps who was one of eight commissioners appointed by the General Court of Massachusetts to govern the new Colony of Connecticut during its first year, 1636. Samuel Clark was the grandson of Daniel Clark who was Secretary of the Colony for several years.

Since the founders of the colony were religious, law-abiding, and hardworking men themselves, they naturally wanted their children to be able to read the Bible and the laws of the colony and to be equipped for "some lawful calling or employment." From the first, they made selectmen responsible for seeing that parents and the masters of apprentices did not neglect the education of children under their care. Selectmen, they said, should question the young people on their knowledge of religious principles.

Under the 1650 Code of Laws, every town with more than fifty households had to have a schoolmaster to teach the children to read and write. Within a few years, the "county towns" of Hartford, New Haven, New London, and Fairfield had to provide grammar schools, which offered courses above the elementary level for students preparing for college. At this time the term "school" referred to a teacher and students, not necessarily to a schoolhouse.

A town the size of Simsbury during its early years was not required and probably could not afford to have even an elementary school. The children of pioneers like Sergeant John Griffin had no teachers but their parents. And parents had little time to spare from the daily struggle for subsistence for tutoring. Consequently, some of their children never learned to read and write.

Sergeant John Griffin could write his name, as illustrated by his signature on a document in the Connecticut State Archives. Probably none of his children learned to write as youngsters. His four sons and two of his daughters affixed their marks to the distribution of his estate thirty years after his death. On later documents, his sons Ephraim and John Griffin, Jr., signed their names.

School attendance was not compulsory, so, even in towns like Windsor that had a schoolmaster from a very early date, some of the children remained untaught. Then, again, school lessons could easily fade from memory in an isolated, beginning settlement where they had little application. Stephen Winchell of Windsor, probably the first settler east of the Mountain, sometimes signed with a mark. He owned books as shown by the inventory of his estate.

A 1700 law required all towns, regardless of size, to hire schoolmasters to teach reading and writing. It also required each town to collect a tax for schools of 40 shillings per £1000 of its Grand List. If the money raised was not enough to support adequate schools, the town, parents of the schoolchildren, and any "estate bequeathed for that use" were to make up the difference. The expected proceeds from the copper mines that were allocated for education in Simsbury might be classified loosely under the last category.

Simsbury chose a committee "to agree about the measure and method of a school and choose a schoolmaster and agree with him according to the rules of the law." John Slater, town clerk and surveyor, became Simsbury's first schoolmaster. He was expected to teach the children "to read, write, and to cipher, or to say the rules of arithmetic as are capable." Sergeant Griffin's grandchildren and Thomas Holcomb's children probably attended the classes he held "on the plain" west of the Mountain for three months of the year while their contemporaries in the southern section of town went to the three-month session in Weatogue. To be sure, no session interfered with planting and harvesting.

The very young children usually did not attend the schoolmaster's class. Groups of these little boys and girls gathered throughout town in the homes of women capable of teaching them the rudiments of reading and writing. In 1704 the Town of Simsbury officially recognized these dame schools, as they were called.

At this time a girl's formal education usually did not extend beyond dame school. Boys usually went on to the schoolmaster's "common school."

By 1725 the children in Turkey Hills were being instructed in schools close to home. That year John Holcomb was in charge of distributing tax revenues among the schools in this section of Simsbury.

Three years passed after Turkey Hills became an ecclesiastical society before the parish held its first annual election of a school committee. It consisted of blacksmith Timothy Phelps, miner John Christian Miller, and ferryman-miller Joseph Alderman. This committee hired teachers, decided where schools should be held, and managed school funds. By then ecclesiastical societies had the legal right and obligation to raise taxes for their own schools.

At least until 1749 any teacher in Turkey Hills held school at home or in someone else's home in a room rented by the school committee. At that time the society voted "to give liberty to set up a schoolhouse near the meetinghouse." If a schoolhouse was built, it may have been the "small schoolhouse" at the Center which is mentioned in later parish records. Its location is not known. A 1757 entry in Captain John Viets' daybook also mentions a schoolhouse.

In 1751 the society voted "to hire a schoolmaster to keep school for four months in the winter season at the Center as near the meetinghouse as may be." Before this time, Turkey Hills may have had only dame schools. Soon the parish had five school districts, two on the west side and three on the east side of the Mountain. Each had its own dame or common school.

Children learned their first lessons from a hornbook. This was a small board shaped like a short-handled paddle with a printed sheet attached to each side and covered with a transparent sheet of horn. Usually the alphabet, the Lord's Prayer, and some one- and two-syllable words were printed on the hornbook. Textbooks in the common schools included the Bible, books of psalms, catechisms, and spelling books. Paper and ink being scarce, young scholars sometimes substituted birch bark and charcoal as writing tools.

Turkey Hills did not have a grammar school, so ministers usually prepared local boys for college. Four from Turkey Hills were graduated from Yale before the Revolutionary War. Captain John Viets sent his son Roger "to learn and board" at the home of the Reverend Samuel Tudor, the Congregational minister in Poquonock. He paid Tudor £8, a deer skin, and a pig. The Reverend Nehemiah Strong prepared Timothy Phelps' grandson Alexander Gillet for Yale. Estate inventories included books on law, Latin, medicine, history, geography, grammar, and religion—subjects studied by these advanced students.

Most boys did not go to college. Many learned trades from their fathers or became apprentices to other craftsmen.

Both in school and at home, discipline was strict and corporal. Manners and morals were important. Children were taught courtesy and right from wrong. According to Daniel Barber, a Simsbury soldier in the Revolutionary War, this early training paid off. In his reminiscences of the war, he writes of his arrival at Roxbury, Massachusetts, shortly after the Battle of Lexington:

Having . . . surveyed . . . the military and warlike appearances on all sides, our first inclination was to sit down, and . . . write home . . . a description of everything . . . interesting. The New England boys were all taught the use of pen, ink and paper. . . . There were many private soldiers, who were young gentlemen of education and handsome fortunes. And further, as a token of Connecticut good habits and moral instructions early inculcated, not a soldier of our regiment was put to any punishment during this campaign.

4

Early Livelihood

ALTHOUGH individual colonists were usually jacks-of-all-trades with more than one marketable skill, farming was the principal occupation of most of them during the 18th century. This was especially true of the inhabitants of small, interior settlements like Turkey Hills. An article in the *Courant* of April 25, 1768, praises these tillers of the soil:

Farming or husbandry is the method of life our Creator first assigned us. The farmer uses no corruption but manure; he hatches no intrigues but poultry; he brews no mischief but beer; he fears no beasts of envy, though he dreads the blasts of heaven and instead of fortifying cattle he fences fields, because he hath no enemies but vermin.

To begin a farm in a wilderness like Turkey Hills in the early 1700s, a family cleared the brush and scrub from a plot of land and stripped sheets of bark from the larger trees to kill them. The following spring the farmer steered his ox-drawn plow between the trunks and planted his first crop. Then season after season, he chopped down and uprooted the leafless forest in his field. No eyebrows would be raised nor would there be loss of face should the farmer's wife or daughter take a turn at the plowing or hauling.

A yoke of oxen provided the muscle the farmer needed to pull stumps, drag boulders, and fence in his cropland. Horses were a luxury to be used for light work and riding. Since domestic animals did not prosper on forage in the forests and marshes as game animals did, the settlers imported seed to grow nutritious English hay.

For their own food, the farm family planted Indian corn, beans, squash, and pumpkins, as well as peas, cucumbers, carrots, parsnips, beets, barley, wheat, rye, and oats. According to the Viets family genealogy, Captain John Viets, who ran a trading post, may have introduced the potato to this area, bringing the seed from Rhode Island in his saddlebags.

Each household made its bread from the grain it sowed, reaped, threshed, and winnowed by hand. When there was no gristmill nearby to grind the grain into flour, the settlers used a mortar and pestle or a simple hand mill called a quern. Each household also made its own butter and cheese.

As soon as a family could, it planted an orchard. The earliest land transfers in Turkey Hills list house, barn, and orchard, in that order. Fruit trees were so prized they were mentioned individually in wills. In 1736 Isaac Owen's widow, Sarah, inherited part of his orchard near 23 East Street, including "one certain apple tree a sweet belo-bound [*probably an incorrect spelling of* bellibone *which was the English form of the French* belle et bonne] about the middle of the orchard, the middle one of three."

In like manner, Moses Holcomb, who died in 1752, left his widow, Elizabeth, "one-third of a pear tree standing near the house." This house stood near or on the site of the house at 33 North Main Street.

Apples were used fresh or they were preserved by drying or making them into apple butter, vinegar, or cider. Because the colonists believed water might be unhealthy to drink, even small children drank fermented cider. To make this drink, cider makers dropped apples into a cider mill; i.e., two upright cylinders that were notched so that they meshed. A horse attached to the mill by a long wooden arm turned the cylinders as he walked around them in a circle. As the apples fell through the mill, they were ground to a mash called "cheese." Operators removed the cheese from the mill and placed it in a cider press with alternating layers of straw. They laid a heavy board on top of the cheese and applied pressure to the board by tightening, with a long pole, large wooden screws. Freshly squeezed cider ran out of the grooved bottom of the press and drained into barrels.

To supplement what they could grow, a farm family gathered wild foods in the woods and along the watercourses. They harvested maple sap and wild honey, berries, nuts, mushrooms, Jerusalem artichoke tubers, and salad greens, such as watercress, cowslip, milkweed, dandelion, and fern.

Families in Turkey Hills and neighboring communities also relied heavily on the fish and eels they took out of the Farmington River, Salmon Brook, and other local streams. The Colony of Connecticut demonstrated a protective interest in fishing in the Farmington River through legislation. In 1681, when Ephraim Howard wanted to build a mill on the south bank in Scotland, the Hartford County Court granted permission with the understanding that he was not to obstruct the passage of fish, including large numbers of shad and salmon which came up the river every spring to spawn. During the 1700s the General Assembly regulated dams and the use of nets and weirs, particularly at the mouth of the river in Windsor.

The settlers had good hunting in those early days, too. They augmented the beef, pork, and poultry they raised with venison, bear, squirrel, rabbit, goose, duck, pigeon, and turkey. One very early record mentions that Sergeant John Griffin hunted moose. Old inventories often list pigeon nets. Passenger pigeons, now extinct, were once so abundant they were a nuisance to farmers. Efforts have been made recently to reestablish the wild turkey, once plentiful, in New England. The last native turkey in New England was reported shot on Mt. Tom in Massachusetts in 1851.

The everyday dinners of the early settlers were of plain fare, especially during a winter following a lean harvest. Preservation of food was a constant problem and time-consuming chore. The settlers relied on smoking, drying, pickling, and salting (sometimes called powdering) to keep food edible. They used herbs and spices to make it palatable.

Salt was an imported and sometimes scarce item. Like spices, sugar, molasses, and rum, it was brought at considerable expense from the West Indies.

In addition to their fields and orchards, the early settlers depended heavily on their woodlots. With wood they built, furnished, and heated their homes, cooked their meals, and fenced their land. They used homemade wooden plows and harrows, spades and shovels, hoes and rakes, sickles and scythes, pitch and dung forks. If they could get imported or native metal, they made, or had a local blacksmith make, iron teeth and blades. The iron parts of implements were handed down from generation to generation.

Wills often limited the amount of wood heirs could cut each year in the family woodlot. The minister's annual pay usually included a specified number of cords of wood. Even the right to collect driftwood along the Farmington River had a price.

During the first century of the settlement's existence, families produced most of their own clothes and household linens. Each spring farmers washed their sheep and sheared their thick winter fleece. Throughout the rest of the year, farm women carded the wool and spun it into yarn, which they wove into cloth for sheets, bed rugs, and clothes, or knitted into stockings.

Also each spring the farmers planted a crop of flax which added a brilliant splash of blue flowers to their fields. After the fall harvest, the farm families soaked their flax plants in a stream or pond to soften the tough outer coating of the stalks. Then they broke open the stalks with a flax brake to expose the inner fibers. They hatcheled, or combed, these fibers and spun them into linen yarn. The fabric they wove became bed linens, towels, napkins, handkerchiefs, shirts, gowns, petticoats, aprons, and bonnets.

Women made soap from animal fat and lye leached from wood ash. They dipped bayberry and beeswax candles and sent their children to hunt the resinous, flammable knots in decaying pine stumps.

In time, small commercial enterprises lessened the rigors of self-sufficiency. Mills, especially, were welcome additions to any new settlement. As early as 1730, Turkey Hills men began to build several types of mills along the area's streams.

Dr. John Viets built his linseed-oil mill on his home lot east of Salmon Brook in the early 1700s. Salmon Brook was a millstream in 1751 when Joseph Wilcoxson, Jr., grandson of Sergeant John Griffin, and Brewster Higley, Jr., grandson of Captain John Higley, dammed its waters to make a millpond. By 1784 this site behind 115 Hartford Avenue had two gristmills and a sawmill. Muddy Brook had a sawmill south of Turkey Hills Road by 1752.

In 1766 the town granted Deacon Asahel Holcomb liberty to build a dam across Trout Brook (now Creamery Brook) "and to raise a pond and turn the stream for the use and benefit of setting up a corn mill." This mill would have been on the west side of North Main Street just north of the Center.

Within a few years there was a gristmill near the site of the West Iron Works on Stony Brook at the Simsbury-Suffield line. John Lewis, his son Hezekiah, and his son-in-law Lemuel Bates were involved in building and operating the mills. In addition to local mills, residents on Copper Hill used the mill at Westfield, Massachusetts. They probably traveled there along the shore of The Ponds (Congamond Lakes).

Although local millers did not harness the power of the Farmington River until a later time, many of them built close to the river at the mouths of their millstreams. The 1732 map of Simsbury shows Thomas Holcomb's gristmill north of the Falls. Around 1750 Jeremiah Case built a gristmill and a sawmill at what would become Tariffville.

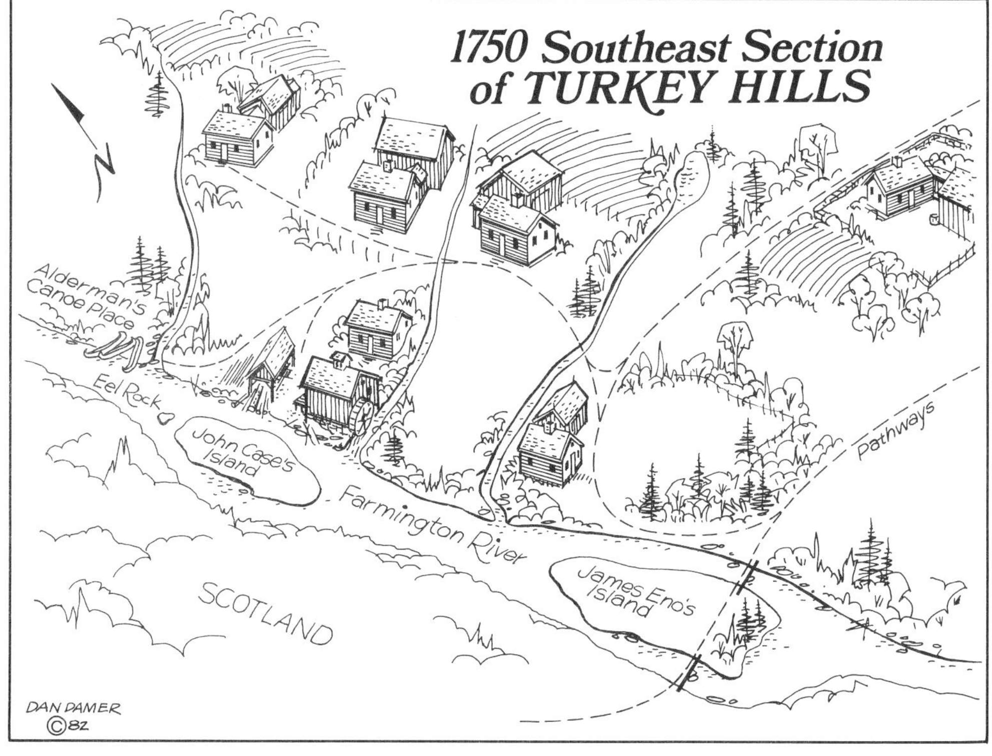

Artist's concept of millsite on the Farmington River. This section of town later became known as Spoonville after the Cowles Manufacturing Company built a factory across from James Eno's Island.

Down river at Poquonock were the Rainbow Mills. Turkey Hills men, Matthew Griswold, Isaac Gillet, Lemuel Bates, and Hezekiah Lewis, were among the owners of these mills from the early 1730s to the close of the century.

By 1749 Daniel Granger, originally of Suffield, had obtained permission from the Hartford County Court to dam a stream that flows from the north into the Farmington River. Its mouth is near the island just west of the present Spoonville bridge. Part of the foundation of either the sawmill or the gristmill he built still stands there. During the 1750s Joseph Alderman, Elisha Winchell, and Joshua Holcomb were part owners of this enterprise. It seems to have been unprofitable because, when blacksmith Thomas Griffin bought the property in 1759, the mills were described as much out of repair. Evidently Griffin was more successful, as he continued to operate the mills and an adjoining fishery until his death in 1803.

The Farmington River transported much of the timber to the sawmills along its shores. Skilled loggers usually cut timber during the winter—hauling the logs to the riverbank was easiest when the ground was frozen hard and paved with snow. Anywhere from eight to twenty yoke of oxen were necessary to pull a sled carrying one of the huge logs destined to become the mast of an oceangoing ship.

The logs were twitched into the Farmington River while it was swollen and swift during the spring thaw. Much of the smaller timber was delivered to nearby sawmills while the mast logs went on to shipbuilders on the Connecticut River.

In December 1762 London Freebody mortgaged land to Joseph Griswold for £60 with this understanding: "that if the said London shall well and truly bring down the river from Hartland 300 white pine logs that lie on the bank of the river . . . belonging to said Griswold and deliver said logs to Mr. Joshua Holcomb, Jr., at a place called Pickerel Cove . . . the foregoing deed of conveyance should be void." The £60 was probably the capital Freebody needed to undertake this business venture. He evidently put up his land as security for the loan.

Another agreement, between Jonathan Higley, Dr. Higley's son, and Eliphalet Michelson, describes the start of a fishery on the Farmington River. In it Higley agreed to cut a channel through a certain rock in the river by Michelson's land on the south side of the river. The channel near Eel Rock was to be "for the use and design of catching and taking of fish that may be annually swimming up and down said river." Higley also agreed to pay "one-half of the cost and expenses in making and maintaining proper and convenient wooden works, fish garth, pots or nets for the catching of fish—taking one-half of the profits of said fishing place." Just a year and a day from the date of this agreement, Higley's brother-in-law Edward Thompson recorded in his diary: "Brother Jonathan Higley drowned in attempting to swim across the river with his frock on at Alderman's canoe place July the 8, 1771, and [*was*] taken up about six days after on a small island near the sawmill—an island about 3 or 4 miles down the river."

The "canoe place" mentioned was at the mouth of a brook a bit west of Thomas Griffin's mill and fishery. Joseph Alderman ran a ferry service there, which was the means in that locality of crossing the river. Once across, a traveler could go the rest of the way to Windsor on foot along Griffin's Path.

By 1719 there was a bridge from Turkey Hills to the island that lies just east of the Spoonville bridge and another bridge from the island to Scotland. The present dirt road along the north bank of the river at this place is called Old Church Road. The name probably stems from the fact that the road led to these early bridges and was the route Turkey Hills Episcopalians traveled to St. Andrew's church in Scotland.

Early residents crossed the river regularly for neighborly visits as well as to worship. They also crossed to trade. All local families, which were consistently large, tried to produce surplus crops, livestock, and handiwork to barter. They traded with other households or with professional traders, who could provide them with items that could not be produced locally.

Captain John Viets was probably Turkey Hills' first commercial trader. By 1738 he was running a trading post in one of the two houses he owned on the west side of the Copper Hill before he built the house now known as the Viets Tavern, 106 Newgate Road, around 1763. His account books show the variety of his wares and the extent of his business. The earliest book also indicates that Abel Forward, who lived near the present house at 43 Newgate Road, was Viets' partner in some trading ventures. Viets' and Forward's trading trips took them to the frontier towns of Schenectady and Albany in New York; to Boston, Cape Cod, and Martha's Vineyard in Massachusetts; and to Rhode Island.

Viets equipped many local homes with woodenware and earthenware. He bought horses from farmers all around the countryside and drove them to market in Boston, where he traded for the imported allspice, indigo, beads, thread, pins, needles, silk,

Viets Tavern

velvet, lace, quires of paper, books, and jackknives with which he stocked his post.

Many local families kept a running balance on account and paid Viets in labor, produce, and homecrafted products. Women brought in weaving, sewing, and knitting. Men brought cider, tar, woodenware, and animal skins, including muskrat, beaver, raccoon, fox, bear, and deer. Local blacksmiths shod his horses; shoemakers, tailors, and seamstresses outfitted his family; joiners made furniture for his homes. Neighbors cleared, fenced, and cultivated his land—all in return for the merchandise of his trading post.

Captain John usually settled a customer's balance with a notation in his daybook witnessed by both parties. One of his more dramatic notations reads: "Then balanced all books from the beginning of the world to this day between William Ross and John Viets."

After he moved to Turkey Hills, in about 1745, Richard Dana Gay* set up a mercantile shop which was probably a refinement on Viets' early trading posts. Gay's shop was in his home, which stood near 129 North Main Street. Gay's first account book is not extant but his second, dating from 1789, gives a description of his varied wares.

He sold items such as soap grease (animal fat for rendering into soap), buckles, ribbon, cloth, cloth shoes, homespun coats, meat, vegetables, grains, butter, cheese, cider, wine, and brandy. He also sold services. He would "hoop your barrel," "bottom your chair," mend saddles, pasture animals, and rent a horse and oxen. He even rented half a house at £1 per year. Most of Gay's transactions, like Viets', were settled by barter rather than cash.

Though the Viets and Gay establishments offered imports and the convenience of a variety of goods, they handled only part of the trading done in colonial Turkey Hills. Townspeople bartered for products and services at almost every house in town.

The men who lived along the path that is now North Main Street are good examples of the numbers and kinds of artisans, entrepreneurs, and professionals in Turkey

*Richard Dana Gay, brother of Suffield pastor Reverend Ebenezer Gay, Sr., was one of the few colonists born before the Revolution who had a middle name. In Europe, where the population was denser, they came into use earlier.

Hills just before and during the Revolutionary War. Their account books and the inventories of their estates list tools and other particulars that show the several types of work each did, in addition to farming, and other aspects of their lives. Sometimes the records reveal when and how they built their houses, shops, and farm buildings.

Traveling down the street today it is still possible, with a little imagination, to envision the scene that was familiar to those farmer-tradesmen more than 200 years ago. They had built their houses in the middle of their rectangular farms and had worn a path from one dooryard to the next. The meandering dirt lane skirted a stump here and a boulder there.

During the spring thaw, the path was an almost impassable morass of mud and ruts. When it was dryer, cows, sheep, horses, swine, and poultry came to feed on the grassy, flowered strip between the two dirt tracks which were packed hard by cart wheels. The animals were allowed to graze there because roadways were considered part of the town commons. Ownership of the wandering livestock was ascertained by an earmark each owner registered with the town clerk. The swine had rings in their noses to prevent them from rooting and yokes around their necks to keep them from wandering too far, as colonial law required.

On either side of the path were tree-shaded houses, wells, and barns. Like all New England settlers, Turkey Hills farmers housed their livestock close to their own residences so that the animals could be tended easily during the winter. Kitchen gardens also grew close to the houses, while stone- or wood-fenced fields surrounded the homesites. Fruit trees grew near at hand in orchards. The far reaches of each homestead along the mountain ridge to the west usually were not cleared of trees nor drained of marshes. These acres served as woodlots and hunting grounds.

At the northerly end of the path, where it intersected the Suffield border, a trail forked to the west. David Winchell of Suffield used this access to the swamp lying at the foot of the Mountain. Here he gathered the reeds he wove into baskets.

The northernmost farm on the path comprised the north half of lot 1 of the land grants of 1688 and about 50 acres of the lot to its north. All belonged to Nathaniel Phelps who had come to Turkey Hills from Northampton, Massachusetts, about 1715. Like all of the Turkey Hills Phelpses, he was a descendant of William Phelps of Windsor. The 1732 map of Simsbury shows his house on the east side of the path. He may have specialized in weaving. When Joseph Cornish, Sr., recorded his daughter Elizabeth's dowry in his account book of 1747, one item was £1 7s to Phelps for weaving.

The present house at 229 North Main Street is built over an old brownstone block foundation that is laid dry. Originally, this was probably the foundation of the home of Nathaniel Phelps, Jr. Another son, Ebenezer, lived in his father's house until 1788 when he moved to South Grand Street in Suffield. According to a 19th century deed, Ebenezer was buried on Round Hill. The house at 212 North Main Street probably was built in 1806 by Ebenezer's son Eber.

John Granger came over from Suffield in 1735 and bought a house John Owen had built about 1720 on the south portion of lot 1. The Granger family eventually had

212 North Main Street

two houses by the path and one back on the Mountain. These buildings are gone now.

The Forward family lived on the second grant. In 1738 Joseph Forward bought a house, now gone, that stood near the one at 195-197 North Main Street. In 1762 Forward's son Joseph hired Joseph Cornish, Jr., to help build another house on the same property. This may have been the brick house that is mentioned in later records.

Forward, one son, and a grandson—all of them named Joseph—specialized in the messy, smelly art of tanning leather. Local farmers traded animal skins and tree bark used in the tanning process for products the Forwards made. Men of that day used leather breeches, jackets, and aprons as well as shoes, boots, saddles, harnesses, and other leather items.

Some Forwards turned to a profession rather than a trade. The first Joseph Forward had a son Justus, who was ordained a minister at Belchertown, Massachusetts, in 1755. He served there until his death in 1814. His cousin Abel Forward, Jr., preached in Turkey Hills for a few months before becoming the first minister of the Congregational church in Southwick, Massachusetts, in 1773. According to Southwick historian Gilbert Arnold, after Forward died in 1786, his widow preached in his place. However, like any other woman, she was not allowed to vote on church matters.

Samuel Strickland lived on the east side of the path, south of the Forwards. His son Joseph was a weaver who would board with a family for weeks at a time while he wove cloth for them. In 1779 Samuel's grandson Eli Strong built a house and blacksmith shop on or near the site of the house at 173 North Main Street.

173 North Main Street

Just south of this house is a brick one (171 North Main Street) which James Moor, a cooper, built in 1770. Joseph Cornish, Jr., sold him timber and carted brick for the house from Windsor. According to family tradition, the Moor house was used as a tavern.

171 North Main Street

The Cornish farm was a bit farther down the path. Joseph Cornish, Sr., a grandson of the first schoolmaster at Northampton, Massachusetts, bought 177 acres here in 1736. He first built a small house, now gone, then a larger one—a common practice at the time. He sold 67 acres of his land, 44 of which became James Moor's home lot.

The senior Cornish was a tailor who stitched leather breeches for the men of Turkey Hills. He was also employed as a carter, to haul goods. As his children became old enough, they also worked for their neighbors. His son Joseph helped construct houses, and his daughter Elizabeth spun yarn for the John Thralls and quilted for the Forwards. Everyone's work, which was carefully entered into the family's account book, was bartered for the needs of the whole family.

143-145 North Main Street

Cornish's son Joseph remained on the farm after his father's death in 1759 and built himself a house in 1765, presently 143-145 North Main Street. He continued the account book which shows he prospered as a builder and a potash maker.

To make potash, which was used in making soap and glass, Joseph Cornish, Jr., bought wood ashes from people in Turkey Hills and nearby towns. He leached these ashes with water to get a lye solution which he boiled until the water evaporated, leaving the potash, or "black salt," on the bottom of his pot.

Historian Albert Carlos Bates recalls the equipment used in this operation:

In the writer's boyhood days there rested against a low bank in front of the old Cornish house . . . two or three iron kettles; I would call them cauldrons rather than kettles. They were in the shape of a shallow hemisphere with a wide flat rim around the top and my recollection is that they would hold nearly or quite a barrel.

After his potash was loaded into barrels, it was drawn by oxen to a river town—his account book names Windsor, Hartford, Rocky Hill, and Wethersfield—and shipped to a seaport, usually New York. Because wood was scarce in England, potash was one of the few products the English government encouraged the colonists to produce and export to the mother country. Joseph Cornish's account book indicates he was well paid for his product and paid in specie, which was scarce. Since he used the money to pay other local people for their ashes and for helping to make the potash, his enterprise invigorated the local economy.

Richard Dana Gay, the shopkeeper, lived below the Cornishes. His brick home is now gone, as are his barns on both sides of the path and his cider-mill house, where he stored his empty cider barrels, his cider mill, and press. His son Richard's house (123 North Main Street), built about 1779, is still owned by one of his direct descendants.

Richard Dana Gay and his neighbor to the south, Lemuel Bates, were among the largest landowners in Turkey Hills. Both lived on lot 7 where Timothy Phelps had built his cellar home seventy years before.

123 North Main Street

In 1760 Lemuel Bates bought Timothy Phelps' home from his heirs. Then in 1773, Bates built himself a larger home (116 North Main Street) which is now owned by his great-great-great-granddaughter, Kathleen Bates.

116 North Main Street

Lemuel Bates ran a tavern in his home. Innkeepers were licensed by the General Assembly. At one time an innkeeper was not allowed to serve more than half a pint of wine to a person at one sitting, and he had to watch that no patron drank for more than half an hour or after nine o'clock at night.

For local people, the several inns in town served as informal meeting places where they could learn the latest news. Dates of town meetings, election results, and new laws were posted on their walls along with notices of auctions, house raisings, and husking bees. For travelers, the inns served as stopovers where they and their horses could rest and dine.

Besides being an innkeeper, Bates was a saddler, a mill owner, a soldier, a frequent officeholder in the town and parish, and a trader. He and Phineas Griswold built a sloop on the Farmington River with timber cut on the Bates farm. Griswold sailed it to the West Indies several times to purchase sugar and molasses which Bates sold.

Lemuel Bates bought three houses south of his that William Moor, James Moor's father, once owned. The houses are now gone. Dr. John Howe and his wife, Lydia Gay Howe, lived in one that stood north of 95 North Main Street. Dr. Howe was Turkey Hills' fourth doctor, succeeding John Viets, Samuel Higley, and John Nelson. Dr. Nelson, who died in 1766, lived on South Grand Street.

The Samuel Forward family owned the next lot to the south which is now part of 81 North Main Street. The second Samuel Forward, who died in 1762, was a chairmaker and a cooper. Coopers were important artisans in an age when most food was stored in wooden barrels, tubs, firkins, pails, buckets, and kegs. Local families needed special containers for butter, cheese, and suet; as well as tubs in which to do the powdering, the washing, and so on. Joseph Phelps even had a "bear barrel."

When the first Joseph Phelps, a housewright, came to Turkey Hills, he bought lots 10 and 11 and the land adjoining them on the Mountain, at least 250 acres in all. The home of his son Joseph stands today as the kitchen of the house at 71 North Main Street.

Joseph Phelps, Jr., who died in 1775, three years after his wife Deborah, left an inventory that suggests he was both a carpenter and a shoemaker. The clothes

71 North Main Street

listed show what a well-to-do couple might have worn in colonial Turkey Hills.

Joseph left his four coats, a cloak, three vests, three jackets with sleeves, three pairs of breeches—two of them leather for working outdoors—eight shirts, six pairs of stockings including one blue linen pair, leather gloves, caps, boots, shoes with silver buckles, knee buckles, and silver sleeve buttons. He also had a wig. Some of Deborah's clothes had probably been disposed of by the time Joseph died. Left to be recorded in his estate were her mitts, gloves, five caps including a nightcap, four hoods, four aprons—one each of linen, holland, and muslin, and one of tow and wool combined—one gown, two shifts, and a striped wrapper.

A grandson of Joseph Phelps, Sr., Ezekiel Phelps, Jr., was finishing the present house at 39 North Main Street when he died in 1789. This Phelps was a blacksmith. No doubt he made the finely wrought latch and hinges on the unusual cupboard built into the base of the chimney of his new house. He evidently made brass clock movements as his inventory lists "old bellows, vice, anvil, and bickhorn with all the materials belonging to clock making" and a small amount of old brass.

39 North Main Street

In 1776 Samuel Booth bought the house of the first Joseph Phelps that stood near the entrance to East Granby Estates and built a shoemaker's shop near it. When he died two years later, he left eighty pounds of sole leather, a side of upper leather, five sides of horse leather, calf and sheep skins, and animal hides. His three cords of "tanner's bark" suggest that he, like the Joseph Forwards, did his own tanning.

The number of Booth's livestock shows he was also a prosperous husbandman for his day. He owned a sow and four shoats, thirty-two sheep, four horses, three yoke of oxen, fourteen cows, and a bull. Few early inventories included bulls as each section of Simsbury had a man appointed "to provide bulls for the benefit of and use of their respective squadron."

The Holcomb family lived south of the Phelpses and Booths on lot 12. John Holcomb, Sr., had a small house with a cellar, two rooms on the first floor, and one on the second. It stood on or near the site of the present house at 33 North Main Street. His son Moses, who inherited the house, was a cooper.

At the south end of his father's lot, John Holcomb, Jr., built the house at 27-29 North Main Street after 1736. John Holcomb, Jr., was a tailor. Captain John Viets' daybook credits him "for cutting out a coat for Jonny my boy" and again "for cutting out a coat and waistcoat for the same boy."

33 North Main Street

The artisans, traders, and tavern keepers along North Main Street are but a sampling of men who conducted business from their homes and shops in the town before the end of the Revolutionary War. Many of the men who lived west of the mountain ridge on the pine plains and along the east branch of Salmon Brook were millers, loggers, and turpentine makers.

In the Copper Hill area, Benoni Viets, who as a child was a ward of Dr. John Viets, became a skilled blacksmith and a horse trader in partnership with Captain John Viets. Benoni Viets built his first house and blacksmith shop just north of the entrance to the gun club on South Main Street. The cellar hole, now overgrown with sumac, marks the site at present. About 1746 he moved to a house on the east side of the southern end of Newgate Road. Older townspeople remember this second home as the "house under the Mountain."

27-29 North Main Street

Captain Viets' brother Henry worked as a shoemaker and a blacksmith at his home near 31 Griffin Road. The house now on this site was built by Henry's son, James Viets. It stayed in the family until 1915. Thomas Stevens, son of one of the copper miners from Great Britain, lived near Henry Viets. As an early commercial farmer, he sold quantities of grain to townspeople.

31 Griffin Road

Ezekiel Phelps, Sr., who lived at 38 Holcomb Street, was a weaver, tailor, carpenter, and stoneworker, as well as a farmer.

Along Turkey Hills' eastern boundary, Stephen Winchell and John Thrall raised horses, possibly for sale. Their estate inventories list more than a farmer's usual number of horses. Horses were one of Connecticut's major exports at the time. When he died in 1749, Thrall left the tools of a carpenter, a blacksmith, and a shoemaker. Matthew Griswold, who bought Thrall's house in 1768, was a brickmaker.

At 62 Rainbow Road, Nathaniel Mather fed and housed an occasional traveler while he did weaving and tailoring for his neighbors. Barnabas Meacham, who lived in a house that stood across from 82 Rainbow Road, was the settlement's only known collier, or charcoal maker, from this era.

Few Turkey Hills men of this time joined the professions. Rather than consult doctors, townspeople usually treated themselves with lotions, ointments, plasters, and potions made from wild plants and garden herbs according to old family recipes. Midwives assisted during childbirth. Sometimes laymen even debilitated the sick by bleeding, a treatment confidently employed by many certified physicians.

The smallpox cemetery on the mountain north of Hatchet Hill Road is a reminder of one scourge of the times. It was perhaps located in this remote spot to quarantine deceased victims. The headstones that once marked it have been taken.

Captain John Viets and Deacon Joshua Holcomb and four of his grandchildren were among the many Simsbury people who died of smallpox during the 1700s. Local doctors inoculated people against the disease by transferring the fluid from the rash of a smallpox patient into the blood stream of the person to be immunized. Often the procedure was successful, but sometimes the inoculation itself resulted in the recipient's death.

Colonial Turkey Hills had no lawyers, as such, but most townsmen seem to have been well aware of their legal rights and eager to exercise them. Men of better than average education prepared and served legal documents in numerous suits over property and debt. Jonathan Higley, Jr., a self-taught attorney who lived near 61 Spoonville Road, gave legal advice and made out writs in civil cases.

Unlike colonial doctors and lawyers who could train under the apprentice system, ministers needed a college education to be hired by most congregations. The community looked to its minister and any other man with a higher education to tutor young men who were bound for college.

Deacon Samuel Owen, who lived in the house at 82 Rainbow Road, tutored young Turkey Hills scholars. He was also employed by the Turkey Hills Ecclesiastical Society to cut brush in the cemetery. Regardless of education, wealth, or social standing, no townsman who disdained or was inept at manual labor would have been well accepted in colonial Turkey Hills. The labor of one's hands was too necessary for the continuation and growth of the community.

5

Property and Prosperity

THE ENGLISH colonists who founded Windsor came there with few personal possessions and very little money. Once there, they received grants of free, unimproved land that started many on the way to prosperity. Year by year with hard work, they improved their land, built homes and outbuildings, and accumulated personal property. Generation by generation they added to their material wealth and improved their living conditions. Slowly Windsor and its offspring towns such as Simsbury evolved from harsh outposts to more comfortable villages.

Sergeant John Griffin, the first European settler in the area now East Granby, died intestate in 1681. In England at that time Griffin's eldest male heir would have been entitled to his father's entire estate. In the Colony of Connecticut, however, all his ten children, both sons and daughters, were entitled to shares.

Two disinterested townsmen inventoried Griffin's estate, valuing his land (more than 1000 acres) at £120. In comparison, his second most valuable possession was 6 acres of Indian corn, priced at £9. His three horses were worth £5 and his three guns, £1 each. No house was itemized in the inventory.

Historian Lucius I. Barber points out that Griffin had no table or chairs. He speculates that Griffin may have had a puncheon on four legs or one fastened to a wall and a rude bench or stools. Barber also noted the lack of a looking glass and crockery.

Griffin's sons John and Thomas paid their father's debts by making pitch and tar on his land. They were later reimbursed for their labor with land parcels from the estate. In 1698 and again in 1711, the heirs met to work out the division of Griffin's land. (The married daughters were represented by their husbands.) They set out parcels of land during the first division and, in true Biblical fashion, drew lots for the ownership of each. The men of the court approved this amicable distribution of the largest land holding in the history of the local area.

One record concerning the settlement of Sergeant Griffin's estate mentions that John Griffin (probably John Griffin, Jr., then a bachelor in his mid-twenties) had a "sellar," most likely a cellar house. Settlers all over New England used similar dwellings as temporary homes. To make a cellar house, a man dug a three-walled excavation, open at the top, into the side of a hill or embankment. Then he constructed a fireplace and chimney at the rear of the cut and lined the dirt walls with rough planking.

He also enclosed the open front with planking, leaving spaces for a door and perhaps a window or two. He covered the structure with a peaked roof of sod or thatch supported by spars. This made a nicely insulated one or two room home. In many instances, these rude quarters became the cellars beneath more permanent dwellings.

Timothy Phelps' cellar house, located by "T. Phelps" on the 1732 Simsbury map, was two rooms wide. He built it into a bank just south of the house now at 116 North Main Street. Some time before 1746, Phelps incorporated the old cellar into a mansion house, as a house of finer construction was called. This wooden structure, which no longer exists, was two stories high on its north side and one on the south. Colonial laws and deeds sometimes mandated that a landholder build a mansion house within a specified period of time after taking possession of his land.

Another type of temporary dwelling used in colonial New England was the log house. It was made of square-hewn logs, or logs that had been hewn flat on two sides. Log houses built in this, the English manner, took more time and tools to construct than did cabins of untrimmed logs as introduced by Swedish settlers in Delaware about 1638. Trimming made the naturally tapered logs uniform in thickness, so that, when they were placed on top of one another, their flat sides were flush without the gaps that builders of cabins had to chink. The ends of the logs were either lapped or dovetailed together and did not protrude beyond the corners of the building. The windows in these houses were small, and loopholes for firearms sometimes dotted the walls.

Although built to be family homes, these solid structures could, and did, double as garrisons. They were generally built in areas where settlers feared enemy attack. Early block forts and log prisons were also constructed of square-hewn logs.

Amos Moor's inventory mentions a log house he built about 1738 on lot 23. Before he died in 1785, Moor also built a mansion house on the same lot. The log house is gone, but when Alexander H. Griswold built the house at 175 South Main Street in the mid-1800s, he may have incorporated the mansion house into it. L. Mazie Viets remembers that her father-in-law, Willard W. Viets, who bought this house from the Griswold family in 1904, always spoke of the back section as "the old house."

175 South Main Street

As Turkey Hills achieved a measure of prosperity and new, local sawmills began to provide lumber in quantity, the number of mansion houses also began to increase. Some of these have since been lost to today's town, yet many remain as cherished family homes. Their massive construction, large central chimneys, steeply pitched roofs, and cut stone foundations are distinctive. Their variety of design, soundness of construction, and simple dignity of line reflect the practicality and good taste of the colonial townspeople who built them.

The house Samuel Clark built at the

Samuel Clark house

Center in 1737 was one of Turkey Hills' finest structures. Five generations of Clarks lived in this house on South Main Street

Room from Samuel Clark house as reconstructed at Yale University Art Gallery

where the Combustion Engineering offices are today. In 1920 Francis P. Garvan, a noted New York financier and collector of antiques, bought the house. He had it carefully dismantled and he donated six of its rooms to the Yale Art Gallery. Two rooms were reconstructed and displayed for a time. A newspaper account calls the rooms strikingly good examples of the best architecture of upper class homes of their period.

The layout of the Clark house was characteristic of houses constructed in that era. It was built around a massive central chimney which served three fireplaces on the first floor. A rear addition, which housed a summer kitchen and buttery, was built some time between 1790 and 1800.

Because the house was built to serve as a tavern as well as a home, one of the first floor rooms was a beautifully paneled taproom. When the Clarks needed a ballroom, the partition between two of the second floor bedrooms was swung upward until it lay flat against the ceiling, where it was fastened with iron hooks. Two other colonial houses in town had similar partitions, the Gay house at 123 North Main Street and the Moor house at 171 North Main.

38 Holcomb Street

33 East Street

23 East Street

56 East Street

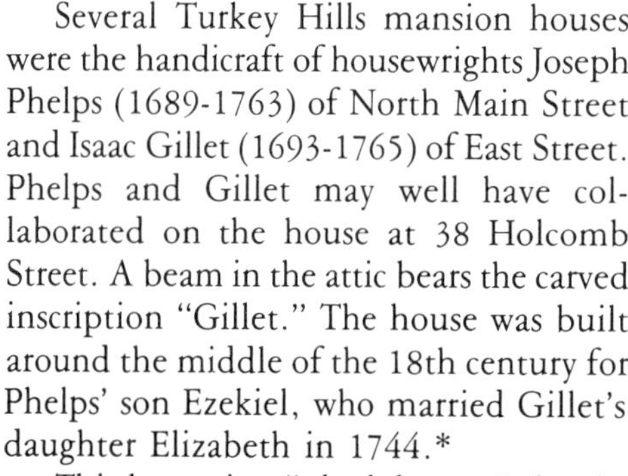

Several Turkey Hills mansion houses were the handicraft of housewrights Joseph Phelps (1689-1763) of North Main Street and Isaac Gillet (1693-1765) of East Street. Phelps and Gillet may well have collaborated on the house at 38 Holcomb Street. A beam in the attic bears the carved inscription "Gillet." The house was built around the middle of the 18th century for Phelps' son Ezekiel, who married Gillet's daughter Elizabeth in 1744.*

This house is a "plank house," that is, it has no studs in its walls. Instead, 2-inch thick planks run two stories from the sill at the ground floor to the plate below the attic floor. The clapboards are nailed to the planking. Inside, the walls in the old kitchen and one of the front rooms are covered with beaded sheathing. Many boards used in the sheathing are 30 inches wide, and the corner and chimney posts are 1 foot square at the supporting girts. These dimensions speak of the size of the first-growth trees the builder had at his disposal. The stone fireplace in the kitchen is 7 feet wide and has an oven in its rear wall.

The house at 39 North Main Street was built for Joseph Phelps' grandson Ezekiel Phelps, Jr. Clues to both the age of the house and the men who helped to build it appear in the probate records at the time of Ezekiel's death in 1789. The inventory of his estate lists "dwelling house, boards and clapboards prepared for the buildings and window frames and sashes." Under a list of creditors to the estate is: "To Mr. Reuben Phelps on a contract made by the

*This house was restored by its present owners, Mr. and Mrs. G. Winthrop Wilson, and was placed on the National Register of Historic Places in 1982.

46 East Street

83 Spoonville Road

2 Old County Highway

82 Rainbow Road

deceased—£11 8s." The only other large debt (£32 11s 1d) is to Reuben Barker, a local joiner who probably crafted the paneling, window frames, and other woodwork in the house.

Joiner Reuben Barker bought Elijah Owen's homestead at 23 East Street in 1792. Judging by its architecture, either Owen or Barker could have built the house that stands there today. Its elaborately framed and beautifully detailed front entry is impressive.

Master builder Isaac Gillet settled near the house at 33 East Street in the 1730s. He and his sons (or, at least, one of his sons) may have built the present house before Gillet's death in 1765, as his inventory credits him with owning only half of the house. Raised paneling and ceilings 8½ feet tall add to the graciousness of this Georgian-style home.

Gillet's neighbor John Thrall built his house, now 56 East Street, in the 1740s. The great fireplace in the kitchen has a hole built into the rear wall for the disposal of ashes which, when dropped through the hole, collect in the base of the chimney so that they may be removed. This somewhat unusual feature is also found at 38 Holcomb Street and 39 North Main Street.

John Thrall's grandson Luke Thrall is the first known occupant of the house at 46 East Street. The elaborate trim around the front doorway is original. The windows are unusual in that they have half-sized panes of glass at the tops and bottoms. The Samuel Clark house had similar windows.

One of the very few colonial lean-to houses in the area stands at 27-29 North Main Street. John Holcomb, Jr., built it

1 North Main Street

235 Hartford Avenue

115 Hartford Avenue

20 School Street

sometime between 1736, when his father gave him the land, and 1765, when he sold the property to his brother Asahel Holcomb.

An unusual style of architecture sometimes called the "meetinghouse" type makes the house at 2 Old County Highway unique in town. This plank house stands four-square with a hip roof. Unlike most colonial fireplaces which are flush with a wall, each of the four fireplaces in this house runs diagonally across the corner of a room. The house may have been built as early as 1747 by Samuel Higley's son, Jonathan.

The Georgian house at 83 Spoonville Road is unusual in that it is only one and one-half stories high. This was built by Hezekiah Skinner at the time of his marriage to Miriam Alderman in 1790.

The small gabled ell to the rear of the lean-to house at 82 Rainbow Road is very old. This was the home of Samuel Owen, who probably built it about 1736. At his death in 1787, his widow received "the west or old part of the dwellinghouse, both lower room and chamber with the entry or passageway out of the house to the southward." The exterior wall of the original house is still intact and may be seen from an attached shed on the south side. In 18th century deeds this little homestead is called "the Pine Tree Place."

Six early dwellings with gambrel roofs remain. In three of them, 23 East Street, 1 North Main Street, and 115 Hartford Avenue, an older ell with gambrel roof has now been incorporated into a more substantial structure. The ell of the house at 1 North Main was built about 1778 by

4 North Road

Deacon Asahel Holcomb. The back ell at 115 Hartford Avenue and the house at 231 Hartford Avenue seem to be the only remaining 18th century homes of the dozen or more that once stood along Salmon Brook. (Land records indicate that the house at 235 Hartford Avenue was built about 1807, although it, too, may be an older house.)

Whole houses displaying this roof style are those at 171 North Main Street (built in 1770), 20 School Street, and 4 North Road. The architectural and structural features of the last two indicate that they were built during the late 18th or early 19th centuries. Since most of the Granby land records are missing for these years, it is hard to date them precisely.

DWELLINGS, both temporary and permanent, tell a great deal about the Turkey Hills settlers' varying modes of life. Inventories of their personal property also yield telling information. Some of these lists, usually made during the settlement of a man's estate, as the Griffin inventory was, show households humble to the point of starkness. Others give a picture of comfort, even of luxury, for the time.

By 1713 Dr. John Viets, the German immigrant, had a house, outbuildings, orchard, and linseed oil mill on the land near Salmon Brook that he had bought from the Griffins. He probably used linseed oil, pressed from flax seed, in his practice of medicine. He also held the first license in Turkey Hills to run an inn.

Dr. Viets died in 1723, leaving a small estate for his widow, two sons, and two daughters:

waring aparil
cut lash
one bedsted and furniture, one old beadticking and blanket
sadel and bridel, one colar and traces, one horsecart irons and cart saddel
one sleadg, three wedges, one ax, 3 stubing hoes
one payr of andirons, old iron, one chisel
fiveteen boocks written in iarmen Jarmin language The worth not known by us
two peuter platters, five peuter plates, quart cup and pint cup
one iron pot and pot hook, one tramel, one littel pot, and one bras cittel
three bouls, two dishes, eight trenchars, one plater, one earthen jug and earthen pot
one hand belle, one tabel, one marter and iron pessel
one trunk, one old chest
one litel whel, one great whele
five broken chears, two payles, all vials, lumber in the chamber,
one brass candel stick, four pigs, one golen botel
one picture

Seventy eight acers of land, part of a building with sum boards by it
The above inventary was taken by us the subscribers being under oath being declared thereto by the widow viett this thirty first day of December 1723

Thomas Holcomb, Ephraem Griphen, Samuel Griswold

(Note that spelling of the day was largely phonetic and that punctuation played no great part in ordinary written text. In most quotations printed in this book, spelling and punctuation have been modernized for the sake of readability.)

The inventory suggests the family cooked their food in an iron pot hung on a pothook or trammel in the fireplace, ate much of their food with their fingers, and drank from a common cup. Dr. Viets may have used his sledge, three wedges, axe, and stub hoe to clear land for the structure it appears he was building at the time of his death. His wife, Catherine, ground grain in the mortar with the pestle and wove the cloth for her family's wearing apparel on the little wheel and the great wheel. Since there seems to have been only one bed, the children probably slept in straw, perhaps in a loft. With only one blanket, it is reasonable to believe that they, like many of their contemporaries, slept with their clothes on.

Dr. Viets left behind in Germany whatever family ties he had there and probably arrived in Turkey Hills with his family and all his possessions easily fitting in his horsecart. In contrast, Isaac Owen, who settled near 23 East Street about 1714, was a member of a family of second and third generation American colonists who had prospered just a few miles away in Windsor.

When he died in 1736, Isaac Owen's inventory listed over 385 separate items, such as: eleven spoons, two knives, and three forks, as well as household utensils of brass, pewter, earthenware, iron, wood, and glass. His linen supply included curtains, tablecloths, towels, napkins, featherbeds, pillows, twenty sheets, blankets, coverlets, valances, and shag rugs. (Valances, for the settlers, were draperies hung around a bed for warmth and shag rugs were used as bed covers. Some of today's townspeople can remember the comfort of a featherbed!)

Obviously these contemporaries, Viets and Owen, enjoyed differing degrees of comfort in their daily lives. Other inventories show much variety of fortune among the first settlers.

The 1743 inventory of the estate of Sergeant John Griffin's grandson Stephen Griffin shows he had amassed a considerable number of possessions and much finery by the time he died at thirty-four.* This sea captain had three possessions of particular significance—three Negroes.

Black servants—the word slave is seldom found in the records—were not uncommon. At least seven are mentioned in the wills and inventories of Turkey Hills men before 1760. Master builder Joseph Phelps showed his concern for his servants in his will dated March 14, 1760:

And furthermore I do order that my Negro man servant Zickery and my Negro woman servant Citty, that are husband and wife, shall not after my decease be parted asunder but

*Tradition has it that Indians pushed Griffin into the Farmington River at the Falls and drowned him. The Griffin genealogy says he left a wife, Mary DeLacy, who was part Spanish and the daughter of a "Prince" in the West Indies.

51-53 Rainbow Road

have liberty to choose their master and mistress among my children to live with, and also that my slave servant Newport shall also have liberty to choose his master or mistress . . . the said Negroes shall be treated kindly.

One of Stephen Griffin's slaves, London (also referred to as London Negro and London Freebody in the records), served in the French and Indian War. He may have gained his freedom in return for his service, a policy that was followed later during the Revolutionary War. At one time London Negro owned a house, orchard, and 35 acres of land in Griffin's Lordship. A 1790 record of the Congregational church reads: "Also baptized Catherine a Negro child daughter to London Freebody deceased. This child was dedicated by Captain Matthew Griswold and Abiah his wife who had taken this child to educate." This second London Freebody was probably the London Negro who had once belonged to the second Isaac Owen of 51-53 Rainbow Road;* Abiah Griswold was Owen's daughter.

Historians believe that most slaves in New England were well treated. They usually worked and ate with their owners and slept under the same roof. In 1784 the Connecticut General Assembly passed a law that all slaves born after March of that year should be freed by the time they were twenty-five years old. The 1790 census lists no slaves in Turkey Hills.

Most property on record before the Revolutionary War belonged to men. When a woman owned property it was usually inherited from her father rather than her husband. After 1723 a husband could not transfer property that his wife had inherited without her signature on the deed.

A settler's wife shared her husband's land, house, and household goods, and bore him children. When widowed she received whatever he provided in his will for her use until she remarried or died. The husband usually left her one-third of his household goods and a dower right to part of his real estate "so long and only so long as she shall remain my widow." Often the family house—even the barn—was divided room by room among heirs so that the widow received only the use of specified rooms and the right of passage through others.

Ephraim Phelps, who lived on the southeast corner of the intersection of Spoon-

*An old chimney and the framework in the cellar of the house at 51-53 Rainbow Road indicate an original structure with one or two additions. Owen probably built the first house in the early 1730s.

82 South Main Street

91 South Main Street

99 South Main Street

74 South Main Street

ville and Seymour roads, was particularly liberal toward his wife. He gave some of his money to his children, to be paid when they came of age,

and all the remainder of my estate that I have or shall die possessed of both personal and real—lands, money, goods, chattels, and all my estate . . . I give to Sarah Phelps my true and loving wife and that forever to be to her own use and behoof and to her free disposing after my death. And I do nominate, choose, and ordain Elijah Owen and my true and loving wife Sarah Phelps to be sole executor and executrix.

John Thrall, who died in 1749, showed his confidence in his wife when he appointed her, rather than a man, as sole guardian of their children.

A prenuptial agreement, a rare document in the 18th century, made between Samuel Forward and his second wife, the widow Martha Winchell, appears in his will dated April 10, 1738:

I will and ordain that whereas there was a jointure made with my said wife Martha and myself before our marriage wherein I was obliged to let her have the use of one room in my house and the use of one acre of grass land and one acre of plowing land, the liberty pasturing for one cow, and the use of my cellar and well and the apples to fill two barrels of cider and apples for her own use all she shall have occasion for during the full term of two years after my decease; and like in said jointure I will give her twenty pounds money to be hers forever as her own property.

An even rarer case of property ownership involves Mary Thompson Higley who was a granddaughter and heir of the Reverend Edward Thompson, the former Simsbury minister. After she married Jonathan Higley in 1747, Mary Higley bought land in her name alone. The couple were living on her land, in her house, which stood on the west side of Spoonville Road north of Miller Road, when Jonathan drowned in 1771 in the Farmington River.

Mary Thompson Higley seems to have been a resourceful daughter of an independent mother, Hannah Thompson. As a widow, Mrs. Thompson came with her three teenage children from Gloucester, Massachusetts, about 1739. She claimed and settled the land at Turkey Hills that the town of Simsbury had given to her father-in-law, Mr. Thompson, forty years earlier. According to Mary Coffin Johnson, they came on horseback, so their possessions were few. Mrs. Johnson writes that they first built a log house on lot 19, and then a frame one, which is probably what constitutes the north ell of 82 South Main Street. (They had come into funds through the sale of 160 acres of lot 24 which had been granted to Mr. Thompson also.) They and their descendants lived in these houses and in those they built later at 91, 99, and 74 South Main Street for over 200 years. (The very old house at 103 South Main Street may have been moved there by the Thompsons. If so, its original location is unknown.)

In the course of little more than a hundred years, the pioneers in Turkey Hills and some of their descendants had freed themselves from the rigors of their early struggle for subsistence in a wilderness. They had cleared their land for homes, crops, and roadways; outlined and divided their homesteads with fences; raised their houses, barns, mills, and other buildings; and established their meetinghouse as the center of local government and worship. Most had acquired a measure of wealth and a comfortable standard of living for their time. Yet they were by no means soft. When their fellow American colonists found the time had come to overthrow English rule, the men of Turkey Hills were ready. They had put down their roots; next they sought independence.

6

The Revolution I: Turkey Hills' Patriots and Loyalists

WAR WAS NO STRANGER to the people of Turkey Hills. By the time the shooting started at Lexington and Concord, they could look back over a succession of colonial wars extending for almost 140 years. Some Turkey Hills settlers were descended from the men who had gone out from Windsor to help subdue the Pequot Indians. Later, others of their antecedents had suffered the burning of Simsbury during King Philip's War. More recently some of their own number had gone off to defend New England in the French and Indian War. For years past they and their predecessors had been building defenses in Simsbury against all manner of attack.

One of the earliest orders of the Connecticut General Assembly required the men in every town to train at least once a month for military duty. The unskilled were to train more often. The trainbands served primarily for "watch and ward" in their own towns, but they supplied able fighting men to colonial forces when called upon.

Because Simsbury's trainband was too small to defend the town effectively during its first settlement and later rebuilding, the General Assembly required the town, and other vulnerable frontier settlements, to garrison a troop of about ten soldiers in each place. Simsbury's trainband not only grew into a militia unit that could protect the town from the threat of an occasional Indian attack, but by 1716 was large enough to divide into two companies. By 1737 there were three companies totaling 202 men. Two years later, when colonial regiments were formed, Simsbury became part of the 1st Regiment. At the beginning of the Revolutionary War, militiamen of Simsbury, New Hartford, Hartland, Barkhamsted, and Colebrook constituted the 18th Regiment of Connecticut Militia.

At least thirty Turkey Hills men fought on the British side in the French and Indian War, 1754-63, and twenty-one of them were direct descendants of the early settlers. Five Winchells fought. Timothy Alderman, Joseph Alderman's youngest son, died while in the army. Sergeant John Griffin's grandson Nathaniel Griffin, who joined the Bateaux Service, was injured "at the Little Falls" on the Mohawk River in upper New York State. During the launching of a laden bateau, a roller on which the flat-bottomed boat was being moved ran over and crushed his foot and leg. Because he was crippled for life, the General Assembly granted him £20.

In 1762 Samuel Thompson and Andrew Hillyer went to Cuba with a British expedition that captured Havana. At the time Cuba was owned by Spain, an ally of France. Of the forty-seven men who went from Simsbury and neighboring towns, twenty-two died, many of yellow fever. Hillyer and Thompson survived.

The Treaty of Paris, signed in 1763, gave French Canada to England and ceded Cuba to Spain in return for Florida. This was new territory to govern and defend, and England was already deeply in debt from its prolonged wars in Europe and in the colonies. Since the newly acquired land would benefit the colonies as well as the mother country, England felt the colonials should help bear the anticipated expense. To that end, Parliament enacted a series of laws to draw tax revenue from the colonies.

While trying to rid themselves of these tax laws, the colonials formed private and public associations such as the Sons of Liberty, the Stamp Act Congress, the Committees of Correspondence, and, finally, the First Continental Congress. Such organizations, both jointly and severally, helped to unite the colonies in resistance to England, eventually resulting in the Revolutionary War.

In May 1773 the Connecticut General Assembly appointed a standing Committee of Correspondence and Enquiry to encourage communication among the governments of the various colonies "on all matters where the common welfare and safety of the colonies are concerned." At a special town meeting on August 11, 1774, held to protest the closing of the port of Boston by the British after the Boston Tea Party, Simsbury formed its own Committee of Correspondence. Turkey Hills men Asahel Holcomb and Ezekiel Phelps were among the committee appointed. Committees of Correspondence would play a very important role in keeping the flame of protest alive, especially in areas far removed from hot spots like Boston.

At the same meeting, townspeople of Simsbury also declared their continued support of the king, but only as long as he did not violate their sacred rights under the Charter of Connecticut. They concluded:

The Parliament of Great Britain has no legal right to lay taxes or duties on our persons or properties without our consent. Therefore we resolve that our brethren and friends at Boston are now suffering under the evil hand of oppression and arbitrary government, in having been condemned unheard, contrary to Magna Carta and the Royal Charter that had been granted to said Province. We therefore from a tender feeling for the inhabitants of that great Town of Boston do judge it our duty to contribute of our substance for their relief under their present sufferings.

At its annual town meeting in December 1774, Simsbury voted to abide by the Continental Association, an agreement proposed by the Continental Congress that called for ceasing trade with Great Britain, Ireland, the British West Indies, and the East Indian Company and ending the consumption of their products. The townspeople also agreed: "We will, in our several stations, encourage frugality, economy, and industry, and promote agriculture, arts, and the manufactures of this country, especially that of wool." Traders agreed to keep their prices reasonable if scarcities should develop. Everyone who raised sheep pledged to raise as many as possible and, rather than eating or exporting any surplus animals, to sell them at reasonable terms to their neighbors, "especially the poorer sort." The Congress recognized that many colonists depended on woolen cloth imported from England and that an increase in domestic production would be vital.

At the same meeting, Simsbury appointed Asahel Holcomb and the second Joseph Forward to a Committee of Inspection in accordance with the 11th article of the Association:

That a committee be chosen in every county, city and town, . . . whose business it shall be attentively to observe the conduct of all persons touching this association; and when it shall be made to appear to the satisfaction of a majority of any such committee, that any person within the limits of their appointment has violated this association, that such majority do forthwith cause the truth of the case to be published in the gazette; to the end, that all such foes to the rights of British America may be publicly known, and universally condemned as the enemies of American liberty; and thenceforth we respectively will break off all dealings with him or her.

Later, during the war, the General Assembly ordered anyone traveling outside his home town to have a pass which Committees of Inspection, or Committees of Safety as some were called, were allowed to issue. A committe member could stop anyone traveling without a pass and bring him before his committee "to be further examined and dealt with as the nature of the case in . . . their opinion may require." Obviously these committeemen were allowed great discretion in the application of their authority, and abuses resulted in harassment of and harm to many people who sincerely opposed the severance of ties with England. Some of the men imprisoned in Turkey Hills at Newgate Prison during the Revolution were Loyalists condemned by such committees.

With their formal support of the people of Boston in their defiance of the Boston Port Act and their concurrence with the Continental Association, the people of Simsbury, after thoughtful deliberation, chose to fight rather than compromise their asserted birthrights. When the first shot of the Revolutionary War was fired at Lexington on April 19, 1775, the colonists living in Turkey Hills could not have been surprised that a showdown with the British army had finally come.

At War: 1775

Of the approximately thirty-three families who lived on the original twenty-four lots along the main street of Turkey Hills east of the Mountain, at least fifteen sent men to Massachusetts in response to the alarm resulting from the Battle of Lexington. Eli Strong (Samuel Strickland's grandson), the second Joseph Forward, the second Joseph Cornish, Richard Gay, Uriah Pease (William Moor's son-in-law), Samuel Booth, Asahel Holcomb, Jr., Andrew Hillyer, and Daniel Willcox went from North Main Street.

Reuben Clark, who lived in his grandfather Samuel's house at the Center, joined them and other men from South Main Street: Oliver and Nathaniel Winchell, Simeon Lewis, Benjamin Thrall, Zaccheus Gillet and his son Nathan. Elijah Owen, Matthew Griswold, and Luke Thrall went from the Windsor Half Mile. These men marched as part of a company under Captain Zaccheus Gillet. Most of them were in their twenties and thirties; the officers were older, with Captain Gillet at fifty-one, the eldest.

This company and two others from Simsbury are recorded on the Lexington Alarm

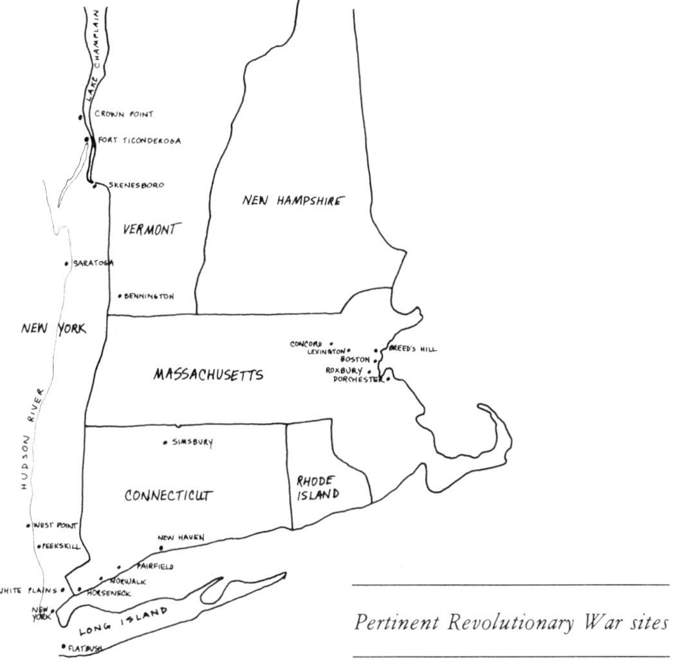

Pertinent Revolutionary War sites

List in *Record of the Service of Connecticut Men in the War of the Revolution,* with sixty-four men altogether. It is certain that other men of the area also went but were not listed in this reference as the records of the Revolutionary War are incomplete. For example, Hannah Weir McPherson says in her genealogy of the Holcomb family that Hezekiah Holcomb, Jr., served under Captain Lemuel Bates at Lexington.

These Simsbury men served from one to six days during the Lexington Alarm. They evidently returned home when they learned that the British had retreated to Boston. Since they had marched on short notice, they could have had no time to arrange their affairs at home for a long absence. It was planting time, and they depended on their crops for food. Later, though, some joined the thousands of Connecticut troops who encamped around Boston and contained the British there for almost a year.

One of the most immediate needs of the colonial army was artillery. Without the approval of the Continental Congress or even of the Connecticut General Assembly, a group of Connecticut men organized and financed an expedition to capture British-held Fort Ticonderoga on the western shore of Lake Champlain. They hoped to acquire cannon and a stronghold against invasion from the North. Intending to enlist men along the way, a small group left Connecticut at the end of April. Noah Phelps of Simsbury and Bernard Romans were sent ahead to find recruits, while a message relayed to Ethan Allen and his Green Mountain Boys brought their support. At the same time, and unknown to the men from Connecticut, Benedict Arnold started out from Boston with exactly the same plans. Before recruiting any troops, he met the Connecticut group, and Arnold and Ethan Allen joined forces.

Noah Phelps will always be Simsbury's hero of the capture of Fort Ticonderoga. He gained admission to the fort before the attack and reported back to Ethan Allen that the fortress was in disrepair and the British powder was so poor it had to be dried and sifted before it could be used, and even then it could not be relied on. The colonials rushed the fort which fell without a single shot. The same day they took the British post at Crown Point to the north. Some of the cannon from these forts were taken to Boston. Others were used during subsequent battles in New York and the South.

The General Assembly acted promptly in response to the Battle of Lexington. It called up a quarter of the colony's militia "for the special defense and safety of this colony" for service not to exceed seven months. Then it provisioned its troops, at least on paper, with three-fourths of a pound of pork or one pound of beef, one pound of bread or flour, and three pints of beer daily to each man. The beef was to be fresh two days of the week. Each soldier was to receive a half pint of rice or a pint of Indian meal, six ounces of butter, and three pints of peas or beans per week. A soldier could draw one gill of rum per day when he was on fatigue duty. Milk, molasses, candles, soap, vinegar, coffee, chocolate, sugar, tobacco, and vegetables in season were to be provided for the troops at the discretion of the officers.

Few of the troops had uniforms and individual officers provided their own. General Washington directed soldiers to wear variously colored ribbons signifying their rank to promote recognition of and respect for superiors.

Early in May a large company of Simsbury men, perhaps 100, enlisted for seven months under Captain Abel Pettibone and left for Boston. In June when the Americans learned of British plans to invade the Charlestown peninsula, colonial troops rallied there. Some of the Simsbury men fought the British on Breed's Hill in the engagement called the Battle of Bunker Hill. They were under the command of Connecticut's Brigadier General Israel Putnam. The colonial troops were defeated, but the horseman who brought the bad news to Simsbury probably tempered it with the exciting thought that the Americans—made up of inexperienced, poorly trained, and ill-equipped farmers—had held off for two hours an army of four times as many experienced British regulars and that the enemy's losses were much greater than theirs!

In July 1775 the General Assembly authorized the formation of the 7th and 8th Continental Regiments of Connecticut, making a total of 7400 men. The fourth company of the 8th, about seventy-five men, formed in Simsbury under Captain Elihu Humphrey. It marched to Roxbury, near Boston, the same month. Soldier Daniel Barber wrote a description of the departure and march of these men. After describing the Reverend Mr. Pitkin's farewell sermon and the parting from families and friends, he says:

We marched about eight miles that afternoon; at night, put up at James Marsh's Inn. Here, for the first time, I slept, as a soldier, on the floor, with a cartridge box for my pillow. At that period, horse-wagons being very little in use, an ox team was provided to carry our provisions for the way, and a barrel of rum. Our provision was salt pork and peas. Whenever we stopped, a large kettle was hung over the fire, in which the salt meat was put without freshening, and the dry peas, without soaking.

After about nine or ten days marching, in company with our ox team, loaded with salt pork, peas, and candlestick bottoms [hard biscuits] *for bread, and the barrel of rum to cheer our spirits and wash our feet, which began to be very sore by traveling, we came to Roxbury, the place of our destination. There the place of our encampment was already marked out, and a part of our regiment on the spot. For every six soldiers, there was a tent provided. The ground it covered was about six or seven feet square. This served for kitchen, parlor,*

and hall. The green turf, covered with a blanket, was our bed and bedstead. When we turned in for the night, we had to lie perfectly straight, like candles in a box; this was not pleasant to our hipbones and kneejoints, which often in the night would wake us, and beg us to turn over.
Our household utensils, altogether, were an iron pot, a canteen, or wooden bottle holding two quarts, a pail, and wooden bowl. Each had to do his own washing and take his turn at the cookery.

Daniel Barber was fortunate to be assigned a tent, for many of the troops had to improvise shelter from sails provided by the seaport towns or materials they could scrounge—boards, bricks, stones, brush, and even turf.

Less than two weeks earlier, on July 2, General Washington had arrived in Cambridge to take command of the troops. The lack of discipline among them appalled the new commander-in-chief. These recruits were independent men, used to managing their own affairs and taking few orders from anyone. Their officers were usually friends and neighbors who did not expect or demand the immediate and unquestioned obedience to orders characteristic of a professional army. Then, too, most men enlisted for short terms and saw no reason to travel very far from their families. Few Turkey Hills men served more than eight months at a time or went beyond New England. Men went home promptly at the end of their enlistments—sometimes sooner if the crops or other business needed tending to—no matter the state of the battle at the time.

Washington quickly and skillfully introduced the discipline that was necessary to maintain a battle-ready fighting army. However, the days of fall grew short and the possibility of the English attacking before spring grew remote. Fuel ran low and clothing and shelter became inadequate against the cold. Smallpox was already invading the army. Richard Gay was sick as were many others by now. At least four Simsbury men had died; at least two had deserted. In December the men of Turkey Hills and thousands of other Connecticut troops whose enlistments were up must have been happy to head home.

1776

Since they knew the expiring enlistments would deplete their army in December, General Washington and the Continental Congress acted early in the fall of 1775 to reenlist men already in service and to recruit others. Connecticut was to raise eight regiments to serve for one year from January 1, 1776, in a Continental Army.

Both Captain Abel Pettibone's and Captain Elihu Humphrey's companies were included in the eight regiments. The rolls of these are missing, but no doubt many Simsbury men were among the soldiers stationed around Boston at the beginning of the year. They may have been among those who secretly, under cover of the night of March 4, fortified the heights of Dorchester and set up twenty of the cannon that Henry Knox had brought from Ticonderoga in February. At daybreak the British discovered the Americans' threatening position and immediately prepared to attack them, but a storm intervened. When it was over, the Americans were firmly entrenched on the heights. Thereupon the English evacuated Boston, which Washington occupied March 18. He remained there until early April when he left for New York City where he believed, and rightly so, that the English would make their next attack.

By summer Washington was calling for reinforcements for his troops in New York. Ensigns Andrew Hillyer and Nathaniel Winchell from Turkey Hills were part of a Connecticut battalion which was raised in June for service under Washington. They had probably not arrived in New York when the news of the signing of the Declaration of Independence was read to the troops on the evening of July 9, 1776, amid cheers of approval. After the reading, the crowd razed the leaden statue of George III which stood on Bowling Green. The greater part of it was carted to Litchfield, Connecticut, where it was made into bullets.

In July the Continental Congress asked the General Assembly to send all the militia who could be spared to New York to reinforce the Continental Army. Hundreds of Simsbury men responded including many from Turkey Hills under Captains Joseph Forward and Hezekiah Holcomb. Daniel Barber wrote that his company was drafted and ordered to be in readiness at a day's notice to march to New Haven and to embark for New York:

The next year, the war appeared much more alarming, as the British had sent out a large addition of sea and land forces. . . . In this general alarm, I again turned out, with most of my old associates in arms. This was about the month of July. We took shipping at New Haven, I think, the day before the battle began at Flatbush on Long Island; which battle continued for several days. This was, indeed, a very serious time with us. From the place where we were stationed, the loud thunders of the cannon, and the cracking of small arms, while the smoke ascended like the smoke of a furnace, gave us, as might be expected, anxious and trembling fears for the cause of our country, as well as for ourselves. Our army, at length, finding that they were not able to hold their position, made a general and very secure retreat, from Long Island to the city, under the darkness of the night.

Captain Forward's company had not arrived at Long Island until August 24 and Captain Holcomb's until August 26, the day before the actual fighting started. Lieutenant Ezekiel Phelps reported his company was positioned so near the British that he shouted to them, "Shoot straight; shoot to kill, not maim."

By the end of September, New York City, too, was lost. As Elisha Winchell, Jr., would recount in later years, the British came from Long Island and the colonials "all ran for their lives."

Since the official records show that these militiamen were discharged September 25, they were probably home in time to celebrate Reverend Aaron Jordan Booge's ordination in Turkey Hills on November 27, 1776.

The men were in no mood to reenlist, at least not immediately. Dudley Pettibone, a member of a committee to encourage enlistments, reported to the General Assembly a month later that he had called the military companies and householders of Simsbury together and done all in his power to encourage men to volunteer. He concluded, "Yet after all not one in the said town of Simsbury appeared to enlist."

1777

The unsuccessful campaign at New York in late 1776 convinced the Continental Congress of the need for a permanent, disciplined army to augment the Continental

Army. For the new army, to be called the Continental Line, men would have to enlist for either three years or the duration of the war.

At a Simsbury town meeting in March 1777 a committee was chosen to inform the governor and Council of Safety, who were responsible for raising, supplying, and assigning Connecticut's troops, that it would be very difficult to raise Simsbury's quota of men for such a long enlistment. The committee was to request that Simsbury's soldiers be allowed to enlist for only nine months, form their own companies, choose their own officers, and join the Continental Army in a regiment of their own choice. Of course, this is just what General Washington did not want. If anyone ever presented the petition, apparently no one bothered to record it in the minutes of the Council of Safety. They were busy appealing to the state's militiamen to volunteer for just six weeks to reinforce the too few American troops at Peekskill, New York, until recruits could be found to fill the Continental Line. Captain Abel Pettibone's company volunteered for the duty at Peekskill and returned home May 5 in time for spring planting.

One of the reasons men hesitated to join the Continental Line may have been the prevalence of smallpox among its soldiers. In February 1777 the Council of Safety resolved that newly raised troops for continental service would have to be inoculated in the state before being sent into service, as the disease could no longer be prevented from spreading throughout the Army. Inoculation against smallpox was still controversial. At the same time, the inhabitants of Simsbury voted that stopping inoculation might be a prudent means to prevent the spreading of smallpox in their town. Captain John Viets died of the disease in April 1777.

The decisive action that summer began in the North when General Burgoyne arrived from England to lead the British army down the Hudson River to a planned rendevous with General Howe, who was to bring his troops up the Hudson from New York City, thus cutting New England off from the rest of the country. On July 5 Burgoyne and his army occupied Ticonderoga without a battle, proceeded to Skenesboro (now Whitehall) at the south end of Lake Champlain and then started overland toward the Hudson River. Hoping to replenish his supplies by capturing horses, cattle, and grain, Burgoyne sent a detachment of troops to raid the American supply depot at Bennington, Vermont. By some calculations, one-tenth of General Burgoyne's army was killed, wounded, or captured in August during the Battle of Bennington. Seth Griffin and Captains Hezekiah Holcomb, Joseph Forward, and Asahel Holcomb participated in this American victory.

There are no records of Simsbury men participating in Burgoyne's final defeat on Bemis Heights near Saratoga, New York, in October, but Samuel Woodruff, who later moved to Turkey Hills, was there. At the time he was a seventeen-year-old student at Yale. When he learned that Burgoyne was at Saratoga, he and several other students rushed to the scene in time to participate in the final battle.

Fifty-five years later, when applying for a government pension, Woodruff remembered the fighting in detail:

About 11 o'clock in the forenoon of that day, the British troops advanced under the command of General Frazer who led up the grenadiers, drove in our pickets and advanced guards, and made several unsuccessful charges with fixed bayonets upon the line of the continental troops at the American redoubts on Bemis Heights near the headquarters of General Gates.

But meeting a repulse at this point of attack, the grenadiers commenced a slow, but orderly retreat, still keeping up a brisk fire. After falling back two or three hundred yards, this part of the hostile army met and joined with the main body of the royal troops. . . .
Here, on a level piece of ground of considerable extent, called Freeman's Farms, thinly covered with yellow pines, the royal army formed an extensive line with the principal of their artillery in front. By this time the American line was formed, consisting of the continentals, state troops, and militia. The fire immediately became general through the line with renewed spirit, and nearly the whole force on both sides was brought into action. General Frazer . . . received a rifle shot through his body . . . of which he died the next morning. . . .
Soon after the occurrence, the British grenadiers began reluctantly to give ground; and their whole line within a few minutes appeared broken. Still they kept up a respectable fire both of artillery and musketry. . . . A regiment of the Royal Grenadiers, with the brave Major Ackland at their head in conducting the retreat, came to a small cultivated field enclosed by a fence. Here they halted, formed, and made a stand—apparently determined to retrieve what they had lost by their repulse at the redoubts in the commencement of the action. They placed in their centre and at each flank, a strong battery of brass field pieces. The carnage became frightful, but the conflict was of short duration. Their gallant major received a musket ball through both legs, which placed him hors de combat. *Retreat immediately ensued, leaving their killed and some of their wounded with two brass field pieces on the ground. . . .*
The retreat, pursuit, and firing continued till 8 o'clock. It was then dark. The royal army continued their retreat about a mile farther and there bivouacked for the night. Ours returned to camp, where we arrived between 9 and 10 o'clock in the evening.
About 200 of our wounded men had been brought from the field of battle in wagons, and for want of tents, sheds, or any kind of buildings to receive and cover them, were placed in a circular row on the naked ground. It was a clear but cold and frosty night. The sufferings of the wounded were extreme—having neither beds under them nor any kind of bedclothes to cover them. Several surgeons were busily employed during the night extracting bullets and performing other surgical operations. This applicant, though greatly fatigued by the exercise of the day, felt no inclination to sleep, but, with several others spent the whole night carrying water and administering what other comforts were in our power, to the sufferers, about 70 of whom died of their wounds during the night.

The next day Woodruff buried twenty to thirty of the royal grenadiers beneath the cleared field on which they had died. He witnessed the ceremonies of surrender on October 17, 1777. A direct result of Burgoyne's defeat was the French government's decision to ally with the Americans the following year.

In *Newgate of Connecticut*, Richard H. Phelps writes that the British troops who surrendered at Saratoga passed through Turkey Hills and stopped at Lemuel Bates' tavern on North Main Street:

"The British had plenty of money," said Captain Bates, "to pay for the best we had; and my folks were kept busy in distributing pitchers and pails of cider among them. At night all the floors in my tavern were spread over with them." Another portion of the British captives encamped on the premises of Captain Roswell Phelps [71 North Main Street]. . . .

These prisoners of war were an interesting sight and excited an inspiring curiosity in all this region.

Others of these prisoners of war stayed at the home of Daniel Holcomb on Wolcott Road.

In violation of the surrender convention signed at Saratoga, the Continental Congress did not send Burgoyne's defeated soldiers back to England. Many escaped while they were being held in the colonies as prisoners of war. The rest were simply released after the war ended. Most settled in the new United States. One of them, Charles Stevens, came to live in Turkey Hills and worked as a hired man. Since he was particularly adept at digging ditches, the townspeople called him "the ditcher." Richard H. Phelps tell this story:

Two maidens of the neighborhood meeting him one day innocently saluted him with— "Good morning Mr. Ditcher."
The old veteran turned upon the damsels with flashing eye and informed them that he did not acknowledge that title, exclaiming with a haughty look "I am a grenadier of General Burgoyne's army and was a big man before you were born!"

In November 1777 Uriah Pease was killed, probably at the Battle of Fort Mifflin on an island in the Delaware River near Philadelphia. This was just before General Washington's withdrawal to winter quarters at Valley Forge.

1778

Simsbury's militiamen served with the Continental Army from March 1778 to the end of the year. Some were sent to Hudson River forts where garrisons were maintained until the end of the war in expectation of a British attack up the river from New York. About this time some may have been sent to Rhode Island and Connecticut coastal towns where there was action or threat of action throughout the war.

1779

In July 1779 the British invaded southern Connecticut by sea in an attempt to draw American troops away from the highlands of the Hudson where they were entrenched at West Point. Captain Andrew Hillyer and his troop of light horse rushed to New Haven where the British landed. The latter looted and burned while skirmishing with civilians and militia. Next they sailed to Fairfield, which was almost undefended, and burned that town. They then burned and pillaged Norwalk. Connecticut troops on the Hudson were ordered south to counteract the raids, and the companies under Joseph Forward and Hezekiah Holcomb were probably among them. The British had evacuated the area before these troops reached the coast.

Captain Lemuel Bates had been on the coast at Horseneck (now Greenwich) since March. The British continued to threaten coastal towns and in September Bates alerted the Second Company of Alarm in Simsbury "to equip themselves with arms and accoutrements and hold themselves in readiness to march at the shortest notice for the defense of the state." These men were part of an "alarm list composed of men between the ages of sixteen and sixty, with certain exceptions, who could be equipped and ready to march in case of an emergency."

Nineteenth-century historian Royal R. Hinman tells the story of Turkey Hills Captain Andrew Hillyer and Bearmore, a Tory who spied for the British in the vicinity of Horseneck at this time. Hillyer and his troop of light horse were ordered to raid Bearmore's quarters and take him prisoner if possible. They failed to capture Bearmore, and on their way back to headquarters at night, they came upon an American company of about fifty infantry under a Captain White. Hinman says:

At that moment, two scouts that had covered the rear of the light horse, came dashing in among them, one of which was covered with blood, his hand hanging by the skin, having been lopped off at the wrist by a British dragoon; and reported that a squadron of British cavalry were close upon them. Captain White exclaimed, "I am lost, my infantry cannot escape." Captain Hillyer said, "No, that must not be; follow my directions, we will make a stand and fare alike; divide your men and throw them over the stone wall on each side of the road, in a quartering direction, that the fire on one party may not injure the other; be deliberate, and when you hear the word 'charge,' do what you can."

The light horse then stationed themselves across the road out of fire of Captain White's infantry and made ready to receive the British "with swords loosened and pistols cocked." When the British rode up, Captain Hillyer gave the signal, "Charge them, my lads!" At the same time the infantry rose from behind the wall and poured such deadly and well-directed fire on them that many of the enemy were killed. The British retired to form for another attack, but the infantry's continuing fire evidently persuaded them to retreat. Hinman, who was Connecticut's Secretary of the State from 1835 to 1842, adds: "The plunder taken from Bearmore and the British on that occasion was sold for more than $20,000 continental money. Captain Hillyer was presented with a beautiful Yager's Rifle as testimony of his conduct."

1780-83

Simsbury's militia companies were activated again in 1780 and 1781 for service at the Hudson River forts. The men of Turkey Hills accepted service with the militia, but extant records show fewer than ten who joined the Connecticut segment of the Continental Line for the required time of three years or the duration of the war. Two of them, the third Asahel Holcomb and Gad Alderman, were just sixteen years old when they enlisted in Sheldon's Dragoons early in 1781. The fact that these dragoons had been quartered in Simsbury the previous winter may have influenced the youths to join them.

As the war dragged on and the main theater of battle moved farther from New England, filling its quota of soldiers for long-term service became a serious problem for Simsbury. In November 1780, in compliance with instructions from the General Assembly, the town divided itself into as many groups as it lacked men to fill its quota. Each group had to find a recruit to serve for three years or the duration of the war. Those groups of men who did not find a recruit were subject to fine. Within three months a committee had to be appointed to consider and adjudicate all the grievances and controversies that resulted.

In July 1781 the town chose a committee to see if its quota for the Continental Line was filled and to look for deserters. The committee found that Simsbury had sixty-five men in service at the time, fourteen short of its quota of seventy-nine. At least ten Simsbury men had deserted earlier, four of them were from Turkey Hills. In October of that year the American siege of Yorktown, the last major confrontation in the war, forced Cornwallis to surrender to Washington.

Early the next spring, Simsbury voters empowered their selectmen to hire soldiers for a year to fill the town's quota for the Continental Army. Hiring substitutes was an acceptable practice throughout the war. Of seventy-four militiamen detached from the 18th Regiment to the Continental Army in 1778, thirty-seven of them hired substitutes. Abel Forward, who was a Loyalist, offered his slave Zickery Prince his freedom if he would serve in the army in place of his son Jesse Forward. Prince was killed in the army, so the Forwards freed his wife, Citty. Captain John Viets' son Abner hired a substitute.

In May 1782 the town voted 95 to 87 not to fine those groups of townspeople who had been negligent in procuring soldiers the past year. Victory and peace were in sight and the town and colony had already given ample support to the war. In the year 1777 Simsbury, a town of about 4000, had supplied close to 900 militiamen to Connecticut's 18th Regiment, a part of which served with the Continental Army. Connecticut, which ranked seventh among the colonies in population, stood second only to Massachusetts in the number of soldiers she supplied to the Continental forces. The peace treaty signed in September 1783 brought the official close of the war.

At Home

Connecticut's farm wives and their farmer husbands who rushed home from battle to tend their crops played a major role in the winning of the war. Connecticut became known as the "Provision State," as her people provided more food for the American army than did any other colony. Food shortages at home resulted. An inventory of grain in Simsbury in 1779 shows a deficiency "computed as in wheat" of 9145 bushels.

The shortage of salt was most serious, since people depended on it to preserve meat. New England has no natural salt deposits. For years salt had been brought to Windsor by boat from the Turks Islands in the West Indies, but this supply was cut off early in the war by a British naval blockade. The General Assembly offered bounties for salt produced from sea water. Officials were empowered to confiscate it from hoarders, and ships were sent under armed convoy to find it wherever they could.

Clothing for soldiers was conscripted from towns. During the years 1777-80 Simsbury supplied at least fourteen pairs of mittens or gloves, thirty-one frocks, forty-seven woolen breeches, 184 shirts, 208 overalls, and 477 pairs of stockings. This meant extra work from the raising of sheep and flax to the final sewing and knitting of the garments. During the same period townspeople contributed 303 pairs of shoes. They also furnished horses, teams of oxen, and carts.

In response to orders from the Council of Safety, the town authorized taxes to buy blankets, tents, and ammunition, as well as food and clothing for the troops. Townspeople were reimbursed by the state for many of their contributions, but their colony taxes rose steadily as a consequence.

Scarcities created by the loss of imports and the needs of the army raised prices. In 1776 the General Assembly set maximum prices on labor and goods "to prevent oppression by excessive and unreasonable prices on necessities and conveniences of life." Controls, though, did not prevent some speculators from profiting by engrossing, that is, purchasing enough of a product to control its price. And farmers often sold to the highest bidder. Laws which prohibited exporting vital goods from the colony were often disobeyed or circumvented.

Although currency became available to many for the first time through payment of military provisions and services, the paper currency issued by the colonies and the Continental Congress depreciated so quickly that overall there was more economic loss than gain for most people. Residents of Turkey Hills were probably fortunate that they still used barter as their principal means of exchange, at least among themselves.

The war contributed to the secularization of society that had started before the 18th century. Soldiers who had never been out of Simsbury before found different mores among troops from other colonies and countries. Profanity and the free use of intoxicants became more acceptable. Religious habits changed, as Daniel Barber noted:

Now for the first time, we travelled on the Lord's day, under arms, and past meetinghouses in time of public worship with drums and fifes playing martial music; all of which was calculated to afford to a New England man some doubts and reflections, whether God would be as well pleased with such parade and military performance, as if we had stayed at home to read our Bibles, or went to meeting to hear the minister. But military discipline, and the habits of a soldier, soon effected a degree of relaxation in most of us. In process of time, many, once pious, at least in form and appearance, came into the practice of treating all days nearly alike; yet there were some who kept the practice of reading Watts' Psalms and Hymns as a book of devotion.

Outsiders came to Turkey Hills, too. Colonial troops were quartered in Simsbury in wintertime, and some of the British prisoners of war that General Washington sent to the town in 1777 were allowed to live and work among the townspeople. Governor Trumbull had recommended Simsbury as a place to send prisoners because there was an Episcopal minister there.

Among its own residents Simsbury had a number of suspected and avowed Loyalists. Anyone who belonged to the Anglican Church was suspected of being in sympathy with the crown during the Revolution, because the king was the head of the church. This made the Reverend Roger Viets, pastor of St. Andrew's church, a prime suspect.

Mr. Viets, a Turkey Hills native, had gone to Yale, presumably intending to prepare for the Congregational Church ministry, but while there he attended an Anglican church in New Haven. In 1759, a year after his graduation, Viets became a lay reader at St. Andrew's. The congregation liked him, and after two or three years, the Anglican Society for the Propagation of the Gospel in Foreign Parts offered to pay him £20 a year if he were admitted to holy orders. There was no bishop in the colonies, so aspiring Anglican clergymen had to go to England to be ordained. Viets made the hazardous voyage across the Atlantic and back.

After his ordination and return to America, Viets took charge of St. Andrew's parish in 1763 and remained there for twenty-four years. During this time his congregation increased to nearly 200 families. In 1774 only two other towns in the state had more Anglicans than did Simsbury. Mr. Viets also helped establish churches at Salmon Brook and Great Barrington, Massachusetts. Many of his sermons were published, and he became known as a cultured, scholarly man who had one of the best libraries in Connecticut.

Mr. Viets' sister Eunice married Elisha Griswold, a wealthy landowner who lived where Tariffville is today. Their son Alexander Viets Griswold, born in 1766, became one of the first Anglican bishops in America.

During the Revolutionary War, Reverend Roger Viets was fined £20 and sentenced to a year's imprisonment for "aiding and assisting Major French and a number of other prisoners in making their escape," to quote the *Courant* of January 27, 1777. The prisoners were a group of British soldiers whom, by his later admission, Mr. Viets had been "entertaining and secreting." He was jailed in Hartford for about six months, then released on probation after posting a bond of £1000, promising to stay within the Simsbury town limits and not to "do or say anything against the United States" for the remaining months of his sentence.

After the war the Anglican missionary society withdrew support from its American missionaries, but it invited Mr. Viets to take charge of a new parish at Digby, Nova Scotia. He and his family emigrated there in 1787.

Many Turkey Hills families attended St. Andrew's church. A vote taken at a Turkey Hills Society meeting in 1767 shows twenty-four Congregationalists and about thirty of the Church of England present. Among the latter were many Holcombs, Vietses, Aldermans, and Thompsons, some of whom may have wished that a way could be found to reconcile the colonies with the mother country.

However, only one Turkey Hills man, David Eno, Jr., has been accused of raising arms to support the Crown. In a 1785 petition that asked the General Assembly to invalidate a land transfer, David Eno, Sr., charged that his son deserted the American Army and joined the "service of his British Majesty." The General Assembly denied the petition with no explanation. David Eno, Jr., eventually returned home and lived for more than twenty years at or near 11 Seymour Road. He may have built the house that stands there today. He also received a pension from the United States government for serving in the Continental Army.

The genealogy of the Clark and Forward families calls Abel Forward a Tory and says: "One day during the Revolution, he went to Windsor and purchased some tea; on his way home some rebels overtook him, took it from him, and destroyed it. This act he considered very lawless."

Simsbury's Committee of Inspection condemned Joshua Holcomb for his opposition to the Continental Association and recommended that the public treat him "with the neglect and contempt which is so justly due for his incorrigible enmity to the rights of British America." Holcomb, the son of Deacon Joshua Holcomb, was also restricted to his farm on Holcomb Street. When caught off the farm he was shot in one leg and crippled for the rest of his life.

11 Seymour Road

An Anthony Rogers and a John Griffin petitioned the Governor and Council of Safety from the jail in Hartford in June 1777 for a pardon under a resolution passed by the General Assembly that May. The resolution provided that inhabitants of the state who had absconded "and put themselves under the protection of the enemies of this and other states of America" should be pardoned upon taking an oath of allegiance to the state. These men may have been John Griffin of Simsbury, a descendant of Sergeant John Griffin, and the Anthony Rogers who was married to Joshua Holcomb's sister Zilpah. A year later Simsbury's John Griffin enlisted in the Continental Army; Anthony Rogers left the state.

So the people of Turkey Hills had among them both patriots and Loyalists. They also had in their midst a threat to Tories calculated to make the most stout-hearted pale. Turkey Hills had Newgate Prison.

7

The Revolution II: Newgate Prison

EARLY in 1773 the Connecticut General Assembly had decided to convert the main tunnels of the Simsbury Mines on Copper Hill into a prison. Imprisonment in the mine seemed to the members of the Assembly more humane than other forms of punishment then commonly used, such as branding and mutilating. Being practical, the assemblymen reasoned that the prisoners could be put to work digging copper to pay their board. Furthermore, the committee of three assemblymen whom they sent to inspect the mine assured them that for a rather small sum the mine shafts could be made so secure that escape would be next to impossible.

The Assembly purchased the lease on the mine and authorized a committee to prepare the caverns to house prisoners. Local workmen blasted a lodging room about 12 by 15 feet in the main tunnel and had a wooden ladder in a vertical shaft leading to it. For security they installed an iron trapdoor part way down the 25-foot shaft leading into it.

On October 17 the Assembly passed the act that officially opened Newgate Prison, which has come to be regarded as the first state prison in the new nation that was forming. The assemblymen apparently hoped that naming the prison after the notorious Newgate Prison in London would be a warning to criminals and a deterrent to crime. The English Newgate was a medieval horror with stone chambers of injustice and overcrowding. Its population included men, women, and children. Persons merely accused of crimes, many of them political prisoners, were locked up with hardened criminals. Lack of water, ventilation, space, and sanitation bred vile diseases.

Three assemblymen became the new prison's first overseers: Jonathan Humphrey of Simsbury, plus Erastus Wolcott and Josiah Bissel. They were responsible for checking periodically to see that the prisoners had adequate food, clothing, medical attention, work tools, and professional miners to direct them. They were to inspect the prison accounts and to establish a code of discipline.

Captain John Viets became the first prison keeper, or warden. He had served Simsbury as a selectman and achieved the rank of captain in the town militia. He was a mine proprietor and now operated a tavern and trading post at his home opposite the prison. When he became keeper, he was nearing sixty.

Captain Viets was expected to tend to the daily needs of the prisoners and to see that none escaped. He had the authority to shackle unruly men and to whip them, but no whipping was to exceed ten stripes. He also helped to buy prison supplies, to engage professional miners and other workmen, and to lodge at his tavern all who needed quarters, including the overseers on their visits.

According to the record, the Assembly established Newgate to hold convicted burglars, highwaymen, forgers, counterfeiters, and horse thieves. A first offense drew a sentence of no more than ten years; a second warranted a life sentence, except for the lesser crime of horse stealing. The Superior Court handled all these offenses, except horse stealing which could be tried in a county court.

The first prisoner, burglar John Hinson, was put in Captain Viets' keeping on December 22. On the morning of January 10 Captain Viets found the prison empty. A number of romantic tales surround the record of Hinson's escape; the most popular has a lady friend lowering him a rope. Hinson probably did make his way out the 70-foot ore shaft. In their inexperience as jailers, the prison overseers had failed to see the need to hire a night guard and to secure this second shaft. During mining operations ore had been drawn to the surface through this shaft, and it had doubled as a well. There was a pure spring and pool below it.

Viets advertised a $10 reward in the *Courant* for the return of the escapee, whom Viets described as "about 5 feet 6 inches high, has black eyes, dark hair, fair complexion, and about twenty years of age." Viets also offered the same for any of the "evil-minded persons" who he said helped Hinson escape. No one was turned in.

The members of the Assembly had no desire to duplicate the unhealthful conditions of London's Newgate in their colony's prison in Turkey Hills. For added security, however, they voted to allow the construction of a log house over the ladder shaft and the securing of the ore shaft as long as nothing obstructed the "free communication of air." Daniel Willcox and Abel Forward of Turkey Hills did most of the blacksmith work for these alterations, while other local men provided timber and additional building materials.

Viets was without further prisoners until February as the construction was beginning. Local men were hired from time to time as night watchmen at one shilling a night. Captain Viets began to supply the prisoners with bedding straw, blankets, and shoes, probably made by his cobbler brother Henry. Viets' wife, Lois Phelps Viets, began to make woolen shirts for the inmates. (Viets had met Lois Phelps, daughter of Nathaniel Phelps of North Main Street, when she came to see the mines in operation. Apparently they were as much an object of curiosity then as they are now.)

The General Assembly paid for all supplies, hoping to recover the cost with proceeds from future sale of copper ore dug by the prisoners. The prisoners had other thoughts concerning digging. During the night of April 9, 1774, William Johnson Crawford, a horse thief, and Daniel Collyer Humphrey, a robber, attempted to dig their way out of an abandoned mine shaft with the help of three other prisoners. At approximately 3 A.M., the shaft collapsed. Crawford and Humphrey were buried alive, according to the testimony of the other prisoners. Viets advertised for their capture anyway. Since the shaft has never been reopened, whether or not their bones lie beneath the fallen rubble remains a mystery. Later in the month the rest of the inmates made a successful escape with outside help.

In May the overseers reported to the Assembly that the prison was empty again, but that the construction project was complete. The 20x36-foot log house built of 10-inch-square timbers had two rooms, one to secure the iron trapdoor to the ladder shaft and one to house the two miners they had recently hired. The overseers further stated that an iron grating secured with heavy cut stones had been placed over the ore shaft, and every other place they thought might offer a chance of escape had been sealed.

The next October prisoners began to arrive again. Lois Viets resumed making trousers and knitting socks. Captain Viets supplied the prisoners with their meals, including rum rations. At this time he was charging the colony five shillings a week for each prisoner in his care.

The prison inmates had no intention of thanking Captain Viets for his services. On November 21 the six prisoners incarcerated at the time overpowered the two miners in a remote part of the mine and armed themselves with the miners' tools. Then the prisoners made their way up the ladder shaft and into the locked room in the house above. Somehow they summoned Viets, and when he opened the door, they jumped and beat him. Historian Richard H. Phelps says the townspeople rounded up most of the escapees, some of them hiding in trees and some of them trying to cross the bridge over the Farmington River between Turkey Hills and Scotland. A woman whom Phelps describes in 1844 as "an aged and respected matron, then a child and residing but a few rods from the prison" told him: "The news of their escape and capture spread as much terror among the children in the neighborhood as if they had been a band of midnight assassins." After this incident the overseers instituted the use of leg irons on the prisoners.

During its session in May 1775 the Assembly appointed a fourth prison overseer, Asahel Holcomb, Jr., of Turkey Hills, and authorized the sale of copper ore that had been dug. It also formulated a policy for paroling prisoners the overseers deemed repentant and well behaved. The prisoners had to petition for their release and, if granted, post a bond and/or pay a fine of £5 a year for three years.

The first prisoner to benefit from this policy was William Livingston, a horse thief, who refused to join in an escape that June. Two of the three prisoners involved in this prison break were recaptured, but they and two more escaped again in August. All were returned, except for the notorious Richard Steel, a burglar. On this, his third escape from Newgate, Steel was captured by bounty hunter William Alford of Hartford. On their way back to Simsbury, Alford and his prisoner stopped at the Continental Army encampment in Cambridge, Massachusetts. According to Alford, Steel convinced the American generals to let him make his way into Boston "to do evil" among the British.

With the Revolutionary War underway, the rebelling patriots became more wary than ever of those fellow Americans who might undermine their chances for victory. Patriots watched and harassed Loyalists whose only crime was to do nothing to further the cause. Active Tories and disruptive or profiteering outlaws, they jailed.

General George Washington was the first to send what he termed "flagrant and atrocious villains" to Newgate Prison. The three had been tried at a court martial in Cambridge in December. John Short was convicted of desertion and theft, John Smith of attempting to defect to the enemy, and Owen Ruick of aiding Smith in his attempt to defect. Smith was sentenced to six months and the other two for the duration of the war. The men were brought before Simsbury's Committee of Safety and turned over to Captain Viets.

Owen Ruick eventually won his release form Newgate, fought with the Continental forces, and returned after the war to live the rest of his life in nearby Salmon Brook. John Short, on the other hand, died within a month of his incarceration in an attempted prison break.

This time some of the prisoners tried to dig their way out through the mine's clogged drainage tunnel. After removing loose debris, they discovered the passageway was blocked by a large, immovable rock. When they had accumulated four or five bushels of charcoal from their allotment of fuel, they built a fire against the rock, hoping that heat would crack it. Instead, smoke began to fill the mine. The inmates managed to extinguish the fire, but not before three of them were asphyxiated.

About the time the Declaration of Independence was being signed, three men were sent to Newgate for what a British officer described as "being friends to government and social order." After the addition of these Tories to the prison population, the Simsbury Committee of Safety reported to Governor Jonathan Trumbull that a "dangerous situation" existed at the prison and that Captain Viets was "uneasy." The Committee of Inspection of Farmington and New Hartford also petitioned the governor, urging him to increase security measures at the prison. Now that Loyalists as well as common felons might get loose, the local authorities spoke up.

Captain Viets resigned as prison keeper sometime before the October 1776 session of the General Assembly, which passed Connecticut's first anti-Loyalist law. The Assembly declared that all treasonable acts would be punishable by confinement in Newgate, making official what was already happening. It is ironic that while this law was being passed, Captain Viets' son, the Anglican minister Roger Viets, was beginning a sentence in Hartford Jail for harboring British officers who had escaped from there. Shortly after Captain Viets' resignation but while he was still acting as keeper, the three Tory prisoners escaped.

Captain Viets died from smallpox the following April. He was buried on his own land within sight of the prison. Within a short time the Assembly paroled Roger Viets. One reason for the parole was that he was needed to help settle his father's estate. Widow Viets married overseer Colonel Jonathan Humphrey and lived to an active old age.

At its fall session in 1776 the Assembly also approved the building of an addition to the log house and the digging of a well for the prison. It authorized the prison overseers to hire a new keeper, contrary to the wishes of the Simsbury Committee of Safety who wanted to select him.

A man named Purchase Capon probably was the prison's second keeper, since he signed an escape notice published in February 1777. During this escape two fleeing Loyalists burned down the log house. One was recaptured and taken to Hartford Jail; the other remained at large. Although the Assembly authorized immediate rebuilding, the prison was left charred and empty until 1779.

Early that year the Assembly appointed Roger Newberry, Erastus Wolcott, and Turkey Hills' Joseph Forward, Jr., Asahel Holcomb, Jr., and Matthew Griswold to take charge of rebuilding. They were instructed to build a blockhouse "over the mouth of the cavern suitable and convenient to secure and employ the prisoners in labor in the daytime." The Assembly had long since given up the idea of having the prisoners dig copper. The reactivated prison was to receive counterfeiters, who were disrupting the wartime economy, and anyone convicted of selling or importing goods from enemy-held territory.

The building, which was completed in 1780, became a guardhouse rather than a workhouse. The Assembly authorized Governor Jonathan Trumbull to order a guard of not over forty men to the prison. Overseer Roger Newberry ordered Elijah Owen of Turkey Hills to enlist a guard of one sergeant, one corporal, and twenty-four privates. Raising a guard by voluntary enlistment proved impossible. Later Newberry was ordered to draw a guard from his militia unit. He disapproved of this method and found it, too, unsatisfactory. He suggested to Governor Trumbull that men might be induced to enlist as guards if they were exempted from taxes. Newberry was also unable to find a prison keeper for the salary offered. Despite the fact that the guard was often undermanned, the state gradually increased the number of Loyalists, Tory raiders, court-martialed American soldiers, and common felons it sent to Newgate.

On May 18, 1781, twenty-eight prisoners escaped from Newgate in the largest insurrection of the Revolutionary era. That evening the commander of the guard, Seth Smith of Suffield, was away on leave. About 9 P.M., after most of the guards were in bed, Abigail Young came to the prison, ostensibly to see her husband John, alias Mattick, who was confined there. Samuel Lilly, the second in command, brought her into the guardhouse and unlocked the trapdoor over the mine shaft. The prisoners, armed with clubs, rushed the door and one, Ebenezer Hathaway, made it into the guardroom. While he fought off two soldiers in the guardroom, the rest of the prisoners poured out of the mine. Some of the guards were surprised in their beds and relieved of their muskets and bayonets, pistols, and cutlasses. Some ran off "to alarm the neighborhood," as they later testified. One of the guards, Thomas Sheldon, fought valiantly to drive the prisoners back. Ebenezer Hathaway ran him through with a bayonet, mortally wounding him. Six other guards received lesser wounds.

By the time the struggle ended, all the guards who had stood their ground were locked in the mine. Two Tories who had refused to join the insurrection tended the wounded until help arrived. They were released later for meritorious conduct. Of the twenty-eight prisoners who escaped, sixteen were returned in a week. Ebenezer Hathaway, who had three wounds, and a fellow privateer, William Smith, made their way to New York where they gave an account of the prison break which was published June 6 in *Rivinston's Royal Gazette.*

Overseer Joseph Forward arrested Seth Smith and Samuel Lilly for negligence. The General Assembly's investigation revealed possible collusion between the prisoners and some of the guard. A Private Blenden admitted receiving a bribe from counterfeiter Peter Prentice. Mrs. Young claimed she gave $50 to her husband to give to Lilly, but he denied receiving the money. Neither Lilly nor Smith was convicted of any crime. Ironically, overseer Forward was later brought before a grand jury and accused of being too friendly with the Tories and too lax in maintaining security at the prison. He may have been suspect because he was the nephew of Loyalist Abel Forward.

Toward the beginning of the war, the Connecticut General Assembly had written the Continental Congress about using Newgate as a prison for captured British regulars, but none had been sent there. On September 18, 1781, the Congress passed a resolve which would send prisoners of war to Newgate in retaliation for the ill treatment received by American prisoners in this country and in England.

The Congress asked the Assembly to send a plan of the prison and an estimate of what it would cost to strengthen it. Assemblymen Samuel Mott and Roger Newberry filed two reports which described the partially completed guardhouse, the mines, and the general environment. They mentioned that there was fresh air in the prison and that spring water was available. With the addition of a stone wall and other alterations estimated at £1500, Mott and Newberry felt that Newgate could become a "good strong state prison." They felt that the mines would hold only 200 prisoners, however, significantly less than the 500 the Congress wished to place there. The Congress did not proceed with its plans and never stated a reason. Since the surrender of Cornwallis at Yorktown in October ensured victory for the Americans, Congress probably felt it would not need Newgate. The end of the war was near and they had the upper hand.

It is interesting, though, that Congress chose Newgate to use as a threat to the British. Despite the number of successful prison breaks or, perhaps, because of them, Newgate had gained a reputation as black as the Black Hole of Calcutta. Escaping prisoners like Ebenezer Hathaway delighted in describing and embellishing upon the "horrors" they had seen there. Tory propagandists wrote terrifying accounts of the conditions in the prison which circulated widely and are still being repeated as fact today. Incarceration in Newgate was held up to readers of the sensational press in England as the epitome of what the inhuman rebel patriots would do, short of execution, to persecute those loyal colonists who supported the Crown.

The Reverend Samuel Peters of Hebron, Connecticut, an avowed Tory, gave a fanciful description of the prison in his anonymous history of Connecticut published in London in 1781. He said the prisoners were lowered by a windlass to forty yards below the earth's surface. "In a few months," he claimed, " the prisoners are released by death." Another Tory from Hebron, Reverend Simeon Baxter, likened the cavern to Orcus, or hell, in a pamphlet of propaganda which contained an open letter to George Washington urging him to do his fellow men a favor by committing suicide.

The title page of Baxter's pamphlet, which was printed in London, states that it is a discourse which he delivered personally on September 19, 1781, to the Loyalists confined in the mines at Simsbury. While reviewing the papers pertaining to Newgate Prison in the Connecticut State Library and elsewhere, the East Granby Historical Committee's researcher Eugene J. Riccio became curious when he saw no record of Baxter's having been a prisoner or having visited there. After examining papers and writings pertaining to Baxter's movements during September 1781, Riccio concluded that Baxter was more likely in Maine than in Connecticut that month and that the Newgate prisoners probably were never treated to a reading of the fiery treatise.

Despite the lurid pictures painted by propagandists, no prisoners during this time died from the living conditions in the prison; only from attempts to escape. The converted mine was like most mines and caves. Its tendency toward dampness must have made the footing on the sloping rock floors perilous at times. However, even the most severe critics of the place never claimed to see standing water in the area occupied by the prisoners. Supporters often said the mine was dry most of the time.

Of course the mine was pitch dark except for a bit of daylight that filtered in through the various shafts. Candles and fires must have made the place a bit smoky, although the several shafts allowed ample air circulation. Hygiene was probably a problem for any prisoner who was fastidious, but there was clean water in the well for bathing and housekeeping.

The cavern was not overcrowded like its namesake in London. There were rarely more than twenty prisoners in it at any one time. Not more than seventy altogether were committed to Newgate during the Revolution.

The most favorable thing that can be said about conditions in the mine is that, like all subterranean cavities, it has a very constant temperature. No matter how hot or cold it is above ground, the mine never registers below 40° or above 52°. These cavern temperatures were recorded by researcher Lawrence W. Lang, who spent nine years as head guard and guide there after the State of Connecticut reopened the prison as an historic landmark in 1972.

Newgate's population of prisoners decreased after the September 1781 breakout. The size of the guard was reduced to only a sergeant, a corporal, and eight privates, but still the colony had difficulty filling the positions. Governor Trumbull requested an invalid corps from General Washington, thinking that men too incapacitated for battle could guard the prison. Washington, hard pressed for men himself, refused the request. He said the invalids were still of value to the Continental Army.

Daily business went on as usual at Newgate for a while. Matthew Griswold of Turkey Hills was appointed an overseer in May at the recommendation of Roger Newberry, who felt that Joseph Forward should have another overseer living nearby to help him. A counterfeiter, Collins Gorton, was shot trying to escape. Then on November 6, 1782, the prison was burned out once again, and its role in the Revolutionary War came to an end.

The fire was probably set by the prisoners, who were then housed in cells located in the cellar of the guardhouse. The commander of the guard, Abel Davis, released the prisoners for fear they would die. Four prisoners ran for freedom, but several made no attempt to escape. These were later paroled. A detachment of militia under the command of Benjamin Thrall of Turkey Hills placed the guards under arrest; together with the remaining prisoners, the men were marched to the jail in Hartford. Davis was imprisoned, fined, and cashiered for dereliction of duty.

After the General Assembly decided against immediate repair of the prison, it directed Roger Newberry to salvage whatever he could of value from the ruins, sell it, and pay the prison's outstanding debts with the proceeds. Newgate was abandoned until 1790 when Connecticut reestablished the prison.

By that time, Newgate's address had changed. It was now situated in the newly created Town of Granby.

II

The Granby Years

from the incorporation of Granby to the separation of East Granby

1786 - 1858

Chronological Highlights

1786	*Granby incorporated.*
1794	*Reverend Whitfield Cowles ordained Congregational minister at Turkey Hills.*
c. 1800	*First cigars made in Connecticut.*
1800	*Granby Turnpike chartered.*
1816	*Copper Hill Methodist-Episcopal Church established.*
1820	*East Granby Post Office established.*
1822	*Farmington Canal chartered.*
1827	*Newgate Prison closed.*
1830	*Phoenix Mining Company chartered.*
1830	*Present Congregational meetinghouse erected.*
1839	*Present Methodist-Episcopal meetinghouse erected.*
c. 1843	*German silver flatware silver-plated at Spoonville.*
1850	*Canal Railroad opened to Granby.*

8

A Changing People in a Time of Change

EVEN BEFORE the end of the Revolution, most of the Simsbury residents living in the Salmon Brook Ecclesiastical Society and some of those in the Turkey Hills area had been pressing to separate from Simsbury and to form a new town. At a town meeting in July 1781, held as usual in the First Society, the inhabitants voted to petition the General Assembly to divide the town in two, because Simsbury was so large geographically that it was difficult for men to get together to transact town business. The minutes of the meeting do not record any debate on the subject, but subsequent events indicate strong opposition to the proposal.

First came an attempt to accommodate voters of all sections of town by holding town meetings in different parishes. During 1782 the town held one meeting at Salmon Brook and a later one at Turkey Hills. At the first meeting the townsmen chose agents to petition the General Assembly for division. When they met at Turkey Hills, the only business transacted besides choosing a moderator was a vote to adjourn to the First Society. The recorded vote at the reconvened meeting suggests that heated and perhaps bitter controversy preceded it:

Voted for the future that the selectmen of this town shall not have power or authority to warn any town meeting unless at the meetinghouse in the First Society in Simsbury . . . until the town at a lawful meeting held at the last mentioned place shall see fit to vote and resolve to the contrary.

The voters also decided to reconsider their decision to petition the General Assembly.

Agitation for partition continued, although rotation of town meetings did not. The town voted 172 to 149 in 1785 *not* to take up the question of separation, but a year later the minority of 149 had added or changed enough votes to gain permission again to ask the General Assembly. The petition gave two reasons for the request. One was the "large extent" of the town, about 9 by 16 miles. The other was the necessity of holding town meetings at an "extreme part" of town because the geographic center was a "large barren pine plain which is not and probably never will be settled," and, therefore, some people had to travel 12 or 13 miles to vote.

No representative from Turkey Hills signed the petition; two men from the First Society and one from Salmon Brook signed. Just four days before the town meeting, the Turkey Hills Society had voted 30 to 7 "to remain with the south part of Simsbury and not to be separated therefrom in case the town should be divided." The minutes of the meeting do not say who the thirty men were or why they wanted to remain a part of Simsbury—or more to the point, why they did not want to become a separate town with Salmon Brook, but some of the reasons can be surmised.

The two societies had been separate entities for fifty years. Each controlled its common schools, its church, and the maintenance of its highways. Even the careful allocation of town offices among men of the different ecclesiastical societies emphasized their independence.

The Mountain continued to be a barrier to the development of common interests among the families on opposite sides of it. Children went to schools either east or west of the Mountain,depending on where they lived. Many of the Holcombs, Vietses, and Griffins who lived west of the Mountain attended churches in North Bloomfield and Salmon Brook, while the majority of the families east of it supported the local Congregational church. Men on the east side traded in Suffield, Hartford, Windsor, and even Springfield far more than they did west of the Mountain.

In 1786 it was probably the men on the east side who did not want to join with Salmon Brook, which had more than twice the population of Turkey Hills. Obviously, the voters of Turkey Hills would be a political minority, and Salmon Brook would be the political center of the proposed town.

In spite of all opposition, the General Assembly at its October 1786 session joined the Salmon Brook and Turkey Hills ecclesiastical societies as the Town of Granby. The status of the Windsor Half Mile was not affected. It continued to be a part of both the Turkey Hills society and the Town of Windsor. The Assembly provided that Simsbury's money, debts, poor, and "the whole town stock, arms, ammunition, and camp utensils" be divided according to each town's proportion of the current Grand List. Asahel Holcomb, Jr., a Turkey Hills man from east of the Mountain, was appointed to warn and preside at Granby's first town meeting in December. Thus began the seventy-two years that Turkey Hills parishioners were citizens of Granby.

Three of the earliest settlers of Turkey Hills lived to see the birth of the United States of America and the movement which created the Town of Granby. During their long lifetimes William and Amos Moore and Joseph Alderman saw the parish grow from a few families to over 120 and some of their younger neighbors move to less populated territory. They saw miles of virgin forest cut down, the natural fertility of the soil diminished, and the supply of salmon and shad in the Farmington River depleted. They were glad, no doubt, that most of the bears, panthers, and timber wolves were killed or driven away, but the decreasing number of wild turkeys must have saddened them. They had grown up knowing the joys of the turkey shoot.

Anthelme Brillat-Savarin, gastronome, musician, and refugee from the French Revolution, wrote a description of a 1794 wild turkey shoot which a later author, Edwin Valentine Mitchell, conjectured may have taken place in Turkey Hills. Brillat-Savarin wrote that a farmer who lived "in the backwoods" about 5 leagues (15 miles) from Hartford invited him to go hunting. He arrived at the farmer's house in time to share an abundant supper. "There was a superb piece of corned beef, a stewed goose, and a magnificent leg of mutton with vegetables of every description, and at each end of the table, two large jugs of cider."

The next day, he writes, they shot some partridges and gray squirrels before coming upon a flock of wild turkeys. The birds protested noisily at the intrusion as they flew off. Brillat-Savarin shot one, which he took with the other game back to Hartford. At a dinner party for some of his American friends, he served the wings of the partridges *en papillottes* and the squirrels stewed in Madeira. He concludes: "As for the turkey, which was the only roast we had, it was charming to look upon, delightful to smell, and delicious to taste."

T.G. Case of Granby, a 19th-century historian, recorded the legend of what must have been one of the last salmon to swim up Salmon Brook:

The mill on the brook back of Joel C. Holcomb's [at 115 Hartford Avenue] . . . *was the place where Chloe Alderman, wife of Epaphrus, killed a salmon which weighed 18 pounds dressed. She was tending mill. He (meaning the fish) was trying to jump over the dam and she killed him with a stake. Hezekiah Holcomb, grandfather of Joel C., had half the fish. The date of this fish is not fixed except that his death occurred between 1790 and 1802 sometime and the story seems to be tolerably authentic. It is said that salmon were caught frequently in the Salmon Brook. It is said Hezekiah Holcomb used to shoot them.*

The decreasing fertility of their land along with their increasing population was of even more consequence to the people of Turkey Hills than the loss of virgin forests and native wildlife. Decades of insufficient fertilizing, weeding, and crop rotation had taken their toll.

By the same token, not even the most efficient farming methods known at the time could have made the land productive enough to sustain the large families of the first settlers and their immediate families. The seventeen earliest settlers had seventy-two sons among whom to divide their land. Daughters, some of whom also inherited land, were equally numerous.

David and Rachel Clark (Amos Moore's daughter), who lived in the Reverend Mr. Mills' house at 100 South Main Street, exemplify both the longevity and fecundity of some of the colonists. When Clark died, the fourth Isaac Owen recorded in his diary:

Oct. 26. David Clark, aged 94 years. He was married to Rachel Moore in May 1750, with whom he lived 64 years and five months, she dying the 9th of October 1814, aged 83 years. Their descendants are 20 children (one only at a birth) 117 grandchildren, 111 great grandchildren, and 12 great great grandchildren, making the fifth generation. The whole, 260.

Emigrants and Immigrants

The General Assembly opened the northwestern part of Connecticut to settlement in the 1720s when it arranged to sell public lands. Nine of Turkey Hills second generation Moores and Winchells migrated there and to Duchess County, New York, just over the Connecticut border.

During the last half of the century a number of second and third generation Turkey

Hills residents moved north to Western Massachusetts and Vermont. Some ventured only as far as Granville, Westfield, and Southwick, Massachusetts. The third Joseph Forward went to Southwick in the late 1700s as an agent for an English company that planned to drain the Congamond Lakes for the rich soil in their beds. They actually started to dig a drainage canal toward Westfield. Historian Josiah Holland wrote, "The project was never completed, doubtless because it was found entirely impracticable."

Speculators bought large tracts of land west of New England after the Revolution and sold them to prospective emigrants. Oliver Phelps of Suffield was such a speculator and he found buyers among the Granger family of Turkey Hills.

John Granger had moved over the Suffield border about 1735 to settle on lot 1 at the northeast corner of colonial Simsbury. He had owned approximately 100 acres, which eventually were divided among his children. By 1789 one of his sons, Elisha, was supporting his family on fewer than 20 acres—too little land to be divided into farms for his children. So, his sons Pierce, twenty, and Elihu, eighteen, bought some of Phelps' land in the western part of New York State.

According to James N. Granger, author of his family genealogy, much of Pierce and Elihu's trip into New York State was made by canoe up the Mohawk River and across Oneida Lake. After clearing land and building rude log huts, the brothers returned to Turkey Hills through the woods using a compass and blazing trees as they went. In late winter they returned to New York with Elihu's wife and baby on a covered sleigh. They also took with them a horse, two cows, and a hive of bees. With this beginning they founded the Town of Phelps.

The majority of emigrants from Turkey Hills settled on Connecticut's Western Reserve, approximately 3,500,000 acres in northeastern Ohio. This land was reserved by the state in 1786 when it and the other states ceded much of their western land to the new federal government. This agreement ended repeated territorial disputes stemming from the fact that Connecticut's charter, like those of other colonies, had established its western boundary as "the South Sea," i.e., the Pacific Ocean.

The General Assembly granted 500,000 acres in the Western Reserve to Connecticut people whose property had been burned by the British during the Revolution. A group of men organized the Connecticut Land Company in 1795 and bought the remainder of the land for $1,200,000.

Solomon Griswold of Wintonbury Ecclesiastical Society (now Bloomfield) was a partner in the Connecticut Land Company. His brother Simeon was also a land speculator who bought and sold thousands of acres of the Reserve in what became the township of Windsor, Ohio. He purchased at least five farms in the southeastern section of Turkey Hills from the Alderman and Higley families when they moved to Windsor township in 1804.

Mary Coffin Johnson writes that in 1804 the second Jonathan Higley and his family traveled directly to Albany, New York, then in a southwesterly direction toward Pittsburgh, crossing the Allegheny Mountains and entering the Western Reserve on its southern border. "One of the oxen died on the way, and the milk cow was doomed to do double duty, being hitched beside the other ox to help pull the wagon." After a tedious forty-two-day journey, they arrived at Windsor, Ohio, where "a rough, bare log house with a split timber roof which had been put up for temporary protection from the weather and wild beasts by one Ira Forest . . . stood ready for a shelter."

According to Mary Johnson, Higley's wife, Rachel, carried apple seeds to Ohio. She named the fruit of the trees "Jonathan apples" after her husband.

The Higleys' daughter and her husband, Abigail and Samuel Forward, Jr., had emigrated to the Western Reserve the year before. Their four children went with them as did Forward's parents and five of his brothers and sisters. They were the first settlers at what is today Aurora, Ohio. Like many others, Forward left his birthplace because of financial hardship.* He was bankrupt. An auction of his belongings was held at Luther Holcomb's inn (27-29 North Main Street) and advertised in the *Courant*: "1 horse, 1 cow, 1 blacksmith anvil, about 100 horseshoes, some axes and hoes, a good gun and cartridge box, and numerous articles of furniture, some of considerable value and many useful."

The Forward genealogy says their train consisted of two large wagons, "one drawn by a span of horses, the other by two yoke of oxen and a horse on the lead, one saddle horse and two cows." The wagons were so loaded with food, farm tools, and household articles that the emigrants had to walk the many miles to their new home.

They were met in Aurora, Ohio, by Oliver Forward, brother of Samuel, Jr., who had gone there in advance to prepare for the family's arrival. In fact, he had left Connecticut in February, only two days after his wedding to Sally Granger of Suffield, leaving his bride behind.

A letter dated August 22, 1803, from Samuel Forward, Sr., to his son-in-law Israel C. Phelps in Turkey Hills conveys his satisfaction and enthusiasm:

Oliver put up a good log house, the best on the Purchase. They have cleared about 25 acres, have planted almost two acres of corn without plowing or dragging that is as big as any in the home lots in Granby. They have as good a garden of beans as I ever had in Granby and cucumbers, watermelons, and muskmelons as good as I ever saw—almost one acre of potatoes that look exceeding well and two acres of oats sowed the last of June, now beginning to head out, that are equal to any I ever saw and a large supply of green peas.

Five years later, his enthusiasm was unabated. He wrote that he had between 50 and 60 acres cleared and fenced into "suitable fields and mowing ground" and a large orchard of peach and apple trees. He adds:

*Two tons of hay on an acre here is no great thing. It is good for wheat, rye, or corn. I picked on one acre seventy-six bushels of Indian corn.*** I keep nine cows. . . . I have a good flock of sheep of about twenty.*

The town meetings are held at my house. The first sermon ever preached on Sunday in Aurora was at my house. The first white child born in Aurora was at my house. The Fourth

*Historians think that many people outside the established Congregational Church emigrated for religious reasons. This was probably not true in Turkey Hills where members of other denominations, particularly Episcopalians, seem to have been as politically, economically, and socially prominent as men affiliated with the Congregational Church.

**Timothy Dwight in his *Travels through New England and New York* says 25 bushels of Indian corn per acre was the average yield in Connecticut around 1800, although he had seen 118 bushels from one acre. In 1820 the third Joseph Cornish of 143-145 North Main Street raised over 91 bushels on an acre of land for which he won a premium of $10 from the Hartford County Agricultural Society.

of July was kept up warm at my house. We had a great number of people collected. Oliver delivered an oration that gave satisfaction. We had a liberty pole fifty feet high with a large flag waving on her top and a large bower under which we partook of the good things of this life. . . . About sunset they went home with a blooming cheek and a spark of the spirit of '76 in their breasts.

Five of the Forward sons became lawyers. Walter was a member of Congress (1822-25), a Secretary of the U.S. Treasury (1841-43), and a charge d'affairs in Denmark (1849-51).

Migration from Turkey Hills continued through the middle of the century. The population of Granby was 2595 in 1790 and 2408 in 1850. The population was not stagnant, though, as newcomers did move into the society. Some came from other towns in the East to establish businesses or to work for others. Some married into local families.

Blacks came, fleeing more repressive conditions in the South. The censuses of 1800 through 1850 show from fifty-five to 107 "non-whites" in Granby. Some lived with Turkey Hills families and worked as domestics and farm laborers. Others had their own small homesteads.

Foreign immigrants came mostly from the British Isles; a majority of them were from Ireland. Hundreds of Irishmen were imported into the state in the late 1820s to dig the Farmington Canal, which ran through Granby, and the Windsor Locks Canal. Thirty years later, Irish immigrants laid the tracks of the railroads that replaced the canals. Local families welcomed the Irish as domestics and farm workers. Miners came from Great Britain and Germany to work in the local copper mines after they were reactivated in the 1830s.

Skilled craftsmen found work in the new factories. Weavers were needed at the Tariff Manufacturing Company, founded at Tariffville in 1825 "for the purpose of manufacturing wool, cotton, and other manufactures in the most advantageous manner." Makers of spoons and spectacles came to the Cowles Manufacturing Company on the Farmington River in the southeast section of Turkey Hills. Many of these immigrants moved on to larger manufacturing centers in Connecticut, and others joined the migration to the West. Some settled in and around Turkey Hills where their descendants live today.

A Changing Life-style in Turkey Hills

After the Revolution, rural people became less isolated as the means of transportation and communication improved. More and better roads, bridges, and vehicles made traveling easier.

Mail service improved greatly for the people of Turkey Hills. Before 1805 local men picked up their mail at post offices in Hartford and Suffield. Newspapers printed the names of men for whom there were letters waiting. In 1805 the federal government established the Granby Post Office at the center of Salmon Brook parish, and Turkey Hills got its own station in 1820. It was called the East Granby Post Office. The first postmaster, Chauncey Barker, probably operated it from his store at 19 South Main Street.

Erastus Holcomb, the great-grandson of Deacon Asahel Holcomb, may have been the first post rider to deliver mail to the East Granby Post Office. In 1820 he advertised in the *Courant*: "Erastus Holcomb informs the citizens of the towns of Windsor, Gran-

19 South Main Street

by, and Southwick (Massachusetts) that he has commenced riding post from Hartford through the above towns and will be glad to supply them with various newspapers printed in Hartford and do such other business as is usually entrusted to a post rider." Post riders did personal errands for people, and, like ministers, they often took their pay in produce. During the 1830s a regular stage route was established through the center of Turkey Hills, and, thereafter, stage drivers handled the mail.

Before envelopes came into use about 1839, letters were folded over and secured with sealing wax. There were no postage stamps until 1847. For years the recipient of the mail paid the postage after the postmaster determined the amount due according to the distance it had traveled.

In 1809 the Reverend Roger Viets, who was then at Digby, Nova Scotia, addressed a letter to his brother Abner "at Granby near Simsbury, County of Hartford, Connecticut, New England." He concluded his letter with some brotherly advice:

This letter weighs but a little more than half an ounce, and it is a single piece of paper. The post office can demand of you for postage no more than 20 cents or 25 cents at most. If they say it weighs an ounce and demand a dollar postage, insist on seeing it weighed. Most of the postmasters in all countries are a little oppressive and not over honest.

The postage on the letter was 12½ cents.

More newspapers with their editorials, advertisements, and coverage of current events now supplemented the spoken word and tavern notices in informing people and furthering communication among them. The *Courant* was founded in 1764, the *American Mercury* in 1784, and the *Hartford Times* in 1817. All were weekly papers, published in Hartford. It seems that in 1818 there was about one paper for every three or four households. A year's subscription to the *Courant* cost $2.00 in 1832.

By 1761 there was a library at Salmon Brook. Membership was by subscription. Only members, called proprietors, could borrow books, and then no more than three at a time. Books were returned and redistributed by bid at quarterly meetings. There were fines for turning down a leaf of a book and for returning books late, "let the excuse be what it will."

By 1804, and perhaps before, there was a similar library in Turkey Hills. If its books were donated by local families from their own libraries, the collection would have included such titles as: *The Real Christian Hope in Death, Wisdom of God in Permitting Sin in the World, A Dead Faith Anatomized, Mr. Baxter's Call to the Unconverted, A Compendious History of the World, The Indian History, Sir Walter Raleigh, Aesops Fables,* and *The American Universal Geography.* The novels of Jane Austen, Sir Walter Scott, Charles Dickens, and James Fenimore Cooper may have been added during the first half of the 19th century. There may have been collections of poetry by the Hartford Wits. Poetry was a popular form of expression, and a few poems by Turkey Hills men have survived.

As their leisure time increased, men expanded their range of social activities, forming several fraternal and educational organizations. A Masonic Lodge was established at Turkey Hills in 1796 with Andrew Hillyer as its first Master. For twenty-five years these Masons met at his home, which stood a little south of 19 North Main Street.

The Newtonian Lyceum was organized in 1833 for the "moral and intellectual improvement of its members and the more general diffusion of knowledge." At some meetings participants debated current issues. At others they had speakers on a wide variety of topics—religious, political, literary, historical, scientific, etc.

From the time of the Revolution through the early 1900s, singing schools were popular in Turkey Hills, providing both recreation and instruction through singing. Until 1814, when the local Congregational church acquired its first hymnals, worshippers chanted verses from memory. The result was often an unpleasant drone. Records show that parishioners had been aware of the problem and were progressive, but cautious, in their attempt to solve it. In 1773 they voted to sing new psalm tunes half the time and old tunes the other half. The choristers were to "sit below" rather than in the balcony. In 1782 they voted that the choristers might sit where they found it most convenient and "set such tunes as they think proper according to the meters propounded." The singing may have improved, but not to perfection, because eventually the society voted to raise one penny on the pound to hire a singing instructor.

Dancing schools and semipublic balls appeared in the early 1800s. A printed invitation to a Thanksgiving dance in 1823 at the inn that stood north of 9 South Main Street reads: "Mr. __________ presents his compliments to Miss __________ and solicits the pleasure of waiting on her at Mr. C. Buck's hall on Thursday, the 27th instant at 5 o'clock P.M." To those who opposed dancing as immoral, proponents defended dancing schools and formal balls as opportunities to learn and practice good manners.

Many social activities continued to be work-related—barn raisings, house raisings, quilting parties, husking bees, and such. Even the parish's new Nimrod Club had its practical side; the members could eat the game they killed.

Beginning in 1818, Turkey Hills had an annual fall cattle show and agricultural fair at the center of the parish. There were exhibits of vegetables, fruits, and handiwork such as quilts and hearth rugs. Men showed, matched, and traded oxen; and everyone visited with friends, many of whom came from out-of-town.

Independence Day celebrations were modeled on the colonial training days for the local militia, one of the earliest holidays that combined serious business with pleasure. After an inspection of arms and a drill, the trainbands held contests of marksmanship, wrestling, running, leaping, horse racing, and ball playing. They also brought along food, a practice now reflected in the traditional Fourth of July picnic.

Thanksgiving Day continued to be a festive holiday in late autumn. Starting in 1664, governors of Connecticut had designated a day in October or November to give thanks to God for such blessings as good health, peace, civil and religious liberty, and the "fruits of the earth." Eventually church services were combined with the feasting that had been a part of the traditional celebration of days of thanksgiving since the Pilgrims' first Thanksgiving Day.

Christmas was not celebrated by the Puritans, who disapproved of the secularization of the holiday in England and banned its observance in the New World. It became an Episcopalian rather than a Congregational holiday. The first mention of its celebration by Turkey Hills people is in connection with St. Andrews Episcopal church in North Bloomfield.

Horace Clark recorded in his account book* the days his hired men lost in the early 1800s celebrating Thanksgiving, "keeping up" Christmas, and "cooling off from Independence." David Lamberton took a day and a half off to celebrate Election Day (i.e., Inauguration Day) and slept half a day to get over it. Election Day was a spring holiday and a particularly exciting one for people who went to Hartford to see the parade and perhaps attend the inaugural ball.

Lewis Thrall lost a day's work September 4, 1824, when he went to Hartford to see General Lafayette, who arrived with his military escort amid the firing of artillery and the ringing of bells. A newspaper report says that as Lafayette drove to the State House in his barouche drawn by four white horses, "Every window was crowded with ladies waving their white handkerchiefs." At four o'clock in the afternoon he left by steamboat for New York City "amidst the salute of cannon and the shouts of thousands of gratified spectators."

Turkey Hills men went to Hartford to see traveling shows such as "the witch woman" and "the bear dance." For the first time, they saw elephants and other unfamiliar animals. Eventually the biggest show on earth, the circus, came to neighboring towns.

Local people may have attended the plays produced in Hartford following the Revolution. In an advertisement for the opening of the New Theatre on August 3, 1795, the producers assured anyone who might be prejudiced against the stage that their productions would be "a source of moral instruction as well as rational amusement." Members of the General Assembly were not convinced. Five years later they made it illegal to charge spectators money to attend a theatrical show or exhibition, because such enter-

*Horace Clark (1781-1842) kept a diary and an account book all his adult life. Many are extant, as are diaries of his son Elmore (1807-1891).

tainment led to "the deprivation of manners and impoverishment of the people." The law was in effect until 1852 when the legislature voted to allow each town to regulate its own amusements.

The law did not prohibit entertainments such as the one Charles M. Owen attended at West Suffield in 1814. He called it a performance of "two tragedies and a comedy and dialogue acted upon the stage at intervals with music from the violin, closing with a song which was very applicable to the occasion." There were similar productions at the meetinghouse in Turkey Hills.

Weddings and funerals occasioned large gatherings of families and friends. As a rule, both observances were held at home rather than in a meetinghouse. Justices of the peace as well as clergymen performed marriage ceremonies, and, traditionally, wedding banns were published in the meetinghouse although the law required only that they be announced in a public place.

Young men who had not been invited to a wedding sometimes attempted to "steal the bride" during festivities after the ceremony. If they were successful and able to take her to an inn before they were overtaken by the wedding party, the evening was spent in dancing and feasting at the expense of the bridegroom.

Henry R. Stiles in a history of Windsor relates a local incident of stealing the bride. Elisha Griswold and others who had not been invited to a wedding in Simsbury waited outside the bride's house until they saw an opportunity to seize her. Placing her behind one of them on a horse, they raced to an inn in Turkey Hills where they had previously arranged for food and music. The tavern is not named in history, but it may have been the Viets Tavern because Elisha Griswold's uncle, Luke Viets, ran the inn when Griswold was a young man. The abductors' glee changed to chagrin when they discovered that the supposed bride wore men's boots. The wedding party had anticipated their plans and dressed a man in a bridal gown. Nevertheless, the evening was enjoyed by all—but at the expense of the kidnappers.

Much feasting and drinking took place the night before a funeral while "watchers" sat with the corpse. Sometimes the family of the deceased sent invitations to the funeral and gave gifts to those who attended.

Carvings on the gravestones in the Center Cemetery change from death's-heads on the earliest stones to winged heads representing souls and angels and then to the urn and willow that became popular shortly after 1800. Historians believe these engravings reflect a people's attitude toward life as well as death. The acceptance of the rather meaningless urn and willow may have signified man's lessening preoccupation with the hereafter and his growing concern with the material things of the present.

Conditions during the Revolutionary War that had made it profitable and even acceptable to be greedy, aggressive, shrewd, and disrespectful of authority had hastened the rejection of the Puritan ethic. Failure to attend church services, profanity, drunkenness, extravagance, immorality, and the lack of personal industry were decried in the press and from the pulpit.

The Reverend Mr. Booge kept careful records during the nine years (1776-85) he was the minister at Turkey Hills. Three women and eight married couples—respected members of the community—were "received into charity" after confessing to fornication. There were 179 births, eight of which were illegitimate. Illegitimacy was probably a social stigma, but sometimes illegitimate children were acknowledged and provided for in wills. Since church records prior to 1776 are missing, it is impossible to tell whether or not immorality was increasing in the community. Still, both the acts and the forgiving of them seem significant in this time of the questioning of traditional mores.

Victory heightened feelings of independence, self-confidence, equality, and humanitarianism. Political freedom fostered creativity and enterprise. The Connecticut Yankee succeeded the colonial Puritan, and as men changed, so did their institutions in the new United States of America.

9

Political Beginnings

AT THEIR FIRST Granby town meeting in December of 1786, after separation from Simsbury, the voters elected town officials: a town clerk, selectmen, constables (who now doubled as tax collectors), listers, tithingmen, grand jurors, fence viewers, haywards and key keepers (to control stray animals), a town agent, a sealer of leather and one of weights and measures, a packer, and a brander of horses. Turkey Hills men received about one-third of the offices. This apportionment continued more or less consistently while Turkey Hills remained a part of Granby. The town was not so conscientious about holding one of every three annual meetings in Turkey Hills as they had agreed at their first meeting. In fact, most meetings were held in Salmon Brook. Turkey Hills men probably felt that their forebodings about becoming a part of the new town were justified, but they didn't choose to object immediately.

Connecticut's transition from colony to state was equally smooth. The General Assembly absolved the state's inhabitants from any allegiance to the British Crown and dissolved all political connections between them and the King of Great Britain. They also voted:

That the form of civil government in this state shall continue to be as established by charter received from Charles the Second, King of England, so far as an adherence to the same will be consistent with an absolute independence of this state of the Crown of Great Britain; and that all officers, civil and military, heretofore appointed by this state [shall] *continue in the execution of their several offices, and the laws of this state shall continue in force until otherwise ordered.*

Under her charter, Connecticut had enjoyed almost complete self-government. Connecticut and Rhode Island were the only states that did not adopt constitutions after the war.

Political peace did not last long. The issue of federal pensions for Revolutionary officers caused one of the first serious divisions between the people and their elected officials. The inhabitants of Simsbury strongly protested the proposed pensions at a town meeting when they voted "that the officers ought to have a full, just, adequate, and honorable satisfaction for the time they in fact served their country in defence of the United States of America and no longer." They felt one cause of the late war was the "exorbitant and unreasonable pensions granted to particular persons," and, therefore, such pensions would be "dangerous, alarming, and unconstitutional." (The particular persons referred to were, no doubt, retired English civil and military officers to whom Great Britain paid large pensions.) The Continental Congress authorized the pensions in spite of widespread opposition.

The voters of both Simsbury and Granby instructed their representatives to vote against ratification of the federal constitution in 1788. The minutes of the Granby town meeting to elect a delegate to the constitutional convention at Hartford do not include any debate. The minutes of a Simsbury town meeting held for the same purpose probably express the views of Granby's people:

Voted by said meeting that it was the sense and opinion of the same that to adopt the proposed constitution would institute and erect an aristocracy which they fear would end in despotism and tyranny and extinguish or nearly absorb our ancient charter privileges ever sacred and dear to us and that instead of lessening our taxes and burdens, it would greatly increase and augment them and finally prove destructive of our most invaluable liberties and privileges.

It is understandable that people who had fought a war to rid themselves of one strong central government should fear another. When Connecticut became the fifth state to ratify the constitution, Granby's delegate, Hezekiah Holcomb, was among the minority of forty out of 168 who voted "nay."

State laws that favored the Congregational Church caused the greatest dissension between the people and their Federalist leaders; resistance to the church-state government had been fomenting and solidifying for over 100 years. The first so-called Toleration Act was passed in 1669. Under it and succeeding laws, Episcopalians, Baptists, Methodists, and adherents of smaller sects had been allowed to organize, build meetinghouses, and support themselves by levying taxes on their members. As of 1784 dissenters from the established church who certified that they attended and financially supported "public worship with a different church or congregation" were no longer forced to pay taxes to a Congregational ecclesiastical society.

This new law did not appease completely members of other churches who felt they had a *natural* right to attend and support any church they pleased. It certainly did not satisfy men who did not want to be associated with any congregation, since they continued to be liable for the support of the established church.

A law providing that interest on money from the sale of Connecticut's Western Reserve be used for religious purposes aroused so much opposition that the General Assembly repealed it. Many people simply objected to direct financial support of religion by the state. Others opposed the law because they felt that even though the money was to go to all denominations, the established church would control the distribution. Episcopalian Hezekiah Holcomb, Jr., Granby's representative to the General Assembly, was one of the majority who voted for repeal.

Connecticut's anti-Federalists organized the Democratic-Republican Party in 1800. (Records from that time call the party both the Republican Party and the Democratic

Party.) Their primary objective was the separation of church and state and the termination of the Standing Order, as the informal coalition of Congregational ministers and Federalist officials was called.

Other goals developed as the party attracted men with divers grievances against Connecticut's laws and leaders. They called for the establishment of independent executive, legislative, and judicial branches of government to end the power of the General Assembly, which more or less controlled all three functions of government.

They favored wider suffrage and a change in electoral procedures. Under the law of the time, it was almost impossible to unseat a government official. Men from a relatively small number of families had ruled Connecticut since its founding.

The party called for a state constitution to accomplish these and other radical changes. They felt that Connecticut had no constitution, since her colonial charter had never been adopted by a vote of her freemen.

The Democratic-Republicans claimed to represent the lower classes. They appealed to farmers and laborers, the dissenter, the propertyless, and the unenfranchised. They accused the Federalists of acting as an aristocracy and putting their own interests above the good of the people as a whole.

The Federalists defended the status quo. They justified state support of the Congregational Church as a means to ensure a moral society. They opposed extending the franchise and changing electoral procedures that kept them in power. They believed that representative government by an upper class was superior to a true democracy which, they felt, might lead to anarchy.

The failure of Connecticut's Federalist leaders to support the War of 1812 hastened the downfall of their party. The state's entire congressional delegation voted against the declaration of war. When President James Madison requested that some of Connecticut's militia be put under the command of the regular officers of the United States Army, Governor Roger Griswold refused the request as unconstitutional. The General Assembly supported him, saying that the legislators were aware "that in a protracted war, the burden upon the militia may become almost insupportable, as a spirit of acquisition and extension of territory appears to influence the councils of the nation which may require the employment of the whole regular forces of the United States in foreign conquests, and leave our maritime frontier defenseless or to be protected solely by the militia of the states." The Governor also refused to let the militia leave the state when President Madison requisitioned them for an invasion of Canada.

A British blockade of Connecticut's southern shore made the threat of invasion real. Although the enemy never occupied a Connecticut town, they did attack Essex and Stonington. The national government left the defense of the coast to the state's militia.

Connecticut volunteers were allowed, but not encouraged, to join the regular army of the United States. No Turkey Hills men are listed among their ranks in the *Record of Connecticut Men in the War of the Revolution, War of 1812. . . .* Eleven local men are listed as serving in the Connecticut militia. Hartford is shown as the place of service for two of them; no place is given for the other nine. No one served more than ten weeks. C. W. Crankshaw in *An Index of Veterans of Connecticut During the . . . War of 1812* lists ten of these eleven men and nine others from Turkey Hills with no further information.

In May of 1816, in an attempt to bolster their waning support, the Federalist General Assembly repealed the fine for absence from church on Sundays. That October they voted to distribute to the churches most of the money they had received from the federal government for expenses of the War of 1812, which had ended a year before. Members of churches other than the Congregational felt the Standing Order were trying to buy their support. Some, like the Methodists at Copper Hill, rejected their share of the money. The Turkey Hills Ecclesiastical Society voted to spend $30 of their portion for lottery tickets and the rest for repairs to the meetinghouse.

That same year, a coalition of Democratic-Republicans, Episcopalians, and other dissident Federalists united as "Tolerationists" and nominated Oliver Wolcott for governor. Wolcott won the gubernatorial election in 1817 and the reign of the Federalists in Connecticut was over.

Only a new constitution—a restructuring of the state government—could satisfy the grievances that had festered for over thirty years. The freemen of Granby sent Salmon Brook's Sadoce Wilcox and Democratic-Republican Reuben Barker of Turkey Hills to the constitutional convention, convened at Hartford August 26, 1818. They both voted "yea" when the final draft was adopted 134 to 61.

The new constitution provided for the separation of church and state:

Article 1, Section 4: No preference shall be given by law to any Christian sect or mode of worship.
Article 7: It being the right and duty of all men to worship the Supreme Being, the Great Creator and Preserver of the Universe, in the mode most consistent with the dictates of their consciences; no person shall be compelled to join or support, nor by law be classed with, or associated to any congregation, church, or religious association.

Legislative, executive, and judicial powers were divided among three separate branches of government. Laws governing nomination and election of state officials were reformed. Suffrage was extended somewhat, although it was restricted to white male citizens.

The constitution was a compromise, and its acceptance by the freemen of the state remained in doubt until the final count of 13,918 in favor and 12,364 against was tallied. In Hartford County, only five out of seventeen towns voted to accept it. Granby was one of the sixteen towns that repudiated their delegates to the convention when her freemen voted 175 to 132 against it. Richard J. Purcell, in *Connecticut in Transition: 1775-1818,* says, "The hostility of the purely agricultural towns can only be ascribed to the unreasoning conservatism of the Connecticut countryman, which time had scarcely weakened." There can be no doubt that this break with the past was a sad, even appalling, decision for many of these people of "the land of steady habits."

There are few records to show how the majority of Granby's freemen stood politically in the early 1800s. Newspapers as yet did not report votes by party. Edmund B. Thomas, Jr., did analyze the few voting statistics he was able to find. In his dissertation, *Politics in the Land of Steady Habits,* he estimates that from 1803 to 1813 and from 1816 to 1820, Granby's vote remained steady at between 46 and 55 percent in favor of the Federalists. Granby supported the Tolerationists' nominee for governor in 1816, but reversed its vote by a narrow margin in 1817.

There is a strong probability that a majority of Granby's Tolerationists lived in Turkey Hills. It seems likely that almost half the families in the parish were dissenters from the established church. Forty-nine residents whose names appear on a 1785 Grand List were associated with the local Congregational church, thirty-nine with the Episcopal churches at Scotland and Salmon Brook, three with the Baptist church in Suffield, and one with the Congregational church in that town. (These people were not all members of these churches. Sometimes the only record is of a marriage or a baptism. No church affiliation could be found for nine men on the list.)

Some Turkey Hills people traveled great distances to attend the churches of their choice. In 1785 Worthy Thrall joined a society of Quakers in Enfield. There are records of local people attending a Methodist meeting in Granville, Massachusetts, in 1794. About 1799 a Methodist church was formed in West Granby, which some local people may have attended until the Copper Hill Methodist Episcopal church was established in 1816.

For years local Episcopalians had been resisting taxation by the Congregational ecclesiastical society. The Reverend William Gibbs, an Episcopalian minister at Scotland, had taken Congregationalist Joseph Cornish, Jr., to court, charging that Cornish had collected society taxes from Darius Pinney, an Episcopalian, that should have gone to his church. When Reverend Roger Viets certified to the society of Turkey Hills that Eli Holcomb was connected with the Episcopal Church, he added, "And we think it unreasonable as well as unlawful to oblige him to pay rates among you, especially as he attends with us and has his children christened here."

Some local representatives to the General Assembly can be identified as Democratic-Republicans, and there were probably others. From 1787 through 1794, Granby was allowed only one representative to each session of the legislature, which met semiannually in May and October. Between 1794 and 1818, when the October session was discontinued, the town sent two men to each session; one was usually from Turkey Hills. Episcopalians Hezekiah Holcomb and Hezekiah Holcomb, Jr., represented the parish from 1787 through 1799. From 1800 through 1818, twelve other Turkey Hills men were elected of whom at least two, and perhaps four, were Democratic-Republicans. (By the 1840s, a majority of the parish's voters supported Democrats—successors to the liberal Democratic-Republicans—in preference to the more conservative Whigs.)

The *American Mercury* in 1803 reported that the Democratic-Republicans held a Fourth of July celebration in Turkey Hills on the green in front of the Samuel Clark house at the center of town:

The anniversary of American independence was this day celebrated by the Republicans of the town in a manner truly becoming the glorious era. The auspicious morn was ushered in by the discharge of seventeen cannon, placed upon an eminence overlooking the town and commanding a distant prospect. At twelve o'clock a large and respectable number of people from this and the neighboring towns assembled at the house of Mrs. Bathsheba Phelps[*] *(Turkey Hills Society) where a procession was formed to the number of 430 ladies and gentlemen, preceded by a band and martial music—a company of militia commanded by Captain George Owen attended by a field piece. All moved with the greatest order and*

*Widow of Ezekiel Phelps, Jr. She lived at 39 North Main Street.

regularity to the meetinghouse where a sermon was delivered by our worthy friend the Reverend Whitfield Cowles from Galatian v. 1: "Stand fast therefore in the liberty wherewith Christ hath made us free and be not again entangled with the yoke of bondage."
Mr. Cowles discharged the duties of chaplain with much propriety. An oration was delivered by Jonathan Higley, Esq., replete with genuine principles of liberty. Odes were sung appropriate to the occasion.
The procession then returned in the order it advanced to an elegant bower, situated on a beautiful green fronting the house of Captain Joel Clark. Mr. Ebenezer Hickox was chosen President and Reuben Barker, Vice-President, of the day.

The newspaper article goes on to say that a liberty pole was entwined with laurel wreaths and placed in the center of the green. There were speeches and "the most harmonious vocal music attuned to the patriotic song, *Jefferson and Liberty.*" Toasts were drunk to American independence, to President Thomas Jefferson, and to the United States Congress—"May they still open the recesses of the wicked, clear away the rubbish of the last administration, and establish the nation in righteousness." After noting that seventeen toasts were drunk, the reported concluded, "We are happy to add that no accident intervened to damp the joys of celebration."

Newspaper articles, sermons, diaries, and speeches of the time reveal the bitterness of the political war. Although only a few Democratic-Republicans were identified in print, their names represent many different Turkey Hills families. At least five of these opponents of the Standing Order were members of the established church, and one was a Congregational minister, the Reverend Whitfield Cowles. Because of his unorthodox political beliefs as well as his unethical conduct, Mr. Cowles became Turkey Hills' most controversial minister.

10

Religion: Tumult, Decay, and Revival

THE REVEREND WHITFIELD COWLES became minister of the Turkey Hills Congregational church in 1794. He was a native of Southington, Connecticut, with an undergraduate degree and a Master of Arts degree from Yale. He had been licensed by the Congregational South Association of Hartford in 1790. He was thirty years old when he was ordained at Turkey Hills.

Nine "houses of entertainment" were designated for the ordination day. The only ones standing today are at 23 East Street and 71 North Main Street. Asahel Holcomb, Jr., entertained the ecclesiastical council of ministers and laymen from neighboring towns at his home at 27-29 North Main Street. The religious services and the festivities following them concluded with a grand ball in the evening.

Calvin Duvall Cowles, in *The Genealogy of the Cowles Families in America,* painted the following word-portrait of the new minister:

> *Mr. Cowles was a large, fleshy man, full of life and much given to pleasantry. As a preacher, he was popular, and was always heard gladly in his native town. He was emotional rather than logical. His kindred and early companions always warmly espoused his cause and never lost faith in his integrity.*

Things seem to have gone relatively well during the first years of Mr. Cowles' ministry. Although there was some grumbling, most of the parishioners were occupied as usual with repairing and improving the meetinghouse. Individuals were given permission to build seats in the gallery, and steppingstones were added to the front of the building in 1798. The society built a steeple at the north end of the meetinghouse and put a lightning rod atop it, but no bell ever hung in the steeple.

Some who disagreed about the alterations to the building and the expenses involved were very likely people who did not want to be associated with the Congregational Church (or, perhaps, any church at all), yet were obliged by law to pay taxes to the society. General dissatisfaction with government favoritism toward Congregationalism resulted in laws that made it easier for men to transfer their financial support to other churches. This change made it harder for the Turkey Hills Ecclesiastical Society to raise enough tax money to cover its expenses. For the first time, in 1794, the society solicited voluntary contributions in the form of yearly pledges to supplement its revenue.

Mr. Cowles did not approve of the ecclesiastical tax nor of Connecticut's church-state government that made it mandatory. After 1804 he accepted only voluntary contributions toward his salary. He was confident "a generous and Christian people will contribute whatever may be necessary to my support."

Mr. Cowles needed a steady income to support his growing family. He had brought his bride, the former Gloriana Havens of Shelter Island, New York, with him to Turkey Hills. After their son, Rensselaer Watson, was born in 1796, Mrs. Cowles suffered spells of mental illness. She and the baby spent the winter of 1797-98 with her family on Shelter Island. Records of the Presbyterian church on the island show that Whitfield Cowles preached there on twenty-four Sundays during 1798, although his absence from Turkey Hills is not mentioned in local records. Mrs. Cowles died in April 1802, a year after the birth of their daughter, Mary Henrietta. Mr. Cowles then married Desire Brown, his deceased wife's first cousin. They had nine children, two of whom died as infants.

Unfortunately, Cowles' faith in his parishioners' generosity proved unfounded. Both pledges and taxes became harder to collect. By 1806 the voluntary subscriptions towards his salary were so much in arrears that the society brought legal action to collect them. In what was obviously a test case before the Connecticut Supreme Court of Errors, society treasurer Ebenezer Hickox sued Alson Hoskins to force him to pay his $10 annual donation. Hoskins' defense was not that he had not pledged the money, but that Hickox was not the legal treasurer of the society since the meeting at which he had been elected was not legally warned. The court decided in the defendant's favor.

Unable to collect either taxes or subscriptions, the society was forced to borrow money from individuals to pay expenses. When they voted that year to discuss with Mr. Cowles the possibility of his dismissal, people probably were motivated partly by resentment against constrained support of the established church and partly by dissatisfaction with Mr. Cowles himself.

Whitfield Cowles was a political maverick, a Congregational minister who broke with the Standing Order and supported the Democratic-Republican Party. Naturally he aroused animosity. The August 4, 1803, issue of the *American Mercury* mentions him as one of several clergymen who were persecuted for their political beliefs:

No sooner is a clergyman known to be a Republican, (although he preaches no politics on a Sunday, or on Fast and Thanksgiving days,) than Federalists are immediately up in arms against him. Plots and schemes are set on foot—his ruin is decreed—as he is proclaimed an infidel—no vice is too low to be falsely ascribed to him; attempts are eagerly made to oust him from his place or silence him, at any rate to render his life uncomfortable. If, however, he rise superior to their machinations, then their way is to neglect his minstrations, forsake God's house and worship, and even change their religion to accomplish their pious views. . . . A little thing has been noticed . . . their magnanimously refusing to honor Republican clergymen with the usual title of Mr. and of Rev. —Their style more commonly is, that fellow, that rascal, and epithets of similar politeness—This is of a piece with what it is said Dr. Trumbull declared before an association of clergy not long since that sooner than assist in licensing or ordaining a Democrat, he would saw his own arm off. . . .
Mr. Cowles of Granby has experienced treatment from his federal parishioners similar to the foregoing. After endeavoring to make all the trouble in their power, several have changed

their religion and gone off! And all this without any conceivable reason but that Mr. Cowles is a Republican.

But his politics were not the only part of Whitfield Cowles' life-style to which his parishioners objected. The people of Turkey Hills often had been upset by their ministers' secular interests. One reason they dismissed their first settled minister, Ebenezer Mills, was because they were "dissatisfied and uneasy concerning our reverend minister's trading." They faulted Nehemiah Strong for his debts. They complained that Mr. Booge did not prepare his sermons until the morning of each service and that he devoted the rest of the week to secular pursuits.

If they had expected Mr. Cowles to be different, they had reason to be disappointed. Not only was he a trader, he also produced the articles he sold. And he was often in debt.

For a few years he had a shop and house just east of 24 School Street. The only clue as to what he made in his shop is that he had "watering tubs of every description." He may have used them to wet the broomcorn he made into brooms. He may have used them in making tinware; family tradition credits him with crafting tin candlemolds and lanterns. An extant account book shows he raised hogs, butchered them, packed them in brine, and shipped them to New York for sale. He also distilled and sold cider brandy.

Mr. Cowles' parishioners probably were upset at his free-spending ways, too. He was not as practical about money as the terms under which he agreed to settle in Turkey Hills suggest. Before his ordination, he demanded interest on his salary of £86 per year if it were not paid on time; perhaps he had been warned about the parish's casual bookkeeping. After his predecessor, Mr. Booge, had been in Turkey Hills for six years, the society appointed a committee to ask him "what he had received for two years past."

Imagine the consternation of society members when Mr. Cowles bought three or four houses and perhaps added large additions to two of them during his fourteen years as their minister. (Nehemiah Strong had been criticized for buying one farm.) Besides the house and shop on School Street, Cowles owned the Thompson house at 82 South Main Street for a number of years. Entries in the Gay family diaries indicate he bought the original house, now the wing on the north side, and added the large section on the south.

In 1802 he bought the Joseph Griswold, Jr., homestead of approximately 75 acres, running north from the Farmington River on both sides of Spoonville Road. Besides the house on the property—built by Joseph Alderman's grandson Darius Pinney in 1775—there were barns, a cider-mill house, and a distillery. Mr. Cowles built the house at 118 Spoonville Road on the property; part of it may be the Darius Pinney house. The room above the woodshed has always been called the broom shop, presumably because Cowles made the brooms he sold there. (Land records show that he also had an interest in a house that stood near 121 Spoonville Road. Later he owned one that stood opposite it in front of 114 Spoonville Road.)

For years Mr. Cowles ignored his parishioners' complaints against him. He refused to meet with church and society members who wanted to dismiss him from his pastorate. Finally, in the fall of 1808, some members of the society brought twelve charges against him to the North Consociation of Hartford County. At his trial two of them were combined into one and two were withdrawn. Of the remaining nine, Mr. Cowles was found innocent of six and guilty of the following three:

> *That the said Cowles in the latter part of the winter of the year 1808 again transported into the State of Vermont a sleighload of cider brandy for the purpose of selling the same and did then in said State on the Sabbath or Lord's Day without any necessity or urgent occasion for so doing with said load of cider brandy travel the distance of about thirty miles and in open contempt of the moral law contained in the Decalogue and of the Christian Sabbath. . . .*
>
> *That the said Cowles since his ordination as aforesaid and before the date hereof, to wit, on or about the day of January 2, 1804, did propose to the widow Mary Griffin to sell her for the use of herself and family a fat hog and to induce her to purchase the same and falsely affirm to her that the pork of said hog was remarkably good and well fattened and she confidently relying upon said affirmation purchased of him said pork and paid him thereof the full price of the best pork and in fact said pork was soft, ill-fattened and unfit for use all which facts at the time of said sale were well known to said Cowles and wholly unknown to said purchaser which doings of said Cowles were false, fraudulent and deceitful, contrary to the plain principles of common honesty and in direct violation of the Divine Law. . . .*
>
> *That the said Cowles since his ordination and before the date hereof by profane language, by disorderly practices, by idle and vain discourses, and by trifling levity of his general conduct has brought great discredit and scandal upon religion, destroyed all hopes of his future usefulness in said church and society, dissaffected the members of both, and induced great numbers of them to disconnect themselves from said church and society and to unite with other churches and societies being of different denominations of professing Christians.*

The consociation concluded,

> *the flock under his pastoral care and charge and the people of this place are scattered as sheep upon the mountains of Israel without a shepherd; and all prospect of their peace and unity and of his usefulness among them is stained.*

The consociation dismissed him from the Congregational ministry with the provision that he might apply for reinstatement when he showed "a sincere repentance of his past errors and a resolution to be more watchful, faithful, and exemplary in the future."

It is impossible even to guess how many of his parishioners supported Mr. Cowles and how many opposed him. Deacon Asahel Holcomb, Richard Gay, Roswell Skinner, and Appleton Robbins signed the charges against him; eight other local people are named in the document. At a society meeting just before the trial, there was a unanimous vote *not* to dismiss him. The minutes of the meeting do not say how many people attended. Within two weeks after his dismissal, an unknown number of church members voted *not* to accept it and to withdraw the local church from the consociation. (Seven men had signed the warning of the meeting.) They reasoned that the consociation had exceeded its authority and disregarded accepted Congregational Church procedures before and during the trial.

118 Spoonville Road

In their rejection of the consociation's authority, they were following the principles of Turkey Hills men who, in 1776, had approved in general the Saybrook Platform providing for regional associations of churches. At that time the local church reserved the right to question, arbitrate, and even ignore the decisions of its consociation.

The division among the members of the church and within the whole ecclesiastical society was so great that neither body was able to function effectively for the next few years. The diary of the Reverend Thomas Robbins, pastor at the Congregational church in East Windsor, describes the condition of the church during this time:

June 1, 1808. Rode to Turkey Hills. Very cool. Preached in the afternoon. . . . People appear quite attentive, but I fear the work is declining. There is a prospect of an important ecclesiastical trial here.
August 30, 1808. Rode to Turkey Hills. The consociation met here to hear charges against Rev. Mr. Cowles. He used every exertion and quibble to evade the trial. The hearing has been very disagreeable; they did not begin upon the charges.
November 2, 1808. Rode to Turkey Hills. The consociation are here on the trial of Mr. Cowles. He defends with great obstinancy. The evidence appears very bad against him.
November 7, 1808. The consociation at Granby dismissed Mr. Cowles and suspended him from the work of the ministry. I think their decision very judicious.
August 5, 1809. Rode to Turkey Hills. Our association are supplying this afflicted society this summer. (Ed. note: As when a minister dies it has long been a New England custom for each minister of the association to give a Sabbath for the benefit of his family, so it was done here for the benefit of the church.)*
August 6, 1809. The Baptists are making very great exertions here, and have got a considerable number of the people. They are encouraged by Cowles.
August 7, 1809. This society is in a very deplorable state. They have been long chastened. I hope it may be sufficient.

*Dr. Robbins' diary was edited by Increase N. Tarbox and printed in 1886.

Mr. Cowles asked the consociation to reinstate him a year later. Herman R. Timlow wrote that Mr. Cowles asked "forgiveness for his faults so far as he felt conscious of guilt." This was not acceptable to the consociation and they refused his request.

When the local church asked to be readmitted to the consociation in September of the same year, their request was accepted. "The church then voted to request the Reverend Whitfield Cowles to deliver the church records into the hands of the clerk."

The last official church record concerning Mr. Cowles is dated February 5, 1812, when several members of the church asked the consociation for advice "respecting the church standing of their late pastor." The consociation's decision was that Mr. Cowles was no longer a member of the church nor should he be allowed to take communion.

Although the consociation censured Mr. Cowles for unethical and irreligious conduct, his biographers agree that his trial was essentially political. Two of the complaints of which Mr. Cowles was found innocent refer to his political views. One is that he taught "that the legislative power of a state has no right to enforce the observance of any portion of time in a religious manner and as a Christian Sabbath." The consociation acknowledged in its final report that Mr. Cowles did express this belief. "And we do conceive that his expression concerning the Legislature . . . has been highly unbecoming the Christian minister, and calculated to mislead the mind."

In the same vein, another complaint attributes to him the statement that ministers as such "were not entitled to a stated salary, but as teachers of morality had a right to receive a stated salary." This refers to his opposition to taxation for ministers' salaries in keeping with his belief in the separation of church and state.

Some historians have written that Mr. Cowles adopted the tenets of the Universalist Church before he was dismissed from the Congregational ministry in 1808. Two facts dispute this. First, he applied for reinstatement in the Congregational Church in 1810. Second, he informed the Turkey Hills Ecclesiastical Society in 1814, "I do withdraw myself from her, and shall from this date give support to the Baptist Church in Turkey Hills."

Mr. Cowles became a charter member of the First Universalist Society in Granby in 1832. One of the articles of the church's constitution bears his imprint: "No money shall be received for the benefit of this society except by voluntary subscription or contribution."

His obituary notice in *The Universalist* of December 12, 1840, reads:

Died in East Granby, Nov. 20, Mr. Whitfield Cowles, aged 76. Mr. Cowles was formerly the settled Presbyterian clergyman in the parish where he died. He took a very active and independent course in the political struggle which resulted in the election of Thomas Jefferson to the Presidency of the United States, and is believed to have been the first clergyman in Connecticut of his denomination, who embraced and defended Republican principles. This course, it is supposed, led to a dismission from his parish.

The Reverend Daniel Hemenway, the local Congregational minister in 1840, wrote: "Mr. Cowles entered very deeply into the political controversies of that period, espoused the interests of the Jefferson school in opposition to a great majority of the serious portion of his people and was instrumental in fomenting a very unhappy division which the lapse of twenty-two years has not healed."

The Cowles family genealogy concludes that Whitfield Cowles' dismissal from the established church was more political than religious:

He was a Jeffersonian in politics and this fact arrayed many of his society and ministerial brethren against him. Some who at first took ground against him, afterward confessed that such was the fact and affirmed that he was unjustly condemned. He lived in Granby over thirty years after these events and no one pretends to point to acts inconsistent with a high standard of morals.

In 1812 eighteen members of the society, only six of whom were members of the Congregational Church, asked the General Assembly to authorize the society's reorganization. The General Assembly accepted the petition, and the Turkey Hills Ecclesiastical Society became a functioning legal entity again. Eventually it lost any secular function and became solely a part of the Congregational Church. It was legally dissolved in 1953.

A Return To Religion

The reorganization of the Turkey Hills Ecclesiastical Society coincided with the religious reawakening that swept through Connecticut in the wake of what historians refer to as an age of "free thinking and free drinking." In a July 1815 article on recent religious revivals, the *Connecticut Evangelical Magazine and Religious Intelligencer* lists Turkey Hills as one of the societies that "had been favored with special showers of grace."

The Reverend Bennet Tyler describes conditions at Turkey Hills and the effect of this revival in his biography of evangelist Asahel Nettleton:

In the autumn of 1814, Mr. Nettleton commenced his labors in East Granby. This was a waste place. The moral condition of the people was exceedingly deplorable. But God saw fit to turn again the captivity of Zion. Under Mr. Nettleton's preaching, there was a very interesting revival of religion.

The Reverend Jonas B. Clark, the Congregational pastor from 1842 to 1845, portrayed even more vividly Mr. Nettleton's influence on the parish:

The effect of that revival upon the church, and upon the community, was most happy and lasting. The interest of Christ's kingdom had suffered much from an erroneous ministry. The church lost all spirituality and fervency. The community was buried in sinful indifference. When Mr. Nettleton came among them, stupidity and slothfulness prevailed among all classes and ages. The effect of his entrance to the place was electric. The schoolhouse and private rooms were filled with trembling worshippers. A solemnity and seriousness pervaded the community, which had not been experienced for years before. . . .
At this day, we can hardly imagine the effect which his visit had upon this waste place. This seems to have been Satan's chief seat. Infidelity had been infused into the very bosom of the church. Of course, sin in every form abounded.

Thirty-three people joined the church during the year of the revival. One was young Deborah Thrall, a daughter of Worthy Thrall. Miss Thrall evidently had second thoughts about her conversion, for, within a year, her fellow church members brought the following complaints against her; first, that she had played cards frequently; second, that she had not attended public worship on the Sabbath for a long time; third, that she had avoided members of the church when she was asked to meet and talk with them; fourth, that she had associated with "non-professors"; and finally, that she had acknowledged that she no longer hoped to be "renewed in heart by the Holy Spirit," that she lived without prayer, had no desire to remain a member of the church, and was completely unrepentant.

A committee was dispatched to her home certain that their zealous admonitions would reap the desired reward. She thwarted them with her absolute refusal to reform, and thereupon began a battle between church and sinner that lasted nearly ten months.

A second committee appeared at Sister Deborah's armed with a lengthy letter of admonition so overwhelming with its biblical overtones of hell and damnation that even the worst offender would have cringed and repented. However, the accused remained impervious to such beseeching questions as: "Have you seriously reflected that you must one day appear before the judgement seat of Christ and answer to your injured Saviour? Have your carnal joys while at the gaming table never been interrupted with this solemn thought: Can you have peace?" Deborah's sole response was an adamant request to leave the church.

In the ensuring months, various committees steadfastly endeavored to reform Deborah—and Deborah just as steadfastly refused all pleadings. Finally, on November 1, 1816, when she failed to appear before a church meeting, the members conceded defeat and Sister Deborah Thrall was excommunicated from the church.

Even more dramatic was the attempt to save another parishioner. She has no name; nor was any age given her. But for one brief moment she transcended her female contemporaries with a spirited, imaginative independence that must have astounded the small community of Turkey Hills.

What was her distinction? Not her sin—insobriety at a church service—but her response to the reprimand for such wayward conduct. For upon hearing the discourse delivered by a committee dispatched to her home, she excused herself, walked out to the road, gathered a handful of stones, and returned. Applying a skillful knowledge of the Bible and psychology, she gave one to each committeeman, sat down, and asked them to please continue. No one there could have mistaken her message.

The Congregational church at Turkey Hills had always been concerned about the moral conduct of the people in the parish. Its members endeavored to control people's beliefs and actions in a manner inconceivable today in all but the most fanatical churches.

The church regularly elected committees of about five men to assist the pastor in the "inspection of the flock." This entailed far more than sending letters of admonition to those who did not attend church regularly. Church members lodged complaints against one another for offences which ran the gamut of sin all the way from profanity, disobedience to parents, quarreling, and intoxication to stealing and fornication.

The key to this concern about each other's behavior is contained in the Confession of Faith and the Covenant to which all church members had to subscribe. They affirmed their belief in original sin, for instance, and in a day of judgment when "they who have done good shall be absolved and acquitted and made perfectly blessed in the full enjoyment of God forever. But they who have done evil and died in their own inpenitence shall be turned down to a burning hell and lodged there forever." In the Covenant (literally an agreement between God and the church members), the members acknowledged their "sinfulness by nature and by practice" and promised "to live in all respects according to the rules and precepts of the Gospel."

Thus church members believed that those who confessed their sins would be saved from eternal damnation. They were not vindictive, and the records contain many instances of penitent members being "received into charity." Among them was Deacon Asahel Holcomb's wife Dinah "upon a confession for intemperance." Those who refused to repent—such as Nathaniel Mather who broke the fourth commandment by doing "worldly business" on the Lord's Day and repeatedly staying away from church—were excommunicated.

The church's attempt to enforce its own ethical standards was backed by law. In Turkey Hills, Justice of the Peace Andrew Hillyer recorded in 1812:

Lyman Phelps personally appeared before me, Andrew Hillyer, and confessed that he was guilty of a breach of the Sabbath for that he, the said Lyman, did on the twelfth day, being the Sabbath, labour in making hay—fine of $1.67 to the town of Granby and 25¢ cost. Reuben Winchel admitted himself guilty of profane swearing and paid a fine of $1 to the treasurer of said Granby in cash.

The 1818 state constitution prohibited the government from favoring any particular church, but in some ways the law continued to support the Puritan way of life. For example, the revised laws of 1821 reaffirmed observance of the Sabbath and days of public fasting and thanksgiving. On these days, secular business, labor, recreation, and travel "except from necessity or charity" were subject to fine. The law also continued the annual election of tithingmen to apprehend violators. The General Assembly removed the restrictions on days of public fasting and thanksgiving in 1833, but controversy over blue laws such as the one banning the opening of stores on Sundays continued into the 1970s.

Missions

The founding of missionary societies at this time also reflected the spiritual reawakening. The Missionary Society of Connecticut, organized by the Congregational Church in 1798, sent missionaries to new settlements in the United States and to foreign countries. Two of Turkey Hills' native sons who became Congregational ministers were home missionaries. Alexander Gillet (1749-1826), known as a particularly effective revivalist, served in rural areas of Connecticut and in Vermont. Newton Skinner (1782-1825) went to northern Vermont for the summer of 1808.

At the time, Congregational ministers could obtain leaves of absence from their parishes for a few months at a time to serve as missionaries. To pay them, the General Assembly authorized the collection of contributions from all denominations. This was another example of state support for the established church to which members of other churches objected.

Cynthia Thrall, daughter of Luke and Deborah Granger Thrall of 46 East Street, became a missionary. When she was thirty-four years old, she went to the Dwight Mission Station near the present town of Russellville, Arkansas, where the American Board of Commissioners for Foreign Missions had a school for Cherokee Indian children. To reach the mission, she traveled for three months through Ohio, Kentucky, and Illinois in a two-horse wagon "with spring seats and a cushion covered with painted canvas," as she wrote home.

Miss Thrall became a housemother and teacher. When the federal government moved the Cherokees west, she went with them and helped to establish a new mission in what is now Oklahoma. She died there in 1834. The Reverend Charles Chamberlain wrote about her:

Her friends say that among her tribes it was fact that the Indians were inclined to regard her as a god and to worship her. She took under her special care several orphaned children among the Indians whom she named after the members of the church here, as Abiah Griswold, Hervey Skinner, and Joel Clark.

The Congregational Church established the Domestic Missionary Society in 1816 to aid existing churches in Connecticut. The *Courant* reported that its purpose was "to build up the waste places of Connecticut and its vicinity by furnishing the destitute with religious instruction." The church at Turkey Hills received the society's financial help intermittently between 1826 and 1857.

There was increasing concern about the spiritual life of the prisoners at Newgate. Local laymen held prayer meetings in the cavern. The Reverend Roger Viets had ministered to the inmates during the Revolutionary War and other ministers conducted services for them from time to time. Dr. Thomas Robbins wrote:

*August 6, 1809. At five o'clock preached a third sermon . . . at Newgate. It was one of the most affecting scenes I ever saw. There are about fifty prisoners, very dirty and very heavily ironed. They behaved well. Had a large audience.**

Dr. Robbins led the worship service at the dedication of the chapel that the General Assembly built at Newgate:

May 4, 1815. Rode to Turkey Hills with Mr. Wolcott and attended the dedication of the new chapel at Newgate Prison. The occasion was very interesting and joyful. The prisoners (52) appeared much gratified with the prospect of state religious ordinances.

A year later the General Assembly appointed Reverend Eber L. Clark chaplain for the prisoners. At the same time he became the first settled minister at the local Congregational church since Mr. Cowles. He divided his "ministerial labors" equally between the parish and the prison. Each paid one-half his salary.

This arrangement was disrupted when the Democratic-Republicans came to power. They were willing to support a chaplain at Newgate, but Congregationalist Clark was not acceptable to them. Since the society could not pay his full salary, he left the community in 1820. The church was without a settled minister until 1826 when financial

*Editor Tarbox added, "Newgate was the old and half-barbarous State Prison . . . in a very wild and rough district of the town of Granby."

Drawing of Newgate Prison made in 1861 by George E. Townsend showing outside entrance to chapel

support from the Domestic Missionary Society made it possible to hire the Reverend Stephen Crosby.

A manuscript found in the Gay-Moody home at 123 North Main Street sarcastically expresses the feelings of a local poet when the Democratic-Republicans took over the administration of Newgate. Part of it reads:

In the year one thousand eight hundred eighteen
Was witnessed a new and glorious scene.
At Newgate State Prison was acted this farce
To turn out old officer, institute new
And keep strict economy still in their view.

* * *

To save many thousands they loudly proclaim
Seven hundred a year to the sick and the lame.
And paying for preaching fifty dollars a year
Is enough for the guard and the prisoners to hear.

Congregational meetinghouse, built in 1830

Churches and Meetinghouses

Under the constitution of 1818, the relationship between the Turkey Hills Ecclesiastical Society and its Congregational church continued much as before. Together they hired and dismissed ministers, while the society maintained the meetinghouse and managed the finances. However, the society had even more difficulty than before raising money because the constitution made membership completely voluntary.

The society continued to tax members and to solicit pledges. In 1823 it began to "sell" the pews in the meetinghouse on an annual basis. Perhaps half the people who purchased the seats were not church members. Some nonmembers did attend church services; all could claim their seats for town and society meetings and for social occasions.

In 1830 the society of about thirty members made a bold decision. They would tear down their wooden meetinghouse, which was about 100 years old, and build a stone one. This was particularly daring because only a few months before the society had made a special appeal for money to support the gospel and had received no contributions.

According to the Reverend Charles Chamberlain, some people wanted a place to hold a private school as well as a new house of worship. He wrote:

The winter of 1829-30, the friends of religion and the friends of education met to see what could be done about a school of higher order. It was first proposed to create a small building just sufficient for the purpose, supposing that was all that could be done. Another plan was to excavate under the old meetinghouse as that stood on elevated ground and do off

Former ceiling of the sanctuary in the Congregational meetinghouse with fresco secco

a room there. The timbers of the house were examined to see if such a plan would be practicable. "At length," says Deacon Cornish, "someone ventured to say, 'We can build a church and a schoolhouse, too.' When the good minister took our hands on parting that night, he seemed to grasp them with uncommon fervor. 'Pray for this object,' said he. 'It is a noble thought.'"

Connecticut no longer required religious instruction in the public schools. Albert Carlos Bates in his introduction to the *Records of the Second School Society of Granby* writes: "Repeating the catechism was kept up in this society until after 1830, but its study and repetition was not then obligatory. . . . Saturday forenoon was the time then usually taken for this exercise, and only those who chose to do so took part in it." The "friends of religion" in Turkey Hills may have wanted a private school where their children could receive more religious instruction or they may just have wanted a classroom for their Sunday Schools. In 1826 the First School District had voted to allow Methodists, Baptists, Congregationalists, Episcopalians, and Universalists to hold their "religious meetings of every kind and all meetings for moral instruction" in the schoolhouse if they furnished their own wood.

The meetinghouse cost a few cents less than $3500. The bell was an additional $300.66. More than 250 people subscribed labor and amounts of money from 50 cents to $775 each. Over 80 percent of the pledges were less than $10. One hundred and thirty-eight men who signed the first subscription list were residents of other towns: forty-nine were from Hartford, twenty-eight from West Hartford, twenty-five from Berlin,

129 South Main Street

and the other thirty-six from Farmington, East Hartford, Wethersfield, Bristol, East Windsor, and New York City. Joel Holcomb was the only contributor from west of the Mountain along Granby Turnpike. There were no subscribers from Salmon Brook or from towns bordering Turkey Hills.

Two Massachusetts men, Isaac Damon of Northampton and Elijah T. Hayden of Deerfield, were the contractors on the meetinghouse. They had built the Congregational meetinghouse in Southwick, Massachusetts, in 1824 and the one in Simsbury early in 1830. Damon is recognized as the architect of these and other churches, courthouses, and bridges in the Connecticut Valley region of Massachusetts and Connecticut. The square, wooden tower, or belfry, with its louvered openings is a distinctive feature of the East Granby building and of other meetinghouses designed by Damon. The local meetinghouse is in the Greek Revival style of architecture.

The basement of the building had two rooms separated by a brick wall. The one on the west was furnished as a schoolroom with desks and seats. There were two doors on the south side of the basement, but no stairway to the main floor above.

Upstairs there was a small vestibule and an audience room (sanctuary) with galleries on three sides. Access to the galleries was by open stairways at opposite ends of the vestibule. Above this entryway and behind the west gallery—reserved for the choir—was a small room from which to ring the bell.

A high pulpit stood at the east end of the audience room in front of a recess in the wall called a blank window. The square pews from the old meetinghouse stood against the walls. The two tiers of slips that lined the center aisle had paneled doors and cap moldings "similar to those in the South Meetinghouse at Hartford," according to the building contract.

The plastered walls and slightly arched ceiling seem to have been left unpainted. When the sanctuary was remodeled in 1865, an unknown artist covered them with a fresco secco, a mural painted with water-based colors on dry plaster. An article in the *Courant* of September 14, 1930, describes what the author calls an unusual decorative pattern. "In subdued shades of gray, brown, and blue, a remarkable light and shadow effect, creating the illusion of carving, columns and other artistic designs, the church has a scheme of decoration rarely seen in this country."

Copper Hill Methodist-Episcopal meetinghouse, built in 1839

The Reverend Stephen Crosby dedicated the building on May 31, 1831. For the next three or four days, ministers and lay delegates from neighboring churches met at the new meetinghouse. In his *Sketch of the Congregational Society and Church,* Albert Carlos Bates writes that most engaged in "preaching, exhortation, or prayer."

For $150 George Burleigh Holcomb bought the old meetinghouse with the exception of the lightning rod, stone steps, pulpit, and pews. The stone steps were placed at the entrance to the new meetinghouse. Holcomb used some of the lumber when he built his home at 129 South Main Street soon after. Chamfering on the boards in a back shed indentifies them as part of the first meetinghouse.

Horace Clark was particularly happy when he wrote in his diary that he had helped to raze the old building which stood in his front yard. He wrote: "April 4: Myself and boys assisted Burley Holcomb in pulling down the old meetinghouse which fell about 3 o'clock in the afternoon, to my great joy." Clark bought the meetinghouse lot for $100.

Now, for the first time, church bells rang out in Turkey Hills. Thereafter they announced religious and secular meetings, historic occasions, and the deaths of people in the community.

For perhaps twenty years, the society rented the schoolroom to different teachers. Residents of the community gathered there through the years for the various meetings, for school graduations, fairs, strawberry festivals, oyster, pineapple, chicken pie, and maple sugar suppers, chrysanthemum shows, and other social and fund-raising occasions, even as they do today.

Seth Griffin, Aristarchus Griffin, and Calvin Gillet, with their wives, organized the Methodist Episcopal church at Copper Hill in 1816. This church, usually called

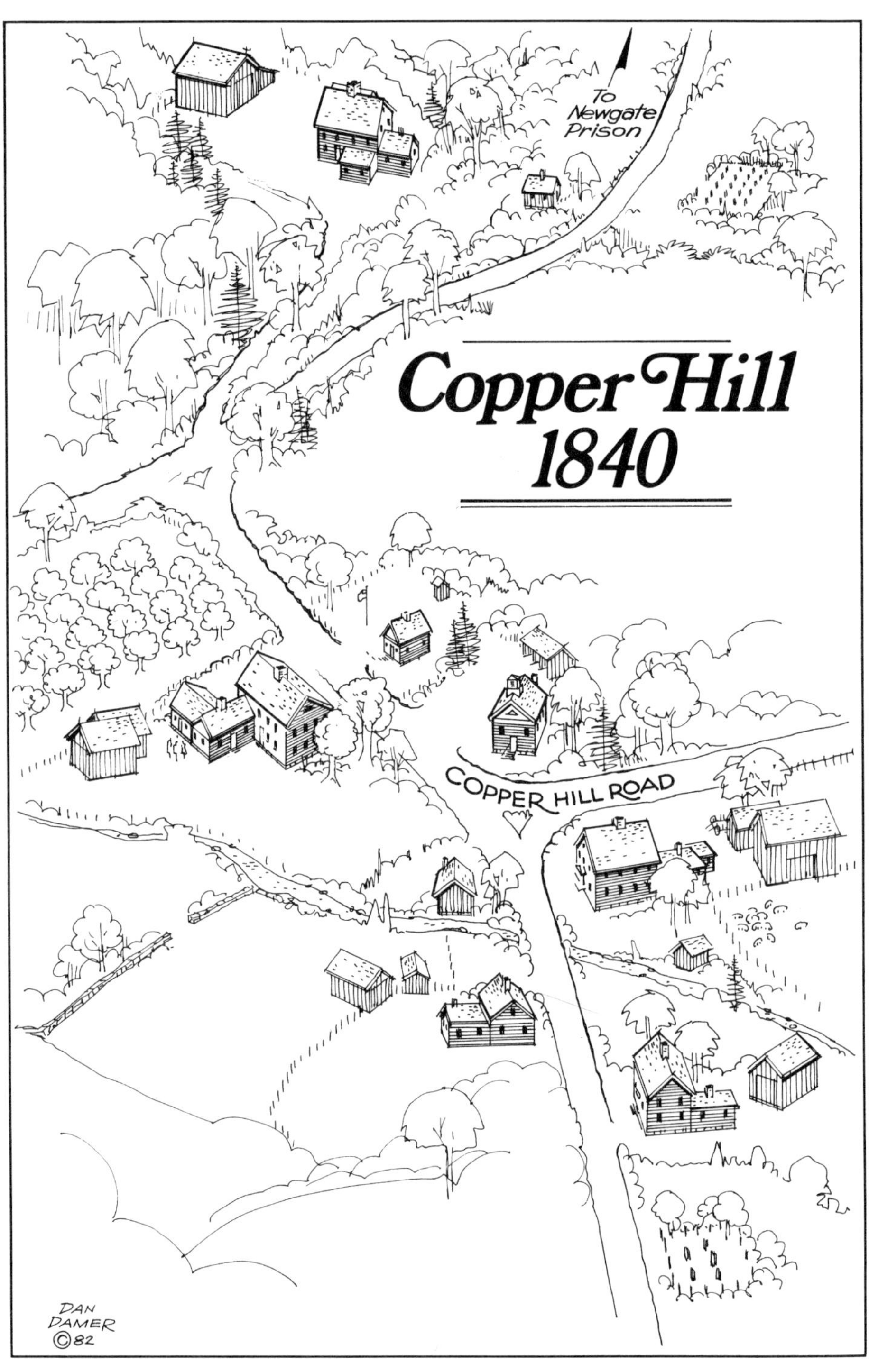

Artist's concept of Copper Hill section of town. Note the new Methodist-Episcopal church with schoolhouse east of it and the prisoner's cemetery toward Newgate Prison

the Copper Hill Methodist church, became part of the Granville (Massachusetts) Circuit and shared a minister with other churches in the association. In 1844 it became an independent station with its own minister.

Members held their meetings in private homes and schoolhouses until 1839 when they built a meetinghouse for approximately $1400. It is of Greek Revival architecture and stands today about 33 feet south of its original location. The congregation purchased their first church bell in 1878 for $325. The lecture room was added later.

Revivals added many members to the Copper Hill church. Charles Horace Clark described one that he attended:

The writer, at a single evening meeting in the church, which lasted from seven o'clock until midnight, witnessed as many as fifteen persons who became apparently unconscious. Some were stretched upon the floor; others were lying or being supported upon the seats. This visitation of "the spirit" was regarded as a great blessing, and it certainly did strengthen the church in numbers.

These gatherings often attracted so many people that they had to be held outdoors. When they lasted several days, the participants camped out nearby. Thus they became known as camp meetings. There were camp meetings at various locations near Copper Hill throughout the nineteenth century.

The Methodist meetinghouse became the social as well as the religious center of the Copper Hill community with its sociables, rummage sales, fairs, and suppers similar to those held at the Congregational meetinghouse.

Then, in 1856, both parishes built parsonages. The one at the Center stood southwest of the meetinghouse on the opposite side of what was then Church Road. It was torn down in 1974 when the road was widened and extended to become a part of Rainbow Road. The one at Copper Hill stood west of the meetinghouse until 1963 when it was razed, partly because of its rundown condition. Members of both congregations built sheds to shelter horses and carriages during meetings.

At least two native sons became Methodist ministers, Gervase Aristarchus Viets and Duane Nelson Griffin. Both were grandsons of Mr. and Mrs. Aristarchus Griffin, who were among the founders of the church at Copper Hill.

Turkey Hills people helped to organize churches at Tariffville during these years. The Congregationalists established the first in 1832 and the Baptists followed a year later. Some of them may have been members of a Turkey Hills Baptist church that had been founded in 1809. This earlier congregation never built a meetinghouse; the last extant record of their meetings is dated 1832. Two local men whose parents attended the Baptist church at Tariffville became ministers. Apollos Phelps Viets was a Baptist minister; his nephew Francis Hubbard Viets was ordained at the Congregational church in Riverton, Connecticut.

The Trinity Episcopal church was organized at Tariffville in 1848. Joel C. Holcomb, Henry L. Holcomb, and Thomas G. Holcomb of Turkey Hills were among its founders. At least two Turkey Hills men became Episcopal ministers: Frederick D. Holcomb and Hugh H. Holcomb. The latter went to West Africa as a missionary in 1856 when he was thirty-one years old; he died there a year later.

These new congregations can be attributed to Tariffville's rapid growth after the

Former Congregational parsonage, built in 1856

Tariff Manufacturing Company bought the Griswold Mills. The new company employed 136 persons in 1832. Thirteen years later, the number had increased to over 450, and the community had become a major manufacturing center.

Some of the employees at the Tariffville company were from the British Isles. Many of them, particularly the Irish, were of the Catholic religion. There were only about 720 Catholics in Connecticut in 1832 with two church buildings and two resident priests. As many as twenty-four of the 720 lived at or near Tariffville where they gathered to worship. The first St. Bernard's Catholic church was built there around 1850.

The Scottish weavers who came to the area were often Presbyterian. They organized a church of that denomination at Tariffville in 1844.

Thus did established churches survive and grow while new ones formed during these years. The separation of church and state did not change the people's religious habits as had been feared. Congregationalists survived without government support, and other sects thrived without government interference.

11

The Second School Society of Granby

LAWS PASSED by the General Assembly between 1793 and 1799 changed Connecticut's system of public education significantly. They divided the state into school societies, which superseded towns and ecclesiastical societies as overseers of the public schools. Turkey Hills, including the Windsor Half Mile, became the Second School Society of Granby.

The new society had six school districts, three on each side of the Mountain, with boundaries approximately as shown on the 1869 Baker & Tilden map of East Granby. The school districts retained control of the everyday workings of their schools. Each chose its teachers and set their salaries, determined how long its schools would be in session, and decided when to build and repair its schoolhouse.

The legislators decided at this time to put the money from the sale of Connecticut's Western Reserve into a perpetual fund. The interest from the fund was to be used to support either public schools or "the Christian ministry or the public worship of God." The choice was left to the new school societies. As might have been expected, they all voted to use the income for public education. This income was distributed to the school societies according to the "list of polls and ratable estate of such societies." After 1820 the money was apportioned according to the number of children between the ages of four and sixteen in each society.

The legislators voted in 1799 to return annually to the school societies some of the tax revenue the state collected from the towns. Each society was to receive $4 for every $1000 of its Grand List. When the interest from the School Fund exceeded $62,000 in 1821, this return from local property taxes was discontinued.

The increase in state aid at the end of the 1700s helped the people of Turkey Hills build public schoolhouses. A road layout of 1798 mentions one near the intersection of Hatchet Hill Road and Hartford Avenue in the Sixth School District. Two years later the Second District built one just south of 139 North Main Street, and the First (or Center) District raised one east of 20 School Street about the same time. There was a schoolhouse in the Fourth District near 3 Old Road by 1817. Residents of the Third District built one about 1820 at the site of the present one at 32 Spoonville Road.

A history of the Methodist Church at Copper Hill says that its congregation met in schoolhouses at Copper Hill and Hungary (a section of Granby west of Copper Hill)

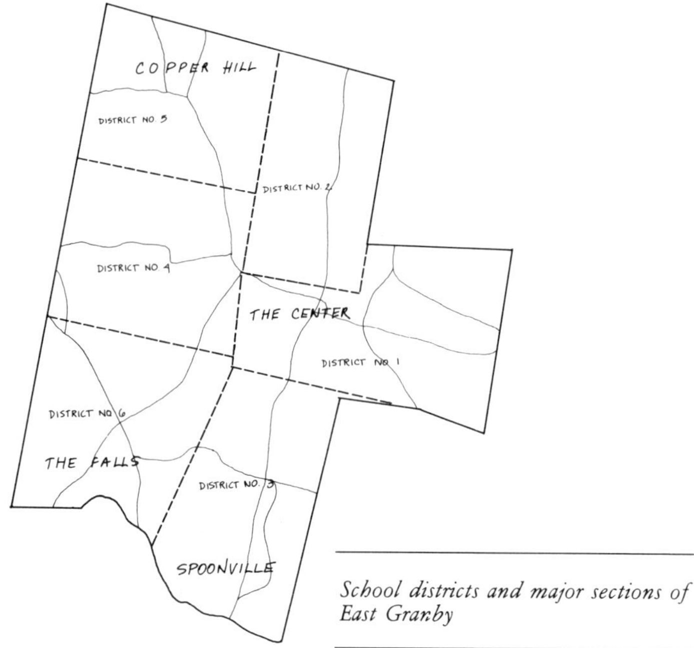

School districts and major sections of East Granby

in 1833. A new one was built in the Fifth District near 23 Copper Hill Road in 1840.

Albert Carlos Bates describes these early schoolhouses in his introduction to the minutes of the meetings of the Second School Society:

Inside, a desk slightly inclined and with a narrow level place at the top was attached to the wall and extended along three sides of the room. In front of this was a long form or bench without back on which the older pupils sat. They were thus seated facing the wall and with their backs towards the teacher. At times these pupils were allowed to turn about and sit facing the middle of the room.

Inside of the bench or form on which the older pupils sat was another lower one which was occupied by the smaller children who were seated facing the center of the room. The children seated on this bench had no desks. In most, probably in all, of the schoolhouses in this society the bench and desk for the larger scholars were on a platform raised two steps above the floor of the room. In such cases the lower step formed the bench or seat for the smaller scholars. This gave them the advantage of a back to their bench; but this arrangement also had one disadvantage for them. When the larger scholars sat facing the middle of the room, each one was afforded opportunity to poke his toes into the back of the luckless child seated just in front of him.

The teacher's desk, whose height made it necessary for the teacher to stand behind it or to sit upon a high stool or a raised platform, was near the fourth side of the room. Its hinged cover could be locked down to preserve its contents from inquisitive eyes and fingers. The fireplace was also located at this side of the room. The stove succeeded the fireplace before 1830, the change probably taking place during the decade previous.

Later, within the memory of some now living, the long benches and desks were replaced

Center District schoolhouse, built in 1844, and pupils of a later vintage

by desks and benches suitable for two scholars and arranged in rows all facing the teacher's side of the room. The present writer can certify to the discomfort of these desks with their accompanying narrow seats and straight, perpendicular backs.

The schoolhouse in the Fourth District was torn down and a new one built in 1840. These structures were not so sturdy as the community's colonial homes that have stood for over 200 years. Most had to be repaired every few years and replaced within fifty years.

Taxpayers of the Center District solved this problem in 1844 when they replaced their wooden schoolhouse with a brick one. It had two rooms and cost about $470, approximately twice the price of a one-room wooden one. The new building stood for over 120 years.

Samuel A. Clark bought the old schoolhouse for $69.50 and moved it to a location south of his ancestral home at the Center. After dismantling the chimney, he drew the building on sleds or stone boats pulled by oxen. Neighbors pitched in to help Clark with the drawing, which took three days. The old schoolhouse became a home for Clark and his bride, the former Ruhama Marilla Dibble. It stands today as the back ell of the house at 8 South Main Street.

Money to build and maintain these schoolhouses came from a tax on the property owners of the districts in which they were located. The actual expenses of schooling such as teachers' salaries were paid with money from the state and from the parents of the students. The parents' tax was based on the actual number of days a child attended school, and children whose parents did not pay the tax were not allowed to attend.

Parents had to furnish textbooks for their own children, to provide firewood, and take their turn boarding teachers. Families who could not supply firewood or a place

8 South Main Street

for a teacher to stay were taxed instead. Children whose parents did not fulfill their obligations in some way were not allowed to attend school. Youngsters with "the itch" (lice) were also excluded until they were cured to the satisfaction of the itch committee. Disobedience of orders was also a valid reason for expulsion.

Schools held both winter and summer sessions. The winter one began in November after the crops were harvested. The summer one started in early spring. They were from three to five months long, depending on how much money was available to pay for teaching and other expenses.

School societies appointed "visitors" to monitor the common schools. Their job was to certify teachers and ensure that they effectively instructed their charges in "letters, religion, morals, and manners," as a 1799 law decrees. After the adoption of the constitution in 1818, religion was omitted from the requirements. The local common schools were using textbooks in spelling, reading, grammar, arithmetic, geography, history, natural philosophy, astronomy, and chemistry in 1839.

Few men or women made teaching a career. Out of 1292 common school teachers who responded to an 1839 questionnaire, only 100 had taught more than ten years and only 341 had taught in the same school twice. Most women made a career of marriage and homemaking. For young men, teaching was a way to earn money during the winter months when their fathers did not need their help on the farms. (Women taught summer sessions.) When the men married, they found ways to earn more than a teacher's salary.

It seems that teachers, like ministers, sometimes had difficulty collecting their pay. The minutes of one meeting of the First School District read:

Voted that Alfred Owen shall have the privilege of drawing $3.45 from the public treasury *as a reward in full for teaching school a winter past provided there remains so much unappropriated money in the treasury.*

There were no normal schools before 1849, and teachers generally were untrained, many having only common school educations. Carlos Bates was comparatively well educated. He attended the private classical academy that Lemuel Cicero Holcomb kept at his home on the east side of Old Hartford Avenue. He also attended Westfield Academy. His certification from Westfield attests:

This certifies that Carlos Bates is qualified to instruct in the first rudiments of learning as the law directs:—in addition to this, in French, and some branches taught in grammar schools.
Westfield Academy—Oct. 23, 1829 *Emerson E. David, Precept.*
West. Acad.
N.P. C. Bates sustains a fair moral character, has been a member of the Academy a few months and studied Nat. Philosophy, Astronomy, Logic, etc. and etc. E.D.

According to his family genealogy, Mr. Bates taught in a number of district schools around Turkey Hills and was "particularly successful in those requiring discipline." Discipline was important when one person taught as many as fifty children in one room.

The number of children over four and under sixteen in the Second School Society declined gradually (with fluctuations from year to year) from a high of 352 in 1826 to a low of 188 in 1854. In 1839 there were 269 youngsters in this age group; 205 were enrolled in the common schools. The average attendance was 150, or 75 percent. Thirty did not attend any school; the remaining thirty-four may have gone to private school.

Turkey Hills and neighboring communities provided private schools for children of all ages. There were many dame schools for young children. The record of one is preserved on a sampler on which is embroidered:

Wrought in the school of
Miss Susan Pinney
Granby Turkey Hills
Connecticut
**1833
Aurelia Barnard's sampler aged 12 years

Susan Pinney was the daughter of Joseph and Eleanor Griswold Pinney. She probably held her dame school in her parents' house that stood on the west side of Spoonville Road opposite Miller Road. Aurelia may have been the daughter of George and Sally Higley Barnard of North Bloomfield. She is referred to in some official records as Amelia.

Abiah Griswold's dame school is mentioned frequently in old documents. Miss Griswold lived at the home of her parents, Matthew and Abiah Owen Griswold of 56 East Street.

Men held select schools in their homes as well as in the basement of the new Congregational meetinghouse. These were for older children who would be of high school age today. The Reverend Daniel Hemenway, who succeeded Congregational minister

Joseph Pinney house

Stephen Crosby, had both day and boarding students at his home at 36 South Main Street.

By 1821 and intermittently for more than thirty years, Lemuel C. Holcomb ran his academy called "The Cottage School." An advertisement for the school assures the reader that pupils

> *will be prepared for entering any of the colleges in the United States, or they may remain in the institution till they have completed such an education as their parents may think necessary to qualify them for their business in life. The number of pupils will be limited to twenty. The expenses of each will be $200 per annum, including tuition, board, and washing, to be paid quarterly in advance.*
>
> *Every attention will be paid to their morals, and their health; and horses and carriages will be furnished gratuitously that they may ride out with their instructors on Saturday afternoons and other hours of recreation. . . . In connection with the Ancient languages will be taught Ancient Geography and Ancient History. The mathematical course comprises arithmetic, algebra, geometry, plane trigonometry, spherical trigonometry with its application to nautical astronomy, analytical geometry, and the differential and integral calculus.*

Genealogists of the Holcomb family write with pride of this educator and classical scholar, who, when he was eighty years old, translated a little Greek and Latin every day so as not to become rusty.

Some local young people attended the Granby Academy, established at Salmon Brook in 1794. It was one of Connecticut's earliest coeducational academies. An advertisement in the *Courant* describes it as a place where "youth of both sexes may be in-

36 South Main Street

structed in the various branches of literature." Parents were assured "that the manners and morals of their children, as well as any branch of education they may reasonably require, will be attended to."

Turkey Hills students also attended nearby Suffield Academy. This school was organized in 1835 as the Connecticut Baptist Literary Institution.

Critics of the public school system grew more and more outspoken during the 1820s and 1830s. They felt that the abolition in 1821 of the school allotment from local property taxes contributed to the public's growing apathy toward the common schools during the succeeding years. Critics felt, in other words, that when people no longer had to pay an annual school tax, many of them became indifferent to the quality of public education. As one school visitor reported to the state, "That which costs them nothing, they consider and use as nothing worth."

The General Assembly responded to such criticism in 1837 by authorizing a study of the common schools. As a result of this survey, they appointed a Board of Commissioners of Common Schools who were to keep the public and the legislators informed of conditions in the schools. Teachers were to keep better records of the students' attendance, school visitors' supervision, etc. The visitors were to make regular reports to their school societies and to the commissioners.

At the same time, the General Assembly ruled that no child could be kept from attending school because his parent, guardian, or master was unable to pay a school tax or assessment. They voted in 1842 to allow district committees to provide books for needy students. Seven years later they established the state's first normal school, now Central Connecticut State College.

Additional income came to local schools in 1837 because of a situation that is hard to imagine today. There was surplus money in the federal treasury! Congress voted to lend some of it to the states. Connecticut, in turn, voted to lend its share to her towns, and Granby decided the money should be used for mortgages with the interest from them going toward expenses of the common schools. When East Granby became a town in 1858, its share of the Town Deposit Fund was $2,183.84. The town continues to choose an Agent of the Town Deposit Fund. The money is on deposit today at the Winsted Savings Bank.

The General Assembly in 1854 reinstated the town property tax for public schools that they had discontinued thirty-three years before. Towns were required to raise a school tax of one cent on each dollar of their Grand Lists.

In a move to centralize control of the schools, two years later they abolished most school societies and returned supervision of public education to the towns. Local school visitors reported to the Commissioners of Common Schools that there was some improvement in their schools shortly thereafter. Yet they concluded:

Some of the greatest hindrances to raising the standard to that degree of excellence most desired come from parents and guardians. They are not so anxious to know how well a teacher is qualified as to know what he asks for his services. They do not feel as willing to pay wages enough to obtain teachers every way qualified to teach, as they are anxious to know if they have public money to keep their schools long enough for all purposes without resorting to district tax. If the people would only give as much thought to the right education of the children as they do to almost everything else, the whole cause of complaint would be removed and the common schools of our town would be a common blessing.

12

Transportation: Land, Water, and Rail

LOCAL PEOPLE whose lifetimes spanned the seventy-two years that Turkey Hills was a part of Granby saw marvelous advances in transportation. One of America's first turnpikes, one of its first canals, and one of its first railroads passed through the town.

The town's many brooks and the Farmington River had always been obstacles to overland traffic. Floods often washed away the bridges over them, and the structures that survived the pressure of water and ice had to be replaced every decade or so because their timbers had rotted. (Turkey Hills never had covered bridges. After 1801 when a new law required railings on bridges "raised above surrounding ground" such local bridges had high wooden sides.)

Bridges were financed by town taxes, private subscriptions, and lotteries. The last had to be approved by the General Assembly.

Subscribers built the first single bridge over the Farmington River between Scotland and Turkey Hills in 1780. It was at the foot of Spoonville Road.

The first bridge at the Falls was built by subscription ten years later. When Simsbury men had petitioned the legislature unsuccessfully in 1769 for a lottery to finance a bridge there, they had complained, "Where the highway crosses the river, it is rough and rapid . . . and in a great proportion of every year, said river is utterly impassable for horses, carriages, and cattle." The petition continued that, as a result, the "great travel, concourse, commerce, and business" between Hartford and towns to the north had to be discontinued for long periods at a time.

The first bridge at the Falls was only seven years old in 1797 when the selectmen of Granby informed the public in the *Courant:* "The bridge over Windsor Ferry River at the Falls (so called) is out of repair; and as it was not built by the Town of Granby, nor considered by said town as a place where they are obliged to support a bridge, they do not consider themselves responsible for any damage that may occur to any individual by passing or attempting to pass said bridge."

The people of Granby and Simsbury agreed that a new bridge was needed, but they disagreed about who should pay for it. Granby wanted both towns to build it and petitioned the General Assembly to so decree. Simsbury countered by reminding the legislators that when Granby was incorporated, the new town had accepted the responsibility of building and maintaining a bridge over the Farmington River somewhere between Pickerel Cove and Windsor. The General Assembly sided with Simsbury, whose taxpayers were already supporting five bridges across the same river, and Granby had to build the bridge alone.

The new bridge became part of the Granby Turnpike, which was chartered in 1800. The turnpike ran from Hartford through the center of Bloomfield to Tariffville, along Hartford Avenue to the center of Granby, and then through North Granby to the Massachusetts line. A number of local men were partners in the company that built and maintained it. They collected a toll for its use. There were at least two toll gates, one in North Granby and one in Scotland, but none along Hartford Avenue. The toll charges were:

	cents	*mills*
Every traveling four-wheeled pleasure carriage	*12*	*5*
Every chaise, chair, or sulky	*8*	*0*
Every loaded cart or sled	*12*	*5*
Every loaded two-horse wagon	*8*	*0*
Every pleasure or traveling sleigh	*6*	*2½*
Every empty cart, wagon, or sled	*4*	*0*
Every single horsecart or sleigh	*4*	*6*
Every man and horse	*4*	*0*
Horses, cattle, and mules in droves	*1*	*4*
Sheep and hogs	*0*	*5*

People did not have to pay a toll when they used the road in their day-to-day business such as going to their fields, to gristmills, and to religious and political meetings. The section of the turnpike in Granby reverted to the town when the General Assembly annulled the company's charter in 1845.

Turnpikes were usually better built and maintained than other roads. In 1817 the General Assembly considered a petition that promised to improve the highway between the centers of Salmon Brook and Turkey Hills by turning it into a private turnpike. The petitioners cited the need for better roads between towns west of Granby and the bridges over the Connecticut River at Springfield and Suffield for transporting "iron, bark, coal, lumber, and other heavy commodities." To prove their point, they added:

To present some idea of the travel in the direction above stated, it may be said with truth that no less than 200 tons of iron with other ponderous articles is annually transported from the towns of Winchester, Norfolk, Colebrook, and Canaan to Newgate Prison and to the armory in Springfield, Enfield, and other towns east of the Connecticut River, passing the bridges as aforesaid.

The legislators decided in favor of a route through West Granby center and then northeast to Suffield in preference to the one through Turkey Hills.

A turnpike over the Mountain could have made a great difference in the lives of the people of Turkey Hills. A better road would have made business and other interchange between them and the residents of Salmon Brook much easier. The route might have become the major east-west artery for out-of-town traffic that the petitioners envisioned. When the General Assembly denied the petition, Turkey Hills may have lost its only chance to become a crossroads of commerce. As it was, most of the traffic through the parish continued to move on the main roads that ran north to south on each side of the Mountain.

Other roads changed somewhat during these years to better define a corner, to shorten or straighten a route, to lessen the grade of a hill, to accommodate a new house, etc. What to do about the road from Newgate north to Copper Hill caused much controversy. Originally this road turned west a little north of the prison and ran down a steep hill before continuing northeast by a house that stood near 165 Newgate Road.

For four years beginning in 1844, townspeople argued over the best way to avoid what they called "the long hill." Some favored building a new road west of the hill from the Copper Hill meetinghouse directly south to Old Road. Others wanted to move the road to the east where the incline was more gradual. They finally left the decision to commissioners of the Hartford County Court, who decided on the eastern route. It was another seven years before Julius G. Viets built the new section of Newgate Road north of the prison for $1.20 per rod. The railing along the road was extra.

There was no controversy over a new road and bridge at the south end of town, because they cost the townspeople nothing. The Tariff Manufacturing Company bought the Ellsworth Mills (including Thomas Griffin's gristmill) on the Farmington River in 1827. Shortly after 1840, the company built a roadway (Tunxis Avenue) and a bridge over the river (called the Middle bridge) to connect the mills with their factory at Tariffville. The road and bridge became town property in 1848.

Vehicles increased in number and variety. Carts, two-horse farm wagons, sleighs, and sleds were common in Turkey Hills in the 1700s, but there were few carriages until the second quarter of the next century. The second Joseph Cornish may have owned the first one in the parish. By 1772 he had a chair, a two-wheeled vehicle, usually without a top. Whitfield Cowles had a chaise, which a 1799 tax receipt describes as a two-wheeled vehicle with a top and wooden springs, drawn by one horse. Most affluent men had carriages by the middle of the 1800s, but one-horse wagons, which were introduced early in the century, continued to outnumber carriages.

Stagecoaches provided the first commercial transportation after post riders. A stage ran west of the Mountain through Simsbury and Granby by 1806. The first mention of a route through the Center appears in Horace Clark's diary under the date of April 2, 1837: "First time a stage ever ran from Westfield to Hartford through Turkey Hills." The route ran from Turkey Hills through Rainbow to the center of Windsor and then to Hartford. Dana L. Paine, who once owned a house that stood south of 46 North Main Street, drove the stage for over thirty years. By 1856 Turkey Hills people could go to Hartford and return with him on the same day.

A new and very different horse-drawn vehicle appeared in Granby about 1829. It was a canalboat.

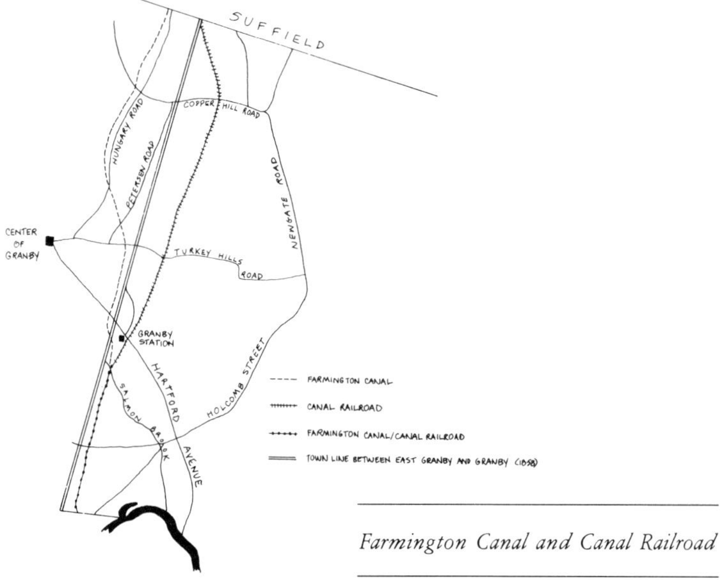

Farmington Canal and Canal Railroad

The Farmington Canal

Perhaps nothing in the history of East Granby excites the imagination quite as much as the thought that 150 years ago a canal over 30 feet wide, flanked by a 10-foot-wide towpath on one side and a 7-foot berm on the other, ran through the town. Canal-boats up to 74 feet long and 12 feet wide pulled by as many as four horses carried freight and passengers across the plain at Floydville and over a culvert that spanned Salmon Brook. Six locks raised them across Hartford Avenue just west of the Granby-East Granby town line and up the hill toward Turkey Hills Road. From there the canal ran north-west across Petersen and Hungary roads and then north through Suffield to the state line.

The ruins of Newgate Prison, colonial homes, and abandoned railroad tracks are obvious reminders of the past. Except for the lockkeeper's house at 86R Hartford Avenue, the remains of the canal are less apparent—an embankment near Floydville Road, a pile of large red stones in Salmon Brook above Granbrook Park, and a ditch here and there along Hungary Road.

As planned, the Farmington Canal was to run 58 miles from Long Island Sound at New Haven north through Cheshire, Farmington, Simsbury, Granby, and Suffield to Massachusetts. There it was to connect with the Hampshire and Hampden Canal, which would run through Southwick to the Connecticut River at Northampton for a combined length of 80 miles. Promoters hoped that eventually the waterway would continue north along the Connecticut River to Canada. The charter for the Farmington Canal included a branch from Farmington north to the Massachusetts state line at Cole-brook. There it was to connect with a canal that would run from Boston west to the Hudson River where it would link up with the new Erie Canal leading to the Great Lakes.

This interstate waterway promised to open new markets and stimulate both agriculture and industry throughout the region. Although it would be navigable only eight or nine months each year, a canal would move freight and passengers faster than they could be transported over the highways of the day or even on the Connecticut River whose shoals and rapids made passage difficult. New Haven men welcomed the canal as a means to divert to their city the trade from northern New England that now went down the Connecticut River to Hartford. Promoters foresaw prosperous factories and trading centers with stores, warehouses, and hotels along the canal. Men would have new jobs building, maintaining, and operating the waterway and the boats that would travel it.

On the Fourth of July in 1825, Connecticut's Governor Oliver Wolcott turned the first spadeful of dirt at the state line in Suffield. After an appropriate ceremony in the center of Salmon Brook, between two and three thousand people formed a parade 2 miles long and proceeded to the Suffield-Southwick border. Led by the Simsbury Artillery, some walked, some went on horseback, and some rode in carriages and wagons. Dignitaries rode in a canalboat mounted on wheels and pulled by four horses. The fact that Governor Wolcott broke his spade as he turned the ground was recalled later as an omen of the misfortunes that befell the canal. Afterward 300 of the celebrators returned to Salmon Brook for an outdoor feast on the green under the traditional bower.

Engineers laid out the route of the Farmington Canal and determined construction specifications for the ditch and the twenty-eight locks that were to raise the water 220 feet from the harbor at New Haven to the state line. The canal was to be 20 feet wide at the bottom and 34 feet to 36 feet wide at the top with a depth of at least 6 feet. The locks were to be lined with wood and surmounted with stone walls of dry masonry. Eighty feet long, they were to be 12 feet wide and 6 to 10 feet deep. The six at Granby were among the shallowest with a total lift of 37½ feet. The next lock to the south was in Southington, and the intervening 28 miles became known as the Long Level.

Different men contracted to build sections of the canal, and there were workers in Granby by the fall of 1825. They dug the waterway and piled the dirt into embankments as high as 60 feet with the tools of the day—picks, spades, shovels, and wheelbarrows as well as scoops and "canal carts" pulled by draft animals.

The next summer they started work on the locks and the stone arch culvert over Salmon Brook north of Granbrook Park. A late summer flood washed the culvert away before workmen had completed the dirt canal, towpath, and berm above it. In rebuilding the culvert, they increased its span from 30 to 40 feet and laid the stone in water cement made from limestone that had been discovered only recently in Southington. Another flood washed away this second culvert in 1828.

Joel Holcomb was one of the contractors on a third culvert, 40 feet long, which carried boats and later railroad cars for over 100 years. This arch was the largest and most imposing of the thirteen culverts on the Farmington Canal. It must have been 30 to 50 feet wide; only the 280-foot-long aqueduct that carried the canal across the Farmington River at Farmington was greater in span. A flood destroyed the culvert over the Salmon Brook in September of 1934. At the time it was considered the oldest stone arch railroad bridge in the country.

Local men furnished labor, stone, and chestnut and oak timber and planking for the locks. Joel and Thomas Holcomb did the "puddling" (waterproofing) around the piles, using a thick paste of clay and water called "puddle." Men also trampled it into the bed of the canal to lessen seepage. The Holcombs received $245 for their work, which must have been extensive considering that a load of stone cost less than a dollar and a man worked for $1 a day or $2 if he used his own team of horses or oxen. Even the contractors worked for $1 a day plus mileage; i.e., 3 cents a mile for horse and wagon. The Irish immigrants who dug the ditch worked for as little as 30 cents per day.

There were five turnouts or basins where passengers and cargo could be loaded and unloaded between the Simsbury town line and Hartford Avenue. There were two large warehouses, one near 91 Hartford Avenue where the canal crossed the highway and another near the so-called Granby Station.

Segments of the canal opened as they were completed, and openings were occasions for celebration. At each town along the waterway, cheering bystanders, ringing church bells, booming cannons, and clamorous band music greeted the first boats to come through. The section in Granby was navigable by 1829. It was another six years before the waterway opened all the way from New Haven to Northampton.

There were all sizes of boats on the canal from rowboats to packets. Some barges were small enough to propel with poles or long sweeps. Larger boats, which were pulled by horses, might have a captain as well as a crew. Often boys and girls called hoggies led the horses along the towpaths. As a general rule, horses were changed every 10 miles.

Passenger boats had cabins with sleeping bunks, dining facilities, etc., and the tops of the cabins served as decks. Since there were many bridges over the canal that gave little clearance, loungers on the decks had to scramble below when they heard the warning shout, "Low bridge!"

Freighters traveled at about 2½ miles an hour and passenger boats a little faster. By 1839 packets made the 80-mile trip from New Haven to Northampton in twenty-four hours. (Passengers paid $3.75 apiece, bed and meals included.) Because the packets' speed generated a high wash that damaged the banks of the canal, the canal company set a limit of 4 miles an hour.

At least five Turkey Hills men operated boats on the canal. An old receipt credits Thomas G. Holcomb for boating thirty-three cords of wood from the Massachusetts state line to a landing west of the Daniel Holcomb homestead off Wolcott Road. He charged $13.86. Milton Phelps and Lyman Griffin were co-owners of the *Union*, and Griffin owned a second boat. Daniel B. Holcomb and Gaylord Holcomb owned the *Neptune,* which carried both freight and passengers. Old records describe it as using two horses and two hands and worth $450.

Some historians belittle the amount of traffic on the canal. Others feel that business was good and steadily improving through 1847, the last year it was completely navigable. Freight for the years 1830-45 averaged 20,000 tons a year. In September and October of 1839, 222 boats left New Haven with over 7,817,000 pounds of goods.

One fact is certain. From the chartering of the Farmington Canal in 1822 to its abandonment twenty-five years later, the waterway was a financial failure to its stockholders, most of whom never recovered their investments. It is said the directors declared only one dividend. They cut and sold the grass on the banks of the canal one summer and then distributed the proceeds among the stockholders.

Canals were new in America, and most of the contractors had never worked on one before. Historian Charles R. Harte wrote in his *Some Engineering Features of the Old Northampton Canal:* "The Erie Canal [completed in 1825] was almost the only

Railroad bridge over Salmon Brook

large project up to this time, and while some of the contractors on the Farmington Canal came from the work on the Erie, others were local men entirely unaccustomed to work more extensive than the excavation of a large cellar."

Construction costs greatly exceeded the estimated expenditure of a little over $420,000. Part of the trouble was that there was never enough capital. Men bought stock for a small down payment with the understanding they would pay the rest of the purchase price in installments as the company needed money. Often stockholders failed to pay the installments, probably feeling they would be throwing good money after bad. This lack of public confidence was widespread and made it difficult to raise money.

When the company could not pay its contractors, the contractors had to skimp on materials and labor. Inferior materials and workmanship led to breakdowns in the operation of the canal later. For example, they agreed to remove all vegetation such as stumps, bushes, and roots from the embankments so they would be as watertight as possible. When this was not done, seepage and washouts resulted. Locks were made of wood rather than stone to save money, and when the wood rotted it had to be replaced with stone.

Problems at the Granby locks may have been typical. The contractor in charge complained to his partner that he needed masons and more stone and wood. The lumber he did have was not seasoned, and he had to set up a kiln to dry it. He seems to have kept his sense of humor as he closed his letter of complaint with, "Fear not the world, the flesh, nor the directors." The two men contracted to have the locks done in 1826, but they were not finished until a year later.

In 1836, the first full year the canal was navigable from New Haven to Northampton, both the Farmington and the Hampshire and Hampden canal companies declared themselves insolvent and their ditches and locks "in a state of dilapidation and decay." The New Haven and Northampton Company organized to take over the repair and operation of the waterway.

Still, finances did not improve. The canal companies collected transit duties on cargo and tolls on all boats, but because they did not own the boats, they received only a small proportion of the overall transportation charges. Their revenue seldom covered more than operating costs. It was never enough to pay for repairs needed because of damage done by floods, freshets, muskrats, and men.

Among the human enemies were property owners whose land the canal companies confiscated without paying what the owners considered a fair price. Sometimes the waterway ran between a man's farmyard and his outlands. This meant he had to drive cattle and wagons over farm bridges that were often narrow and steep. Water from the canal sometimes flooded a man's property, and, conversely, it sometimes took water a farmer depended on for his crops and farm animals. Angry men sued the company for their losses and physically damaged the canal in retaliation. Someone once cut loose the 700-foot floating towpath across one of the Congamond Ponds!

Another enemy was drought. The Granby section of the canal had to close for three months in 1832 when a dry spell lowered the water in the Ponds. In 1845 severe drought interrupted navigation the length of the canal for two to three months. Every disruption meant a loss in revenue and public confidence in the canal.

The canal never went above Northampton. There was never a branch between Farmington and Colebrook, and a railroad — rather than a canal — ran along the northern border of Connecticut. And in the end, it was the railroad, not financial difficulties, that dealt a final blow to the canal.

The Canal Railroad

The first railroad tracks on Connecticut's soil were laid across the southeastern tip of the state in 1837 as part of a rail line between Providence, Rhode Island, and Stonington, Connecticut. Two years later, the Hartford and New Haven railroad ran between Hartford and New Haven, and in 1844 the line extended to Springfield.

Soon after the train ran through Windsor Locks for the first time, Elmore Clark wrote in his diary with unusual enthusiasm, "Took forty bushels of corn to Windsor Locks, and while there I for the first time in my life saw the 'cars' pass there on the Springfield and Hartford Railroad." Clark would have seen the engine crew standing on an open platform with only a small railing for protection and the brakeman riding on the outside of the cars ready to set the brakes by hand or foot when the engineer "whistled for brakes."

The earliest passenger cars resembled stagecoaches, but their design changed quickly. Probably those Elmore Clark saw already looked like the long cars of the 1900s. Inside a narrow aisle ran lengthwise between rows of seats, each of which accommodated two people. There were small windows, candles or lanterns for light at night, and at

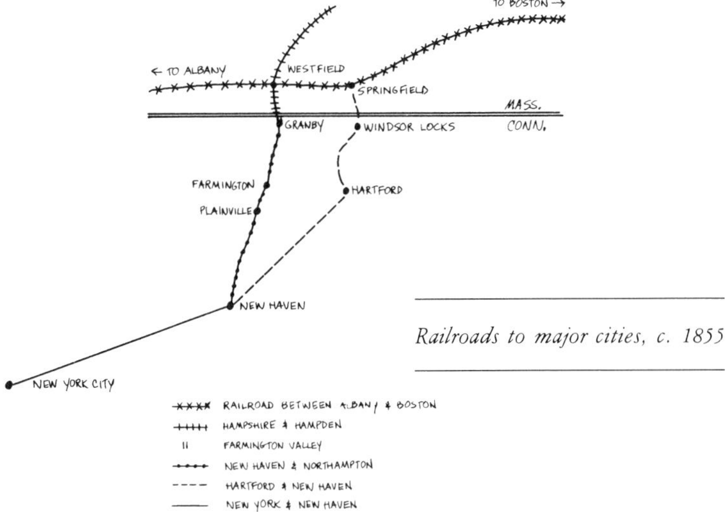

Railroads to major cities, c. 1855

least one wood stove in each car with its smokestack passing out through the roof.

Officials of the New Haven and Northampton Company recognized the inability of their canal to compete with the new railroads and decided to join what they could not successfully rival. In 1846 they petitioned the General Assembly for the right to lay railroad tracks along the canal. For a short time they operated the railroad and some of the canal simultaneously with the horses walking between rails laid along the tow path, but this arrangement proved impractical. The section of the canal through Granby closed by April of 1849 when townspeople voted to take down the bridges and fill in the ditch.

The Canal Railroad, as it was called, followed the route of the waterway across Floydville Plain and over the Salmon Brook culvert. At that point it left the canal's tow path, ran directly north, and ended at Hartford Avenue about half a mile east of the canal. When the rail line was extended beyond Hartford Avenue a few years later, it continued north as much as a mile east of the canal ditch and crossed the Granby-Suffield line about a half mile east of it. When East Granby became a separate town from Granby in 1858, the legislature set their dividing line between the old canal way and the railroad, so that whereas the canal ran through the present town of Granby, the railroad ran through what is now East Granby.

The railroad station at 121 Hartford Avenue was built about 1853. It is still called the Granby Station although it has been in East Granby since shortly after it was built.

The Canal Railroad played an interesting part in the competition between the Hartford and New Haven and the New York and New Haven Railroad, which was chartered in 1844. When it opened to Granby in 1850, the New York and New Haven was operating the line under a lease from the New Haven and Northampton Company. The rival Hartford and New Haven had opposed the chartering of the Canal Railroad as a threat to business on their rail line along the Connecticut River. Now they fought its extension to the state line and the chartering of the Hampshire and Hampden Railroad north from there through Westfield to Northampton. Their terminal at Springfield connected with rail lines running between Boston and Albany. With tracks to Westfield,

Granby railroad station

the Canal Railroad would have a competitive connection with the Boston to Albany route.

The two railroad companies reached an agreement whereby the Hartford and New Haven would pay $12,000 of the $40,000 a year rent for the Canal Railroad, and the New York and New Haven would use its influence to prevent the extension of the road. They also agreed not to divert business from each other.

But Joseph E. Sheffield, at one time the largest stockholder in the New Haven and Northampton Company, was not to be deterred. He was behind the chartering in 1852 of the Farmington Valley Railroad Company with the right to build a rail line from the terminus of the Canal Railroad at Hartford Avenue north to the state line where it would connect with the proposed Hampshire and Hampden Railroad. Joel C. and Thomas G. Holcomb, sons of Joel and Thomas Holcomb, respectively, who were involved in the building of the Farmington Canal, were among the incorporators.

As soon as the line was completed in 1855, the Farmington Valley Railroad Company leased it to Sheffield for $10,000 for 999 years. Four years later he transferred the lease to the New Haven and Northampton Company whose section of the Canal Railroad between New Haven and Granby was still under lease to the New York and New Haven. Within a few years this last company controlled the Canal Railroad from New Haven to Northampton.

New and better means of transportation brought many benefits to Turkey Hills. As they facilitated communication and contacts among people, they lessened the isolation of families and the community as a whole. For most people, visiting and sightseeing, business trips and vacations either increased or became possible for the first time. The Farmington Canal introduced daylong outings and longer excursions, which the railroad continued. A trip on the canal was a favorite with honeymooners.

Stagecoaches, canalboats, and the railroad all carried mail and freight as well as passengers. They and the traditional wagons brought a variety and quantity of food, household goods, clothing, farm tools, etc., that earlier residents had never known. These vehicles carried the farmers' produce as markets expanded. They imported raw materials necessary for the area's developing businesses, and they exported some of the finished products. The proximity of the Farmington Canal was one of the reasons that the Tariff Manufacturing Company located nearby and that the Phoenix Mining Company reactivated the mines at the Copper Hill a few years later.

The improvements in transportation generated jobs directly connected with them and opened up other work opportunities as well. They were largely responsible for the change in the way men earned their livings as Turkey Hills entered the industrial age.

13

Livelihood: Moving Toward Specialization

THE DEMAND for any single product or skill was limited in a small, rather remote community like Turkey Hills around 1800. However, as the size, number, and accessibility of potential markets increased during the 19th century, local men had more incentive to concentrate on a particular manufactured or agricultural product, a business, or a service. Although each homestead still produced much of what it needed, self-sufficiency was being replaced slowly by specialization.

The Farmers

A new tree—one from which men harvested leaves rather than fruit—appeared in Turkey Hills at this time. It was the mulberry tree, and with it came a new agricultural business, the raising of silkworms.

The production of raw silk had begun in the South in the 1620s and had spread to New England in the 1700s. After the Revolutionary War, Connecticut's General Assembly offered bounties to encourage the raising of silkworms and the cultivation of mulberry trees. (Raw silk comes from the cocoons of silkworms, which feed on mulberry leaves.) Connecticut men produced only a small amount of raw silk until the 1830s when the business became a speculative craze with the introduction of a new variety of mulberry tree that propagated easily, grew quickly, and produced unusually large leaves.

This new enterprise came to Turkey Hills by August of 1835 when Samuel W. Brown of Hartford and John R. Lee of Berlin, Connecticut, bought 154 acres of land along with Eli Strong's house and blacksmith shop at 173 North Main Street. The house that stands there today seems to have been built over the blacksmith shop about this time. Brown and Lee planted mulberry trees and built a small, two-story building in which to raise silkworms. Marie Case Sheldon remembers her grandfather Henry A. Case saying that someone raised silkworms in another small building that stood near 20 Tunxis Avenue.

The few account books that remain from the 1830s show that local men were raising mulberry trees, but they do not record the sale of leaves, silkworms, cocoons, or raw silk. Therefore, the extent to which townspeople participated in the business is uncertain. This was a cottage industry, and families often raised the silkworms in their homes. Sometimes they reeled the raw silk from the cocoons, but usually they sold the cocoons to silk manufactories, one of which opened at Hartford in 1835 and another at Windsor Locks in 1838.

The financial depression of the late 1830s and the fact that the new mulberry trees usually were not hardy enough to survive New England's winters contributed to the failure of silk production in the state. A fatal blight in 1844 killed almost all of the mulberry trees in the country. After that silk companies imported raw silk. Today one lone mulberry tree stands in a field behind 173 North Main Street as a reminder of an almost forgotten cottage industry in Turkey Hills.

Men continued to harvest fuel from woodlots, as the advent of the woodburning locomotive brought a new market for firewood. They also produced, as before, lumber, fence posts, hoop poles, and shingles. Daniel Willcox and Eli Strong specialized in making staves for shipment to the West Indies. There the staves were made into barrels and returned to New England filled with sugar and molasses.

Cider brandy became a very popular drink during these years, and the demand for apples grew correspondingly. By 1828 Granby had fifty-two distilleries. These were not all separate buildings. Often a man merely added a still to the apparatus he stored in his cider-mill house. Whitfield Cowles wrote in 1796 that at $20 to $22 a barrel, cider brandy was cheaper than rum. The men who inventoried Levi Pinney's estate in 1805 appraised it at 40 cents a gallon, and Elmore Clark sold it for 27 cents a gallon in 1845.

Farmers also increased their production of other crops to sell commercially. Joseph Forward, Jr., grew flaxseed, one of Connecticut's major exports before cotton cloth became generally available, decreasing the demand for linen. By 1850 local families were raising almost 34,000 bushels of corn, rye, and oats with some buckwheat and wheat each year. The market for potatoes grew as they became one of the most popular of all vegetables. Over 13,000 bushels were harvested in Turkey Hills in 1849.

These were the peak years for the cultivation of grain, and output diminished by one-half between 1850 and 1860. One reason was that the market for local grains decreased as steamboats, canals, and railroads brought wheat from the West into the area. Another reason was the success of a cash crop that eventually would displace most others. It was tobacco.

The Indians were using a native tobacco when the first settlers arrived at Windsor. The newcomers found the Indian leaf bitter, and they soon replaced it with a variety of tobacco from Virginia. Usually they smoked it in pipes, but they also rolled the leaves to smoke, chewed it, and used it as snuff. It seems they did not continue for long the Indians' practice of steeping it in water and drinking the beverage.

For the first 150 years or more, families cultivated enough tobacco for their own use, but only a few raised extra to trade. At the same time, the tobacco business did increase enough to prompt the General Assembly in 1753 to order all towns to choose inspectors to insure the quality of tobacco that was to be exported. It is estimated that in 1801 the Connecticut Valley produced about 20,000 pounds. By 1845 Granby was raising over 35,000 pounds a year. Five years later twenty-two Turkey Hills men alone raised 23,605 pounds; in 1860 eighty-seven produced 212,353 pounds.

The introduction of cigars and their immediate, widespread popularity were major reasons for this increase in the growing of tobacco. Israel Putnam is credited with importing the first cigars into the colony when he returned from the expedition against Havana in 1762. The *Courant* published the first advertisement for "segars" of domestic manufacture in 1799.

Roswell Viets of East Windsor and Simeon Smith Viets, both natives of Turkey Hills and grandsons of Captain John Viets, were among the first cigar makers in the state. Hezekiah Spencer Sheldon tells of the beginning of Simeon Viets' business in *The Memorial History of Hartford:*

A foreigner, Spaniard or Cuban, of intemperate habits—a cigar maker by trade and a tramp—drifted to West Suffield and in some way made the acquaintance of Simeon Viets, who was a man of enterprise and a Connecticut Yankee. The result was that Viets bought a little Spanish tobacco, gave the man a job, and began the manufacture of "genuine Spanish cigars," the first industry of the kind in the Connecticut Valley, if not in New England. Girls were taken as apprentices and instructed by the Cuban in the art of making a "Principe" cigar. This was 4½ inches in length with a "kink head." To make the "kink" was such an accomplishment that when it was mastered, the trade was acquired.

Men and women soon found they could make cigars at home and sell them to cigar manufacturers like Simeon Viets or trade them to peddlers and local storekeepers. To make these early, rather crude cigars, they placed pieces of tobacco on a larger piece of leaf, rolled the two parts together and twisted them with a kink at one end. Sometimes they applied glue to the length of the cigar before rolling it. As they perfected their product over the years, manufacturers learned how to wind cigars so that they stayed together without kinks and glue. The fine quality cigars that evolved have three parts; filler, binder, and wrapper.

Ideally a cigar is filled with flavorful tobacco cut in long, unbroken strips so that it tastes good and draws well. It is bound with a single piece of tobacco which is both elastic and tough enough to hold the filler together and keep the cigar's shape. Then it is wrapped in a piece of unblemished leaf of fine texture and attractive color.

Hezekiah Sheldon writes that by 1830 the cigar table and cutting board had displaced the spinning wheel and the loom in many households. He says that this cottage industry continued until about the time of the Civil War. By then most cigar making was done in factories and shops.

Storekeeper John J. Viets bought cigars for resale from individuals and manufactories. He paid as little as $2 per 1000 for those made from native tobacco, called Supers, and as much as $12 per 1000 for cigars made in whole or in part with tobacco from Cuba, Santo Domingo, Missouri, and Kentucky. The length and quality of the cigar also affected its price. In October and November of 1846 he shipped by railroad and steamboat to New York City almost 70,000 cigars. He could have sold more. He complained to a prospective customer at the time, "Good cigar makers and cigars are scarcer than *wooden nutmegs,* and the more they cheat, the better they consider the business."

Another major reason for the increase in tobacco farming was the fact that the soil and climate of the Connecticut River Valley are particularly favorable to the cultivation of tobacco. Men were able to develop Connecticut Valley Broadleaf, a tobacco with a large, finely-textured, aromatic leaf. It was particularly suitable for cigar wrappers.

By the time Horace Clark's sons inherited his land in 1842, they were probably planting this improved tobacco. In his diary Elmore Clark details the tedious hand-work involved. He prepared and seeded his tobacco bed in early spring. In June he transplanted the young plants to the open fields and began his constant battle against worms and weeds. As the plants grew tall, he topped and suckered them to maximize the growth of the remaining leaves. In late summer and early fall, he cut the plants off at the base of the stalk; "stuck" them, or speared their ends onto a wooden lath; and hung them upside down to cure. During the winter months, he took the plants down, stripped the stalks, and bundled the leaves for hauling to market.

Clark fertilized with manure, plaster, lime, and ashes. One year he used guano, which he went to New Haven to purchase. Once he bought some "Castor Pumace" in Hartford to put in his tobacco hills and 100 pounds of "Bond Dust" at Bloomfield, also for the tobacco. Another time he covered his newly planted tobacco with hay, removing it later. "An experiment," he noted. In his small way, Clark was typical of the Connecticut farmers who experimented to improve their crops and livestock.

He brought his tobacco stalks into his back kitchen to stick and he hung them in his barns and cider-mill house to cure. Other farmers, too, converted their outbuildings and even rooms in their houses to accommodate this cash crop. In 1854 Clark went to the raising of Renselaer Pinney's tobacco shed northwest of the Pinney home at 36 South Main Street. This must have been one of the first of the tobacco barns that have been a distinctive part of the town's landscape ever since.

During the 1850s Clark seems to have planted about an acre of tobacco each year and harvested around 1500 pounds, which he sold for $200 to $300. The better leaves, which could be used for wrappers, brought as much as 22½ cents per pound; the poorer leaves, for filler, as little as 3 cents per pound.

Clark sold his tobacco to dealers from as far away as Baltimore, Maryland. Usually, though, he sold to cigar makers and tobacconists in Suffield, which was at one time the marketing center of the business.

Turkey Hills also had its tobacco dealers. Anson Bates became the community's first a little before 1840. For the next twenty years, he bought, packed, and sweated tobacco (to ferment it) before reselling it.

Elmore Clark's nephew Charles Horace Clark built a tobacco warehouse in front of the cider mill and distillery that stood just north of Trout Brook on the east side of North Main Street. There he stored tobacco before reselling it or making it into cigars. Albert Carlos Bates writes in his *Historical Sketch of Turkey Hills* that it was a substantial frame building, two stories high, painted white, and standing on a high brick basement close to the highway. He adds:

A number of cigar makers were regularly employed as well as other persons to handle and care for the tobacco and girls to stem the leaves. Even at this time, the cigar makers were members of a union. The cigars that were made were packed in rather large boxes, which bore a label carrying a large picture of Mr. Clark.

Clark employed as many as seventeen people. One year they produced 800,000 cigars, valued at $32,000. In 1883 the building was moved to Tariffville where Gordon C.

Willoughby converted it to a gristmill and installed a steam engine for power. Willoughby used some of the doors from the manufactory in the house he built at 15 Old Hartford Avenue a few years later.

Another local cigar manufacturer was Peter Grohman, a German immigrant. He may have had his cigar shop at his home that stood on the northeast corner of Turkey Hills and Newgate roads. Grohman employed four cigar makers and produced around 100,000 cigars a year.

While cultivating more tobacco, farmers also increased the number of farm animals they raised. Almost every family had at least one milch cow, and some had ten or more. They turned much of the milk into cheese and butter, over 40,000 pounds in 1850.

Farmers raised extra hogs, cattle, and sheep for sale locally and out of town. Sometimes they sold to drovers who stopped at the local inns on their way to river and seaport towns. Horace Clark, who kept his family's old inn at the Center, wrote in his diary:

> *October 3, 1818. Drove of cattle from Granville, keeping cost $4.*
> *September 19, 1819. Kept fifty-four cows for Barsley and Holt.*
> *October 24, 1820. Kept 311 hogs last night.*

According to *The Heritage of Granby,* the house at 231 Hartford Avenue was once an inn for drovers, and it was not unusual to see 100 oxen in the pasture nearby.

The Landlords

Innkeeping continued as a typical occupation in the 1800s while running hotels and boarding houses began in this century. Most of these lodging places were located on the main thoroughfares through Turkey Hills, what are now South and North Main streets and Hartford Avenue.

On South Main Street, Horace Clark took down his tavern sign in 1821, perhaps the one that had invited people to his family inn for eighty years or more. Across the street from him to the east (north of 9 South Main Street) was a house built about 1809 by shoemaker Benejah Phelps. Phelps and a succession of landlords, including John J. Viets and ending with Francis Granger, ran an inn or hotel there for the next hundred years. It was more than an overnight haven for travelers; many single men who worked in the community made this inn their home. At 5 North Main Street, Charles P. Clark, Horace Clark's son, ran an inn for a year or two around 1837.

Blacksmith David Latham welcomed paying guests at his home on the west side of Hartford Avenue opposite Hatchet Hill Road, and at least six of the Holcombs who lived nearby used their homes as taverns through the years.

Joel Holcomb's inn at 115 Hartford Avenue must have done a brisk business while passengers waited for boats to go through the nearby locks of the Farmington Canal. (Holcomb had added the large front section of the house in 1809.) Boats from Westfield often stopped their first night out at Granby where some of the passengers

Inn that stood north of 9 South Main Street. The photo shows an unheated second floor addition for a tubercular patient

and crew may have slept at Holcomb's and at his brother Abraham's inn at 231 Hartford Avenue.

Joel B. Holcomb, Joel Holcomb's grandson, built Turkey Hills' first hotel, probably about the time he received his innkeeper's license in 1852. It stood on the east side of Hartford Avenue opposite the Granby Railroad Station until 1978 when the East Granby Volunteer Fire Department razed it. Holcomb offered food, drink, and lodging to the businessmen and other travelers who came to town on the train and on the stage, which stopped at his hotel.

On Newgate Road, the Viets Tavern almost always had accommodations for visitors to the prison and the mines. Luke Viets, one of Captain John Viets' sons, ran

5 North Main Street

the family inn until a year or so before his death in 1835. His grandson Benjamin F. Barker was operating it as B. F. Barker's Hotel when he died in 1856.

Factory workers and other laborers from out of town lived in the community's first boarding houses. Whitfield Cowles built one on the Farmington River east of Spoonville Bridge to accommodate the workers at his nearby wire factory. Some of the workers in the textile mill at Tariffville boarded at homes across the river, including 22-24 and 26 Old Hartford Avenue.

David Latham house

Storekeepers and Peddlers

Appleton Robbins, a native of Wethersfield and a Hartford merchant, opened the community's first general store when he bought the Deacon Asahel Holcomb house, the back ell of 1 North Main Street, around 1790. He also purchased the Daniel Willcox house across from his new home on the east side of North Main Street. He evidently used the Willcox house as a store until he built a new one south of it sometime after 1810. This newer building stood in front of the Congregational meetinghouse. It was used as a house for perhaps 100 years before it burned in the 1950s.

Farmers traded their excess foodstuffs to Robbins. He, in turn, took large quantities of cheese, rye, corn, and preserved beef and pork to Hartford to be sold there or shipped to commercial towns and southern plantations along the eastern seaboard and to the West Indies and other foreign countries.

Within the next few years, there were at least four more stores at the Center. Grove Griswold had one on the east side of North Main Street near Trout Brook. Elisha Winchel, Jr., operated one in Whitfield Cowles' former shop on School Street,

Holcomb Hotel

and Perley Holt and Alfred Owen had one at their gin distillery, which stood near 4 Church Road.

About 1816 Reuben Barker built the store that stands today as a house at 19 South Main Street. His son, postmaster Chauncey Barker, managed it. Six years later Charles T. Hillyer bought the business with the financial help of his future father-in-law, Appleton Robbins. An advertisement in the *Courant* announced the change in ownership:

Charles T. Hillyer has taken the store formerly occupied by Mr. Chauncey Barker, where he has just received from New York, and now offers for sale on the most accommodating terms, a general assortment of dry goods, groceries, crockery, hard, hollow and stoneware, drugs and medicines, paints and oils. Boots and shoes made for customers on the shortest notice.

John J. Viets was operating the business in 1837 when he raised his own store that still stands at 9 South Main Street. An extant letter book contains copies of his business letters along with debits and credits of cash and merchandise. The book shows he was both a retailer and a wholesaler, who dealt with suppliers and customers from Vermont to Georgia.

He was a horse trader in the tradition of his great-grandfather Captain John Viets. Although men brought horses into the area from the West for sale, Viets preferred horses from Canada and northern New England, and he went there to buy them. He sold them locally and as far away as Providence, Rhode Island. (By the early 1800s, most families had at least one horse for transportation and farm work.)

Viets bought from many sources. Local people sold or bartered their produce and other wares. Some of his shoes and boots came from Benjamin Harger's cobbler's shop just north of Harger's home at 22 South Main Street. He bought larger quantities from Truman Allen's shoe manufactory on the corner of Wells Road and North Granby Road in the Salmon Brook parish. His account book describes the footwear as Indian rubber shoes (rubbers), strap shoes, pumps, booties, slippers, brogans, cow boots, buskins, and half-gaiter boots. The average price was about $1 a pair.

Peddlers stopped by to sell or exchange goods. Salesmen, called agents, from out-of-town manufactories brought small orders of portable items and took orders for larger items such as farm tools. Viets ordered from wholesalers in Hartford and New York City either in person or by mail.

He often instructed his suppliers to

leave goods at an address in Hartford or another nearby town where he could arrange pickup with a wagon. At least three times a week, he would drive to Hartford or send someone in his place.

Viets' business arrangements were informal by today's standards. His dealings with Lambert Hitchcock of Hitchcockville (now Riverton), Connecticut, were typical. Viets stocked Hitchcock's crickets (small footstools), tables, wash stands, and "plain stands" along with chairs defined as Boston rock, roll top fancy, tea color cane seat, flat top maple, sewing, etc. He paid with either merchandise or cash.

Viets might go to the factory to select the furniture; he might order by mail or buy from one of Hitchcock's agents. One letter reads:

Hitchcockville
31 July 1839

Mr. Viets
Dear Sir, I send you by the bearer Mr. Wright a load of chairs which please receive and sell on commission at prices annexed. I may perhaps when I see you conclude to make an exchange for cigars.

Even at prices as low as $2.75 for a Boston rocker and 75 cents for a plain chair, the furniture did not sell. Viets complained:

We have complaints every day that the prices are too high. The consequence is we rarely sell at all. Please do direct what reduction of prices may be made . . . as I wish to sell (and not keep) as low as others.

Hitchcock obligingly reduced the prices to $2 for the rockers and 60 cents for the plain chairs.

Some barter, some cash, and a great deal of credit moved goods in and out of Viets' store. When he bought 226 gallons of cough medicine from Festus Viets for $117.92, he paid him with $50.92 in cash, a personal note for $37, and a "due bill in goods" for the remaining $30. When he bartered with John T. Knox for a top buggy ($111.50) and fifty bushels of oats ($20), he traded him a Belcher buggy ($75) and a coat ($15), relinquished a note he held from Knox ($31.50), and credited the remaining $10 to Knox's account at the store.

In this pre-checking-account era, dealing with out-of-town suppliers and customers was even more complicated.

Viets Store

Evidently Viets did not find the mails dependable unless he knew the post rider or stagecoach driver personally. He advised one of his debtors to deposit the money owed him in a bank at Worcester, Massachusetts, and to send a proper receipt from the bank to him. He could then exchange it for a note at a Hartford bank.

Money, like merchandise, could be left at designated places to be picked up later. Still, Viets found the safest and most convenient way to send cash was by "private conveyance." This meant that he found a trusted acquaintance who happened to be traveling in the right direction and asked him to deliver or collect the payment personally.

By the 1840s Lemuel C. Holcomb and

his son-in-law, Henry Merwin, had a drygoods and grocery store east of Old Hartford Avenue on the north bank of the Farmington River. The more than 400 men and women who worked at the Tariff Manufacturing Company across the river were ready customers for the general store. They also provided a market for the farmers who brought their produce to the factory and sold it from their wagons.

Another retail business of the day was peddling, a popular occupation among the young men of Turkey Hills. They traveled throughout New England, the South, and the West, selling Yankee notions and larger items from saddlebags, peddlers' boxes, and wagons.

Clocks were their most common merchandise. Madison Cowles, a son of Whitfield Cowles, was peddling when he died in Virginia in 1836. Claims against his estate show that he owed more than $2700 to three of Connecticut's most famous clockmakers: Daniel Burnap, Chauncey Jerome, and Eli Terry, Jr. Clocks at that time sold for as little as $5 apiece.

John J. Viets outfitted peddlers at his store, and sometimes he provided the means of transportation as well as the merchandise. One agreement with a peddler reads:

Granby
Feb. 6, 1846

John J. Viets and William Gabriel this day make the following arrangement for going on an excursion, or peddling trip, to Vermont the present winter with shoes, boots, dry goods, and cigars.

Said John J. Viets is to furnish horse and sleigh vs. said Gabriel's time and services in the campaign and both to share equally in expenses, profit or losses of the excursion—and equally furnish cash and capital.

The value of peddler Gabriel's merchandise was $141.50. Yard goods were as little as 8 cents a yard; castor oil was 6 cents a bottle, and pocket knives 20 cents apiece. There are almost 100 entries charged to Gabriel in the account book. Each is for one item, which might be as small as a paper of pins or as large as over 90 yards of calico.

The Professionals

Attorney Grove Griswold became Turkey Hills' first member of the Hartford Bar Association in 1805. Samuel Woodruff was already a member when he came to the community around 1808 and married Chloe Phelps, the widow of Roswell Phelps.

Tobacco dealer Anson Bates was a practicing attorney with one office in Hartford and another at his home on North Main Street. (According to an entry in Alfred Gay's diary, Bates built the house at 88 North Main Street in 1860.) Albert C. Bates wrote of him in the family genealogy: "When it was time for the courts to sit, he would journey from his home to Hartford, often traveling the 15 miles on foot, and remain there during the sessions." Anson Bates may have been Turkey Hills' first commuter.

88 North Main Street

Besides representing people in court, Bates' practice consisted largely of drawing

103-105 Hartford Avenue

22 South Main Street

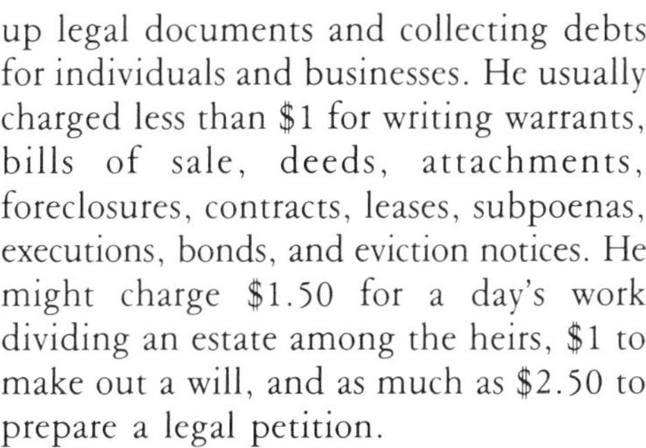

up legal documents and collecting debts for individuals and businesses. He usually charged less than $1 for writing warrants, bills of sale, deeds, attachments, foreclosures, contracts, leases, subpoenas, executions, bonds, and eviction notices. He might charge $1.50 for a day's work dividing an estate among the heirs, $1 to make out a will, and as much as $2.50 to prepare a legal petition.

Holcomb genealogists call Thomas Holcomb a lawyer, although the federal censuses label him a farmer. At least two of his sons became engineers, and much of their work was on bridges and railroads in the South. One of them, Richard Erskine Holcomb, probably built the house at 103-105 Hartford Avenue around 1850.

There were at least six doctors in Turkey Hills during these years. All lived near the Center with the exception of Dr. Lafayette Johnson who lived in the John Pinney house that still stands east of 101 Spoonville Road in the Windsor Half Mile.

Dr. Eliphalet Buck came to Turkey Hills around 1790 and stayed until a year before his death in 1844. He was a charter member of the Hartford County Medical Society, founded in 1792. His home at 42 South Main Street burned in 1904.

Dr. Lewis Badger came from Suffield and built the house at 22 South Main Street in 1829. His extant letters indicate that he came at the request of local residents who promised to subscribe to his support. When he emigrated to Ohio in 1831, he evidently sold his practice (his subscription list) to Dr. Chester Hamlin. Dr. Hamlin occupied the houses at 11 and 17 South Main Street. Appleton Robbins built these at that time, perhaps to attract a doctor to the community. Dr. Hamlin bought the houses from Robbins' estate in 1851 and continued his practice there until he died in 1872.

After the Copper Hill Methodist church became an independent station in 1844, they had resident ministers. The Congregational church, too, had ministers almost without interruption after 1826 when they began to receive financial help from the denomination's domestic missionary society.

The center of town, with 11 and 17 South Main Street in foreground.

Teaching, particularly in the public schools, probably was not considered a profession as it is today. Most teachers were relatively uneducated and did not teach for long. For ministers like the Reverend Whitfield Cowles, teaching was a secondary occupation. Even classical scholar Lemuel C. Holcomb is called a teacher on only one federal census; usually he is called a farmer.

Artisans

Artisans continued to work in shops in or near their homes. There were at least seven shoemakers in Turkey Hills during these years. They saw the advent of factory-made footwear that eventually limited their craft to shoe repairing.

In contrast, work for the community's nine or more blacksmiths increased. There were more oxen and horses for them to shoe. Although manufactories soon produced many of the tools and hardware their predecessors had made, the repair of these and the new metal articles such as farm implements, water pumps, and stoves fell to them. They worked closely with the community's eight or so wheelwrights and wagon and carriagemakers who prospered, too, as these vehicles became more common.

At the west end of Holcomb Street and south along Hartford Avenue, there was a small community of these artisans. Joel Eno, who lived near 2 Washington Ridge Road, made wagons and carts as well as furniture, sleds, and coffins. He was also one of the parish's first professional painters. He was not expensive by today's standards. Labor to paint two rooms was $2.50. If he furnished the paint, he charged another $7 or so. His recipe for japan, a varnish, was:

Take one gallon of oil, one-half pound red lead, one-half pound of umber pulverized together. Boil them together—say three hours—then drop in moderately one pound of gum shellac. When over the fire, thin down with one quart turpentine.

Blacksmith David Latham ironed tires onto the wheels of Joel Eno's carts and wagons. He did this by heating iron strips and fitting them around the wooden wheels. As the iron cooled, it shrank and adhered to the wood.

Sometimes Latham employed Joel Eno to make the wooden parts of vehicles, then Latham added the metal parts and sold them. He advertised in the *Courant* of December 17, 1816, for two blacksmiths. They were to be faithful, trusty, and acquainted with shoeing and the various branches of country work. He added that he would "furnish anyone with one- or two-horse sleighs or wagons, made to any pattern, to suit the buyer, finished with beauty and taste—likewise ox-carts."

David Latham may have owned the plow factory that appeared on Granby's 1845 Grand List. The 1850 census shows he made 40 plows, valued at $320, the previous year.

The Merwin and Holcomb blacksmith shop stood behind 14 Old Hartford Avenue. It belonged to Lemuel C. Holcomb, but since he was already busy with his tavern, his store, his academy, and his farm, Merwin may have been the blacksmith. The shop employed two men who did about $1200 worth of custom work a year.

The Aldermans who lived near 119 Holcomb Street also worked with wood and metals. Oliver Alderman was a carpenter and a contractor on large construction projects according to the Alderman genealogy. The author adds: "He was said to have been the only one in the community who could make the drawings and carve out to make a perfect fit the large wooden cider press

Thompson wagon shop, built in 1817

screws used in those early days." His son Clydon was a wheelwright with a shop near 241 Hartford Avenue.

East of the Mountain, four of the descendants of the Reverend Edward Thompson became carriagemakers. Three of them lived all of their lives on his grant on South Main Street. George W. Thompson lived as an adult at 82 South Main Street; his wagon shop stood south of his home. Edmund Thompson, Jr., lived as an adult at 99 South Main Street, and his son, Edward P. Thompson, lived at 74 South Main Street. Father and son shared a shop that stood just south of Edmund's house. The 1817 contract for the building says it was to be 20 feet by 40 feet, to be modeled on Chauncey Barker's new store, and to cost $140. It was torn down in the 1970s.

117-119 South Main Street

In the *Courant* of July 13, 1819, Lot Thompson and Edmund Thompson, Jr., with blacksmith Walter Thrall of 46 East Street advertised:

The subscribers having this day formed a connection in business under the firm of Thompsons and Thrall, respectfully invite those who may be pleased to favor them with their custom to call at the shop lately occupied by the Messrs. Thompsons in Granby, Turkey Hills Society, where they may be accommodated with any kind of work in their line, viz., chaises, pleasure wagons, peddler's wagons, etc. of every description, which they engage shall be as good as recommended at the time of sale.

The shop was employing seven men in 1820. They would have included joiners, blacksmiths, and apprentices: the joiners to make and repair the bodies, called boxes, and other wooden parts; the blacksmiths to make and repair axletrees, springs, tires, and other metal parts; and the apprentices to help while learning a trade.

Among the apprentices was Charles A. Tudor. He came to work for Edmund, Jr., in 1843 when he was seventeen years old. Twenty years later he bought George W. Thompson's shop, moved it across the street, and set up his own carriage business. About the same time he built the house at 117-119 South Main Street.

Edmund Thompson, Jr., worked at the shop for more than forty years. His account book shows he made as many as twenty-nine vehicles in a single year, although fifteen was a more usual number. Some are called simply "wagons" and some wagons with various prefixes such as "one-horse," "two-horse," "buggy," "Belcher," "lumber," and "peddler's." Buggies are characterized as having "open fronts," "elliptic springs," "side springs," and "scroll

Artist's concept of the Center of East Granby in 1831

A cidermill and cider brandy distillery are shown on the east side of North Main Street, north of Trout Brook, and a house later used as an inn by Charles P. Clark stands south of the brook on the opposite side of the road. Directly south are Appleton Robbins' houses from which he ran his store. In the center foreground is the old Clark farm, for many years a tavern, and across the road is the Benejah Phelps inn to the northeast and the Barker-Hillyer store to the southeast. In the right foreground is the new home of Dr. Lewis Badger, which would later house a shoemaker and a wagon maker. North of the road to Windsor (now School Street) at its intersection with Church Road stands the Holt & Owen gin distillery and store. The small shops on the south side of the road were used by storekeepers and blacksmiths, shoemakers, wagon makers and other artisans at different times. William Rockwell's tannery on the same side of the road by a brook completes the picture.

bodies." There are also cutters, chaises, carriages, sulkies, sleighs, carts, and coaches. Prices range from around $40 for a cart to $165 for a four-wheeled carriage.

Judah D. Viets purchased the house at 22 South Main Street in 1846 and raised a wagon shop. The 1850 census shows he had three men working for him. They had made twenty carriages, valued at $1500, the previous year.

Oliver Moor was a versatile craftsman—glazier, locksmith, cabinetmaker, and occasional cartwright. In 1820 he employed three men in his shop that stood in back of his home at 20 School Street. His most popular product was a washing machine. This was a wooden tub with a rounce—a wooden cylinder connected to a hand crank—which the operator moved to agitate the wash. Later, blacksmith and wagon maker Bradley Perkins occupied Moor's shop and house.

William Rockwell's tannery was on the brook that runs east of the house he built by 1790 at 28 School Street. Local men brought him the skins of their domestic animals. Sometimes he returned the hides to them, sometimes he made them into leather products for sale. His house and shop were advertised for sale in the *Courant* of July 23, 1822:

Tan works, dwelling, etc. for sale. The stand and place occupied by Mr. William Rockwell at Turkey Hills near the meetinghouse. There are about 10 acres of land, a well-built, two-story dwelling house, a barn, etc. together with the tan works, accompanied by water at all times, a shoemaker's shop, etc. It is believed there is no better situation than this for a tanner and shoemaker.

Rockwell may have been Turkey Hills' last tanner.

Joel Ackley and Eleazer Rice made potash at their works south of 61 Rainbow Road. As a teenager Rice had learned the trade from Joseph Cornish, Jr. He also further refined potash into pearl ash, which was used in making soap and glass.

28 School Street

At his shop opposite 23 East Street, joiner Reuben Barker employed as many as seven men at a time. Some were apprentices. He advertised in the *Courant* of October 12, 1801:

Run away on the 4th instant. Apprentice named Samuel Dunn about seventeen years, a stout boy 5 feet 2 inches, short hair . . . rather apt to be talkative and fancy. Wore away a short brown coat, striped swansdown vest, drab overalls, a new fur hat, silk velvet hatband fastened with a silver clasp with the initials of his name engraved thereon. Generous reward offered.

Barker made furniture as well as the woodwork for the interior of houses. Account books credit him for making clock cases, Windsor chairs, and desks.

Israel C. Phelps, who lived in his father Ezekiel's home at 39 North Main Street, was the community's first tinsmith. He bought imported sheet tin from James Ward of Hartford and made it into coffee pots, kettles, bake ovens, pails, basins, dippers, graters, colanders, candlemolds, candlesticks, and pudding, milk, and "sheet pie" pans.

Millers and Manufacturers

A few manufactories joined the sawmills and gristmills along local streams and the Farmington River during the first half of the 19th century.

David Ellsworth of Windsor bought Thomas Griffin's gristmill on the Farmington River in 1804. During the next fifty years, various owners and lessees operated a gristmill, a sawmill, a distillery, machinery for manufacturing spoons, and carding machines at the site. (Carding machines were replacing hand cards for combing wool to prepare it for spinning.) By 1850 two millers, Albert Clark and Henry A. Case, were running the gristmill. With three millstones, they ground 37,500 bushels of grain into flour and meal that year. Case and his brother Edward B. owned and operated the mill from 1855 to 1874, when Henry became sole owner. By then they had added or reactivated a sawmill and replaced the old up-and-down saw with an improved circular one, the first in the area according to the *Encyclopedia of Connecticut Biography*.

At the Willcox mill place on Salmon Brook behind 115 Hartford Avenue, a group of local blacksmiths ran a wire factory around 1810. They drew ductile metal through holes to make wire of specific sizes. Beside the mill was an annealing shed and a coal house that blacksmith John T. Knox, who married the wayward Deborah Thrall, later occupied.

The brothers Festus and Horace Viets had a sawmill and a shingle mill just north of the Granby-Suffield border and northwest of the family home on Griffin Road. This may have been the same mill that Seth and Aristarchus Griffin once operated.

At Stony Brook, a sawmill replaced the earlier gristmill. Farther south on the stream, Duane S. Barnard built a gristmill, called the "Red Hook Mill," where he used a treadmill to grind grain. To the east and just north of Nicholson Road, Erastus Hamlin, a brother of Dr. Chester Hamlin, ran a brass mill. Little is known about what he manufactured. Albert C. Bates in his sketch of Turkey Hills mentions andirons and also brass knobs that men put on the horns of cattle. Elmore Clark recorded in his diary that he had a teakettle and a boiler mended there. Like other local artisans, Hamlin probably spent as much time repairing articles as he did making them.

These were the principal occupations of the men of Turkey Hills, but they were not the only ones. Local records of the time also mention occupations such as printer, bookbinder, mechanic, machinist, mason, boat builder, lock keeper, clock repairer, tailor, railroad laborer, depot agent, fireman, section boss, baggagemaster, stage driver, butcher, silversmith, silver-plater, burnisher, spoon maker, and "speck maker" (a maker of spectacles). These last five are from the records of the Cowles Manufacturing Company during the era when Turkey Hills made its most serious bid to become a mill town—or even one of Connecticut's major manufacturing centers.

14

Spoonville: The Beginning of Silver-Plating

IN A WAY, the Reverend Whitfield Cowles was responsible for the Cowles Manufacturing Company even though he died in 1840, five years before the company was founded. Mr. Cowles had continued his manufacturing ventures after he left the ministry. By 1811 he was making both hand and machine cards at his home on Spoonville Road and selling them as far away as Maryland.

The following year he moved his business across the Farmington River to Griswoldville, as Tariffville was called at the time. By then the Jeremiah Case mills had become the Griswold Mills. There was a complete clothier's business with carding machines, fulling mill, dye house, and finishing shop on the site by the time Cowles became a partner. Both the spinning of the yarn and the weaving of the cloth were done in homes, although Roger Griswold did consider installing spinning machinery in 1808.

Cowles and his various partners also built a wire manufactory at Griswoldville. They advertised American wire of superior quality in all sizes from 1 to 34, also "refuse wire suitable for horse chains." Company records show that between February and October of 1812, they produced 7425 pounds of wire, which they used themselves, probably in making cards. They sold over $9580 worth of wire during the year beginning July 1, 1812. Their business extended from Rutland, Vermont, to Albany, New York, and into southern Connecticut.

At least thirty-eight different men and women worked at the wire factory between 1812 and 1815 for from $5 to $25 a month, which probably included board. Whether or not an employee provided his own "washing, mending and spirits" helped to determine his salary. Some men bound themselves to the company for one year and agreed "to work five days in the week from daybreak until nine o'clock so long as the nights are longer than the days and from sunrise to sunset the rest of the time."

The owners of the Griswold Mills, like those of most early industries, were handicapped by lack of capital. Whitfield Cowles' business correspondence reveals the typical financial difficulties of the time caused by the scarcity of money, particularly specie, the lack of a uniform and stable currency, the existence of counterfeit money, and the financial instability of banks. At least sixteen different men bought and sold their interest in the mills during the three years Cowles was involved. This rapid turnover of investors indicates that no one profited greatly, if at all.

In 1813 Cowles, Lincoln, & Mills—as the business was called at the time—moved their card factory to Hartford. Within six months the name was changed to Lincoln & Mills.

Soon creditors were attaching property at Griswoldville that belonged to the three men. Constable Ambrose Adams levied an execution on 3063 pounds of their wire and posted a notice of its sale on the public signpost in December 1814. He recorded in the town records:

And at the end of twenty days after such posting, I repaired to the sign post and caused due and legal notice to be given to customers to come to the sale thereof, but none appearing, I adjourned the sale to January 24, 1815, when I again repaired to said sign post and caused a drum to be beaten to give notice to persons to come to said sale.

Adams sold the wire and distributed the money to creditors. At the same time Cowles deeded about 40 acres of land near his home on Spoonville Road to eight individuals to satisfy their claims of approximately $2300 against him.

Cowles sold his last interest in the Griswold Mills soon after. He continued to make cards and wire in a factory he built at an unknown location near his home. His agents and, later, his sons sold the cards to cotton and woolen mills in southern and western states.

In 1829 Cowles built a new factory east of the present Spoonville bridge and about 200 feet north of the Farmington River. Joiners Roger and Anson Filer agreed to "shut up" the factory "in a plain but fine and tight workmanlike manner" for $40 in "goods, eatables, and drinkables." The factory was two stories high with a basement. It had twenty-five windows, two large doors and two small ones. Cowles dammed a small stream that ran into the river beside the new factory to power an overshot waterwheel.

Cowles and his sons Madison and Gilbert were operating under the name of Whitfield Cowles & Sons by 1832. Their wire and card business reached its peak about this time, and the company built a boardinghouse west of the factory to accommodate its employees. Whitfield Cowles deeded the business to his sons in 1833. After Madison's death three years later, Gilbert sold the factory to his younger brother William B. Cowles.

About 1840 the new owner began to manufacture flatware of German silver, a varying combination of copper, nickel, and zinc. James H. Isaacson, a former partner with W. H. Pratt & Co., platers of Hartford, and Asa Rogers, an experienced silversmith, joined Cowles in 1843. Soon they were silver-plating German silver flatware by a new galvanic process using batteries. The process had originated in England and reports of it appeared in scientific journals in America shortly after 1840. These men at what became known as Spoonville probably accomplished the first commercially successful electroplating in the United States.

As Wm. B. Cowles & Co., the three men built a second factory nearer the Farmington River. To power their waterwheel, they built a dam from the north bank of the river to the eastern end of Pinney Island, as James Eno's Island was now called.

The three men with John D. Johnson, a manufacturer of brass and German silver in Waterbury, Connecticut, formed the Cowles Manufacturing Company in November of 1845 "for the purpose of manufacturing German and silver-plated spoons, forks, butter knives or any other article in the same line made from German silver and other metals." The new company brought needed capital to the business by issuing 280 shares of stock at $25 apiece for a total of $7000. Isaacson bought forty-six shares; Rogers and Cowles, forty-seven each; and Johnson, 140. Johnson was the only one of the four men who did not work at the factory. His Waterbury company supplied much of the German silver for the Spoonville operation.

From an extant list of the machinery in the two factories, it is possible to deduce how German silver and silver-plated flatware were made at the time:

One engine, lathe, and fixtures in the new factory on the first floor; also one rolling mill in the same room with gear wheels, pulleys, and fixtures complete. Also fourteen sets of cutting out dies for tablespoons, dessert spoons, teaspoons, table forks, gravy ladles, cream spoons, mustard spoons, salt shovels, sugar shovels, and butter knives, napkin rings; one striking up die for butter knife handles. Those dies are in the first floor of the new mill or the basement of the old mill. Twenty solution baths, twenty-four stone pots, and jars, one stove and fixtures. Sixty batteries with apparatus complete for plating, three sinks, connecting wires in the plating room in the new mill. One large polishing frame in the north room of the new mill second floor with shafts, pulleys, stands, wheels, arbors, buffs, and butts complete; also in the room in the northeast corner on the same floor one rolling mill with gear pulleys and wheels and butts complete; also on the same floor in the southeast room one polishing frame painted blue with shafts, wheels, buffs, pulleys, and butts complete—also in the old factory second floor south room, one grinding frame with shafts, pulleys, butts, and twenty-four emery wheels complete—also in the north room same floor—one stove and pipe for soldering butter knives.

By 1850 the company had added a "cutting-out press."

The Cowles company may have used the rolling mill to reduce German silver to the proper thickness. They also may have used it to thin the blanks workers cut from the metal with the cutting-out press and shaped into individual pieces of flatware with the cutting-out dies.

Probably workers shaped butter knife handles and perhaps stamped a pattern on them with the striking-up die. They would have used the stove and pipe in soldering knife blades to the handles. The emery wheels on the grinding frame sharpened the blades.

The company used the solution baths, the stone pots and jars, the batteries with apparatus complete for plating, the sinks, and the connecting wires in silver-plating. Earl Chapin May in *A Century of Silver* describes the process:

The row of earthenware vessels were filled with an alkaline (cyanide) plating solution transparent as water. Underneath, upon the floor, was a corresponding row of jars. Each jar contained a plate of copper and zinc which produced a galvanic circuit or current. A thick bar of silver was suspended in the alkaline solution in the upper row of vessels, and in the same vessel from the opposite end was suspended a cup fashioned from the new alloy [i.e., German silver]. *Two wires were now placed in the lower, or galvanic jar, and the ends brought up and placed in contact, one with the silver, the other with the cup. The silver had passed—in a liquid, transparent, invisible form—through the water to reform itself again in solid metal upon the cup's surface.*

Polishing frames were used in the many buffing and polishing operations that were necessary in making German silver flatware and in silver-plating. The quality of the finished product depended heavily on the amount of polishing and the skill of the burnishers. In fact, most of the operations called for skilled workers of whom there was a shortage in this pioneer industry. The company needed experienced die makers, engravers, platers, and machine operators, as well as burnishers.

Four experienced spoon makers, brothers by the name of Kenworthy, came to Turkey Hills about 1845 from Birmingham, England, where Elkington & Co. had originated the electroplating process. In 1932 William G. Snow, an historian for the International Silver Company, interviewed James Kenworthy, the son and namesake of one of the four brothers, who was born at Spoonville in 1850. He said that his father was the first person to stamp spoon handles with a figured die instead of engraving them by hand.

James Kenworthy, Sr., was one of the men associated with the local factory who owned their own machinery and did piecework for the company; Egbert W. Sperry of Salmon Brook was another. Sperry received 33½ cents for every dozen German silver butter knives he made with the company furnishing the materials. The company then sold them for $2.75 or silver-plated them and sold them for $6.

Sixteen women and ninety-eight men worked for the Cowles Manufacturing Company in 1845 and 1846. Only a few were natives of Turkey Hills. The others either commuted from neighboring towns or lived at the company's boardinghouse and in nearby homes. Thomas Cushman, who seems to have been the company's head bookkeeper although he is listed as a silversmith on the 1860 census, probably built the house at 116 Spoonville Road in 1845. James B. Abbott, another mill worker, built the one at 153 Spoonville Road about the same time. Gilbert Cowles ran the general store that was a part of every mill community. He operated it from the cellar room of his house on Tunxis Avenue that was built into the bank where the abutment to the Spoonville bridge now stands.

The Cowles company made and plated teaspoons and tablespoons; dessert, mustard, and salt spoons; sugar scoops and tongs; cream, gravy, and soup ladles; butter knives and fish knives; and dessert, table, and pickle forks. They bought hollowware and plated it with silver. Some of their items were casters (stands for holding cruets), cake baskets, fruit dishes, tea and coffee pots, napkin rings, tea sets and communion ware (cups and plates used in religious services).

The Cowles factories also produced spectacles. Eyeglasses with either convex or concave lenses ground from common glass were not uncommon even in the early 1700s. At Spoonville they probably made spectacles very much like these earlier ones, although they also could have made bifocals, an invention of Benjamin Franklin's. They did make sunglasses. Frames were of German silver and some were silver-plated. Glasses sold for from $2.25 to $3.50 a dozen, wholesale.

Cowles boarding house

116 Spoonville Road

153 Spoonville Road

Cowles store

On October 9, 1846, the *Courant* reprinted an article from the *New York Commercial* that praised the durability, economy, and beauty of the Cowles silver-plated tableware and challenged readers to distinguish it from solid silver. The *Courant* endorsed the recommendation and added that the Cowles plated ware was "becoming celebrated throughout the country."

The Cowles company had agents in many of the larger towns with at least three in Hartford at different times. Their salesmen traveled throughout New England and as far south as South Carolina and west into Ohio. William B. Cowles spent much of his time on the road. He wrote from Cleveland, Ohio, in 1847 that he had journeyed from Buffalo on the steamboat *Nile,* which had been using the company's spoons for three years. He added that forks were not used very much on boats.

From Cowles' correspondence it is clear that in 1844 the company was already selling significant quantities of silver-plated flatware. In 1845 sales amounted to almost $64,000. The 1850 census shows a capital investment of $9000 and an annual product of 2000 gross of spoons valued at $65,000 and 182 gross of spectacles worth $6500.

In spite of these seemingly impressive figures, the Cowles company was never a financial success. It became one of the many small companies in Connecticut that sprang up, struggled, and died during these years.

William B. Cowles was plagued by the same business conditions that had hampered his father's manufacturing ventures. Although transportation had improved, the network of communication, finance, and distribution that made the industrial age possible was only beginning to develop.

Insufficient capital was perhaps the biggest impediment to success. The younger Cowles did not inherit any money from his father in 1840. In fact, he had to mortgage the estate to pay claims of more than $1600 against it. The $7000 raised by the incorporation of the Cowles Manufacturing Company in 1845 did not keep the business out of debt for long. John D. Johnson immediately mortgaged his shares of the business, presumably to raise the $3500 he contributed. In less than a year Cowles mortgaged the factory property to William Rogers to cover notes for $5150. Asa Rogers mortgaged his interest to his brother William for $1545 shortly thereafter, and soon creditors were demanding money and threatening suits against the company.

Inefficient management and the lack of skilled and responsible labor added to the company's woes. James H. Isaacson left the business in disgust in 1846. In a letter to Asa Rogers, he complained bitterly about conditions at Spoonville:

Our financial affairs are bad . . . but what with that and the position of things at the factory . . . I can see no hopes of our salvation. . . . A front view presents a factory full of stock, with machinery to work at least a reasonable quantity of it . . . but a back view presents the horrid picture . . . of machinery failing . . . the object for which it was designed. In a word a meaner lot of work . . . could not be found. . . . Something must be done. To . . . permit . . . [the] *hands to go on without any oversight must soon be our ruin. . . . The whole interest of every single hand here is to cheat us . . . in the pleasantest way possible. . . .*

But what are we to do? We have a large lot of spoons . . . but positively they are not fit to go into the market even if anybody would buy them. It would be dangerous for an insect to run across them for it would get so deep in the cavities that there would be no chance of his getting out. . . . I am positive that [the ware] *would never be found on a . . . dark day, . . . for there is not polish enough to reflect a particle of light.*

Let us get in some shape before others are ready to jump in the market. The work is so bad I have no hopes of it being sold . . . and I give everything up entirely until some system and responsibility can be had in the work.

Historian William G. Snow wrote after his interview with James Kenworthy:

At that time everything was in a state of turmoil. Nearly every operator or man in authority was jealous of the others, and many things were carried on under cover rather than to give anyone an idea as to what was transpiring.

For instance, early [after Kenworthy's association with the Cowles company], *he was only able to get the necessary German silver of the proper alloy from New York by boat at New Haven. He went to New Haven by team, carried the metal to Waterbury where it was rolled at a mill run by a water wheel which is now in the center of Hamilton Park there. Then he took it after dark, going to Tariffville so that Rogers or no other individual would know the source of his metal.*

There were more than a few makers of flatware in Connecticut ready to experiment with the new silver-plating process. They worked in silver, pewter, German silver,

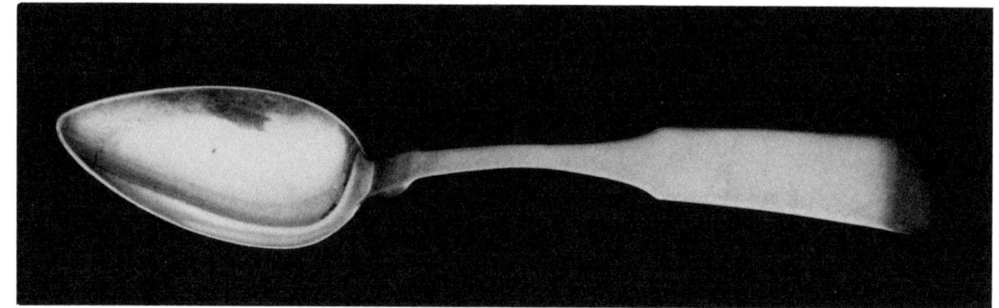

Spoon made by Cowles Manufacturing Company

and Britannia metal, a white alloy containing tin, antimony, and copper. Many were in Hartford or southwest of Hartford, and their general location gave them an advantage over the Spoonville company. They were nearer the producers of German silver and nearer their principal markets in the South and the West, since New York was the distribution center for Connecticut's industrial products. They were near to or a part of the state's largest manufacturing centers—Hartford, New Haven, Waterbury, Bridgeport, Danbury, Norwalk, Stamford, and Middletown—with their pools of skilled factory workers. One successful enterprise attracted another in the same business or using the same materials. Many of Cowles' competitors were nearer to or in the Naugatuck Valley, already the center of both metal processing and metalworking.

Ironically, it was Asa and William Rogers—one a partner in and the other a financial backer of the Spoonville company—who presented the stiffest competition. Asa Rogers, as well as Isaacson, left the company in 1846. Isaacson went to New York, and Rogers returned to Hartford where he joined his brothers William and Simeon in making silver-plated ware. Silver-plated spoons with the trade mark "Rogers Bros." appeared early in 1847. That fall the Rogers brothers won the prize for the best silver-plated ware at the Hartford County Agricultural Fair.

William B. Cowles complained that the Rogers brothers were trying to steal his customers and circulating the rumor that the Cowles company had failed. He bitterly accused one of the company's Hartford agents of discouraging customers from buying his products and other competitors of slandering his German silverware by calling it a "yellow, half-finished mess of trash not fit to be seen much less to be used."

A year after its incorporation, William B. Cowles was the only original shareholder active in the operation of the Cowles Manufacturing Company. The break was not a complete one, because the Rogers brothers bought German silver flatware from Spoonville for another two years. In the fall of 1848, the brothers wrote Cowles: "The forks ordered 9/11 we shall not want as the time has gone by. Will you do us a favor to send us our name punch at first opportunity—hand it to the stage driver directed to us and obliged."

Addison Harger, William B. Cowles' brother-in-law, became a part owner of the company in 1849 and assumed management of the factory while Cowles continued as a traveling salesman. By the end of the next year, Harger was indebted to thirteen different men and companies for $1200. He mortgaged land, factory buildings, and some of his household furniture to pay his debts. At the same time, he mortgaged the machinery and stock in the factories to Joseph D. Sanford, a storekeeper at Tariffville. Sanford seems to have managed the business for the next eight years or so without making a financial success of it.

Charles Benedict of Waterbury (John D. Johnson's son-in-law) acquired the land, buildings, equipment, and stock from the various owners and mortgagees in 1858. Evidently he was no more successful than his predecessors for he sold all within two years.

Land records do not include machinery for manufacturing and plating tableware after the early 1860s. An 1873 deed says that the personal property on the premises had been destroyed by fire. Only one factory is mentioned in that deed and in subsequent deeds, and it burned down sometime between 1895 and 1897. The Cowles Manufacturing Company was officially dissolved by act of the legislature in 1905.

The Rogers brothers continued to manufacture silver-plated ware during the remainder of their lives. When twelve silver companies united to form the International Silver Company in 1898, the new company included all the active concerns with which the Rogers brothers had been associated. In a short history of Spoonville prepared for East Granby's tercentenary celebration in 1935, William G. Snow wrote:

In giving full credit to the various units now a part of the International Silver Co. that were concerned in the first successful production of silverplated spoons, forks, etc., and in the development of this great industry, the importance of the work done by the Rogers brothers in East Granby from 1843 to 1846 should not be overlooked. Modest in its origin and almost forgotten in the passage of the years, it was, as a matter of fact, of inestimable value.

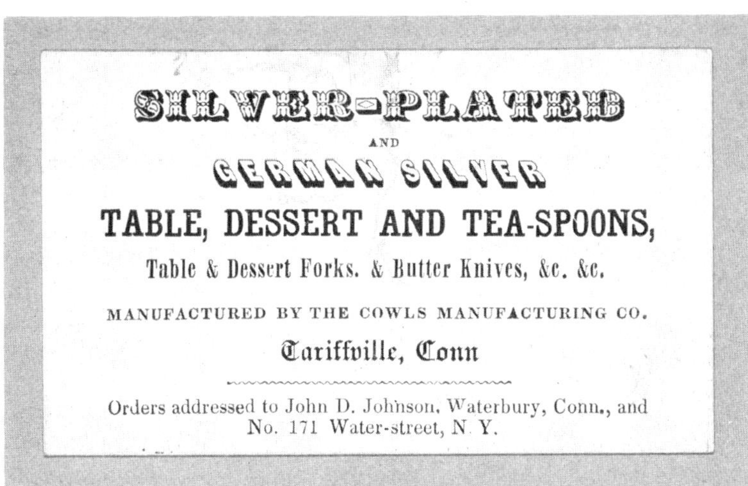

15

Return to Copper Hill

APPROXIMATELY 7 miles from Spoonville, near the northwest corner of Turkey Hills, another manufacturing community developed during these years. It was on the Copper Hill and the workers were convicts.

The ruins of Newgate Prison had remained undisturbed for eight years after the burning of the buildings near the end of the Revolutionary War. Then in 1790 the General Assembly acted to reopen this "public gaol and workhouse," and again the prisoners were to pay their way, if possible. Instead of mining copper, though, they were to make wrought-iron nails for sale.

The crimes for which men were to be incarcerated were the same as in 1773: burglary, robbery, counterfeiting, forgery, and horse stealing. (Arson and rape were added in 1792.) The term for a first offense was to be no more than three years and for a second, no more than six years. A third offense and burglary or robbery involving violence or a dangerous weapon meant life imprisonment. Three overseers, a keeper, and a guard of no more than ten men were to manage the institution.

The overseers reported to the General Assembly in December of 1790 that their workmen had removed the rubbish from the caverns and built two new rooms within them. The first, near the bottom of the old ladder shaft, could accommodate about a dozen prisoners, they wrote. The second, which could hold twenty or more prisoners, was lower and on a steep descent, so the wooden floor was built in steps. Along the walls were bunks with roofs and sides of heavy planks. Each bunk contained berths for a number of prisoners.

Above ground, the workmen had cleared away the overgrowth and charred rubble and erected new buildings. An engraving made by counterfeiter Richard Brunton about 1800 while he was a prisoner at Newgate shows the reconstructed prison yard. The building near the center of the engraving was called the guardhouse. It was of brick and had two rooms at the rear for the guard and two in front for the keeper and his family. These were at ground level with a garret above. Two trapdoors in the floor of the guards' rooms provided the only access to an area called the "stone prison" (later called "the jug") underneath. One opened into an infirmary and the other into a smaller "passage room." In the floor of the passage room was the heavy, iron-sheathed trapdoor that covered the old ladder shaft leading down to the caverns.

Engraving of Newgate Prison by counterfeiter Richard Brunton

The building shown to the right and in back of the guardhouse is the workhouse or nail shop where as many as thirty-two prisoners at a time made nails at eight forges. The three smaller buildings in clockwise order are a blacksmith shop, a bakehouse, and a coal house.

The prison yard was somewhat less than half an acre. Around it was a picket fence made of posts 10 inches square and 11 feet long, topped with 5-inch iron spikes at 3-inch intervals. Brunton shows a large gate, wide enough to admit carts and carriages.

At the whipping post, a guard applies a lash to a prisoner's naked back. Up to ten lashes at one time was the punishment for not performing assigned work, for disobeying orders, insulting or abusing the jailors, carrying or concealing a weapon, quarreling with other prisoners, stealing, and for cutting restraining irons. A reduction in food and solitary confinement in the dungeon with only bread and water to eat and drink were other punishments.

All the prisoners in Brunton's engraving are fettered. When Edward A. Kendall visited Newgate in 1807, he watched the shackled prisoners as they came out of the caverns at 4 o'clock in the morning. He wrote:

They came in irregular numbers, sometimes two or three together, and sometimes a single one alone; but, whenever one or more were about to cross the yard to the smithy [workhouse], *the soldiers were ordered to present in readiness to fire. The prisoners were heavily ironed and secured both by handcuffs and fetters and, being therefore unable to walk, could only make their way by a sort of jump or a hop. On entering the smithy, some went to the sides of the forges where collars, dependent by iron chains from the roof, were fastened around their necks, and others were chained in pairs to wheelbarrows.*

The engraving shows some of the more tractable inmates working in the prison yard. They were allowed to work under guard outside the prison walls, too, and neighboring farmers frequently hired them to labor in their fields. Richard H. Phelps in *Newgate of Connecticut* writes that when one of these "better sort of convicts" had saved enough change, he might persuade a guard to cross the street to Viets Tavern with him. There both could enjoy themselves at the bar.

These outings away from the prison afforded opportunities for escape, and even the prison itself with its spiked palisade and 14-foot-deep ditch behind it was not secure. At least eight men escaped from it before 1800.

The prisoners helped to tear down the fence in 1802 and build a 12-foot high wall of hewn stone, which increased security and enlarged the prison yard to ¾ of an acre. Phelps writes that the prisoners were allowed to join in the celebration when the wall was completed. According to him, one of the prisoners offered this toast: "Here's to Lieutenant Barber's great wall. May it be like the walls of Jericho and tumble down at the sound of a ram's horn." (A Lieutenant Calvin Barber was the contractor in charge of building the wall.)

The walls did not tumble down—at least not while there were prisoners at Newgate—but neither did they discourage all attempts to escape. Turkey Hills' Dan Forward was the hero of an uprising that occurred about the time the wall was built. All the guards except Forward were sick, and he was carrying on alone with occasional help from men in the neighborhood. One evening two of the convicts attacked him as they were about to go down the ladder shaft. As Phelps tells the story:

> *He* [Forward] *was a robust, stout fellow, over six feet high, and always ready for any contest; and instead of retreating, he returned their compliments, taking one by the neck and another by the heels, and dashing them down into the shaft upon the rest, who had now begun to come up. The neighbors hearing a scuffle at the prison, ran over to his assistance; but their aid was unnecessary, as Forward had vanquished his foes and turned their course into the dungeon. It is very likely that all could have escaped if Forward had betrayed the least sign of fear, or had resorted to any other mode of persuasion.*

Newgate's overseers reported regularly to the General Assembly, and from time to time the legislators appointed committees to investigate conditions at the prison. Their reports usually concurred that the prisoners' food and clothing were adequate. At the recommendation of a committee in 1810, rice, fish, and fresh vegetables in season were added to the regular rations of beef, pork, bread, potatoes, peas, beans, and cider. They suggested that the allotment of winter clothing—one woolen shirt, one woolen short coat, a pair of pantaloons, and shoes and socks when judged necessary by the keeper—should be increased. They considered the summer clothing—two tow cloth frocks and two pairs of trousers—sufficient. An extra shirt in winter and shoes and stockings for both seasons were added soon after.

The committee regretted that they did not find the prisoners clean. "They have no accommodations for bathing and are universally filthy and afflicted with vermin." The overseers responded that the prisoners' "shirts, summer frocks, trowsers, and stockings are shifted and washed once in each week and are boiled in strong lye made of ashes, which effectually destroys the vermin." They felt this would eliminate the problem "were it not for the frequent recruits from the county prisons." The General Assembly ordered the overseers to provide suitable bathing places for the prisoners. Still, a later committee reported that some prisoners who appeared to love filth were inclined never to change their clothes or wash their bodies.

The inmates complained of the dampness, the fleas, and the darkness in the caverns. Committee members admitted that water dripped from the rocks and fleas inhabited the straw in the prisoners' berths. One committee concluded on the positive side: "As to the total darkness, it tends to incite terror, one great object of punishment, and will operate to prevent the commission of crimes."

These advisory committees agreed the prisoners had adequate blankets and clean straw for their berths. They felt the caverns were temperate and the prisoners generally healthy. The fact that only a few died while at Newgate supports this last conclusion.

The most general afflictions noted were swollen legs and tumors "which frequently become running sores." The committees attributed these to "obstructed perspiration occasioned by want of cleanliness and by damp lodgings, the wearing of shackles about the legs, the constant confinement of the prisoners every day in the year and through the day at their blocks, and their employment which requires them to stand on their feet the greater part of every day."

A foremost concern of the overseers and the legislative committees was that the prisoners had to be lodged together at night. As a result, they said, the prisoners had

Newgate Prison and Viets Tavern

too much time alone between checks by the guards to plot uprisings and escapes.

One well-plotted attempt to escape in 1800 failed. The plan was to make keys to all the locks on the leg chains that secured the convicts to blocks in the workhouse. At a given signal, the prisoners were to unlock their fetters, overpower or kill their jailors, plunder and burn the buildings, and then escape with weapons and loot.

Making the keys was the most ingenious part of the scheme, and at that the prisoners were successful. They took impressions of the locks with soft, damp bread. Then at night, using a sharp piece of metal, they transferred the impressions to smooth pieces of pine boards. The keys had to be of metal, so they secretly collected pewter spoons and buttons. Heat to melt the pewter before casting it in the pine molds was not readily available in the caverns. The prisoners overcame this problem by smuggling pork from their rations along with flint and steel into the dungeon. When they burned the pork in metal cups, the heat was enough to melt the pewter they held in iron spoons above it. Although the keys were made and successfully tested, they were never used, because the plot was discovered shortly before the prisoners were to carry it out.

Three brothers, experienced key makers who, it was said, could open the door to any store in New Haven, almost succeeded in a similar attempt to escape a few years later. At a given signal, about thirty prisoners in the nail shop unlocked their fetters with pewter keys the brothers had made. In the ensuing struggle with the guards, a prisoner was shot through the head. The bloody sight so unnerved the other would-be escapees that they gave up.

The fact that all the prisoners had to sleep in the dungeon meant that first offenders and hardened criminals were thrown together indiscriminately. The following is a typical report to the General Assembly on the subject:

There can be no doubt that at least in some cases, compunction soon follows the commission of the crime, and the offenders repent and might under suitable treatment be reformed. In this frame of mind, he is sent to Newgate for a short period and thrown into a most execrable dungeon and amalgamated with a gang of the most corrupt, depraved, and incorrigible wretches that ever disgraced the human form. The consequence naturally and almost necessarily follows that every remnant of virtuous feeling is soon obliterated and all susceptibility of good impressions wholly destroyed.

He finds no discrimination between himself and the vilest offenders with whom he is incarcerated and amongst whom it is impossible for him to exist unless he manifests and cherishes the most infernal disposition. Thus neophytes in sin placed in this school of iniquity soon become confirmed and inveterate villains and after one or two years apprenticeship under the most accomplished instructors, are let loose to prey upon the community a thousandfold more depraved than before their confinement.

The General Assembly responded to recommendations from committeemen and overseers by periodically appropriating money for additions to existing buildings and for new ones. By 1806 there were three new buildings: a combined kitchen and hospital, an "upper prison," and a larger workshop.

Even with a kitchen, the prisoners continued to cook their meat at their forges. Edward A. Kendall observed them:

I found the attendants of the prison delivering pickled pork for the dinner of the prisoners. Pieces were given separately to the parties at each forge. They were thrown upon the floor and left to be washed and boiled in the water used for cooling the iron wrought at the forges. Meat had been distributed in like manner for breakfast.

Since the new hospital freed the underground infirmary, prisoners could stay there after they finished their daily quotas of work and before they went into the caverns at sundown. Some could sleep there, too. The upper prison had separate cells; but because they were not secure, the building became a storehouse.

Even the larger workshop was inadequate a year later when there were forty-four prisoners with more expected. There was a need, too, for other occupations with appropriate work places.

Making nails had not proved profitable for a number of reasons. The iron rods from which the nails were made were expensive compared to other raw materials such as wood, and they had to be hauled in wagons from Salisbury, Canaan, and Litchfield. The prisoners, either through ineptness or carelessness, wasted almost half of the rods. (At one time the state paid each man a penny for every pound of nails he produced over his quota. This incentive was discontinued because it "induced them to slight their work and to steal nails from each other at the forges.") Finally, the introduction of cut nails seriously lessened the market for wrought nails. To meet the need for more occupations, the prisoners helped to add a cooper and cabinetmaker's shop, a shoemaker's shop, and a wagon shop.

In 1815 they also built the chapel that has been mentioned. This was a large room with an arched ceiling and seats for 250 people. Outsiders often attended services there.

In spite of these additions, a year later the legislators commissioned plans for a new penitentiary just north of the Viets Tavern with forty-six cells to accommodate ninety-two inmates including women and paupers. Men convicted of less serious crimes would have been imprisoned there, while more hardened criminals would have been confined at the old prison. The lawmakers rejected the proposal, primarily because of the estimated cost, $35,000.

When the Democratic-Republicans came into power in 1817 as champions of the underdog and supporters of social and economic reforms, Newgate was a natural target for their attention. They soon ousted the Federalist overseers, including Samuel Woodruff, and replaced them with members of their party, including Reuben Barker. They also dismissed keeper Charles Washburn, the husband of Andrew Hillyer's daughter Betsy. Although the changes were obviously political, the new legislators justified them as a move to improve conditions at the prison.

They also appointed a committee to suggest different work for the prisoners and plans for altering or erecting buildings. At the committee's recommendation, they enlarged the guards' quarters and the stone prison under them. In 1824 they added a four-story building at the rear of the prison yard. This included berths for fifty convicts. For the first time Newgate had female prisoners and a cell was set aside for them. Three were committed for adultery; a fourth for killing her husband with an axe.

With the additional room in the stone prison and the new building, at last no prisoner had to sleep in the caverns. Still, some prisoners preferred to sleep there, and counterfeiter William Stuart explains why in his autobiography:

We chose those lower huts in the summer for sleeping because . . . we could digest our plans unmolested. The loudest cry could not be heard above the ground, as the upper surface of the shaft was closed by a trapdoor fastened from above. We would pick up tallow in the daytime and carry it down to give us light in the pitchy darkness that overspread the vast cavern. Some nights were spent in gambling, others in fiddling and dancing, others in arranging schemes to obtain our liberty, and others in devising plans to punish that world by whose arbitrament we were excluded from the enjoyment of life.

The prisoners' work was diversified further. Reports to the General Assembly in the early 1820s classify them as nailers, blacksmiths, shoemakers, coopers, wheelwrights, machine makers, stonecutters, basket makers, tailors, plow makers, sawyers, wagon makers, and knife makers.

In 1823 the legislators appropriated $3000 for a treadmill so that the prisoners could grind grain for use at the prison and for sale. Holt and Owen's gin distillery at the Center was a customer. To turn the millstones, about twenty men at a time had to tread the horizontal flanges of a wheel, which was 20 to 30 feet long. A man worked for ten minutes and rested for five. The prisoners abhorred running this stepping mill, because it required severe physical exertion and was very tedious.

Even with the diversification of work, income at the prison did not meet expenses. The average annual deficit was about $3800 for the first twenty years and increased to over $7000 in succeeding years. Even the treadmill was not a financial success.

A legislative committee appointed in 1824 and reappointed in 1825 concluded that Newgate would always be a heavy expense to the state. Furthermore, the members of the committee were extremely critical of conditions at the prison. Echoing past committees, they denounced the confinement of prisoners together at night where they were "allowed an intercourse of the most dangerous and debasing character." Under the circumstances, they said, the prison became a school of criminality rather than reform.

They reported that the prison was overcrowded, since the number of convicts had doubled over a period of three years as new laws sent men convicted of additional crimes

Engraving of a typical treadmill, published in 1824

such as manslaughter to Newgate. (There were 124 inmates as of May 1824.) They felt "the respectable class of our citizens" who believed the notoriety of the prison deterred crime were mistaken. As proof, committee members noted that nearly one-fourth of the inmates were at Newgate for a second time.

The buildings, they said, were old, dilapidated, and insecure. The "night rooms" with their poor ventilation and vermin of various kinds were "excessively offensive and loathesome."

They [the buildings] *are obviously no part of any entire design, but seem to have been erected and altered and amended and patched, at the whim of the various keepers. . . . In this way, the place has become insensibly a thing of shreds and patches, and so much abounds in nooks, and corners, and bye places, and weak points, that almost every facility seems to be furnished for secrecy and escape. A force of twenty-two persons, which is the present number, and which is a larger guard than is maintained at any other prison in New England, seems here scarcely sufficient to restrain and coerce the prisoners.*

They reminded the legislators that the original reason for selecting the copper mine for a prison had been the caverns. These were no longer used except as punishment, and the committee felt that for humanitarian reasons, they should never be used again on a regular basis.

The General Assembly accepted the committee's recommendation that the prison be moved to another location, and they voted to build a new one at Wethersfield. It was to be patterned after the state prison at Auburn, New York. Many states were considering prison reform at this time, and the penitentiary at Auburn was regarded as a model of security and economy. There each prisoner was confined in a separate cell at night. During the day convicts worked together at productive employment, but in complete silence.

Some local people strongly objected to abandoning the prison in Granby. Anonymous letters to the editors of Hartford's papers—presumably from these people—

insinuated that Martin Welles, a member of the legislative committee, was not impartial in his recommendation that the prison be moved to Wethersfield, his hometown. There were also letters of support for the move such as one that appeared in the *Courant:*

> *I observe that the commissioners on the state prison have been repeatedly attacked in the* Hartford Times *for something which is said to be wrong in relation to that subject. . . . The fact is this prison at this location has long cost the state some eight or ten thousand dollars a year, and these Granby people were engaged in a most bitter quarrel with each other as to who should have the privilege of picking this great state bird—she has been a rare bird to them—and now when this source of emolument is to be removed and this drain upon our treasury stopped, there are a few there who are ready even to tear in pieces any man who has been active in the removal.*

Others besides those who worked at Newgate and those who supplied food and raw materials for its operation were upset over the move. People in the area found the prison a convenient shopping center, for it resembled to some extent a modern mill outlet where all the products and services of the prisoners were for sale to the public. The prisoners received some of the income from the sales. Richard H. Phelps remembered that they were allowed to work for themselves and for others after their daily assignments were accomplished: "A little cash or some choice bits of food from people in the neighborhood procured many a nice article of cabinet ware, a good basket, a gun repaired by the males, or a knit pair of stockings by the female convicts."

Evidently counterfeiter-engraver Richard Brunton could be engaged to paint portraits. The Connecticut Historical Society owns two by him. One is of Reuben Humphrey, a keeper at the prison while Brunton was held there, and the other is of Humphrey's wife, Anna.

The prisoners also made wooden and metal knickknacks to sell to the many visitors to Newgate. The overseers estimated that in 1810 an average of not less than 450 persons visited the prison monthly. It was the practice to admit visitors at all times for a fee, which was divided among the keepers and officers.

A last attempt at escape ended in death the night before the prisoners moved to Wethersfield. Convict Abel N. Starkey was sleeping in the dungeon at his own request. When a guard heard a loud noise from the caverns, he went below and found Starkey dead at the bottom of the well shaft. Starkey had attempted to climb up the shaft with the help of a rope attached to a bucket used for drawing water. When the rope broke, he had fallen into the water below and the bucket had struck his head. The guard found that the hatch over the well shaft had been unfastened. It was common information that Starkey had $100, but there was only $50 on his body. The missing $50 was evidently the bribe he paid his accomplice to open the hatch.

Local men took the remaining convicts to Wethersfield under armed guard in 1827. Handcuffed and fettered with those considered most dangerous chained to the timbers of wagons, they formed an unforgettable procession for the people who gathered along the way. Memories of this event have been passed from one generation to the next so that local people still speak of the day the prisoners left Newgate.

Mining Again

In 1829 rumors spread through the area that someone was planning to reactivate the old copper mines. Members of the Viets family reported that a William Dubois of New York had approached them about leasing the mineral rights to almost 600 acres of their land along the Copper Hill. Some of the Griffins and the Phelpses confirmed that they were about to lease the old Samuel Higley mine and land around it off Holcomb Street to Mr. Dubois. When queried, Granby's town clerk, Thomas Holcomb, said John O. Pettibone of Simsbury was the man to ask about the rumors since he had just bought the prison property, 5 acres that included the prison yard and the caverns.

John Pettibone said yes, he and attorney Dubois and George Bacon, also of New York, were going to ask the General Assembly to charter the Phoenix Mining Company at its next session. He and his partners had already sent samples of copper ore to three companies in England and to a Thomas Humphries in New York to be assayed, and the returns were encouraging.

When skeptics asked Pettibone why he thought he could make the mines profitable when no one had been able to before, the reply was that advances in geology, metallurgy, and chemistry that could be applied to mining and smelting would make a big difference. The new steam engines would make it easier to pump water out of the mines and to crush and smelt ore. Also, the new Farmington Canal, which ran only a few miles from the mines, would be an asset in transporting raw materials, copper ore, etc. Why, he concluded, there was even something new called safety fuse that promised to take most of the danger out of blasting.

Pettibone added that he planned to recruit miners from Europe. While awaiting them, the company would collect the ore that was lying on the surface. If it were sufficient, the partners would erect a crushing machine immediately to prepare it for smelting. They might smelt the ore at the mine, or they might send it to smelters in Taunton, Massachusetts, or even to Swansea, Wales.

People had reason to be pleased with John Pettibone's plans. Activity on the hill always had brought employment and an outlet for raw materials, food, and other provisions. Reactivating the mines would be a boon to local families.

The General Assembly chartered the Phoenix Mining Company in May of 1830, and its directors appointed Richard Bacon of Simsbury their agent to supervise the mining operation. Miners started working a year later. A few were local men, and perhaps fifty came from England, Ireland, Wales, and Germany between 1831 and 1836.

Extant records of the company do not tell the quantities of ore that were mined and smelted. George Viets was probably only one of a number of men who hauled ore to the Farmington Canal. His account book shows that he took about ten tons between 1832 and 1834. Richard Bacon wrote in a letter to two directors of the company in November of 1833 that the mine had produced an estimated 1000 tons of ore, which, he felt, should yield 10 percent copper if properly smelted.

Bacon went on to say that with the new steam engine, it would be possible to smelt ore at the mine, something the company had not done before. He recommended building a smelting works near the Farmington Canal and using water power, which he thought would be more economical than steam. Also, a works at the canal, he wrote, would eliminate the expense of hauling raw materials such as coal, iron, lime, and wood from the canal to the mine.

Bacon predicted that with an additional investment of $20,000 to $30,000, the company could build twenty furnaces and smelt the 5000 to 10,000 tons of ore that would be available annually if all the old mines were reopened. (This would include the Higley mine, the mines at the prison site, and the North Hill and Castine mines about a half mile northeast of the prison.) He concluded that unless the business was expanded, the company would only justify the public's opinion that it was engaged in a wild and foolish enterprise.

Although most of Bacon's suggestions were not implemented, the company evidently did smelt some of the ore. Richard H. Phelps wrote that the directors "expended many thousands of dollars in digging extensive levels, building furnaces, and constructing engines and machinery to facilitate their operations in raising, pounding, and smelting the ore."

The company ceased operation in 1836, primarily for financial reasons. To raise money the directors had sold stock for a small down payment with the understanding that they would call for additional installments as needed. Even though stockholders had to pay their installments within sixty days of notification or forfeit their shares, the arrangement invited speculation, and it did not produce the necessary operating capital or any capital reserve. A number of stockholders defaulted when the company did not pay a dividend after a year or two of operation, and the directors had to borrow money periodically to pay the company's debts. The country-wide depression that began around 1836 was a final blow to the mining venture for the time being.

The end of the mining operation left Richard Bacon with time to pursue a new, albeit related, enterprise, the making of the new safety fuse. William Bickford of Cornwall, England, had patented safety fuse in 1831 and had begun to manufacture it shortly thereafter. He twisted layers of textiles such as jute and cotton yarn around a core of black powder and dipped them in a waterproofing material such as tar. The result was fuse that burned more slowly and predictably than the goose quills filled with powder that were used at the time.

Bacon went to Cornwall in 1836 and became the American agent for Bickford's company. To keep the price of fuse as low as possible, it was decided to build a manufactory in Simsbury and to incorporate Bacon, Bickford & Company, predecessors of Ensign-Bickford. Bacon became the manager of the new company, which was the first to manufacture safety fuse in the United States.

The parent company sent over ten casks of fuse after Bacon visited Cornwall. John E. Ellsworth speculates in his history of the Simsbury firm that much of this first shipment was used by the Phoenix Mining Company at Newgate. It is possible that Bacon made fuse at the mine while a factory in Simsbury was being built. True or not, when this first factory burned in 1839, Bacon did manufacture fuse at the copper mine while building a new one.

Like most of his contemporaries, Richard Bacon pursued more than one occupation at a time. He farmed, he managed Bacon, Bickford & Company, and he soon returned to mining.

The Phoenix Mining Company took some ore from the mines in 1845 while Bacon was negotiating for additional mineral rights and the outright acquisition of more prop-

Interior of mine at Copper Hill

erty on the Copper Hill. A year later he became the sole owner of the prison property after he recovered judgment against the company for $2,335.25. George Bacon and John O. Pettibone continued their financial backing until the early 1850s when they sold their interests to Richard Bacon.

Bacon operated as Richard Bacon & Company until 1855 when he and Ezra Clark, Jr., of Hartford founded the Connecticut Copper Company. Besides the Newgate property, they had a mill and ore house on two acres of land west of 38 Copper Hill Road. The new Farmington Valley Railroad, which ran along the west side of the property, provided convenient transportation.

No records remain of the Connecticut Copper Company to show how extensive the operation was, although an extant list of the company's personal property gives some indication:

One twenty-horse engine and two boilers with furnace; one ten-horse engine, chimney stack and cistern; two steam gauges; one stamp battery of twelve heads with cam shaft gear, driving pulleys, shafts and ore pit [to crush the ore]; *one elevator with iron buckets and shafting; two pairs of mill stones with driving gears, conveyors, and other machinery connected therewith* [also to crush ore]; *one elevator with tin buckets; two circular screws with shafting and pulleys; one flat screen with shafting and two launders* [wooden water troughs used to wash ore] *with screens; two distributing tubs with gearing, shafting, etc; ten separators with fixtures* [for separating the copper ore from the rock]; *100 feet of shafting with pulleys, etc.; belting from 2 to 12 inches in width connected with shafting.*

The company also had iron "heating pipes" for warming the mill, 100 tons of Cumberland coal, a pair of Fairbanks hay scales, and a variety of hand tools.

The Connecticut Copper Company operated for only a few years before it, too, failed. Dr. E. Francfort of Middletown, Connecticut, examined the mines at this time and submitted a detailed report to the company. He states emphatically that although the rock was rich in copper, the way in which Clark and Bacon were preparing the ore for smelting was "entirely erroneous." Francfort enthusiastically assured the owners that if his instructions for dressing the ore were followed, the mine would become one of the most valuable known.

Dr. Francfort's suggestions were never carried out, and the mines were abandoned again. The reasons probably included two familiar ones, the scarcity of money and inadequate or misapplied technology. N. H. Egleston wrote in 1886: "The discovery of the larger and richer deposits of copper of Lake Superior rendered the working of the Simsbury [*sic*] mines unprofitable."

An observation of one historian may hold more truth than humor. He concluded that mining at Newgate was doomed because the ore in the caverns was as refractory in nature as the men who had been imprisoned within them.

Verces Made Upon Newgate Prison

The court in fact have passed an act in 1790
Old Newgate to repair.
And those that break the peace must make
Their grim appearance there.
Bound in a chain they must remain.
And this must be their fate:
With hammer and tongs make good the wrong
Those wretches do the state.
Down in this den those guilty men
Will groan in sad despair
And curse the day that ever they
Was doomed to enter there.
Being void of light, eternal night
In those dire regions rein,
While rocks and stones will wrack their bones
And torment them with pain.
Unwholesome damp their limbs will cramp,
Their faces pale as ashes;
Their inward part will also smart
When guilty conscience lashes.
Hunger and thirst they suffer most,
And when the lice previel,
Then they with skill will learn to kill
And crack them with their nails.
God grant that I may strive and try
In wisdom to excel.
And shun with horror that place of sorrow,
That true emblem of hell.

A grim picture of the prisoners' lot in Newgate was graphically described by this old poem of unknown origin which appeared in the Windsor Locks Journal *of June 29, 1900. Whitney D. Viets, proprietor of the prison at the time, had sent a copy to the* Journal *hoping to publicize the prison further as a tourist attraction.*

16

Fortune and Misfortune

REAL PROPERTY continued to be the principal measure of wealth for the people of Turkey Hills. They lived during a time when business investments often yielded poor returns, paper money was unreliable, and specie was scarce. The federal government and the states minted coins, but not in sufficient quantity to meet demand. Yeoman's *A Guide Book of United States Coins* estimates that there were fewer than one United States coin per person in the country in 1830.

The federal government did not issue paper notes until 1862. Banks issued them, backed by their own deposits of gold and silver, but since these institutions were not regulated closely by any government, the value of their notes was not stable. Historians have estimated that by the 1860s there were perhaps 7000 kinds and denominations of legal notes plus thousands of counterfeit ones throughout the country.

Barter and credit continued to be the foremost means of exchange among local people. In their dealings with each other, they settled accounts either with cash or personal notes every few years. Since they used the notes as currency, a personal note might pass from one person to another until the death of either the owner or the signer of it when, hopefully, the estate could collect or pay the debt. A single business transaction often took many years to complete.

The third Isaac Owen was one of the area's most prosperous men. When he died in 1816, his estate valued at $116,500* included $324.50 in silver coins and $23,453 in personal notes. Owen was one of a small number of local men who could be considered as a moneylender or financier. They had the means to invest in personal notes, home mortgages, real estate, and businesses. The names of these men appear frequently in land and estate records. Most of them were commercial farmers and storekeepers, although blacksmith David Latham was among them. When banks were few and at a distance, these men played a vital role in the community's economy.**

*In 1792 the federal government made dollars and cents the country's official monetary units. For the ordinary man, the changeover from pounds, shillings, and pence was gradual and probably difficult. It was not until 1815 that Richard Gay, used dollars and cents consistently in his account book, and not until 1857 that the Congress withdrew legal tender status from the monies of other countries.

**Note at foot of next page

44 Hatchet Hill Road

Some commercial farmers accumulated large land holdings during these years. First of all they needed acreage for planting and grazing. By now any public land that all men had once used belonged to individuals, but for a few years there was a common field of privately owned parcels of land that included much of the Windsor Half Mile and extended north into Suffield. In 1782 the owners of this area of more than 3½ square miles formed an association to arrange for its fencing so they could pasture their animals within it.

Men like Isaac Owen also bought land as a legacy for their children. Owen lived on South Grand Street, south of Stony Brook, in Suffield. His home was one of the twelve farms he owned in Suffield, Windsor, and the Turkey Hills section of Granby. His eleven children inherited these and the farm at 56 East Street on which he held a mortgage.

Owen acquired some of his farms from the emigrants who left the area, and Levi Pinney did the same at the southeast corner of Turkey Hills. His 380-acre homestead lay west of South Main Street and ran from north of Hatchet Hill Road south to the Farmington River. On the land were four houses, two of which are still standing. One is at 27 and the other at 44 Hatchet Hill Road. Both these houses were probably built in the 1760s. The first has not been changed a great deal. The second has been added

**The Hartford National Bank was founded in 1792. An article in the *Courant* of July 6, 1819, announced the establishment of the Savings Society of Hartford, the first savings bank in the state. "The design of this institution is to afford those who are desirous of saving money the means of employing it to advantage without running risk of losing by lending it to individuals, who by misfortune or fraud, pay neither interest or principal. No sum above $200 will be received in the course of any one year. . . . This is because the object of the institution is to aid and assist the poorer and middling classes of society in putting their money out to advantage."

105 Newgate Road

to and remodeled periodically. The house at 30 Tunxis Avenue is built over the foundation of a third one that belonged to Pinney. When he died in 1805, his estate was divided among his six sons and two daughters.

By this date a few Holcomb families owned much of the land along Hartford Avenue that once had belonged to Sergeant John Griffin. Samuel Clark held title to hundreds of acres of Griffin's Lordship along Holcomb Street. He lived in the Ezekiel Phelps house at 38 Holcomb Street, and his homestead extended from Turkey Hills Road to Hartford Avenue. It was only part of the 680 acres he acquired before his death in 1827. Clark's nephew Horace Clark at the Center accumulated over 500 acres through inheritance and purchase, and his sons Elmore, Charles P., and Samuel A. continued to farm the property after he died in 1842. On North Main Street, the heirs of John Holcomb, Richard Dana Gay, and Lemuel Bates worked their ancestral acres for another 100 years or more.

At Copper Hill the descendants of Thomas Stevens, Henry and Captain John Viets, and Nathaniel Griffin redistributed the land among themselves through purchase and sale, intermarriage and inheritance. Some of them farm there today. (John Christian Miller's land went to Thomas Stevens, Jr.)

As this pattern of accumulation and division repeated itself throughout the parish, homesteads became smaller. An agricultural survey from the 1850 census lists fourteen men in Turkey Hills with more than 200 acres of land. In 1860 there were only eight; in 1870, six. At the same time professional men, storekeepers, artisans, and other entrepreneurs, who could support themselves on smaller plots of land, inserted homes and work places between those that already stood along the dirt roads. Farmers, too, built

61 North Main Street

new houses, and men of all occupations modified older ones in the latest architectural styles.

Many of the early houses of this period were of Federal architecture. The Federal Cape at 105 Newgate Road with its large central chimney was probably built at the end of the 18th century, perhaps in 1798 for Luke Viets, Jr., and his bride, Abigail Phelps.

The house Whitfield Cowles built after 1802 at 118 Spoonville Road is Federal with a central entrance hall that originally ran from front to back. Instead of a massive central chimney, there are twin interior brick chimneys between the front and back rooms on either side of the hall. This home is still owned by one of Mr. Cowles' direct descendants. (Major exterior additions such as the front porch, entry portico, side veranda, and pillars were done early in the 20th century.)

The Federal house at 61 North Main Street also has a central hall and twin interior chimneys. This was built for Orson P. Phelps in 1814. Horace Clark recorded in his daybook that he worked at framing the building. He charged $1.25 a day and "victualled" himself (provided his own food).

The farmhouse at 81 North Main Street is an interesting combination of the old and the new. It was built around 1827 for Edmund Bidwell on the site of the Samuel Forward house that is shown on the 1732 map of Simsbury. The back ell is much older than the main part of the house. The newer part originally had a central chimney similar to those in colonial homes, but its gable end—rather than its long side—is toward the street. This is a characteristic of the new Greek Revival architecture that Turkey Hills builders were adopting at the time.

There are eleven Greek Revival homes on South Main Street alone. The tops of their gables usually have full pediments that enclose tympanums with lights of various designs. The front entry is usually in the gable and with only a hall and one room facing the street. The house at 152 South Main Street, built by Lemuel Bates for his son Zophar about 1795, is typical.

The new style of architecture inspired men to remodel their homes, sometimes making it difficult to date them precisely. For example, in spite of the Greek Revival details of its entryway, the house at 62 Rainbow Road was probably built by Nathaniel Mather, Jr., before 1785. At 74 South Main Street, carriage maker Edward P. Thompson seems to have added the portico to his older house at the same time he built the large Greek Revival addition. Across the road at 99 South Main Street, it is obvious that Edmund Thompson, Jr., added the portico with its Doric columns and pedimented gable to his Georgian home during this period.

In contrast, the unusual Greek Revival house at 121 Spoonville Road with its twin symmetrical wings seems to be a completely original structure. There was an older house on the property, but it was not incorporated into the newer one.

The distinctive stone house at 119 Turkey Hills Road was built by George Viets for his son George W. in 1843. The date is verified by an entry from that year in John J. Viets' letter book: "Uncle Geo. has finished the stone work of the new house."

Greek Revival gave way to Victorian architecture in the second half of the 19th century, and the balloon frame made of two-by-fours gradually displaced the post and beam frame. The houses at 281 Hartford Avenue and 192 Holcomb Street are examples of early Victorian architecture. The first, a brick house, is of the Italian villa style with its low-pitched roof that is almost concealed by a wide overhanging cornice supported by sawn brackets. The arcaded columns of the side entry porch are also Italianate.

John Boyle, a native of Ireland, built this brick house between 1850 and 1855. Boyle was a superintendent over the Irish immigrants who laid the railroad tracks through town at that time. He had come to Southwick, Massachusetts, in 1826 to work on the construction of the Farmington Canal and its extension to Northampton, first as a laborer and then as a contractor. He left Granby in 1857 to continue his work in railroad construction throughout the East.

According to Edgar Seymour, Henry L. Holcomb built the Gothic Revival house at 192 Holcomb Street in 1858. Its sharply pitched roofs and decorative bargeboards that cover the end rafters of its gables are characteristic of this early Victorian style. Seymour's grandfather Chester Seymour bought the house in 1860 and the family lived there for the next 105 years.

These newer houses had smaller chimneys for the stoves that were displacing fireplaces, which had been used up to this time for heating and cooking. In other ways, too, homes became more comfortable and housekeeping much easier than it had been before the Revolutionary War.

Personal Property

Estate inventories show that floors, usually of bare wood or even of earth in colonial days, now had rag rugs and carpeting. (Imported rugs had always been available, but they were rare in Turkey Hills.) Women wove their own carpets, using homespun yarn and yarn from nearby mills such as Joel B. Clark's at Rainbow. Thrifty housewives

152 South Main Street

62 Rainbow Road

121 Spoonville Road

119 Turkey Hills Road

281 Hartford Avenue

192 Holcomb Street

saved worn-out clothing, blankets, and linens to weave into rag rugs. Commercial carpeting became available from mills like the New England Carpet Company, which owned the Tariff Manufacturing Company mill for a time. The factory was making about 132,000 yards of carpeting a year by 1839.

People now had more and a greater variety of chairs, tables, chests, desks, mirrors, and other furniture. Glassware, stoneware, crockery, earthenware, and chinaware appear more frequently in inventories than do the once predominant woodenware and pewter. The number of spoons, knives, and forks increased. The newer containers and implements of durable, lightweight tin plate were a decided improvement over those of wood, iron, and other metals.

Oil lamps and lanterns succeeded pine knots and grease lamps. People still used candles, and many housewives continued to make them even though they were now available at stores. Similarly, families continued to make soap, but stores did sell it.

An inventory of merchandise in the new general stores is impressive considering that only a few years before these conveniences and necessities had to be made by hand locally or imported at great expense. Most were from Connecticut's new, small manufactories and some were available for the first time. Among the items mentioned in John J. Viets' letter book are many different kinds of yard goods, sewing accessories such as buttons, ribbons, lace, tapes, thread, papers of pins and needles, hooks and eyes, bodkins and thimbles, elastic garters and suspenders; jewelry, gloves, handkerchiefs, socks, veils, shawls, cravats, collars, corset lacers, hats and hat boxes; brushes and knives of all kinds; shaving cream, razors and razor strops; iron, wood, and horn combs; cologne and soap; pocketbooks and wallets; key rings, watch keys, spectacles and sunglasses; toothpicks; boxes for snuff, tobacco, and jewelry; carpet bags and umbrellas; pocket rulers, pens, pencils, crayons, pen holders, and India ink; letter paper and reams of wrapping paper; scrapbooks, account books, numerous almanacs, and other printed books; garden seeds, tinware, thermometers, hand tools, padlocks, and fish hooks; lamps and oil for lamps, carpeting, stove blacking, friction matches, washboards, mop handles, twine, shears, candles, tablespoons, and teaspoons; rheumatic plasters and corn plasters, patent medicines, snuff, and laudanum; sleigh bells, whips, toy watches, Jew's harps, flutes, and harmonicas; fire crackers and percussion caps.

The availability of cotton and woolen material from nearby mills enabled most families to give up the hard and tedious chore of making linen by the 1830s. Some people continued to raise sheep and spin and weave woolens for another decade or more.

Women continued to sew for their families even though they could now buy ready-made clothes and household linens. Seamstresses and tailors were still on hand for people who preferred custom-made apparel. Both Elmore Clark and Alfred Gay, who lived at 123 North Main Street, patronized a tailor by the name of Morse. Gay wrote in his diary: "Went to Tariffville to get Morse to cut a coat and vest. Paid 75¢. Bought trimmings of Viets. Paid $5. Got Mrs. Achsah Moore of Spoonville to make them. She charged $2.25."

Gardens and orchards yielded a greater variety of food. Diaries and account books now mention celery, lettuce, peppers, tomatoes, sweet corn, and onions. Men added peaches, cherries, rhubarb, quinces, grapes, currants, and plums to their orchards and farmyards.

Fish was one of the few foods families had to buy if they wanted it in any quantity after the early 1800s. Each spring they bought lamper eels and shad to preserve in salt. In the early 1820s Horace Clark could buy shad for 12 cents and eels for 3 cents apiece. He might buy 230 eels and 50 shad in a season. Alewives, clams, and oysters were also available.

As winter set in, Clark's cellar might contain a dozen fifty-gallon barrels of cider, bushels of potatoes and turnips, plus barrels of salted fish, pork, and beef, and smaller quantities of beets, carrots, squash, onions, apples, cabbages, pumpkins, dried beans, nuts, and popcorn. Families without cellars or with smaller ones stored their winter food in root cellars. It was during these years that local men began to harvest ice and pack it in straw and sawdust in icehouses for use in warm weather.

Families enjoyed esthetic improvements in their homes as well as the new creature comforts. Local and itinerant artists decorated inside walls with stenciling and primitive paintings. A bedroom in the house at 99 South Main Street has willow trees and coral red flowers stenciled on its gold walls. The work is signed "L. W. Langdon." There is a basket of fruit stenciled on a black background over the fireplace mantle in the parlor. An unknown artist once painted a picture on the wall above a fireplace in the house at 2 Old County Highway.

Eunice Griswold Holcomb Pinney, a granddaughter of Captain John Viets, was a self-taught primitive painter whose work has gained national recognition. Mary Black calls her "the most skilled and creative of the lady amateurs who painted for their own pleasure." Her first husband was Oliver Holcomb, son of Asahel Holcomb, Jr. Holcomb drowned while fording a stream on his way to Ohio, and his widow married Butler Pinney in 1797.

Eunice Pinney was almost forty years old when she began to paint, and her style reflects her maturity. Art critics describe her paintings as distinctive with originality of design, carefully balanced composition, bold lines, vigorous color, and a wide range of subject matter. More than fifty of her watercolors are owned by her descendants, museums, and private collectors.

Improved agricultural implements and methods made even a farmer's exhausting work somewhat easier during these years. In 1817 Turkey Hills men were among the founders of the Hartford County Agricultural Society whose purpose was to help farmers improve their land and the quality of their produce and domestic animals.

At the time most men prepared the soil and planted, cultivated, and harvested their crops much as their fathers, and even their grandfathers, had. A man walked behind a plow that had a wooden moldboard, covered with sheet iron or tin plate to protect it from wear and tipped with an iron share that formed the cutting edge. He evened the land with the metal teeth of a wooden harrow. He planted and sowed his seeds by hand, weeded with a hoe, harvested his grains with a scythe, and threshed them with a flail. By now men had fanning mills to winnow the seeds from the husks. They also had the new wide cradles attached to their scythes to catch the grain as it was cut so that it could be laid gently on the ground.

Cast iron plows became available during the 1820s and steel ones by 1840. George W. Thompson had a threshing machine in 1839. This was probably one of the first in town, because Elmore Clark did not use one until eight years later, and then he rented it.

Clark was one of the men who tried a cultivator—also called a horse hoe—that

John J. Viets had for sale that year. Viets observed: "Cultivators are used here by some, but not as much perhaps as in some places."

Horace Clark was enthusiastic about a corn sheller he bought in Agawam, Massachusetts, for $10.50 in 1841. In his diary he wrote: "One thing I am satisfied of fully is that I gain five bushels if not ten in a hundred in measure by using the machine."

Planters or drills, mowing machines, hay rakes, and reapers appear in records dated shortly after 1850. These machines were expensive. Men shared the few they had just as they shared hand tools, horses, oxen, wagons, and work. Machines lessened, but by no means eliminated, a farmer's hand labor.

Economic Diversity

Overall, a majority of homeowners in Turkey Hills managed to live more or less comfortably with a little money and a great deal of hard work. They bought on credit what they could not barter or pay cash for, borrowed money from acquaintances and relatives as needed, and mortgaged or sold some of their land as a last resort.

Men who did not inherit property found it hard to save money enough from their wages to buy land and a house. A farm laborer earned an average of $12 a month with board in 1850.* The following is a typical contract between a farmer and his hired man:

April 1, 1853. The subscribers made the following agreement, viz., *William Leaky agrees to labor faithfully for Walter Thrall one year from this date for the sum of $144 and the use of the house where he now lives and the use of the east part of my garden the same as occupied the last year, and said Thrall agrees to give the same for such services as rendered. Leaky boards himself Sundays and does his own washing.*

During the year Thrall deducted the cost of some food, wood, clothing, and the rent of a horse and wagon from Leaky's pay. Leaky may have stayed another year. When they balanced their account in March of 1855, Thrall owed his hired man just $10.

Landless laborers like Leaky included members of established local families, newcomers from other eastern states, and immigrants from Europe. Many moved on to larger towns and to the West. Madison Cowles wrote to his brother Sylvester at Worthington, Ohio, in 1827:

I think the prospects are not very flattering in New England for a young man that has arrived at the age of twenty-three without the knowledge of some profession or trade. Many of the young men of your acquaintance are scattered up and down the world. Some on the canal, others peddling and Ogden and Wareham Griswold are trading at Springfield on borrowed capital, or so I understand. Clytus P[inney] *is at home. Luther P*[inney] *is a contractor on the Rhode Island Canal. Chester Adams has taken the jail tavern at Hartford.*

*A female domestic at the time received an average of $1.25 a week with board. Male teachers who boarded with parents might receive $12 to $16 a month; female teachers might receive half that. Men who worked at the Cowles Manufacturing Company earned an average of $26 a month; women averaged $5 a month. A carpenter earned an average $1.25 a day. These wages were without room and board, which cost about $1.50 a week for men.

101 Spoonville Road

Some who remained in Turkey Hills did acquire property either through inheritance or purchase. Weavers Charles and Peter McKinney from Ireland built homes on 60 acres of land west of Miller Road. One of their houses stands today at 101 Spoonville Road. Peter McKinney was a selectman and a representative to the General Assembly from East Granby before his death in 1878.

Irishman Richard Milhenning built the house at 17 Miller Road, and his countryman James Holmes became his neighbor when he purchased the house at 83 Spoonville Road. Caine Mahoney, listed as a laborer from Ireland on the 1850 census, built the house that stands today as a barn at 49 Russell Road. During the last half of the century, men like Michael Kelly, Patrick Carroll, James McGarrity, James Kavenaugh, and Dennis MacNamara added their names to the town's lists of homeowners and voters.

The 1850 census lists four black families in the parish. The men are described as farm laborers except for one who is called a farmer. They had none of the inherited wealth that contributed to the prosperity of many local whites. They were not skilled craftsmen like the local artisans and the immigrants who came to work in the factories at Spoonville and Tariffville. They were at the bottom of the pay scale, yet all four families owned houses—however small—in Turkey Hills at one time or another.

Common Adversity

Poverty, sickness, and death were impartial companions to all regardless of race or nationality. Families who could cared for their indigent members, including those who were physically and mentally disabled. Sometimes they were able to send the handicapped to private institutions such as the American School for the Deaf, incorporated in 1816, and the Hartford Retreat, founded in 1824. There were no state institutions for the handicapped until the 1860s.

17 Miller Road

Towns were responsible for any of their legal inhabitants who became impoverished or disabled if their immediate relatives could not take care of them. At a Windsor town meeting in 1788, the voters decided that the selectmen should rent a house or houses for the town's poor "that an experiment may be made of the expense of supporting them together." They may have chosen a house on Hazelwood Road in the Windsor Half Mile, because by the early 1800s, a homestead there was called the Conscience Town Farm. The road was called Conscience Town Road until the present century.

Granby paid families to care for paupers in their homes, and in 1827 the town voted to establish a poorhouse. The town poorhouse was never located in Turkey Hills, but local families did house one or two paupers at a time at town expense.

The state assumed responsibility for people called "the unsettled poor," those who had no legal residence. In the 1800s the state comptroller auctioned these state paupers to the lowest bidder. The maximum payment allowed by the state under an 1821 law was 50 cents per week for anyone under fourteen years of age and a dollar for anyone over fourteen.

For thirty years or more, state paupers lived in sheds behind the houses at 5 and at 27-29 North Main Street. They were all ages with a variety of physical and mental disabilities. Census records show that in 1860, thirty-seven, ranging in age from two to 100 years, lived at 5 North Main Street. Seven of them were insane; one was blind.

The prevention, diagnosis, and treatment of disease were still relatively primitive so that illnesses were more frequent, of longer duration, and more likely to be fatal. Families continued to raise herbs for medicinal purposes, and now they could buy any number of commercial medicines. John J. Viets sold bitters, usually an alcoholic liquid made with herbs or roots and used as a tonic. Horace Clark's account book contains a recipe for Stoughton Bitters:

Take ½ lb. of bitter orange peel, ½ lb. of ginseng and ½ lb. of red sanders [sandal wood], *or as much as is necessary to get it the proper colour. Steep the above in French brandy till it is fit to use.*

Mr. Viets also stocked cathartic and camphor lozenges and ones labeled for coughs, worms, and dysentery. He had itch ointments, croup and cough syrups, and rheumatic salves for headaches and catarrh. Laudanum was available over the counter.

Doctors continued to bleed or cup their patients. They dispensed pills, applied mustard plasters as poultices, and recommended "sweats" or "spirit vapor baths" over burning alcohol to rid the body of whatever might be causing an illness. Operations are not mentioned in extant local records. Local doctors still pulled teeth, but people also went to dentists in nearby towns to have their teeth filled, cleaned, pulled, and replaced with false ones.

Diaries attribute deaths to dysentery, numb palsy (paralysis), canker rash (ulcers in the mouth), bilious colic, smallpox, cholera, dropsy, erysipelas, heart disease, cancer, and lung fever or consumption. Some women and many infants died at the time of childbirth. Children succumbed to croup, scarlet fever, mumps, and measles. Sometimes two or three in a family died within days of each other. There were accidental deaths from falls off wagons and high beams in barns, from gunshot wounds and explosions in nearby powder mills. Drownings in the Farmington River were not uncommon.

To meet the need for more burial grounds, the Holcomb family opened a cemetery on Hartford Avenue and Copper Hill families established one on Griffin Road.* A number of families subscribed three dollars apiece to purchase land that is now the north half of the old cemetery at the Center. (The second Isaac Owen had deeded the south half to the Turkey Hills Ecclesiastical Society in 1770.) They divided the property into plots and assigned them among themselves. In succeeding years men of the community bought palls and a hearse and built a small structure at the Center Cemetery to house the hearse.

Drunkenness affected every family in the parish at some time. The first temperance unions were formed early in the 1800s as people recognized and acknowledged that the excessive use of alcohol was a social problem. The Reverend Stephen Crosby organized the Turkey Hills Youth Temperance Society around 1830. Its sixteen charter members pledged that they would

abstain from the use of distilled spirits, except as medicine in case of bodily hurt or sickness; that we will not allow the use of them in our families, nor provide them for the entertainment of our friends, or for persons in our employment, and that in all suitable ways, we will discountenance the use of them in the community.

Elmore Clark was the president of either this or a similar organization in the 1840s. He wrote in his diary on October 13, 1844: "I this day declared I would drink no more spirit or wine only in sickness. I hope I shall stick to it."

*There are nine known graveyards in East Granby: Center Cemetery, Holcomb Cemetery, Copper Hill Cemetery, Elmwood Cemetery on Nicholson Road, Viets Cemetery opposite Newgate Prison, prisoners' cemetery behind 165 Newgate Road, the smallpox cemetery off Hatchet Hill Road, Beth Hillel Memorial Park, and the Hartford Mutual Society Memorial Park, these latter two off Wolcott Road.

The Congregational Church continued to excommunicate men and women for drunkenness. At the trial of Horace Phelps, his wife testified that she lived in fear her husband might kill her when he was drunk. Her only recourse, she said, was to hide from him in some place such as the barn. A witness testified that he saw bunches on her head "which she said were occasioned by her husband's swinging her round the house so as to raise her from the floor by the hair."

It became easier for women and men to free themselves from an unhappy marriage after 1843 when the General Assembly added habitual intemperance and intolerable cruelty to the grounds for divorce. Legislators had provided for divorce early in the colony's history, and they actually granted four between 1636 and 1665. For over 150 years, though, the only grounds were "adultery, fraudulent contract, willful desertion for three years with total neglect of duty by the other party, or in case of seven years' absence of one party, not heard of."

Chloe Viets Barker took advantage of the new law to divorce Reuben Barker, Jr., in 1843. Their divorce may have been only the second one in Turkey Hills. Addison Harger had divorced his wife two years earlier, presumably on grounds of desertion as she had left him over three years before.

Because people were dependent on their crops for food, the weather was a constant concern. Men noted each day's weather in their diaries and read the forecasts in their almanacs as faithfully as they had once read their Bibles. Each growing season brought the threat of crop damage from hail, wind, frost, drought, and excessive rain. Floods damaged more than crops. Elmore Clark recorded that on April 17, 1854, there was a severe snowstorm and the brooks rose to new heights:

Oats not sown, fences not mended, feed cattle as in winter, and now we are drowned out. I have 1½ feet of water in my cellar. The Connecticut River is higher than it was in 1800, what was called the Jefferson Flood. Scotland and Tariffville bridges are gone, and I hear that nearly every bridge on Salmon Brook is gone. Covered bridge at Windsor is gone.

Lightning storms took their toll of animals, trees, and buildings, and there was only a bucket brigade to fight the fires it caused.

Horace Clark also appreciated the gifts of nature. Each year he recorded the arrival of the individual species of birds, the greening of the different trees, and the blossoming of the various flowers. The longest and most eloquent entries in his diary are often about unusual weather conditions:

June 16, 1806. Total eclipse of the sun. In the time of the greatest observation, the dew fell, hens went to roost, the whippoorwill sang his morning song, the cock crowed as for day, and finally everything wore the appearance of a new day.

III

The East Granby Years

After the incorporation of East Granby

1858 -

Chronological Highlights

1858	*East Granby incorporated.*
1861-65	*Civil War.*
1882	*East Granby Creamery opened.*
1899	*Hydroelectric plant on Farmington River began operation.*
c. 1900	*First shade grown tobacco raised.*
c. 1900	*Roads first paved.*
1902	*Branch of Central New England Railway opened through East Granby Center.*
1904	*First telephones installed.*
c. 1908	*First automobile purchased by East Granby resident.*
c. 1910	*First electric lights installed.*
1914-18	*World War I.*
1922	*East Granby Library Association organized.*
1929	*Stock market crash presages Great Depression.*
1930	*East Granby Volunteer Fire Department founded.*
1939-45	*World War II.*
1951	*Housing boom in East Granby started.*
1968	*Newgate Prison returned to state control.*

17

Separation from Granby

THE CIVIL UNION of the people of Turkey Hills and Salmon Brook as the Town of Granby was never a completely happy alliance. Seven times between 1786 and 1857, Turkey Hills men unsuccessfully petitioned the General Assembly for permission to separate from Granby. Finally the legislators granted an eighth petition, and East Granby became the 159th town in the State of Connecticut in 1858.

Through the years the would-be secessionists offered different plans to reach their goal. In 1793 they requested simply that Granby be divided into "two distinct towns." In 1820 they asked that about three-quarters of a square mile along the parish's eastern border in Suffield be joined with the Turkey Hills sections of Granby and Windsor to form a new town. In a petition three years later, they omitted the Suffield area.

The Turkey Hills petitioners usually lived east of the Mountain, although a few men from Copper Hill signed in 1823. Even though most Turkey Hills men who lived west of the Mountain evidently did not want to separate from Granby, their land had to be included to give a new town a sound economic base. The petitioners were careful to assure the legislators that towns losing territory as well as proposed new towns would be of good size with large Grand Lists.

The reasons given in the petitions were familiar. The signers from Turkey Hills said they had little in common with the people of Salmon Brook. They complained of the long distance they had to travel to town meetings in the western parish and of the road over the Mountain, which was sometimes impassable.

In 1820 and 1823—but never again—a majority of the voters of Granby gave their support to the division of the town. The majority must have been small, because members of the General Assembly who recommended that the petition be denied in 1823 noted that about half the inhabitants of Granby were against it. They also concluded that the petitioners did not suffer any more inconvenience in attending town meetings than did citizens of many other towns.

Almost twenty years passed before Turkey Hills men again approached the legislators. Seventeen who lived at the northeast corner of the parish asked to be joined to Suffield in 1843. They cited their proximity to the center of Suffield and the good level road thereto, along with their close ties to the people of that town. Twenty-five Suffield men endorsed this unsuccessful petition.

At about the same time, in 1842 and again in 1851, families living east of the Mountain asked that their section of town be annexed to the Town of Windsor. In 1851 every voter east of the Mountain signed the petition. Opposition statements from the residents of Granby and Windsor bring out for the first time an economic issue—the cost of building and maintaining highways and bridges—that was central to the controversy over partition.

Windsor residents opposed the annexation in 1851 because they did not want to assume Granby's share of the expense of the Spoonville and Middle bridges over the Farmington River. (Bloomfield paid one-half of the expense.) They also feared that any increase in the size of their town might lead to its division. Even without the additional land, their fears were justified when the northern section of Windsor, including more than one-third of the Windsor Half Mile, broke away to become the Town of Windsor Locks three years later.

Roads and bridges were a major expense for Granby. The cost of building and maintaining bridges across the Farmington River and that of building new roads usually came from special appropriations. The expense of maintaining roads and building and repairing smaller bridges came from an annual highway tax, which was often as much or more than the general tax for all other town expenditures.

For various reasons Salmon Brook's highway expenses that were paid with the annual tax were greater than Turkey Hills'. Her area was almost two and one-half times that of her counterpart; and over her large expanse, she had a labyrinth of roads in contrast to Turkey Hills' four north-to-south arteries with two or three crossroads. Salmon Brook had forty or so bridges across her many miles of streams; Turkey Hills had six or fewer. Opponents of partition in 1851 informed the General Assembly that Granby would be left with thirty-eight bridges and very expensive roads, while the land to be annexed to Windsor had only one-half of two bridges and roads that could be kept in repair at little expense.

How to collect and disperse the highway tax was decided at annual town meetings where the voters of Turkey Hills were a minority. Occasionally the decision was to put the money into the town treasury and let the selectmen decide on which highways and bridges to expend it. This arrangement probably seemed unfair—and the results may have been unfair—to the people of the eastern parish, who had only one representative out of three on the board of selectmen.

In most years, though, highway surveyors collected highway taxes in their own districts either in labor (evaluated at 10 cents per hour) or in cash and applied both to the roads and bridges therein. Since Turkey Hills was usually a separate district, this system must have seemed the most equitable to its people. Antagonism resulted when Turkey Hills' surveyors collected their taxes and kept their roads in good repair, while Salmon Brooks' failed to collect all of their taxes and then requested money from the general treasury to pay their highway expenses.

Furthermore, since Turkey Hills' per capita share of Granby's Grand List was at least 50 percent* more than Salmon Brook's, her families paid a comparatively larger share of town taxes. Harold A. Pinkham concludes:

Because Turkey Hills had twice the per capita valuation of its neighboring society and required less in appropriations from the total tax levy, the Turkey Hills Society felt it was carrying the burden of Salmon Brook on its own tax shoulders. Conversely, Salmon Brook, with a less wealthy group of citizens, found itself dependent upon Turkey Hills' contribution to meet the town's fiscal requirements. With political power being determined by the size of the voting population and not by the total wealth per capita, Salmon Brook with twice the population could dominate all decisions made in the town meetings. Although Salmon Brook recognized the concept of minority representation and granted at least one seat on each town agency or committee to Turkey Hills, Salmon Brook dominated the decisions of town government.

Turkey Hills' taxpayers may have been bitter about other town expenses over which they had little or no control. For example, sometimes town funds were used to repair the Episcopal church building at Salmon Brook where town meetings were held for many years. Voters east of the Mountain resented the fact that town meetings were almost never held in their meetinghouses, which often needed repairs, too.

The 1854 law that reinstated the town property tax for education and the 1856 law that eliminated school societies fired anew Turkey Hills' determination to separate from Granby. In 1856 the town collected $315 from a school tax based on the Grand List. Of this, Salmon Brook probably contributed $183 and received $206 in return, while Turkey Hills would have paid $132 and got back $109.** Money from the state for the common schools had been distributed in proportion to the number of children in each society since 1821, but this was a new, direct tax, and its disproportionate return must have been more obvious.

The 1856 law was particularly upsetting to the parents of children in Turkey Hills' district schools. Since the end of the previous century, the two parishes of Granby had been separate school societies with autonomy over their own schools. Now a board of education, elected by the voters at large, assumed the powers and duties of the societies. These included the distribution of school funds and the formation of "rules and regulations for the management, studies, books, classification, and discipline" of the schools. Although school districts retained their traditional functions, the board could "form, alter, and dissolve" districts. Each district still chose its teachers, but members of the board had to certify them, and the board also could annul their certifications.

Through the years students from Simsbury, Windsor, Windsor Locks, and Suffield had attended the common schools in Turkey Hills. Their parents had been active in their districts and in the First School Society. Now they would have no vote in electing Granby's board of education, nor could they be members of the board.

*Per capita valuations are estimates, because exact censuses and Grand Lists from this time for the two societies are not available. No complete tax lists remain, either.

**	Estimated Grand List	Number of Children	Special Appropriation	Pro Rata Distribution
Salmon Brook	$18,000	406	$31	$175
Turkey Hills	13,000	169	36	73

John J. Viets emphasized that this latest law on education caused "unnecessary expense and delay in getting our school business transacted" when he asked the General Assembly to divide Granby in 1857. Ninety-seven men—approximately half of Turkey Hills' registered voters—supported his petition. They were from both sides of the Mountain and from all sections of the parish except the Windsor Half Mile, which was not included in the proposed town. Only a very small number of the approximately 300 men who signed a dissenting petition were from Turkey Hills.

While the General Assembly met that spring, the people of Turkey Hills had reason to believe that at last their plea for independence might be granted. The Senate easily passed a resolution incorporating the new town, but members of the House were not as compliant. They first amended the resolution, then tabled it, and finally rejected it. Both chambers subsequently reaffirmed their votes and appointed representatives to a committee of conference, who also failed to agree. Debate resumed as the 1857 session came to a close, but neither side would change its vote. East Granby was not to be for another year.

Debate in the General Assembly brought out state-wide issues not mentioned in the petitions. Opponents of the new town argued that the State Houses in Hartford and New Haven were overcrowded and that Connecticut already had an unusually large number of towns in proportion to its size. They pointed out that the House of Representatives had a disproportionate number of members from small towns, and they were unwilling to add to this rural majority, which, they felt, ignored the needs of the urban populations. If the resolution had passed, the approximately 2500 people of Granby and East Granby would have had three representatives, while New Haven's 39,000 people would have had only two.

Many Democrats in the legislature probably opposed the formation of the new town because they might lose politically if Granby were divided. Salmon Brook's Republican majority would almost certainly send two of their party to the General Assembly, while East Granby with its Democratic majority would be allowed only one representative. Since Granby had elected two Democratic representatives almost without exception every year for the previous twelve years, the Democrats would lose one vote and the Republicans would gain two.

Locally, though, political considerations were not the issue. Where a man lived was more important than his political affiliation. The possibility of gaining two Republican seats in the House did not change Salmon Brook's opposition to separation, and the possibility of losing a Democratic seat did not diminish Turkey Hills' support for it.

The Joint Standing Committee on New Towns and Probate Districts made a change in their resolution of incorporation that may have been politically motivated. On the extant resolution, the name they first proposed for the new town, "Turkey Hills," is crossed out and "Frémont" is written over it. John Charles Frémont was the presidential candidate of the new Republican Party in 1856. He won in Granby by sixteen votes and in Connecticut by a majority of over 5000, although he lost nationally to Democrat James Buchanan. The name Frémont may have been an attempt to win the support of the large number of Republicans in the legislature. One newspaper reported that the name occasioned some laughter in the General Assembly when one legislator suggested "Frémont and Jessie" might be preferable. Frémont's wife, Jessie, was a well-known, independent woman. She had been active in her husband's campaign as his confidential secretary, and her popularity had brought him votes.

Turkey Hills people did not like the name Fremont, and when John J. Viets submitted his successful petition the next year, he specified the name, "East Granby." Within the new town, he included about 2¼ square miles from the west side of the Town of Windsor Locks. This area contained the northern 1½ miles of the Windsor Half Mile, which was a part of the Turkey Hills Ecclesiastical Society. Its residents had had religious and educational ties to the parish for over 100 years.

Exactly how much opposition came from Windsor Locks is hard to determine. At a town meeting in April, attending voters agreed unanimously to give up their land if the General Assembly divided Granby. Later, opponents said that only seventeen men had attended the meeting and that sixty or seventy remonstrants from Windsor Locks had appeared before the committee on new towns. "A limited number of voters" from Windsor Locks submitted a petition against the partition, but the committee's majority report discredits it as having been circulated "by interested parties from West Granby."

The majority report recognizes complaints the people of Turkey Hills had been expressing for the past sixty-five years and more. The report acknowledges that the Mountain isolated and alienated people living east and west of it. Furthermore, voters on the west side united against those on the east to hold all town meetings at Salmon Brook. "The people in the east are compelled to submit to unjust and unreasonable burdens, in taxes and otherwise, imposed upon them by the numerical strength residing in the west society." The report cites as an example of what they considered unfair taxation the distribution of the highway tax for five years beginning in 1856 *"whereby over $1000 is to be expended on roads in the West,* and only $305 in the *East."*

The minority report accepts the distribution as fair and uses these figures to support its contention that Granby would be left with an unfair amount of highway expenses if she were to be divided. The majority report counters that it would cost East Granby almost twice as much to maintain its three bridges over the Farmington River as it would cost Granby to support its forty-seven small bridges. Therefore, "the new town will take more than its share of town expenses, but this they are willing and agree to do."

When a majority of the committee acknowledged that there were already too many members of the General Assembly, they justified their support of the new town by writing:

But they cannot feel that such a consideration should deter this Assembly from doing justice *to a portion of our fellow citizens, in a case as* clearly existing *and* strongly made out *as this by the petitioners, and being in number and wealth larger than many of the present towns of this State, and where such release or division will not injuriously affect the rights of others connected with them.*

The minority report mentions two aspects of the situation that the majority report does not address. One was the fact that there were eighty voters on the west side of the Mountain who would have to cross it to get to the center of the new town. Since many of these electors registered in favor of the division, the complaint perhaps seemed

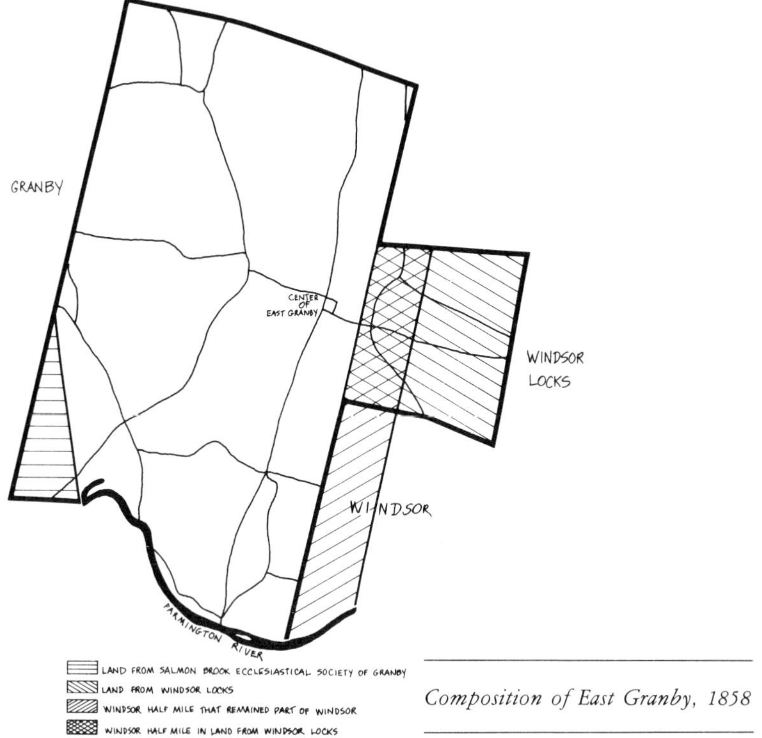

Composition of East Granby, 1858

irrelevant to the majority. The anticipated tax relief evidently outweighed the inconvenience of getting to town meetings. Henry L. Holcomb may have spoken for other large property owners who lived west of the Mountain when he admitted he supported the separation only because he felt it would decrease his taxes. (At least one man who lived west of the Mountain changed his mind within a few years. Jeremy H. Holcomb of 135 Hatchet Hill Road and other unnamed men unsuccessfully petitioned the General Assembly in 1865 "to make the Town of East Granby, or a part thereof, a part of Granby.")

Another objection in the minority report is that the Farmington Valley Railroad would be entirely in East Granby, "which if of any advantage, would principally accrue to the new town." The quote suggests that whether a railroad went through a town or a few yards outside its borders might be relatively unimportant. The minority report does not mention the copper mine or the factory at Spoonville, probably because they were so unprofitable as to be negligible.

The General Assembly incorporated the Town of East Granby as of June 2, 1858. It encompasses most of the Turkey Hills Ecclesiastical Society plus some land from the Salmon Brook Ecclesiastical Society along its western border. The town's eastern boundary is the same as that of the original Town of Granby with the addition of the aforementioned land from Windsor Locks, which includes the northern part of the Windsor Half Mile. The southern section of the Half Mile, which was also a part of the Turkey Hills

Ecclesiastical Society, remains a part of the Town of Windsor. (In 1873 Windsor men who lived there petitioned the General Assembly to annex this part of the Half Mile to East Granby. The petition was denied.)

Besides setting the boundaries, the articles of incorporation made the new town a part of the third senatorial district and of the probate district of Granby, empowered justices of the peace residing therein, and provided for the division of assets and liabilities. The people who remained in the Town of Granby found consolation in section eight, which specifically states that East Granby "shall hereafter forever maintain a good and sufficient bridge, at the sole expense of said town," across the Farmington River, northwest of Tariffville. This costly bridge had never ceased to be a bone of contention between Granby and Simsbury, and the people of Granby were glad to relinquish responsibility for it.

Entries in Elmore Clark's diary convey the excitement that pervaded Turkey Hills in the spring of 1858. Clark went to the legislative session in New Haven four times between May 12 and May 20. On the last day, he recorded: "I came from Hartford to Windsor Locks and then home. Was sent for to come back to New Haven about 4 p.m. Carried I. P. Owen to Hartford and we went to New Haven. Six of committee in favor and three against new town." When the time came to celebrate on June 3, though, his practical side prevailed. He recorded that his two hired men went to the "new town celebration" while he "attended to" the crows that were eating his corn in the fields.

Lighted windows, waving flags, torchlight parades, ringing church bells, booming cannon, and marching bands were a part of political celebrations by 1858. After the many years of anticipation and disappointment, there can be no doubt that most of the residents of East Granby celebrated the birth of their town with appropriate exuberance.

18

The Civil War

EAST GRANBY held its first town meeting a scant week later, on June 9, 1858, in the basement of the Congregational meetinghouse. Some of the traditional offices of the new town, such as hayward and fence viewer, were already becoming obsolete, and after 1888 the few still considered necessary were filled not by election but by appointment by the selectmen. Most of the remaining elective officials are familiar today: town clerk and registrar of vital statistics, treasurer, agent, selectmen, assessors, school visitors (board of education) with a school fund treasurer, constables with one designated a tax collector, grand jurors, registrars, auditors, and a board of relief (board of tax review).

The town's new officials in 1858 and 1859 were involved in negotiations with Granby and Windsor Locks over responsibility for paupers, distribution of town debts and deposit funds, and boundary lines—particularly the one between Granby and East Granby. These local and relatively minor disputes soon paled before the national crisis that threatened the country—the Civil War.

Unlike their forefathers who answered the call to Lexington in 1775, most of the men in East Granby were not prepared to take up arms in 1861. Few had attended a training day since 1847 when the militia had been divided into two classes, the active and the inactive. Only a few men enrolled in the active branch; instead, most paid a fee, called a commutation, which exempted them from duty.

The Civil War was not as popular as the Revolutionary War had been. Whereas Turkey Hills had its Loyalists in 1775, they were a minority. A majority of East Granby's voters in 1861 supported the Democratic Party, which opposed the war. The town never gave a majority of its votes to President Abraham Lincoln or to Connecticut's Governor William A. Buckingham, both members of the Republican Party, which supported the war.* Nor were the voters of East Granby alone in their opposition. Many people in Connecticut felt the war was a mistake for economic, political, and even moral reasons.

*A man who had lived in Spoonville as a boy during the war recalled years later that officials had come looking for a young man from Germany who was a draft evader. The townspeople knew the German was hiding on the island near the Spoonville factory, but they did not betray him. When the boy asked his mother why their neighbors had lied about the man, she replied, "We are good Democrats who are in sympathy with the South."

Buckingham's majority in 1860 was a slim 531 out of over 88,000 votes cast, and Lincoln's was less than 2500 out of over 87,000 in 1864 even though a Northern victory seemed assured by then.

The people of East Granby had personal reasons for opposing war with the South besides the obvious one that war is horrifying—and a civil war particularly so. Many local people had close relatives living in the South, and some had made friends there while trading, especially peddling. The South also provided a market for local manufactured and agricultural products. Democrat Richard H. Phelps wrote in December of 1860 just before the Confederate States seceded:

It is astonishing that our Northern friends cannot realize the comparative helplessness and ruin of our business interests there, when the great South becomes a separate nation, holding free trade with Europe, the slave trade revived in full operation with no conservative check upon it by this nation or any other. Then we will see the practical result of the sickly, sentimental philanthropy of the slavery abolition party—a party which has thus far served the positive purpose of tightening the shackles of the slave, the more they have abused the South. The financial result of all this, the nation already begins to feel to their sorrow in the stoppage of Northern manufactures, in the diminished market for the produce of every farmer and in a depreciation of the price of produce and property throughout the nation of hundreds of millions of dollars.

The complicated issue of slavery, with its economic and moral implications, is considered by most historians to be the principal cause of the war. Through a series of laws beginning in 1774, Connecticut provided for the gradual abolition of the institution within its borders and made it increasingly difficult for people to participate legally in the slave trade. The number of slaves in the state decreased from 2759 in 1790 to 310 in 1810 to seventeen in 1840. National censuses show five slaves in Granby in 1800 and none in 1810 and thereafter. The General Assembly finally outlawed slavery in 1848.

Most Northerners, both Republicans and Democrats, were not abolitionists, but they did feel that slavery should be confined to the states where it already existed. Supposedly the extension of slavery into new territories in the West was settled by the Compromise of 1820. At the time Maine was admitted as a free state and Missouri was authorized to adopt a constitution with no restrictions on slavery. The remainder of the Louisiana Purchase, the land north of 36° 30', was to be forever free.

The annexation of Texas in 1845 and the War with Mexico (1846-48) added territory where slavery was economically practical and raised the issue again. Both the annexation and the war were unpopular in Connecticut. Fewer than 700 Connecticut men served in the Mexican War; six were from Granby, but none from Turkey Hills.

The Compromise of 1850 settled the question of slavery in some of the territory acquired as a result of the war. California was to be admitted to the Union as a free state. Utah and New Mexico were to be organized as territories with their voters to decide the question at a later date. Slave trade, but not slavery, was to be outlawed in the District of Columbia.

As part of the compromise, a second Fugitive Slave Act strengthened the original law of 1793. Under it anyone, even without a warrant, could take an alleged runaway slave before a federal commissioner, who had the power to decide whether or not the accused should be returned to the state or territory from which he may have escaped. The accused had no right to a trial by jury and could not testify in his own behalf. The oath of the alleged owner of the accused was to be taken as proof of guilt. Furthermore, the law set a fine of up to $1000 and a prison sentence of up to six months for anyone who helped a suspected or convicted runaway to escape and civil damages of $1000 "to the party injured by such illegal conduct."

The law added: "and all good citizens are hereby commanded to aid and assist in the prompt and efficient execution of this law, whenever their service may be required." Thus everyone was legally liable to help in apprehending a suspected fugitive. Also, since there was no time limit, no matter how long a person had been free, he or she was subject to arrest.

There were at least eighty-two blacks in Granby at the time, and suddenly the people of Turkey Hills must have thought: "Does the government expect me to help arrest my neighbors like Thomas Sharp who has lived here for twenty years?" Men who had dealt with slavery only on an intellectual level now faced it on a personal level. Perhaps as a result of the second Fugitive Slave Act, local votes for the Abolitionist Party's candidate Francis Gillette rose from one in 1845 to twenty-four in 1853. Seven years later Abolitionist Morton Cornish received average minority support when he ran for representative to the General Assembly from East Granby.

For members of the Underground Railroad, fugitive slaves had been of personal concern for many years. The late Irving Griffin said they hid in a tiny room under the floor of an upstairs closet in the house at 23 East Street. This tradition could be ignored along with the one that held that George Washington slept at the Viets Tavern except for some supporting evidence. East Granby was on a route that ran between Farmington, the center of the Underground Railroad in Connecticut, and Springfield, a center in western Massachusetts. Second, Abolitionist Morton Cornish lived in the house during these years. (A former house at 23 East Street, or perhaps the back ell of the present one, was the birthplace of abolitionist John Brown's paternal grandmother, Hannah Owen Brown.)

Connecticut practically nullified the second Fugitive Slave Act in 1854 by authorizing a $5000 fine and five years imprisonment for falsely representing a free person to be a slave and by requiring the testimony of two credible witnesses, "or its equivalent," to prove a claim to a Negro. That same year Congress passed the Kansas-Nebraska Act which allowed settlers in the new territories of Kansas and Nebraska to decide whether or not they wanted slavery. This effectively repealed the Compromise of 1820 because these territories were north of 36° 30'. The law incensed Northerners, split the Democratic Party into Northern and Southern factions, and led to the death of the Whig Party. It also inspired the birth of the Republican Party, which opposed the extension of slavery but did not advocate its abolition. The *Courant*, a Republican newspaper, summed up the feelings of Republicans and many Democrats in the North after Abraham Lincoln's election in 1860:

The success of the Republican party in the late election has definitely settled one thing — that a majority of the people of the United States are opposed to the extension of slavery over our territories. It has settled nothing else. . . . The existence of slavery in the sovereign states, much less its forcible expulsion from them, was not an issue in the election.

Most Northerners, then, were not ready to go to war to abolish slavery in the South, and perhaps not even to prevent its extension into the West. They were willing, though, to fight to keep the country intact after the secession of the southern states. Connecticut's House of Representatives gave its support to the war "not for conquest or subjugation, nor for the purpose of overthrowing or interfering with the rights of any State, but to defend and maintain the supremacy of the Constitution and to preserve the Union with all the dignity, equality and rights of the several states unimpaired."

To prevent the South from permanently seceding from the United States was the reason Sidney H. Hayden, the son of Oliver and Jane Owen Hayden of 56 East Street, enlisted in the Northern army in 1862. Furthermore, his extant letters emphasize that he was fighting "to support the Constitution of the U.S." and "to put down treason," not to free slaves.

On the Home Front

Hayden's letters show that the division in his hometown over the war was sometimes bitter. Even the churches were affected. Methodist ministers had been outspokenly anti-slavery for a long time. The Reverend Theodore A. Lovejoy left the Copper Hill church in 1862 after members of his congregation asked him not to preach on political matters. Rather than comply, he asked for and received a transfer to another church.

As a result of political dissension in the Congregational church, voluntary contributions were insufficient to pay the minister, and he had to be supported largely by the Connecticut Home Missionary Society. Hayden wrote in response to a letter from his mother, a member of this church:

I think that at the end of the war there will be the end of slavery and then people will get through harping on that evil that has caused so much disturbance and bloodshed. Certainly there will be no need of saying anything about it in the pulpit.

Women of the local Soldiers' Aid Society met at the Congregational church. They rolled bandages, sewed and knitted clothes, and collected food for the soldiers. Donations like these from every town in the state were an invaluable contribution to the war effort. Virgil Cornish, brother of Morton, was an agent of the Soldiers' Aid Society, stationed in Washington, D.C. He carried food, supplies, and mail to Northern soldiers in the South.

East Granby residents shared in the state's overall economic prosperity during the war. The market for the wool of their sheep increased when cotton was no longer available from the South. Besides the usual civilian need for cloth, the military needed large quantities for uniforms and blankets. The former Cowles factory at Spoonville was one of the many mills converted to the manufacture of shoddy, an inferior cloth made from used woolen materials.

As men moved to nearby towns and cities to work in busy factories, the market there for farm produce grew and prices rose. Tobacco prices also increased as Southern tobacco disappeared from the market.

Sidney Hayden wrote enviously of the men who "stay at home and get big prices for tobacco. Everything is lovely and we three-year-chaps get $13 a month and board ourselves." He scorned radical Democrats, called Copperheads, who advocated peace at any price and potential draftees who left town or paid money to avoid military service.

There was no need for a draft when President Lincoln called for volunteers in the spring of 1861 shortly after the bombardment of Fort Sumter. Men in the North were eager to put down what they considered a rebellion that would be over in a few months. When the rebellion soon turned into a full-scale war requiring an ever-increasing number of recruits, the federal government called upon each state to supply its share.

Connecticut's General Assembly in May of 1862 enacted legislation to register and draft, if necessary, all men with certain exceptions between the ages of eighteen and forty-five. Each town would have a quota to be filled by volunteers or draftees. Republican Governor Buckingham with the support of prominent Democrats initiated statewide recruitment rallies. Caught up in the pervading patriotic fervor and attracted by a bounty of $100 from the town, seven East Granby men volunteered; Sidney Hayden was one of them. They were mustered into the 16th Connecticut Infantry.

When Governor Buckingham threatened to invoke the draft if quotas were not met, the town raised its bounty to $225 for men who volunteered for nine months and $325 for those who volunteered for three years. Twenty-four additional men enlisted from East Granby.

Congress passed the first federal Conscription Act in March of 1863. Again, each town had its quota to fill. Most physically able married men between twenty and thirty-five and unmarried ones to forty-five were subject to the draft if volunteers did not fill the quota. A draftee could pay a commutation of $300 to avoid one draft call, or he could buy a substitute and be exempt from all drafts.

These loopholes for those who could afford them helped to make the law extremely unpopular, and avoiding the draft became serious business. Draftees bought questionable medical exemptions, and many, including at least one East Granby man, fled to Canada. Individuals donated money to help recruit volunteers, and towns gave money to residents who were drafted and did not want to serve so they could pay a commutation or buy a substitute. Towns also hired substitute brokers to find nonresident replacements. Substitutes had only to reside in a town a short time to qualify as part of the town's quota. They came from the cities, from Canada, and even from Europe and received as much as $1000.

Hiring a substitute pleased the drafted man because he did not have to go to war. It pleased the town because it helped to fill the quota, and it pleased the substitute because he received money for enlisting. It did not, however, please the army. Substitutes who enlisted only for the money were often of questionable character. Most were poor fighters who cared little for the Union cause. Some became bounty jumpers who enlisted in one town, received a substitute's fee, and then deserted from the army. Later they would appear in another town and enlist as a substitute again.

East Granby, like most towns in Connecticut and in the rest of the North, was the scene of at least some of these activities. By the time of the first federal draft in

1863, nearly all the local men who were able and willing to serve had already volunteered. Of the eighteen men who enlisted to fill the town's quota in 1863, the name of only one person appears in East Granby's census records or on lists of local voters and resident volunteers. In the same year blacks became eligible for service, and five of the eighteen were Negroes.

Only one of the thirty-nine volunteers from East Granby during the first two years of the war deserted, and he was the only one who was not a bona fide resident of the town. During the last three years, forty-two men enlisted. Of these, thirty-eight were nonresidents, and seventeen of the thirty-eight deserted.

In all East Granby paid over $10,000 to procure men to fill its quotas before the General Assembly outlawed town bounties because they feared the municipalities might go bankrupt. East Granby had to borrow most of the money paid for bounties, but the fact that the town was able to repay this debt by 1869 shows the economy was good.

At the Battle Front

Although East Granby's soldiers did not participate in many of the largest battles of the Civil War, smaller engagements took a heavy toll in men killed, wounded, and captured. President Lincoln's military strategy had three objectives. One was to blockade and capture Confederate ports in the South; a second was to take Richmond, Virginia, the seat of the Confederate government; and a third was to gain control of the Mississippi Valley. Local men fought in all these theaters of the war.

Since the South was dependent on supplies from Europe, control of her ports was crucial. Twenty men from East Granby belonged to artillery batteries that participated in attacks on coastal cities throughout the war.

The heaviest fighting involved attempts to capture Richmond. Northern forces launched a costly and unsuccessful offensive against the city in 1862. After forcing the Union army under George B. McClellan to retreat from the Richmond area, Robert E. Lee took his Confederate troops into Maryland, hoping for one big victory that might convince the North to give up the fight. The two armies met in the Battle of Antietam on September 17, 1862, the most costly single day of the Civil War when over 25,000 men fell dead or wounded.

For the seven East Granby infantrymen in Connecticut's 16th Regiment, this bloody battle was a gruesome initiation to war. After only twenty-three days in the army—eighteen of them on a forced march across Maryland—these men were thrown into the fight, untrained and only partially equipped. One East Granby man was among the many wounded in the heavy Confederate fire that broke up the regiment and forced its retreat.

Sidney Hayden's letters describe the shock and suffering of these raw recruits:

September 20, 1862. We were ordered into a cornfield to support a battery and the Rebels got close on us. Many dropped by my side and bullets, shells, and grape canisters came thick as hail. It is an awful sight to see so many young men slaughtered and crippled, but it is so.

September 26, 1862. Our company is much diminished by sickness and death, having left Hartford four weeks ago with 98 well men and now numbering only 26 fit for duty. It is affecting to hear the names of letters for the dead read in our company when the mail arrives.

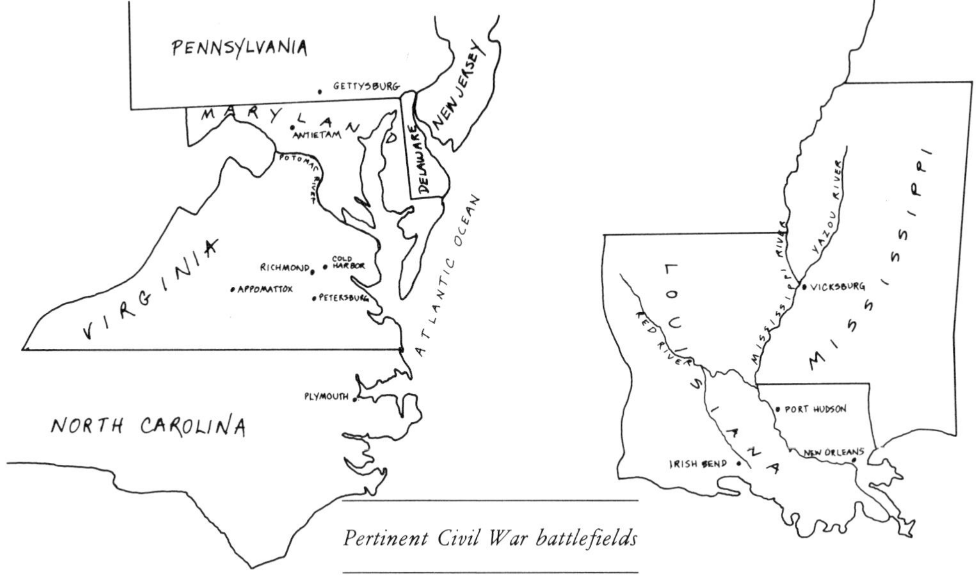

Pertinent Civil War battlefields

Boys that marched shoulder to shoulder day after day by my side in defense of their country, but their marches are over in this world and their spirits have fled.

Neither side won a decisive victory at Antietam, but the battle did end Lee's invasion of the North. This bit of good news made it an opportune time for President Lincoln to announce his Emancipation Proclamation, granting freedom on January 1, 1863, to all slaves in Confederate territory. The last sentence of the Emancipation Proclamation reads: "And under this act, sincerely believed to be an act of justice, warranted by the Constitution upon military necessity, I invoke the considerate judgment of mankind and the gracious favor of Almighty God."

Lincoln did not get the considerate judgment he desired from the many Northerners who were shocked at the proclamation, which, they felt, ended all hope of reconciliation with the South. In the gubernatorial election in the spring of 1863, Governor Buckingham narrowly won over radical Democrat Thomas Seymour, who ran on an anti-draft, anti-abolition, anti-war platform.

Luckily the news from the Mississippi River front was good that summer. Union commanders Ulysses S. Grant and Nathanial P. Banks planned to attack Confederate forces in the river valley from the north and south simultaneously. Grant was to lead his troops south towards Vicksburg, while Banks moved north from New Orleans. Grant laid siege to the crucial river forts at Vicksburg and by cutting their supply lines, starved the Confederates into surrendering on July fourth.

Meanwhile Banks led a poorly executed advance up the river. With him were twenty-five East Granby infantrymen, twenty-four of them in the 25th Connecticut Regiment, and Richard E. Holcomb, formerly major of the 13th Connecticut and now colonel of the 1st Louisiana, a Union regiment of volunteers. Banks took these men and others on an expedition into Louisiana's heartland where the untried 25th were thrown into the center of an unsuccessful and costly assault at Irish Bend.

From Irish Bend, Banks immediately led his men northeast to the Confederate fortress at Port Hudson. A siege similar to Grant's at Vicksburg was in order, but instead Banks ordered two hopeless attacks on the Confederate entrenchments. Colonel Holcomb was killed on June 14 as he tried to rally his men during the second attack. A month later Port Hudson surrendered, largely because the Confederates could not maintain themselves after the fall of Vicksburg. One-third of East Granby's men in the 25th were casualties of these assaults; three died and five received wounds.

Union victory did not come for almost another two years. In 1864 the conflict turned into a war of attrition, a slow diminution of Southern resources. The Confederacy was forced into a defensive trench warfare, which slowly drained its supplies of food, clothing, munitions, and men.

The South desperately needed to break the coastal blockade that kept it from receiving supplies from Europe. Connecticut's 16th Regiment was among 1600 Federal troops holding the port of Plymouth, North Carolina, on April 17, 1864, when 10,000 Confederate soldiers attacked. In spite of the odds against them, the small band of defenders fought off infantry and artillery attacks for three days before surrendering.

Sidney Hayden and two other East Granby men, Robert J. Holmes and James Odey, were among those captured and sent to prison camps in the South. Lewis Sanford Porter, an East Granby soldier whose company was detached from the regiment at the time, wrote to the Haydens:

The Rebs made six or seven distinct charges upon our works but were repulsed each time excepting the seventh charge when they carried our works. The report is that our men mowed the Rebs down like minnows. . . . Finally it got to be pretty hot work. Our men fought them hand to hand as much as an hour. Finally General Wessells was obliged to surrender the place.

Robert H. Kellogg, sergeant major with the 16th Regiment, wrote about the siege:

The place [Plymouth] *was defended with the utmost gallantry, but one redoubt after another was carried by assault, until on Wednesday morning, April 20th, it was evident that our troops could hold out but a few hours longer. The attempt of the rebels to carry the town by a grand assault in the gray of early morning had been partially repulsed; but they had forced their way into the streets fronting the river, and now from the houses in our rear poured upon us a hot fire. Completely surrounded and exposed to a trying cross-fire, every fort in possession of the enemy except Fort Williams or the citadel, the position of the Union troops was now desperate. All demands for surrender had thus far been met with steady refusal by Gen. Wessells. After the last flag of truce from the enemy had returned to their lines, bearing a refusal to the demand for surrender, a tremendous fire of musketry and artillery was opened on the Union line, and the rebels with their characteristic yells were now swarming through the streets of the town, pouring into the camps and pressing every advantage with the confidence of victory near at hand.*

It was at this juncture, with every hope of escape destroyed, that the color-guard of the Sixteenth, at the extreme right of the line, sheltered from the enemy's fire behind an artillery platform, shouted to Lieutenant-Colonel [John H.] *Burnham, who was in command of the regiment, to know what should be done with the colors. The reply came, "Strip them from the staff and bring them here." To tear each flag from its staff was the work of a moment, but who should carry them through that pelting hail of bullets? It required brave men, and they were not wanting. Color-Sergeant Francis Latimer took the national color, and Color-Corporal Ira E. Forbes the State flag, and crossing the most exposed part of the field under a heavy fire, safely delivered them to Col. Burnham. . . . The strips of the flags, torn into shreds, were distributed among the members of the regiment, and concealed in various ways through the weary days of their imprisonment in Andersonville, Charleston, Florence, Salisbury, and other prison-pens.*

By now Ulysses S. Grant had become commander of all Union forces and had begun to coordinate a final, relentless campaign to take Richmond. Six East Granby infantrymen participated in an attack June 3, 1864, against an entrenched Confederate army at Cold Harbor, Virginia, where 7000 Union soldiers fell in one hour. Gone were the early days of the war when infantrymen fought in open fields. Now soldiers defended their positions from the protection of trenches, which helped them repel attacks by numerically greater forces and inflict greater losses than they themselves incurred.

From Cold Harbor, Grant moved his army to Petersburg, Virginia, a vital Confederate rail junction just south of Richmond. After a boggled assault on Lee's army, Grant resigned himself to an extended siege of the city. Eighteen recruits from East Granby were among the Northern troops who lived and fought under horrible conditions in the trenches around Petersburg for the next nine months. Eleven of the eighteen were blacks.

Lee's army barely survived the winter of 1864-65. There were few supplies coming to Petersburg by this time, and the North was winning its war of attrition. With his army reduced to a skeleton force, Lee made a last desperate assault on the Union trenchworks in late March of 1865. After it failed he abandoned the city, and Union forces occupied Petersburg and moved on to take Richmond. Dogged by Grant's army and still fighting, Lee moved west to Appomattox where he surrendered on April 9. The Confederate army in North Carolina surrendered on April 26, and the Civil War was over at last.

Of the nearly 3,000,000 soldiers in the war, 623,000 died and 500,000 were wounded. The high death rate was due in part to inadequate care stemming from a lack of medical knowledge and a shortage of equipment and facilities. More men died from wounds and disease than were killed outright on the battlefield. Three East Granby men died in battle; ten died off the battlefield.

The number of casualties suffered by local soldiers attest to their participation in some of the bloodiest battles of the war. The following statistics compare their losses with estimates of those of the Union army as a whole:

	East Granby	Union Army
Number killed	1 out of 27	1 out of 65
Number wounded	1 out of 9	1 out of 10
Number captured or missing	1 out of 10	1 out of 15

Sidney Hayden was a prisoner of war for eight months. He spent five months at the infamous Andersonville, Georgia, camp where shelters consisted of ragged, makeshift tents and food was scarce and malnutritious. Thousands of men were crowded into 27 acres of land, much of it swampy. Consequently, disease swept the camp, and as many as 127 men died in a day.

All three local prisoners of war survived their captivity. Shortly after he was exchanged, Sidney Hayden wrote:

December 17, 1864. Our regiment has suffered terribly, and I fear many more will as but a few have been paroled. There were 400 men captured out of which 170 have died or been murdered by the treatment received at the hands of their "Southern Brothers." I have been fortunate to have had good health during my confinement in prison.

During the winter Hayden served out his enlistment in Maryland. His letters are filled with plans for his future in East Granby—plans he never realized. He returned home in March, but on April 4, 1865, he died of typhoid fever.

Shortly after the end of the Civil War, the 13th Amendment to the Constitution of the United States abolished slavery, and the 15th Amendment, ratified in 1870, gave blacks the right to vote. Connecticut changed her general statutes to eliminate the word "white" from qualifications for voters at town meetings in 1871. Five years later she amended her constitution so that no potential elector could be disqualified because of color.

On Battle-Flag Day, September 17, 1879, 8000 of Connecticut's Civil War veterans carried the flags of their regiments from the State Arsenal in Hartford to the new capitol on Capitol Avenue where they remain today. (A public referendum had designated Hartford, rather than New Haven, the sole state capital four years before.) The color-bearer of the 16th Regiment, which had torn up its flags rather than surrender them at the Battle of Plymouth, carried a new flag of white silk. At its center in the shape of a shield surmounted by an eagle are the remnants of the original flags that the captured soldiers were able to preserve during their ordeal as prisoners-of-war.

19

To the End of a Century

IN THE YEARS following the Civil War, East Granby became solidly established as an agricultural town in a state that was becoming more and more industrialized. The population of the town declined from 853 in 1870 to 661 in 1890 as families continued to move to the cities and to the western part of the country. Among those who remained in the community, the number of storekeepers, millers, artisans, and other small entrepreneurs declined. New businesses appeared periodically, but overall the decrease continued as farming became still more the principal occupation.

Farmers adjusted their crops and livestock in response to a changing market as railroads brought in certain commodities such as grain from other sections of the country where they could be produced more cheaply. Local farmers reduced their output of wool, pork, cheese, and grain and increased that of beef, butter, milk, hens' eggs, fruit, potatoes, and tobacco.

Alfred and William P. Gay, brothers who belonged to the fourth generation of that family on North Main Street, were typical East Granby farmers. Their diaries, which cover intermittently the years from 1860 through 1890, show that they no longer bartered the variety of services their great-grandfather Richard Dana Gay had, and they left the trade in such items as cloth and ribbon to storekeepers. Like him, though, they pastured animals for other people and sold wood from the Mountain behind their homes.* In most years their principal cash crop was tobacco.

According to the agricultural surveys from the federal censuses, the number of families in town who raised tobacco increased from twenty-two to 117—two-thirds of the town's 177 households—between 1850 and 1870. Production increased almost tenfold, from 23,605 to 235,370 pounds.

About this time tobacco growers began to plant Havana leaf, which yielded relatively more usable tobacco than Broadleaf. Havana made a strong binder for the filler in a cigar as well as an attractive wrapper. Havana leaf and Broadleaf predominated in the Connecticut Valley for the next twenty-five years.

Prices paid to the farmer varied according to quality and demand. Alfred Gay

*Alfred lived with his wife and five sons as 123 North Main Street. North of this family home, William built a house that burned in the early 1960s; the house at 129 North Main Street is built on its foundation. William married twice; his only child was a daughter by his first wife.

sold his tobacco in the spring of 1864 to a Mr. Watts of New York through local agent Peter McKinney. He got 38 cents a pound for 1274 pounds (1031 pounds of a quality suitable for cigar wrappers and 243 pounds that included some suitable for filler plus some called seconds) for a total of $484.12.

By 1872 he had more than doubled his crop. That year he received a record $1,188.95 for 2937 pounds (2506 pounds for wrappers at 45 cents a pound, 34 pounds for filler at 5 cents, and 397 pounds of seconds at 15 cents a pound). In 1875 he harvested 2843 pounds, but only realized $734.95 from its sale as neither the quality nor the price was as good as it had been three years before.

Local tobacco production increased only slightly between 1870 and 1880 as farmers faced more competition from growers in other sections of the country, chiefly Pennsylvania and Florida. The number of East Granby farmers who grew tobacco decreased by 15 percent to ninety-nine, although the average number of pounds each raised rose from 2000 to 2449. Each grower planted between ½ acre and 3 acres of the crop in 1880.

Then, in the early 1880s, cigar manufacturers began to import Sumatra leaf, and it became more popular than Connecticut leaf for wrappers. Although area-grown tobacco remained in demand for filler and binders, production in Connecticut decreased almost 37 percent from 14,044,652 pounds in 1880 to 8,874,924 in 1890.

Federal tariffs on Sumatra during the 1880s and 1890s helped local growers to some extent, and their output rose again by 1900. Edgar H. Seymour reminisced about these times:

In 1871 a cyclone knocked down a lot of the [tobacco] *barns, and as local farmers were already growing more tobacco than they could sell, they didn't bother rebuilding them until 1892 when a tariff was imposed to reduce tobacco imports. Once there was money in it again, a lot of new sheds were put up, some by my father.*

Usually the Gays did not realize as much income from the sale of their farm animals as they did from tobacco, but the market for them was more predictable. The 1880 agricultural survey shows they had owned forty-six cattle the previous year; of these they had purchased nine and sold seventeen. They sold to farmers and drovers throughout the area, and for many years they slaughtered some for their own use and for trade. (Neighbors killed their animals at different times and traded the meat with one another.) The Gays sold meat to butchers and even peddled it house-to-house from their wagons. By 1880, though, they were selling most of their cattle live and getting beef to eat at a market and from peddlers.

By that time herds of swine as large as twenty or more had disappeared from local barnyards, but many families continued to raise a few pigs each year for themselves and for sale. A farmer could buy a piglet for $2, fatten it on weeds, grain, boiled turnips, and swill for six months until it weighed at least 300 pounds, then slaughter it and eat it or sell the meat for $15 to $18.

One of Elmore Clark's annual fall jobs was to slaughter the two hogs he had been raising since the previous spring. By now the animals might weigh 450 to 520 pounds, and Clark needed the help of two or three men to kill, bleed, and skin them. For a few days thereafter, he would be busy cutting them up, rendering the fat into lard,

Benjamin P. Clark house which stood north of 8 South Main Street

making sausages, and salting the remainder of the meat. Alfred Gay wrote in 1875: "Salted hams according to my old rule—For 100 lbs. of ham, 10 lbs. salt, ¼ lb. sal nitre [*saltpeter*], 1 qt. molasses or 1 pt. of molasses and 1 lb. of sugar." Both Clark and the Gays also smoked hams, evidently in small portable smokehouses.

Alfred Gay was among the twenty-one local families who still raised sheep in 1880. He might earn $50 to $100 each spring when he sold his newborn lambs and the fleece from his sheep. Once in a while the Gays may have eaten mutton, but as a rule men still did not slaughter lambs for food. These animals were a vulnerable livestock; sometimes they drowned in brooks and ponds, and they were an easy prey for dogs. After dogs attacked twenty-five of his thirty-three sheep, Elmore Clark recorded in his diary with grim satisfaction: "In the morning I shot with the long gun Adjutant General Charles T. Hillyer's dog—dead. Hillyer was mad."

The market for perishable farm produce increased in larger towns nearby as they grew and became more industrialized, but getting farm products to them remained difficult. The Gays carted butter, meat, apples, potatoes, and other vegetables to Hartford and Springfield where they peddled them from door to door and to storekeepers and passersby along the streets.

Nearby cider mills and distilleries continued to provide the best outlets for apples, usually those of poorer quality. In 1854 Connecticut passed a law prohibiting the manufacture and sale of liquor with some minor exceptions. The law was violated freely and soon became a dead letter. A new law in 1872 provided for the licensing of liquor dealers, and another in 1874 allowed voters at annual town meetings to decide whether or not there should be licensed liquor outlets in their respective towns. The question came to a vote in East Granby four times before the end of the century. Only once did the town vote in the negative.

Between 1872 and 1879 Benjamin P. Clark operated the distillery north of the Center on Trout Brook. One year he received $1820 for the cider brandy he sold by the barrel to customers from Vermont to southern Connecticut and into New York State.

The Gays traded their eggs and some of their butter at the Viets store in the Center. All but two local farmers on the 1880 agricultural survey had laying hens, producing 17,616 dozen eggs the previous year. James R. Viets, brother of John J., ran the store at 9 South Main Street during these years, and he must have wholesaled most of the eggs he took in trade.

The opening of a local creamery in 1882 provided a new outlet for milk. Creameries, which were new in Connecticut in the 1870s, made butter primarily. The *Windsor Locks Journal** reported:

Some weeks ago a creamery company was quietly formed in this town, and they have been quietly at work erecting a commodious building 50x30 feet and 2½ stories high. Their boiler, engine, and other appliances are purchased and will soon be in operation. Some 500-700 cows, chiefly Jerseys, are pledged by the patrons, and the number will probably be increased to 1000. The milk, instead of the cream, is to be delivered to the factory each morning and evening, where it will be skimmed and churned at the proper state and temperature, thus securing perfect uniformity in color and quality of the butter. The constant hard work of our farmers and their families, which is unavoidable in family butter making, is now to be done by machinery, and all hands are rejoicing thus to be relieved of this care and labor of the household.

Most of the stockholders in the new company were farmers who sold milk to the creamery, making it a cooperative venture. The factory stood south of 19 North Main Street on Trout Brook, which soon became known as Creamery Brook.

The *Connecticut Farmer* announced the opening in its June 3, 1882, edition:

The creamery in this place commenced operations Monday the 22d. Austin P. Stowell, [**] *who is not often found napping in the morning, being the first to deliver milk, and the whistle is expected to sound the time of day before long. Peddlers will make the attempt to sell skim milk in Thompsonville, Windsor Locks, Rainbow and perhaps other places.*

The creamery shipped most of its butter to New York, Springfield, and Hartford. Beginning in the spring of 1886, farmers sold cream rather than whole milk to the factory.

By then farmers were selecting and breeding their cows for richer milk. Cattle that dotted Turkey Hills' pastures before the Civil War were generally a colorful mix described as brindled, spotted, "moldy colored" and black, brown, white and red, alone or in various combinations. The red cattle, Devons, were predominant and men raised

*Hereafter referred to as the *Journal.*

**Stowell was the grandfather of Roger H. Stowell, who now lives in the house his grandfather built at 46 North Main Street in 1881.

Ruins of the Case mills on the Farmington River

them for both beef and milk. The East Granby Agricultural Society, of which the Gays were charter members in 1876, recognized only two breeds of cattle, the Alderney (often called Jersey) and the Durham, when awarding premiums at its annual cattle shows between 1876 and 1895. These breeds were prized for the quality of their milk.

The same issue of the *Connecicut Farmer* that announced the opening of the creamery also reported that Henry A. Case had sold the site of his sawmill and gristmill on the Farmington River to Horace Smith of Springfield, who intended to erect a paper mill and other manufactories there. Business at the Spoonville gristmill had been declining steadily as railroads brought in more flour from the West and local farmers turned their fields from grain to tobacco. Business at the sawmill had also declined, but Case was not ready to relinquish that. Instead he moved the mill to a site behind the new house he built at 16 Tunxis Avenue in 1883 and used steam power.

Some of the business from Case's gristmill probably shifted to Clinton Phelps, then owner of the Red Hook Mill on Stony Brook. The Gay family traded with Phelps and in the back of one diary is a printed receipt from "Clinton Phelps, miller, and dealer in flour, grain, feed and fertilizers." Then in bold print are the words "TERMS CASH," a sign of the new economic era that was slowly evolving from the age of barter. Alfred Gay wrote in 1876: "Pease delivered 6M of shingles bo't yesterday at 5.25. 2 percent off for cash within 30 days."

The Gays often had their animals shod, their tools mended, and their vehicles made and repaired at Thomas H. Lee's blacksmith shop at the northwest corner of School Street and Church Road. Lee bought the shop from blacksmith Homer F. Fox in 1875. When Lee's house next door burned down two years later, William Gay wrote, "I went down to carry Tom Lee some things in A.M., potatoes, pork, bread, cotton cloth, turnips." Lee later built the brick house at 11 School Street.

The years the Gays' diaries portray have a pattern of work and recreation determined by the seasons and accompanied by appropriate moods: the harsh drudgery of winter, the expectation of spring, the urgency of summer, and the excitement of the

16 Tunxis Avenue

harvest—all climaxed with a few days of relaxation before the necessary preparations for winter intruded.

The pressing daily chores that could not be postponed even on the coldest days of winter were milking, feeding and watering the livestock, getting wood from the Mountain, and opening paths and roads. In November or December men put their cattle into their barns for the winter. After that they had to let them out once or twice a day to get water from nearby brooks or troughs in their barnyards. This was a cold, unpleasant job, particularly when they had to break ice, and the Gays complained that sometimes it took most of a day.

The Gays used wintertime, just as their forefathers had, to cut and haul the wood they burned or turned into fence posts and lumber. Even though they bought as many as 4000 pounds of coal a year, they still burned a great deal of wood in stoves and fireplaces, and they supplied many other families, too. During the cold, snowy winter of 1881, Alfred Gay had a particularly hard time. He wrote:

Continued breaking road on the mountain. Cut 3 small trees and chained them on the outsides of the sled and snaked them home the whole length to make a road wide enough so the cattle will not crowd. Split one of the sled runners. It is a hard job. The snow is belly deep to the cattle in the woods, 2 feet, I should think.

Men spent winter days and evenings husking corn and thrashing and winnowing other grains before taking them to a mill to be sold or ground into grist for their own use. As tobacco crops grew larger, they spent more time sprinkling, stripping, and packing tobacco—work they had to do in their cellars and kitchens when the weather was very cold.

A late winter job was "knocking" manure, breaking up the clods for easier spreading. Farmers also enriched their fields with compost and various commercial fertilizers. Many of the latter were worthless, but until the establishment of an agricultural experiment

Lee blacksmith shop

station at Wesleyan University in 1875, there was no one to advise a farmer about their effectiveness. He just had to try the different ones.

In early spring the Gays planted, grafted, and trimmed fruit trees, repaired fences, stone walls, and buildings, and picked up stones the frost had heaved out of the ground during the winter. Late spring brought plowing and harrowing, followed by the sowing of seeds and the setting out of plants. As the plants grew, men spent days weeding and removing the insects and worms that threatened them.

In June, July, and August farmers gathered hay, rye, oats, and buckwheat and stored them in their barns. These were the months when hired help was most valuable, because crops had to be harvested when they were ripe. Reliable workers were comparatively well paid. Summer help got as much as $25 a month plus room and board; winter help got $8 to $10.

Because many young men were leaving town, farm labor was often scarce. Local farmers invested as much as possible in labor-saving machinery; the assessed value of machinery in town doubled between 1860 and 1880. Everyone on the 1880 agricultural survey had some implements or machines. Blacksmith Bradley Perkins' were valued at only $5, while Clinton Phelps' and Chauncey E. Viets' were worth the most, $1000 each.

Viets had died in 1876, but evidently his property, which included the house at 57 Newgate Road and one that stood south of it, had not been sold. His inventory at the time of his death lists a mowing machine ($50), a horse rake ($30), a stump puller ($15), five plows ($10), a tobacco rigger ($2), and numerous small tools. Viets probably lent his equipment to neighbors in return for the use of a cultivator, reaper, etc. Sometimes accumulating the equipment to do a job took as much time as the job itself as Alfred Gay found out:

July 11, 1860. A.M. I went to the store with Lester Griffin. Got 1 rake for .45. Got A. Bates' hook ladder, got shingle nails of father, got long ladder of H. Work, etc. P.M. Patched barn roof.

Usually there was a lull in the work after haying season and before the tobacco harvest began. The Gays took a day or two to go fishing, berrying, and perhaps sightseeing with summer guests. Otherwise they spent the time on routine chores such as painting and shingling buildings; cutting brush; cleaning brooks, hog pens, wells, and cisterns; and repairing barrels for winter storage.

The tobacco harvest began in late August or early September, followed by the gathering and storing of nuts, apples, and vegetables. As the fields emptied, men plowed and fertilized them. Sometimes they seeded them with rye, clover, and grass seed. Invariably a few fall days were spent making cider, still the most popular drink.

In October, day and overnight trips to cattle shows in Massachusetts and Connecticut brought a welcome change from work in the fields. The East Granby Agricultural Society had its annual shows on the grounds of the Congregational meetinghouse and in the basement of the building. It was a day to visit with friends and perhaps win a few dollars in prizes. In 1876 Alfred Gay showed his six-year-old team of oxen, which weighed 3800 pounds, and won first premium of $3. His four-year-old cow won first premium of $2. He added his produce to the exhibits in the basement, but evidently did not win a prize. "A fair show of cattle, 40 yokes, but not as good or as many as there ought to have been. A very good show under the church and the biggest crowd of people for a small place like this." Older residents who could remember fifty-four years before when there had been 180 yokes of cattle at the local show probably longed for the good old days.

Visiting with friends and relatives seems to have been the most popular recreation in East Granby. Women, and less frequently men, exchanged visits regularly for an hour, an afternoon, overnight, or a week or two. Men stopped by on business and stayed for dinner at midday; families came for tea and spent the evening. These were usually impromptu visits as there was no easy way to notify a prospective host ahead of time before the advent of the telephone.

Visits were seldom purely social. An afternoon ride might include stops at two or three homes to inquire about someone's health, the possibility of a woman coming to help with the sewing for a few days, or an exchange of steers.

Men gathered at post offices and general stores to discuss the news, predict the weather, bargain their goods and labor, and settle their disputes. At least five residences and stores at the Center housed the post office at different times during the 19th century. The buildings at 9, 17, and 19 South Main Street were among them.

A post office was established at Copper Hill in 1872 with Philo H. Viets as the first postmaster. His brother, William D. Viets, was postmaster from 1878 until 1903 when the station was discontinued. His office was in his new house at 30 Copper Hill Road. Howard Griffin, who lives there now, tells how the postmaster would put the mail in a bag and hang it on a pole beside the railroad crossing west of his home. The train would then pick up the sack and leave a bag of incoming mail in its place. A quatrain from around 1900 adds a humorous touch to the routine:

Copper Hill has its mailman,
William Viets is his name,
And sometimes you'll see him
Running after the train.

30 Copper Hill Road

The year 1903 also saw the start of Rural Free Delivery (RFD) service in East Granby.

There were visits every few months among relatives who lived near enough to make the trip by carriage or sleigh in a day. Every summer brought former residents and their descendants from other states to town, although one member of a family might make the trip back home only once or twice in a lifetime.

Sightseeing was an important part of any long visit. The Gays took their guests to the Bartlett Tower near Tariffville and the Heublein Tower near Avon, to the carpet factories at Tariffville and Thompsonville, to the Shaker Village at Enfield, to Congamond Lakes, and to what were then called "the ruins of Newgate." Charles Hopkins Clark, editor of the *Courant,* owned the Newgate property in 1886 when N. H. Eggleston wrote the following:

The place is now a picturesque ruin, of great interest on account of its historic associations. The high walls . . . have not been cared for by the later proprietors, and portions of them have tumbled down. The old smithy . . . has become a dilapidated mass, its sides having fallen out, and a portion only of its roof remaining. The floor is heaped with the ore which the more recent miners brought up from the cavernous depths below. The clank of the chains is no longer heard, nor the ring of the many hammers upon the anvils. The old treadmill is silent. The various shops where work of one sort and another was done, and the chapel where religious services were maintained for the benefit of the convicts, are now empty. Doors and windows, to a great extent, are gone. The stair-cases are broken down, and one makes his way among the apartments with difficulty. The sentry's box still stands high on the parapet, but no sentry's tread is heard, nor is the gleam of his musket seen in the sunshine. Grass and weeds have overgrown the court-yard. One building only has been kept in sufficient repair to be occupied. In this, situated in the center of the inclosure, a family dwell, guarding the premises from ruthless depredation, and furnishing candles and needful guides for those who desire to explore the dungeons below. The bell, which originally came from Rouen, in France, and long summoned the prisoners to their work, to their meals, and to their quarters at night, has been transferred to the roof of a factory a few miles distant.

Barn opposite 43 Newgate Road

Infrequently the Gays took trips such as excursions by railroad to Boston and New York City. In 1876 Walter and Lusher, two of Alfred's sons, attended America's first world's fair, the Centennial Exposition at Philadelphia. Alfred borrowed $25 for Lusher's expenses and recorded in his diary: "His fare from Hartford and back on boat $5. Stateroom with Walter .50. Board 1.50 per day and .50 admission per day. He says he spent $16.40 all told."

While visiting seems to have been the most popular social pastime in the 19th century, singing ranked close behind it. Sometimes a teacher went from town to town conducting singing schools in each town once a week and spending nights with the families of the students. People of all ages participated in the lessons and the concerts that usually concluded a series.

Dancing was still somewhat controversial. Alfred Gay worried, "There were 35 at church. What a congregation. I am afraid we shall die out with such a minister [*the Reverend Charles Chamberlain*] and such a wrangle in the society. Now it is about dancing in the hall under the church."

The *Journal* reported in 1880 that Allen A. Alderman of 71 North Main Street planned to dedicate his new barn with a party and dance. "The barn will accommodate some 60-80 couples for dancing with abundance of room for spectators. Refreshments of ice cream, strawberries, lemonade, etc., etc., will be furnished. Good music and prompting will be in attendance." The newspaper believed the barn was the first one ever raised by horse power in East Granby. A barn dance also christened the Victorian barn opposite 43 Newgate Road a few years later.

More barns than dwellings were raised during these years, and some farms were abandoned as the Grand List fluctuated between $450,000 and $500,000. Victorian architecture with its various projections—bays, small gables, dormer windows, porches, etc.—caught the fancy of local families who did build homes. The house at 185 North Main Street, built by James H. Alderman in 1875; the one at 32 South Main Street, built by Renselaer Pinney before 1882; and the house at 42 South Main Street, which

185 North Main Street

Morgan J. Bacon built about 1906, are typically Victorian in style.

The Gays were Congregationalists, and they participated in the usual affairs of the church and often attended both the morning and afternoon services on Sundays. Their diaries never mention Christmas in connection with the church, but newspapers show that in the 1890s most denominations had Christmas trees and entertainments. Even the Hartford Hebrew Association held an annual Christmas ball at the time.

Thanksgiving continued to be the big family holiday in the fall. Although Alfred Gay obviously was disappointed at the size of the gathering at his home in 1872, he must have been pleased with the menu:

Thanksgiving day. Did not go anywhere. Had our 5 boys and Emma Moody and no one else, the fewest that we ever had. We had baked pig stuffed, 4 baked chickens stuffed, baked beef, 2 big chicken pies, baked pudding, apple, mince & squash pies, etc. I forgot the cake.

Emma Moody later became the wife of Gay's eldest son, Walter.

Decoration Day was a new holiday that had its origin in the South with the scattering of flowers on the graves of Union soldiers during the Civil War. The custom spread quickly to the North where May 30 became what is now called Memorial Day. Diaries mention decorating soldiers' graves and holding public memorial services.

The 1876 celebration of the 100th anniversary of the adoption of the Declaration of Independence was a memorable event. A picnic for all the townspeople and their guests at Renselaer Pinney's grove near his home just south of the Center followed a parade to West Suffield and back. Alfred Gay wrote that there was "an old-fashioned drum and fife for music and singing by the choir—America and the Star-Spangled Banner" followed by the usual patriotic poems, readings, speeches, and toasts. A dance concluded the festivities. A few days later the Reverend Charles Chamberlain gave his sermon on the history of the town, parts of which are quoted in this book.

42 South Main Street

Political celebrations were exciting occasions in the late 1800s. After a victory in 1880, the Republicans had a typical torchlight parade around the square; i.e., via North Main, Sheldon, South Grand, East, and School streets. Mounted officers of the Boys in Blue, a Republican organization, led the procession of wagons and carriages, while a brass band from Suffield supplied the music. Everyone stopped at 212 North Main Street where Lois and Sylvester Smith served refreshments.

The Gays furnished the food and drink for a similar parade according to Alfred Gay's diary:

October 26, 1876. Boys fixed for illuminating the house. Friday eve the Boys in Blue are to have a parade. The boys from Granby & Simsbury & Windsor & Suffield are all coming. October 27, 1876. Boys fixed for the parade this eve. The women made doughnuts and biscuits for the Boys in Blue, a half bushel of doughnuts. We trimmed every window in the front & north & south part of the house & lighted it. A fine parade. 390 torches. We fed 500 "& they did all eat and were filled" & coffee to drink.

The Boys in White, the Democratic counterpart of the Boys in Blue, also had their local celebrations. One was a "Hancock Flag Raising" in 1880, attended by Boys in White from Windsor Locks, West Suffield, Simsbury, and Granby.

In 1881 William Gay, then a widower, married Alice Warner, daughter of the Reverend Ransom Warner, rector of the Episcopal church at North Bloomfield. Alice may have been unprepared for the life of a farmer's wife. William Gay mentions that even though his bride didn't know much about "putting up a hog," she did well. For the first year of their marriage, he took the washing to other women to be done, but after that Alice took on the chore with the customary help of her husband or the hired man. In fact, she became adept at many jobs she probably had never done before. For example, she helped with the planting and stripping of tobacco, raked hay, and wallpapered. She was not above walking to North Bloomfield to visit her family when the horse was being used in the fields.

Both William and Alfred assisted their wives with churning, preserving, cooking, spring cleaning, etc., particularly when they were unable to hire domestic help. One spring job was reroping the beds and putting clean straw in the mattresses. In 1891 Alice bought a hair mattress in Springfield for $20. When widow Mary Gould came to sew for the family in 1885, she brought her new sewing machine.

Now there were kerosene oil lamps, although the Gays still used many candles. They heated and cooked with stoves. In 1881 Alfred bought a new cook stove for $33, a No. 9 East Lake with a 10-gallon water tank on the back side. The women liked the new stove, he wrote, "except the oven which is only 20" square (while the old one was 22 by 24) & this is as large as any I have seen. Can't bake but 2 of our *big pies* while we used to [*bake*] 4. The water tank is splendid."

Peddlers continued to bring a variety of food and miscellaneous merchandise to people's homes. Eventually some of them such as the fish peddler, the yeast peddler, the meat man, and the baker came on a regular schedule. Samuel Lathrop describes one:

Maurice Sullivan's baker cart from Thompsonville made regular trips through Suffield to East Granby. This old red cart was drawn by a plodding horse with a cowbell hanging from his neck, clearly audible a mile away, selling for cash or taking eggs in trade. In those days, Baker's stuff, as it was called, was much inferior to present day goods. In most homes it was used only in emergency. Few housewives would serve it to their families as regular fare.

Stagecoach drivers also brought merchandise to people along their routes. Alfred Gay wrote that he paid Harvey E. Dibble 15 cents to pick up a clothes wringer for him in Hartford. Dibble, who lived at 21-23 School Street, started his stagecoach route between East Granby and Windsor in 1869, and ten years later he extended it to Hartford. He kept eight horses just for his business, using four at a time. His stage seated eighteen passengers and the driver with room for mail and express, i.e., packages and larger items.

Both William and Alfred Gay assumed their share of civic responsibilities. At different times they served as clerk, treasurer, and committeeman for the Second School District, supervising the building and maintenance of the schoolhouse, supplying wood, buying supplies, and hiring and boarding teachers. William was also one of those elected at annual town meetings to serve on the board of school visitors, of which one member was chosen to be the acting school visitor, who was paid.

School district taxes, except those for building and maintaining schoolhouses, ceased in 1868 when the General Assembly decreed that towns raise enough money by taxation to make their schools completely free.* A few years later the state began to give towns an annual grant per student in addition to the interest from the school fund. The legislators mandated a minimum number of weeks in the school year in 1872, and by the turn of the century all local schools were in session at least thirty-six weeks each year.

*This law evidently did not apply to textbooks. Not until 1931 did the state require towns to supply free textbooks in public schools, although East Granby had done so since 1905.

Drawing of Harvey E. Dibble and his stage at 21 School Street, from an early photograph

By then, too, East Granby's young people had financial help in continuing their education beyond the elementary level. The General Assembly passed a law in 1897 that any town without a high school should pay at least some of a student's tuition to such a school in another town. The state was to reimburse towns for part of the expenditure. Three local students signed up the first year, and at least one went to Windsor High School, probably in Harvey E. Dibble's stage.

In spite of such progress, annual reports of the school visitors at the end of the century contain many of the complaints that critics of the system had voiced fifty years before. The strongest criticism was that the public in general and many parents of school children were indifferent to the quality of education in the local schools. As a result, they said, district school meetings were poorly attended and the schools poorly managed. School buildings were deteriorating because the individual districts were unable or unwilling to raise the money to repair or replace them. Many children did not attend school regularly or at all, and those who did attend were often tardy. In 1895 the total enrollment was 136 with an average attendance of about 55 percent. Children had been tardy 839 times during the year.

School visitors recommended that the town assume complete control of the schools and consolidate those that had too few students to justify maintaining them. One year there were only seventeen pupils altogether in the three schools west of the Mountain. The acting school visitor in 1893 wrote: "The result is poorer schools with inexperienced teachers and a waste of money which would not be practiced in any other expenditures of the town." To make matters worse, some East Granby students were attending common schools in adjoining towns with the approval of the General Assembly and often at town expense.

Finally in 1900 a town meeting voted to choose a new board of education with the power "to run such schools to accommodate the scholars in the town as they deem necessary and make the necessary repairs on the schoolhouses." In effect, the board of education took over both the duties and the property of the school districts.

The amount expended annually for education between 1872 and 1900 was around $1377 or 29 percent of the town's average operating budget of $4760. Expenses of highways and bridges—not including new bridges—averaged about $1681; salaries for officials, $387; and care of paupers, $406. A significant decrease in taxes occurred after 1888 when the General Assembly suspended the state property tax because the state did not need the money. After that an annual military commutation tax and an occasional county tax together averaged about $136 per year. East Granby borrowed money from the time of her founding, and the interest on that debt was about $200 a year. The tax rate during these years fluctuated between seven and twelve mills.

Because William and Alfred Gay were Republicans, their chances to be elected to public office in Democratic East Granby were limited. William did hold a few minor positions, and Alfred was elected third selectman in 1879. After Alfred died in 1884 and William in 1892, the balance of political power changed so that by the end of the century, the town clerk and first and second selectmen were usually Republicans.

When Republicans were victorious, entries in the Gays' diaries are gleeful:

October 2, 1876. I [Alfred] *went to town meeting & had a good time in seeing the dem's fight among themselves. They did not all like their nomination & we elected our 3 selectmen.*
November 2, 1880. I [William] *went down and voted for Garfield. Also was moderator of the meeting. We elected a Republican Representative from the town for the first time since the town was set off.*

The representative was Gordon C. Willoughby of 44 Hatchet Hill Road and, according to the *Journal,* he received votes from ninety-two-year-old Roswell H. Phelps, who had voted at every presidential election since 1809, and eighty-nine-year-old Alexander H. Griswold. Both had been Whigs and were now Republicans. The votes of these two men represented the slim majority by which Willoughby won the election.

William Gay was even more exuberant in 1886 when he wrote: "The Republicans elected every man to office. A great day for East Granby." Although the Democrats regained control the next year, this election marked the end of Elmore Clark's twenty-eight-year tenure as town clerk, the only town clerk East Granby had ever had. In at least four elections, the vote for him had been unanimous. (Clark also had served as Granby's town clerk before the founding of East Granby.) Clark lived all his life in the old Samuel Clark house at the Center, the fifth generation of Clarks to live there and the last occupant by that name. Albert Carlos Bates remembered him as a model town clerk:

His writing was as readable as print; every letter was carefully formed and extremely legible. He was very precise and accurate in his speech as he also was in his dress and manner. . . . His office was in the southeast front room on the lower floor [of his home] *and entrance*

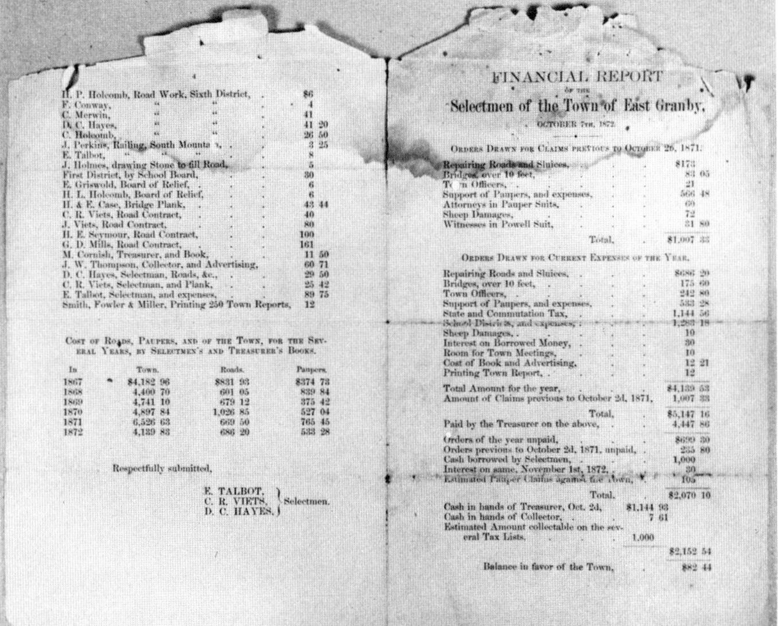

4

H. P. Holcomb, Road Work, Sixth District,	$6
F. Conway, " "	4
C. Merwin, " "	41
D. C. Hayes, " "	41 20
C. Holcomb, " "	26 50
J. Perkins, Railing, South Mounta[illegible],	3 25
E. Talbot, " " "	8
J. Holmes, drawing Stone to fill Road,	5
First District, by School Board,	30
E. Griswold, Board of Relief,	6
H. L. Holcomb, Board of Relief,	6
H. & E. Case, Bridge Plank,	43 44
C. R. Viets, Road Contract,	40
J. Viets, Road Contract,	80
H. E. Seymour, Road Contract,	100
G. D. Mills, Road Contract,	161
M. Cornish, Treasurer, and Book,	11 50
J. W. Thompson, Collector, and Advertising,	60 71
D. C. Hayes, Selectman, Roads, &c.,	29 50
C. R. Viets, Selectman, and Plank,	25 42
E. Talbot, Selectman, and expenses,	89 75
Smith, Fowler & Miller, Printing 250 Town Reports,	12

Cost of Roads, Paupers, and of the Town, for the Several Years, by Selectmen's and Treasurer's Books.

In	Town.	Roads.	Paupers.
1867	$4,182 96	$831 93	$374 73
1868	4,400 70	601 05	839 84
1869	4,741 10	679 12	375 42
1870	4,897 84	1,026 85	527 04
1871	6,526 63	669 50	765 45
1872	4,139 83	686 20	533 28

Respectfully submitted,

E. TALBOT,
C. R. VIETS, Selectmen.
D. C. HAYES,

FINANCIAL REPORT

OF THE

Selectmen of the Town of East Granby,

OCTOBER 7TH, 1872.

Orders Drawn for Claims previous to October 2d, 1871.

Repairing Roads and Sluices,	$173
Bridges, over 10 feet,	83 05
T[illegible]n Officers,	21
Support of Paupers, and expenses,	566 48
Attorneys in Pauper Suits,	60
Sheep Damages,	72
Witnesses in Powell Suit,	31 80
Total,	$1,007 33

Orders Drawn for Current Expenses of the Year.

Repairing Roads and Sluices,		$686 20
Bridges, over 10 feet,		175 60
Town Officers,		242 80
Support of Paupers, and expenses,		533 28
State and Commutation Tax,		1,144 56
School Districts, and expenses,		1,283 18
Sheep Damages,		10
Interest on Borrowed Money,		30
Room for Town Meetings,		10
Cost of Book and Advertising,		12 21
Printing Town Report,		12
Total Amount for the year,		$4,139 53
Amount of Claims previous to October 2d, 1871,		1,007 33
Total,		$5,147 16
Paid by the Treasurer on the above,		4,447 86
Orders of the year unpaid,		$699 30
Orders previous to October 2d, 1871, unpaid,		235 80
Cash borrowed by Selectmen,		1,000
Interest on same, November 1st, 1872,		30
Estimated Pauper Claims against the Town,		105
Total,		$2,070 10
Cash in hands of Treasurer, Oct. 2d,	$1,144 93	
Cash in hands of Collector,	7 61	
Estimated Amount collectable on the several Tax Lists,	1,000	
		$2,152 54
Balance in favor of the Town,		$82 44

First town report, 1872

was obtained by the south corner door. . . . Stepping inside the door, one entered a large room which was almost entirely covered with handsome panelling; a small wood stove stood in front of the closed fireplace and between the two front windows was a large table which served as the desk for his official work as town clerk.

In this room Mr. Clark lived and enjoyed the work which was officially his. He knew his volumes of records thoroughly; could tell in most cases without consulting them as to what deeds had passed during the more than a third of a century that he held his office.

Wilbert was the only one of Alfred Gay's five sons who stayed in East Granby. Helen Gay Moody, Wilbert's daughter who now lives in her ancestral home on North Main Street, remembers that her father gave up his ambition to be a lawyer to stay on the family farm.

Wilbert's brother Frank became librarian and recording secretary of the Connecticut Historical Society and librarian of the Watkinson Library, now a part of Trinity College. He also worked for the Hartford Library Association (the Hartford Public Library) at one time. In the late 1800s all of these institutions were housed in the Wadsworth Atheneum of which Gay was the executive director, 1884-1911.

Gay hired a young friend, Albert Carlos Bates, as an assistant. Bates wrote about his first months at the Atheneum:

I began my duties with the Society Monday, May 2nd, 1892, reserving Saturdays for my own work at home as Town Clerk and Treasurer that year. I took care of my horse, milked the cow and drove the six miles to Windsor Locks, boarding the 7:32 train, returning at night on the train leaving, I believe, exactly at six. This continued until it came dark so

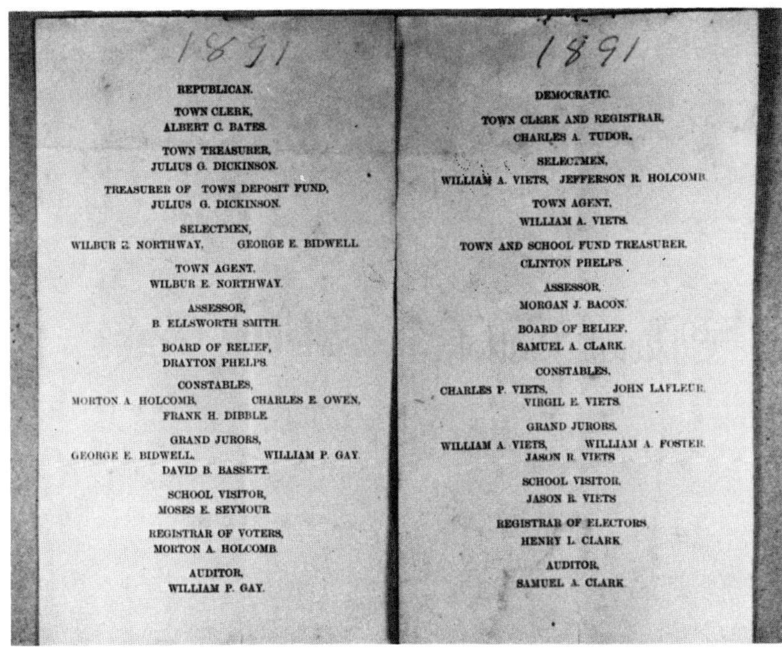

1891

REPUBLICAN.

TOWN CLERK,
ALBERT C. BATES.

TOWN TREASURER,
JULIUS G. DICKINSON.

TREASURER OF TOWN DEPOSIT FUND,
JULIUS G. DICKINSON.

SELECTMEN,
WILBUR E. NORTHWAY, GEORGE E. BIDWELL.

TOWN AGENT,
WILBUR E. NORTHWAY.

ASSESSOR,
B. ELLSWORTH SMITH.

BOARD OF RELIEF,
DRAYTON PHELPS.

CONSTABLES,
MORTON A. HOLCOMB, CHARLES E. OWEN,
FRANK H. DIBBLE.

GRAND JURORS,
GEORGE E. BIDWELL, WILLIAM P. GAY.
DAVID B. BASSETT.

SCHOOL VISITOR,
MOSES E. SEYMOUR.

REGISTRAR OF VOTERS,
MORTON A. HOLCOMB.

AUDITOR,
WILLIAM P. GAY.

1891

DEMOCRATIC.

TOWN CLERK AND REGISTRAR,
CHARLES A. TUDOR.

SELECTMEN,
WILLIAM A. VIETS, JEFFERSON R. HOLCOMB.

TOWN AGENT,
WILLIAM A. VIETS.

TOWN AND SCHOOL FUND TREASURER,
CLINTON PHELPS.

ASSESSOR,
MORGAN J. BACON.

BOARD OF RELIEF,
SAMUEL A. CLARK.

CONSTABLES,
CHARLES P. VIETS, JOHN LAFLEUR.
VIRGIL E. VIETS.

GRAND JURORS,
WILLIAM A. VIETS, WILLIAM A. FOSTER.
JASON R. VIETS.

SCHOOL VISITOR,
JASON R. VIETS.

REGISTRAR OF ELECTORS,
HENRY L. CLARK.

AUDITOR,
SAMUEL A. CLARK.

Official ballots for town election, 1891

early that it was difficult to find the cow on my return home, and I then arranged with the next door neighbor to care for the cow and supply our home with milk. I continued this daily travel through the year, reaching Windsor Locks about sunrise in the latter part of December. Before the end of the year, I was offered the position of Librarian [of the Connecticut Historical Society] *which I accepted, and commenced my duties with the beginning of 1893.*

Bates eventually moved to Hartford where he worked for the Connecticut Historical Society for fifty years. He was an historian, genealogist, editor, author, collector, and bibliographer as well as librarian, recording secretary, and business manager of the society. East Granby is fortunate that he never lost interest in the history of his native town whose public and private records he collected, preserved, and sometimes published. In 1949 when he was eighty-four years old and partially blind, he wrote his *Historical Sketch of Turkey Hills and East Granby, Connecticut.*

William Gay's daughter, Alice Maria, a graduate of the Connecticut Literary Institution at Suffield, sometimes assisted Bates at the Historical Society. She became a noted genealogist, holding offices in at least seven historical associations and societies.

Charles T. Hillyer and his wife, Catharine Robbins Hillyer, left the home they built at 19 North Main Street and moved to Hartford in 1853. Hillyer organized the Charter Oak Bank and became its first president. He contributed land and a large sum of money toward the original Young Men's Christian Association building that stood on the corner of Pearl and Ford streets in Hartford. The Hillyers' children, Appleton Robbins and Clara E. Hillyer, founded Hillyer Institute (later Hillyer College and now a part of the University of Hartford) in memory of their father. Appleton's wife, Dortha

19 North Main Street

Bushnell Hillyer, built the Bushnell Memorial in memory of her father, the Reverend Horace Bushnell.

During the 1890s East Granby's population rose from 661 to 684, reversing a twenty-year decline. Improved means of transportation that lessened the isolation of the community were partly responsible for the reversal. Between 1892 and 1898 steel bridges replaced the three wooden ones over the Farmington River. The Berlin Iron Works erected the new structures at an average cost of $6240 apiece. The state began to assume some control over highways in 1895 and to contribute financial aid for their construction and maintenance. There was even talk of cutting down the road over the Mountain at the turn of the century.

About 1897 an electric street railway began to operate between Hartford and the Rainbow section of Windsor. The people of East Granby drove to Rainbow where they left their horses and wagons or carriages at a livery and took the trolley to Hartford and back. Even more exciting was the prospect of a trolley line from Springfield to Suffield and then down South Grand and East streets to a terminal in East Granby. Work on the line started in 1897, but financial troubles prevented its completion.

The possibility of a railroad from Tariffville through the Center to Feeding Hills, Massachusetts, became a probability by 1899. For thirty years the Central New England Railway,* which ran from Hartford through Tariffville to Millerton, New York, had been planning, surveying, and partially building this branch. East Granby had divided almost two to one against issuing bonds for $10,000 towards its construction in 1869. Opponents defeated a similar bond issue twice more, but by only five votes in 1871 and by only two votes in 1872. Once again people east and west of the Mountain may

*This railroad operated under five different names before 1900. It was chartered as the Connecticut Western in 1869 and became the Central New England Railway Company about this time.

Middle bridge

have been on opposite sides of a question. The Clarks and Gays on the east side of the Mountain supported the branch as a convenient means of transportation for themselves and their marketable farm produce. People west of the Mountain already had the Canal Railroad.

Another exciting undertaking in East Granby at the end of the century was the Hartford Electric Light Company's new hydroelectric plant on the Farmington River at Spoonville. Horace Smith, who had bought Henry A. Case's millsite on the river in 1882, was connected with Smith & Wesson, firearms manufacturers of Springfield. His plans to build a paper factory still had not materialized ten years later when the town voted to abate taxes on the property under certain conditions. Smith added more property in 1893 shortly before he died, and the utility company acquired all of his land in 1896.

The hydroelectric plant, which the company named the Tariffville Station, consisted of a 250-foot concrete dam with a 29-foot fall of water; two pairs of 1300-horsepower water wheels, each connected to a 750-kilowatt generator; and a brick powerhouse. For years the plant sent almost all its power to Hartford over aluminum wires, the first time anyone ever used aluminum to transmit electricity, according to Glenn Weaver in his history of the company. When the plant began operation on Thanksgiving Day in 1899, it became the most valuable enterprise in town, and the electric company became the town's largest taxpayer. The 1910 Grand List valued the property at about $135,000.

A renewal of the search for copper in the Mountain added to the excitement in the fall of 1899. Blasting at Vineyard Notch for the Central New England's railroad tracks had uncovered rich veins of copper, and men were sinking shafts and bringing up ore. Avery Davis of Leadville, Colorado, and Andrew B. Hendryx of New Haven, as the Lenox Mining Company, had acquired the mining rights to 100 acres of land

Cut through the Mountain for the Central New England Railway Branch

off Holcomb Street, and they were negotiating for mining rights at Newgate.

The mining off Holcomb Street did not continue for long. Davis boarded with the John Allisons on Holcomb Street, and Mildred Allison, a daughter-in-law, remembered that ore taken from a shaft at the rear of the old Higley house was of high quality, but water in the shaft was a problem. She felt that the expense of installing a pumping plant at the time was prohibitive.

At Newgate the Lenox Mining Company installed machinery and made arrangements to board miners. The mines reopened for only a few months, though, because the mining company and Charles H. Clark, owner of the mineral rights, could not agree on the distribution of the anticipated receipts from the operation.

Through all these expectations, successes, and disappointments, local families had reasons to be optimistic. Even the Spanish American War in 1898 did not affect them significantly. Evidently few, if any, local men participated in this brief conflict.

The local creamery continued to be a stable outlet for farmers' cream. In fact, the East Granby Creamery received third prize for its butter at the National Butter and Cheese Makers Convention at Cedar Rapids, Iowa, in April of 1896. Later that year the company won second prize at the annual meeting of the National Association of the Exhibition of Livestock at Madison Square Garden, New York.

Connecticut's tobacco production increased significantly during the 1890s and East Granby's farmers shared in the prosperity. Then, at the end of the century, the news came from the Connecticut Experimental Station at Poquonock that Sumatra tobacco grown there under shade was equal to any imported tobacco. The United States Secretary of Agriculture rightly predicted a complete and auspicious revolution of the tobacco business in the Connecticut Valley.

Higley Copper Mine, c. 1900

Property values rose, sales increased, and once-abandoned farms were refurbished as the old home town became more attractive to its native young people. Overall, hopes ran high and optimism prevailed as a solidly agricultural East Granby entered the 20th century.

20

The Heyday of the Cigar

A GOOD CIGAR was many things to men in generations past. It was a token of courtesy and acceptance that one man could offer another, a companion for a lonely peddler, a common bond among spectators at sporting events. It was a necessity for politicians in their smoke-filled rooms, the complement to a good dinner, and the salvation of a poor one. It was an antidote for righteous cleanliness, a badge of substance and success, a comfortable vice, and a simple pleasure.

The first cigars smoked in Connecticut tended to be rather light in color and spotty in quality. Tobacco users preferred pipes, snuff, and chewing plugs. In time tobacco leaf culture and cigar manufacturing improved and cigar smokers increased in number. Soon they had developed particular tastes. By the middle of the 19th century the majority favored dark, very aromatic cigars.

Growers on the small farms in the Connecticut River Valley, including those in East Granby, produced excellent tobacco for the most sought-after smokes. They had imported and improved the heavy leaved Broadleaf tobacco plant and, later, the lighter weight, narrower leaved Havana seedleaf plant that thrived in the soil west of the river. They grew both these varieties in patches and fields open to the sun and sold the best of their crops at top prices to be used as outer wrapper leaves. These gave cigars a highly salable dark appearance and robust scent.

Before the beginning of the 20th century, cigarmakers introduced a fine quality, light colored cigar. It was wrapped in very lightweight, smooth textured, almost odorless leaves grown on the Indonesian island of Sumatra, where low-lying clouds shade the fields and keep them humid. Although these leaves cost cigar manufacturers more per pound than dark leaves, a pound of them served to wrap more than twice as many cigars. The light cigars caught the public's fancy and very soon the market for local tobacco crops diminished.

Just as they had in the past when tobacco grown elsewhere threatened their profit margins, local growers asked for government assistance in the form of protective tariffs. When higher tariffs proved of little use against the growing popularity of the Sumatra leaf, the growers' only recourse was to develop a competitive product. To help them the agricultural departments of both the state and federal governments assigned a number of innovative men to experimental projects. Among them was Marcus L. Floyd.

Floyd was the son of a Florida tobacco grower. He was familiar with tobacco culture there, and with growing plants under artificial shade. Working for the government, he traveled to Europe to observe the tobacco industry there and to help prepare the American exhibit for the 1899 Universal International Exposition in Paris.

About 1900 Floyd arrived in Connecticut to assist with experiments in growing tobacco under cloth mesh tenting, which closely reproduced the humid and shady conditions found naturally on Sumatra. The State of Connecticut conducted one experiment in the Poquonock section of Windsor, and Ariel Mitchelson, a large-scale grower, carried out one in Tariffville. According to Mitchelson's daughter Adelaide Mitchelson Millea, her father had noticed that leaves growing under an apple tree in his field were finer and silkier than those growing in the open, and she believes her father was the first to experiment with growing tobacco under shade. William J. Hayes of Tariffville also did early experimentation in shade growing in that village and in Puerto Rico.

The first-year successes of the experimental fields caused quite a sensation and despite warnings many entrepreneurs jumped into shade growing before all the problems of its culture were identified and solved. This led to many disappointments and considerable loss of money during the first several years of commercial ventures. Finally it became apparent that the cost of erecting poles and netting was beyond the capital resources of independent farmers, with a few notable exceptions like Mitchelson and Hayes, so shade growing passed into the hands of agricultural corporations. These new syndicates of investors bought a number of small farms to form each of their many plantations throughout the Connecticut Valley.

The Tobacco Plantations

The plantation that became known as Floydville was the first commercially successful corporate shade tobacco venture in the valley. Its success was pivotal in the early development of the shade tobacco industry. Floydville was owned and operated by the Connecticut Tobacco Corporation, which was formed in December 1901 with $115,000 capital. The president of the corporation was a Havana importer from New York City, William J. Hazelwood. Its vice-president was a textile manufacturer from New York and Easthampton, Massachusetts, J. H. Lane. Ariel Mitchelson was the secretary-treasurer and Marcus L. Floyd was the salaried general manager. Other directors and stockholders included tobacco importers, growers, and cigar and textile manufacturers. Many were from out-of-state and others were from Hartford. Paul Ackerly, a newspaperman who became quite active in the tobacco business in this area, was from Rockville.

The Floydville Plantation straddled the East Granby-Granby line west of Salmon Brook. This plantation grew to 330 acres while it was held by the original corporation.

Investor Paul Ackerly bought three farms near the corporation's land a year later and formed the Ackerly Tobacco Company, Inc. He apparently put this tobacco land under Floyd's management at first and eventually sold it to the Farren family for whom Farren Road (now Wolcott Road) was named. In 1903 Ackerly bought land near Granby Station and formed the Indian Head Plantation with $30,000 capitalization. According to the *Journal* this brought his aggregate holdings along Salmon Brook to more than 300 acres. Local tradition holds that the plantation took its name from the Indian Head cloth company, which wove cotton mesh used for tobacco tents.

After sterilizing the protected seed beds with steam to destroy weed seeds, insects, and disease, workers sowed the tiny tobacco seeds in late April or early May. Note the large tobacco sheds, or curing barns, in the background.

As the seedlings developed, workers covered the fields with cotton mesh by attaching it to poles, usually made of peeled chestnut tree trunks. Plowing and other soil preparation were done after the cloth was in place.

At harvest time boys picked the green leaves by hand and placed them in baskets. They picked the bottom leaves, which matured first, then returned three more times to pick successively higher leaves.

Mules drew the baskets to the sheds. In the shade tobacco fields today, boys and girls pick the leaves by hand and place them in baskets, which are now usually canvas. Tractors have replaced horses and mules.

A series of photographs from stereographs in Marcus L. Floyd's own collection illustrating how shade tobacco was grown early in the 20th century.

When the danger of frost was past, workers riding on a horse-drawn planting machine set the young plants in the field by hand. Men weeded the tobacco with hoes.

Marcus L. Floyd, shown on horseback, managed the Floydville plantation where these pictures were taken. Begun in 1902, this was the first of three plantations developed by the Connecticut Tobacco Corporation.

With large needles, women sewed a number of leaves onto a string and stretched it onto a wooden lath. The loaded laths were hung in the sheds until the leaves dried and turned brown. Charcoal heaters speeded drying and warded off mold and rot.

The dried leaves were taken down during a "damp", a spell of weather that made them pliable enough to be handled. They were sweated, or fermented, to improve their burn, taste, and color and then sorted by size and color and pressed into woven shipping cartons.

Ackerly put Indian Head Plantation under the supervision of a Windsor native who settled in East Granby, John S. Dewey, and Dewey bought the plantation in 1913. In addition he owned two other farms, giving him a total of about 70 acres on which he did general farming and continued to grow shade tobacco. Dewey was also in the business of buying and packing tobacco.

In 1911 the Connecticut Tobacco Corporation added the Hazelwood Plantation, which straddled the East Granby-Windsor line. This plantation grew to 488.43 acres. Still later the corporation developed the Silver Lane Plantation in East Hartford. The corporation merged with the larger Georgia-based American Sumatra Tobacco Corporation in 1918, and Floyd eventually became a vice-president and director of that company. Later he was the manager of the Cullman Brothers plantations. During his long career, Floyd headed several delegations which represented the Connecticut tobacco growers' interests in Washington, D.C.

Initially, most of the permanent labor force on the Connecticut Tobacco Corporation's plantations was made up of immigrant Polish and Lithuanian families. They usually lived near the Floydville Plantation, either along Hartford Avenue or in Tariffville. Here they could worship in the faith of their homelands at St. Bernard's Catholic church.

By the summer of 1917 the burgeoning shade tobacco industry faced a labor shortage, so Floyd began bringing black families up from the South to both Floydville and Hazelwood. For that era Floyd's labor practices were considered quite forward-thinking and benevolent. He provided small houses with a bit of land for settled families and well-equipped boarding houses for transient labor. Each plantation had a baseball diamond where workers from the two plantations vented their natural rivalry on Sunday afternoons.

Seth C. Sharp, a direct descendant of Thomas Sharp and an independent farmer and tobacco grower in East Granby, thought the opportunity for black people was so good on the plantations that he did what he could to encourage them to come here. Evelyn Edmonds Sharp says that Seth Sharp, who was her husband's grandfather, advanced money to people who wanted to emigrate from the South and many times wrote off the debt.

Rushia West, the granddaughter of Georgia slaves, was one of those who came to the Floydville Plantation in 1917, when she was twenty-five years old. In a taped interview she tells of conditions as they were for her in the South and of the improvements in her life after she came here.

She got better pay, $2 a day rather than as little as 50 cents. She was provided with a better house, with wooden floors rather than dirt, electricity, and running water—but still no bathrooms at first. Her daughter Ruthie got a better education than she herself had gotten, and there was no segregation in the trains, hotels, and public restrooms.

West and her husband were not prepared for the cold winters, and at one point they tried working in a hotel and a department store in Hartford, but they returned to tobacco work because the wages were better. Within ten years they owned 5 acres, a house, and a car, and felt very fortunate. As she explained on reflection, in Georgia the boll weevil infestation was ruining small farmers like her parents and there was "no money because it all went to the war; nothing for the whites to help the colored people. Coming here looked as if [*we might have*] a better chance. People had a little something they could extend to you."

The three plantations, Floydville, Hazelwood, and Indian Head, had a permanent labor force which eventually grew to several hundred. For the harvest each year, they doubled their force with temporary workers. Boys were preferred to men for picking the leaves because they were small and agile enough to move between the rows of plants without damaging them. To further ensure gentle handling, women were hired to string the leaves onto the drying laths. They commuted daily from Westfield, Massachusetts, Hartford, and nearby towns. They were escorted to and from the train stations and supervised closely because, as one newspaper put it, harvest time was "the season when the transient population employed on the tobacco plantations make trouble." The plantations had varying success with importing college men for summer work. Black students from the South worked well, but many students from New York City College quit within a week rather than work overtime.

Harvest time in August was a period of almost nonstop activity on the plantations. In 1909 the Connecticut Tobacco Corporation estimated that their hands, assisted by fourteen mules recently imported from the West, would pick and string a million leaves a day for a total harvest of 50 million. That year the corporation installed electric lights in their sheds so that work could go on into the night.

That year, also, the company had a new sorting shop with a sloping glass roof at Floydville. It was said to be the longest building of its kind with one of the largest skylights in the world. Setting another record, one of the corporation's fields was the largest ever—120 acres—under a single tent.

The Independent Tobacco-Dairy Farms

While the syndicates were developing their large shade tobacco plantations, East Granby's independent farmers continued raising outdoor tobacco because it was by far the most valuable cash crop they could grow. Almost every property in town had a field of tobacco. The fields varied in size from less than an acre to 50 acres, with the typical farm growing 5 to 10. The town had approximately eighty independent tobacco growers during this period. Property owners who did not work their fields themselves leased them "on shares" to these growers, who were either neighboring landed farmers or tenant farmers working toward buying land of their own. Naturally, the prosperity of the whole town depended largely on the prosperity of the season's tobacco crop.

The 1911 and 1912 seasons provide a study of the failure and success of two tobacco crops. The first year a drought slowed the development of the plants, then a severe hailstorm riddled the leaves on about twenty farms. Heavy rains delayed the harvesting of some late-maturing crops and they were caught by an early frost. Hail-cut leaves brought from 4 to 11 cents a pound, frostbitten brought 11 to 14 cents, and high-grade brought as much as 17 cents.

The prices for damaged tobacco did not yield enough cash to fully repay the loans most farmers had arranged in the spring with private businessmen and fertilizer companies to finance seed, fertilizer, and labor. Some farmers cut their losses by plowing their crops under. Those whose fields were so small they could tend the tobacco themselves and fertilize mostly with manure from their own livestock suffered less cash loss than farmers with larger crops. The few growers whose tobacco somehow escaped damage sold their crops as fine-quality wrapper leaves and made about $400 per acre because good tobacco was scarce that year. Encouraged by these few successes, the town's farmers were ready and willing to gamble again in 1912.

There was cash to be made during the winter months hauling fertilizer from the railroad siding in the Center to the Connecticut Tobacco Corporation's new Hazelwood Plantation in the eastern part of town. The fertilizer was manure from horse stables in New York. In November the *Herald* reported: "The haul is now about three miles and three trips daily." The farmers transported 220 freight car loads that winter in their wagons on wheels and runners.

The 1912 tobacco season began inauspiciously with a wet spring, which delayed the transplanting of the young plants from their seed beds to the open fields. In mid-July the farmers began to worry because the fields were becoming too dry. Rain came in time, though, and by the second week in August the success of the 1912 tobacco crop was apparent. "The tobacco buyers having learned that the crop in East Granby was one of the best growing in the state, have been busy in the town all this week," the paper reported. The buyers were offering 22 cents a pound for high-grade and 17 cents for low-grade leaves. Growers went to bed at night secure in the knowledge that their debts would be paid and that they would realize a profit.

The practice of buying tobacco crops in the field rather than after they were harvested and bundled had begun two years earlier at the insistence of the Hartford County Tobacco Growers Association. The association must have thought that it could get better prices for members with this arrangement, but the buyers peppered their sales contracts with loopholes and used them liberally. The *Herald* reported the following February:

Practically every piece of tobacco in town has been sold once, but there are a number of lots of tobacco that have not been delivered and it is not an uncommon thing for a buyer to put in an appearance and find fault with the crop and offer the grower a smaller figure than was agreed on when it was sold last summer in the field. It certainly looks as though the grower was at the mercy of a trust or combination of dealers who will agree to do one thing and then do another.

To be fair to the dealers, the bumper crop of good tobacco that season had begun to flood the market, and prices had begun to fall according to the law of supply and demand.

Along with disease and insect infestations and quirks of weather, overproduction was a constant worry to farmers. On the local level, each grower hoped that his neighbor would plant less tobacco while he himself planted more. On the national level, Connecticut growers tried to surpass those in other states by growing a finer quality of wrapper leaves. The quality of their product was so high that in 1903 the Hartford County growers asked the legislature to require all Connecticut tobacco to be stamped as such to prevent Massachusetts growers from selling their crops as Connecticut's. On the international level, American growers fought for higher tariffs on tobacco imported from other countries where lower labor costs made it cheaper to grow.

When World War I began to disrupt importation, Connecticut tobacco growers immediately realized higher prices. Warren E. Lampson remembered: "I raised 6 acres of tobacco on the Bacon farm in 1914. I thought I was a wealthy man. Had $729 in the spring, put on a derby hat, a blue suit, and got married in March 1915."

The desire to increase profits led progressive farmers to experiment with new methods in every step of production. With the help of the state and federal departments of agriculture and the small state agricultural school at Storrs, farmers learned more about the chemistry of their fields. They began to use fertilizers and other additives more effectively and to try rotating their crops. The government also opened weather forecasting stations in the tobacco region to warn of frosts.

Most farmers now had horse-drawn machines that made it easier to spread manure and to plant tobacco. They also were beginning to use gasoline-powered machines, Francis P. "Frank" Granger having bought what may have been the first gasoline engine in town in 1905. He used it to cut tobacco stalks for farmers around town and soon after bought a bigger engine which could run a gristmill and fill silos. During this period farmers were beginning to replace their shallow, dug wells with more dependable drilled wells. At least six farms had windmills to pump water before gasoline-powered pumps became popular. Benjamin N. Alderman ran a pipe from his mill-filled water tank to his seed bed in 1912, creating the first reported irrigation system in town.

Some individuals, including George E. Bidwell, Henry Z. Thompson, Rollin W. Cowles, and Peter J. Burns, tried harvesting their tobacco by the new method used by shade growers called priming. Primed leaves, picked one by one from the growing plant instead of being stripped from the dry stalk as in the traditional method, were lighter in color, finer in texture, and slightly heavier after curing. Consequently, they sold for higher prices. Priming meant hiring more labor for the harvest, however, so most of the outdoor tobacco growers continued to harvest in the old way.

The older residents in town today remember that during the harvest almost every man, woman, and child worked together in the fields and sheds. Farmers who needed extra hands drove their wagons into Hartford and rounded up men from the streets.

Some individuals in town engaged in aspects of the tobacco business beyond growing. Horace V. Griffin was a financier who became notorious locally for foreclosing on several farms that suffered a series of crop failures. Frank H. Dibble sold hail insurance and Daniel Eagleson perfected and sold a box for pressing leaves into bundles. A few men, including Charles P. Viets and Austin P. Stowell, became expert at sorting leaves; that is, they were paid to separate leaves in a crop and bundle them according to size and color. Louis R. Lobdell built sorting and sweating rooms on his farm at 51-53 Rainbow Road and several other farmers had storage warehouses. It was a common practice to hold a crop a year or two, either because there was no buyer for it or because buyers were offering less than a farmer wanted.

Since tobacco promised great profits but could not be counted on for a steady income, farmers continued to diversify, usually producing perishable products that could not be transported easily from the great farming lands in the Midwest. The town creamery closed after butter started to come into the area in refrigerator cars. In 1905 many farmers began sending whole milk to a plant in Hartford which distributed it throughout the city. The growing market for fluid milk, plus the fact that cow manure was very valuable fertilizer for their tobacco, led some town farmers to develop dairy herds of as many as fifty cows.

To get the milk to Hartford one gatherer collected it from the farms west of the Mountain and put it on the train at Tariffville. At first the gatherer on the east side put his milk on the trolley at Rainbow, and in later years he put it on the train at the depot in North Bloomfield. Burton L. Griffin seems to have been the first gatherer

Lester Kniffin collecting milk for Ernest T. Giddings about 1912

on the west side, followed by Moses E. Seymour, Owen E. Goslee and his son Clifford, and A. Robert Holcomb. Francis P. Granger was the first on the east, followed by Ernest T. Giddings. Some of these men merely owned their routes and hired others to do the actual collecting. The exploits of milk collectors, who were determined to get milk through despite all weather conditions, often made them local heros equaled only by the rural delivery mail carriers.

There were also men who peddled milk door-to-door along routes in places like Poquonock, where many mill workers lived. Usually milkmen poured their milk directly into the customers' containers, but Charles P. McKinnie, who had a route in Windsor Locks between 1908 and 1914, also filled quart bottles at his home. He sold quarts for 8 cents apiece. Most milkmen who sold milk directly from the farmers to the public were put out of business by laws requiring pasteurization.

By 1916 the dairymen who sent their milk to Hartford were upset with the price they were being paid by their current buyer, the Bryant and Chapman Company. They formed a cooperative association in town and about forty of them joined the Connecticut Milk Producers Association. Charles P. Viets was one of the founders of this state organization and its vice-president for many terms.

The next year the dairymen, along with those from other towns, went on strike. They held their milk off the market for eleven tense and unhappy days in April until they found a purchaser who offered a higher price. This was the first of many disputes that arose when overproduction held the wholesale price of milk down or rising production costs rendered it inadequate.

A number of the dairy cows in town were registered thoroughbreds, and each fall local dairymen won prizes for their animals at agricultural fairs. The Holstein-Friezian Association in 1917 congratulated breeder Charles P. Viets on having nine full-blooded heifers that were closely related to the prize cow of the world. A few dairymen, like George E. Bidwell, of 43 Newgate Road, also operated small dealerships that bought and sold cows and show oxen.

The Hiram C. Viets feed and grain business in the Center and Franklin B. Lockwood's store near the Granby Station (now Walter M. Simmons & Sons) supplied some livestock feed, and farmers sometimes bought freight car loads directly from wholesalers. They raised most of their feed, however, and getting in the hay and the corn was nearly as big a production as getting in the tobacco. The silos which sprouted around town during this era kept fodder green during the winter.

Ice was another "crop" important to dairying. Before electrical refrigeration, farmers needed it to keep their milk from spoiling between collections in warm weather. Each dairyman harvested hundreds of tons of ice from ponds around town during January and February. When the ice was 10 to 18 inches thick, men manually sawed it into blocks and transported it by horse and wagon to their icehouses where they packed it in sawdust. Sometimes they hired men like Frank LeMay to fill their icehouses for them. Households that did not have icehouses filled their kitchen iceboxes with blocks bought from peddlers.

Besides cows, horses continued to be part of the economy of the town for both their labor and their sport. Hiram Adams of North Bloomfield was the most active horse dealer in the area, but often East Granby men bought horses from as far away as Michigan for resale in town. Carl B. Tucker and Ernest S. Palmer ran a livery stable behind 22-24 Old Hartford Avenue. People taking the train from Tariffville could leave their horses and rigs there and incoming passengers, like manufacturers' drummers, could rent horses, buggies, and business wagons.

A good many townsmen prided themselves on their fine racehorses. After the demise of the East Granby Agricultural Association around the turn of the century, its fairground with a racetrack at the East Granby-Windsor Locks line was planted in tobacco. Men continued to enter their horses in races at tracks in neighboring towns, however, and challenged each other on summer evenings on South Main Street. The selectmen halted these events in 1912 because they were a hazard to the growing automobile traffic.

With a town full of cows and horses, Dr. Thomas J. Lee was one of the busiest men around. He was a certified veterinarian who also ran his father's blacksmith shop near 15 School Street with the help of assistant smiths. Dr. James H. Prophett, who had his practice in Westfield and Suffield but was related to the Aldermans in town, was called at times to tend sick animals, too. In 1909 E. Frank Rosier built a blacksmith shop near 35 South Main Street. He was also known for handcrafting violins. At the same time blacksmiths continued to occupy the old Merwin and Holcomb shop next to the Tucker & Palmer livery stable.

The number of sheep in town had been steadily dropping for some time and in 1913 Clarence N. Case of 195-197 North Main Street sold his flock. The *Journal* reported it was the last in town although ten years later the paper mentioned that Charles J. Holcomb had a flock of forty-three. Farm families occasionally raised a few sheep and fattened a hog or two for eating while buying more of their meat and fish from ped-

Mr. and Mrs. James McKinnie leaving the Tucker and Palmer livery

dlers and storekeepers. Helen Moody remembers being allowed to stay home from school for the hog butchering and seeing the blood pour onto the white snow. Newell L. DeGray and Seth C. Sharp specialized in butchering during this period. Sharp told the tale of a January day in 1912 which was so cold that as soon as he took the hog out of the scalding water, the tail froze so stiff he could sharpen his knife on it.

All farm families kept chickens for their own use and some raised them commercially for their eggs and chicks. Usually the women and children ran this sideline.

Wild-animal life still had a small economic value to the people in town. Commercial fishing had long since ended, but the local streams yielded plentiful trout and the river provided many good meals of pickerel and eel. Hunting and trapping were necessary in some cases, as well as good sport. On rare occasions panthers, which killed livestock, had to be eliminated. Foxes, which destroyed chickens, were a more common problem; the town placed a bounty on them. Fur of all sorts could be used for warm wraps or sold. The *Herald* reported in 1917 that muskrat brought 50 cents, skunk $4.50, otter $10, and red fox $12.50.

Several fox hunts were staged on the Mountain each fall. Hounds routed the foxes and drove them toward the hunters, who stationed themselves on foot along trails. A coterie of hunters numbering about twenty was lionized by the local press. Of these J. Edward Viets, Seth C. Sharp, Westley and George DeGray, Charles E. Owen, Harry W. Case, Charles G. Sandman, and Francis P. Granger gained additional note by following the hunts in Massachusetts.

Besides fox, hunters shot squirrel, woodchuck, raccoon, owl, crane, and state-stocked partridge. Several of the town's heartier young bachelors spent the winter months in a bungalow on the Mountain in quest of game. The hotel at 28 School Street, where proprietor Richard D. Cannon hung his fox skins beside the mirror in the bar, was a great gathering place for sportsmen. The Newgate Coon Club, which still owns a hunting preserve and lodge in another part of the state, was founded largely by East Granby men.

When a farmer wanted to diversify his field crops, he was likely to grow potatoes. A few put in perishable specialties like asparagus, tomatoes, raspberries, and strawberries. Apple orchards were in decline, often meeting their end as firewood. Most of the town's remaining apple crop was shipped to Massachusetts to be made into cider, cider brandy, and vinegar because all the local commercial distilleries had ceased operation. Cherries, pears, peaches, and walnuts were very small crops; chestnuts, which used to be shipped to New York City by the freight car load, had almost disappeared because of the American chestnut tree blight.

Wood was more valuable than it had ever been because of the amount of development going on in the surrounding cities and towns. Farmers sold the wood from whole woodlots to companies that came to the sites with portable steam-powered sawmills. Their crews produced lumber on the spot using slabwood, their own scrap, to fuel their mills. They also took out poles, railroad ties, and, in the case of an immense oak across from the South District School, shipbuilding material. In 1917 the paper reported the sale of a mountain woodlot in the south end of town that was "one of the few virgin tracts of forest in this section." At about the same time, the state was funding a program to forest "waste land" that resulted in the large stand of white pine which grows today on the sandy plain in the extreme eastern part of town.

The town's farms, themselves, were also rising in value as the tobacco syndicates bought acreage and families leaving behind economic and political turmoil in eastern Europe sought independent farms. The May family is believed to have been the first of this particular wave of newcomers to buy property in town. John May came to this country from Lithuania in the early 1890s and worked as a farm laborer until he had saved enough money to send for his wife and five children. At the time, Russia occupied Lithuania, so the family had to be smuggled out of the country in a wagon of hay. In 1907 the Mays bought the house then at 249 Hartford Avenue. The house burned down within a year, but the Mays rebuilt on the old foundation and made the new house look as much as possible like the old one. Soon more Lithuanian names, like Bartkus, Petraitis, Mulkulkas, Batyte, Narbutas, Padelskas, and Vaitkevich, were added to East Granby's land records.

A Polish bakery opened near the Mays in 1909 in the old stone blacksmith shop on the north side of Hatchet Hill Road near its intersection with Hartford Avenue. The baker, Roman Zawiskowski (or Gawiskowski), came from Hartford and remained in town at least five years before moving his shop to Elm Street in Tariffville. He employed three other Polish men and peddled a variety of baked goods with a horse and wagon.

Families from Poland added names like Bazyk, Stark, Ciemiega, Modzeleski, and Perkowski to the town. They and the Lithuanians had engaged in a variety of occupations in their homelands, but most worked on farms or in factories in this country to earn money to buy land. These immigrants came in far greater numbers than the Irish who had trickled into town during the previous century, and they seemed more foreign because English was not their native tongue. Once they settled, planted tobacco, and started developing dairy herds, they were accepted as hard-working farmers in a community of farms.

21

Transportation and Technology

UNTIL THE BEGINNING of the 20th century, the town's main corridor of freight and passenger transportation was west of the Mountain rather than through the Center. The Granby Turnpike, the Farmington Canal, and its replacement the Canal Railroad, ran north and south along the town's western boundary. To the southeast, a few miles beyond the town line, a trolley took passengers to Hartford from the Rainbow section of Windsor. Only intrepid stagecoach drivers like Francis Granger and Harvey E. Dibble offered passenger, freight, and mail service over the dirt roads that reached the Center.

The Central New England Railway Company Branch

All this changed after the turn of the century when the Central New England (CNE) completed a branch that ran from Tariffville through East Granby Center to Agawam Junction in Massachusetts, where it connected with a line to Springfield. The contest of wills over the railroad's right to build this branch was even more heated than the one that preceded the building of the Canal Railroad in the 1850s. Railroad historian Charles Milmine aptly dubbed it "The Battle of Montague Farm."

Plans for the branch line had been approved by the General Assembly in 1887 and the route was established at that time. The CNE agreed to pay each landowner along the proposed route for right-of-way. Financial problems delayed the start of construction until 1898, after these options had expired; however, all but one landowner honored the agreement. When a railroad official came to settle accounts on the farm at 27-29 North Main Street, he got a surprise. The farm, though unproductive at the time, had just been sold to a Massachusetts man, Charles E. Montague, who would not grant a right-of-way.

Montague, it became apparent, was an agent for the New York, New Haven & Hartford Railroad (NYNH&H), which wanted to block construction of the branch to avoid competition for its own two north-south lines in the area, the Canal Railroad and the Hartford to Springfield line along the Connecticut River. The managers felt that the CNE was building the branch simply to force the entrenched railroad to buy it or the entire CNE system, as the smaller company had once proposed. The CNE claimed that it wished to break the monopoly the NYNH&H had in the area and to provide

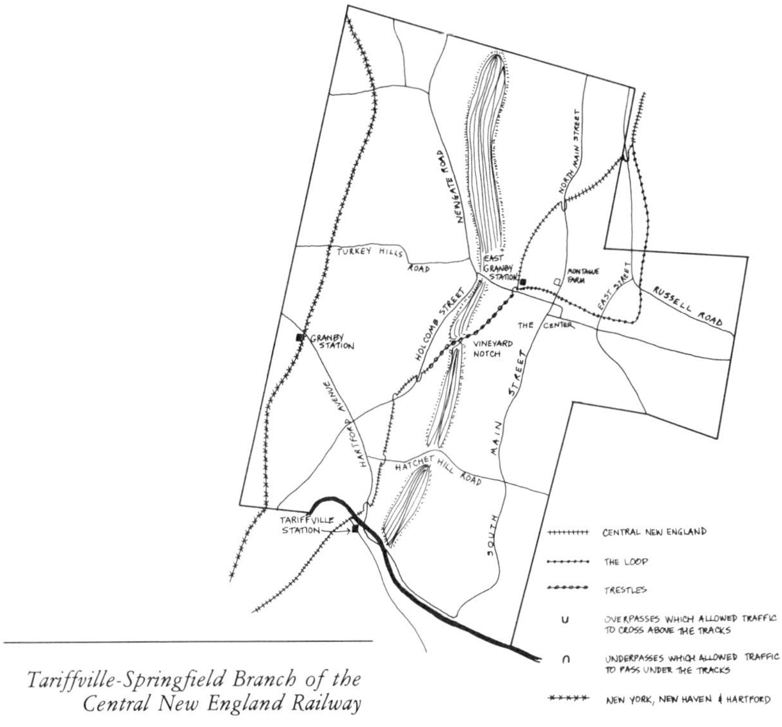

Tariffville-Springfield Branch of the Central New England Railway

towns in northwestern Connecticut with direct service to Springfield. The legal battle that ensued cost the railroads almost half a million dollars, lasted four years, and reached the Connecticut Supreme Court.

Closer to home, the CNE tried two moves to counter the NYNH&H's block. First it proceeded to lay track across the Montague farm and transport its equipment to the other side. One townsman was fond of telling how the entire 300 feet of track was laid across the farm during the time it took his father and him to haul a load of apples to a cider mill. Apparently the CNE officials hoped that when the track had been laid well past the farm, the federal government would back their cause, since the railroad was to carry mail. The NYNH&H got an injunction, however, and tore up the track on the Montague farm.

The CNE went right on laying ties and rails. A number of longtime residents remember the construction or their parents' accounts of it. They recall that the contractor, J. B. Corbett, moved into town to supervise the job and lived for years on East Street. Many of his work crew and later rail repairmen were Italian immigrants who spoke little or no English. They had a contraption powered by twelve mules which caught the townspeople's fancy. It scooped up fill and, using an endless belt, dumped it into mule-drawn wagons.

The first trainload of passengers ran along the branch as far as the obstructing farm in May 1901, according to the *Journal.* The party of about 350 consisted of members of the Connecticut legislature, their friends, and railroad officials. After a few short speeches and time to view the situation, they all returned to Hartford. That same week,

Building the roadbed of the Central New England Railway Branch with mule power in 1899

the first carload of freight, fertilizer for a tobacco farm, arrived on the line.

Soon after, the legislature granted the CNE permission to build a detour to bypass the Montague farm. The East Granby and Suffield Railway Company, with capital stock of $100,000, was formed to lay track for "the loop," as it was known. The long loop left the main track beyond the first temporary station on the Mountain, crossed North Main Street just south of the creamery, and stretched eastward until it crossed East Street. Then it turned northward and rejoined the main track in West Suffield. The route required four bridges, including an iron arch on crushed rock and cement abutments which allowed traffic on North Main Street to cross above the track. The workmen on this project numbered about 100 in full force and they used as many as thirty teams of animals.

After an inspection trip by state railroad commissioners and CNE officials, the branch line, including the loop, was put into regular service in September 1902. The CNE officials immediately proposed laying a track from the loop into Windsor Locks and bought land along the route, but the plan never materialized. Five months after trains started running, the NYNH&H, now called the Consolidated Railroad, sold the Montague farm to the CNE. Track was laid again across the farm and the loop fell into disuse. By 1904 the whole CNE system had become part of the Consolidated Railroad and the loop had been stripped of ties and rails.

Before the merger the CNE had constructed a permanent station at the junction of the main track and the loop, just west of the present entrance to Old Newgate Ridge on Turkey Hills Road. Benjamin A. Krick opened the East Granby station at seven in the morning and closed it at seven in the evening, walking home to 4 North Main Street for meals between trains. Except for one brief period, Krick ran the station the entire time it operated, about thirty years. He was stationmaster, freightmaster, and telegraph operator. His daughter, Helen Krick Root, gives this description:

It was a wooden station with an open platform on both ends. The waiting room held twenty or thirty people. It was heated with soft coal in a potbellied stove that got red hot. My

father had to take care of it.
The telegraph was in the private part of the station and, when storms came, the lightning would really dance off those keys—scare you half to death. I always wanted to learn how to use the telegraph key, the dots and dashes. Phones weren't as accessible then. The telegraph was very active with lots of messages pertaining to the railroad—running times, etc. It was also used for distant message sending—important things.

The CNE train, which chugged through town at a top speed of 30 miles per hour, became a regular feature of town life. It made three round trips daily when service began in 1902, but made only two by 1912. The great black locomotive, No. 29, belched smoke and sparks, which set grass fires in dry weather and threatened the wooden trestles along the way. It tooted its whistle, delighting children and startling horses, and occasionally ran down a stray cow.

The locomotive pulled a mixed train with two passenger cars behind as many as fourteen freight cars. It often left several cars of fertilizer, feed, or coal on a siding at the Center to be unloaded. The freight cars also brought hoboes and in 1912 the *Herald* reported: "The old shack left by Italian laborers some time ago, which has been a tramp headquarters since that time, has been closed to weary pedestrians by the selectmen who have padlocked the door."

Eva L. Pinney was the first person to transport the bags of incoming and outgoing mail between the train and the post office in the Viets store. She and her handcart with bicycle wheels were a familiar sight in the Center.

In 1908 East Granby joined Granby and Avon in sending students to Simsbury High School in the Horace Belden Building on Hopmeadow Street. Hazel Granger Lampson remembers that she and her classmates took the eight o'clock train from the East Granby station, then transferred at Tariffville to get to the high school. School was dismissed shortly after 3 P.M., but the East Granby students did not get home until after 6 o'clock. They used the hours before the evening train to study, she says.

Mazie Viets recalls that "about twenty of us went from East Granby and practically the only other passengers on the train were traveling salesmen." Helen Moody adds that in the morning "very often there would be some chorus girls on the train while we were going to school. They sat in the back."

The students continued to take the train until about 1918 when changes in train and school schedules made it impractical. Passenger service was discontinued in 1927

East Granby railroad station

Turkey Hills Road with railroad bridge in middle distance

and freight was discontinued in 1938. Shortly thereafter the station was dismantled for salvage and the rails were torn up, but traces of the roadbed still can be seen today.

Road Improvements and the Appearance of the Automobile

In the year 1900 all the women in town wore long dresses, the primary means of transportation was the horse, and all the roads were dirt, some refined a bit with gravel. While trailing skirts and spirited steeds imbue the era with romance, the dirt roads are less enthusiastically remembered. Gradually but constantly since the end of the last century, work crews funded by both the town and state have worked to level the grade of the roads, pave them, and amend their courses until the town's wagon ways have been transformed into modern asphalt thoroughfares.

Roger H. Stowell told how the town crews groomed the dirt roads. Every spring, after their icy, rutted surfaces had thawed and dried sufficiently, a crew smoothed them with a scraper. According to Stowell, the scraper had four wheels and a movable iron blade similar to the blade on today's snowplows, but fastened under the midsection of the machine. It was pulled by four horses and operated by two men. The men lowered one end of the scraper into the drainage ditch beside the road and brought dirt up to the center. Later, workers picked oversized stones from the roadway.

During the summer a town crew scattered oil on the roads to keep the dust down.

The roads were scraped again in the fall. They were not plowed in the winter, although crews "broke out" the drifts. People simply put away their wagons and buggies and hitched their horses to sleighs. Even the stagecoaches changed to runners. Travelers often left the roads in winter and struck out over snowy farm fields.

In 1895 the General Assembly addressed the matter of improving inter-town roads by using a combination of state and local funds administered by its newly created state highway department. By 1900 a contractor and crew working under the state aid program were busy with steam drills lowering the grade over the Mountain on Turkey Hills Road.

In 1903 one crew of townsmen lowered Creamery Hill (just north of Creamery Brook on North Main Street) and another raised the grade where Muddy Brook crosses Hartford Avenue. During the first decades of this century, the annual town reports routinely listed expenditures for dynamite and fuse caps, culverts and tile. One by one each hill and quagmire along an existing inter-town road was either blasted or drained.

The first true paving put on the inter-town roads in East Granby was telford, layers of stone and gravel rolled smooth. "I helped put the roads in around here for 50 cents an hour," Warren E. Lampson said. "We crushed the old stone walls for making the roads. We used our own horses and wagons. Then they came along with finer rock to fill in between the bigger rock."

Besides eliminating many stone walls, road contractors had countless carloads of traprock shipped in by rail. They also collected fieldstone from local properties and crushed it by machine, and they bought gravel from several pits in town. Mazie Viets remembered that the gravel pit on the Calkins farm at 62 South Main Street, which her father-in-law worked on shares, was the forerunner of the present Roncari Industries quarry opened in 1952. The Edward Balf Company operated a quarry with a traprock plant on the west side of the Mountain, south of Hatchet Hill Road, in 1916.

Willard W. Viets, Mrs. Viets' father-in-law, oversaw the first road paving crews in town during his tenure as first selectman from 1898 to 1922. In addition to his regular salary, he was paid by the day for supervising work on the state roads and he often worked along with his crew. In 1910 the *Journal* reported: "The roads are still being improved by our energetic selectman W. W. Viets and his employees. East Granby takes no back seat in the matter of good roads."

By 1914 the whole length of North and South Main streets from the Spoonville bridge to the Suffield border had been improved with gravel and telford and accepted as a state-aid road. Hartford Avenue was accepted by the state soon afterward. The town and state shared the financial responsibility for improving and maintaining these roads.

Interestingly, the only fully funded state road in town during this era was a segment of the Grand Trunk Line system, a highway designation established by the state in 1908. The Trunk Line that ran between Hartford and Tariffville via Bloomfield crossed the Spoonville bridge where it intersected with the end of South Main Street and ran for about a mile along the north bank of the Farmington River before leaving East Granby across the Middle bridge. This once heavily traveled strip of road, Tunxis Avenue, is a much less used dead end since the 1955 flood swept away the Spoonville and Middle bridges.

Today traffic going northward from Bloomfield divides before reaching the river.

Cars headed for East Granby Center go over a relocated Spoonville bridge and a new stretch of highway that bypasses South Main Street's former southern end, now called Spoonville Road. Cars going to East Granby west of the Mountain travel south of the River to Tariffville and then cross the Tariffville bridge, which has also been relocated. When the course of Hartford Avenue was adjusted to connect to the new bridge, part of the old turnpike was bypassed and renamed Old Hartford Avenue. A number of other roads in town have similarly been bypassed and some have been abandoned.

At the annual meeting in October 1912 the town voted to instruct its representative to the General Assembly "to endeavor to get a bill passed to have the state build and maintain the bridges on the Trunk Lines of the state roads." Since the Spoonville and Middle bridges were then on a Trunk Line, that would shift the responsibility for them to the state, leaving only the Tariffville bridge in the town's care. Owen E. Goslee sought and won election in 1914 as East Granby's representative, and his son H. Clifford Goslee remembered that the hard feelings over which towns should be responsible for the bridges had not abated with time. "My father was anxious to go [*to the General Assembly*] so he could fight and get East Granby down to one out of three. And he did. That's all he went for." By 1917 Hartford Avenue had become part of the Trunk Line system, so the Tariffville bridge, which Granby had been glad to get rid of when East Granby became a separate town, also became the state's responsibility.

Once the town's main street went on the state rolls for aid, it was just a matter of time before it was blacktopped. The work of blacktopping began at the old Spoonville Bridge and progressed northward. It was done in two sessions, the first reaching what is now 63 Spoonville Road and the second completing the job in 1917.

Soon after the main street was blacktopped, the town began to plow it in winter. Mazie Viets remembers the town crew operating a V-shaped wooden plow with a metal edge drawn by two horses. The side roads were left mostly alone, she says, and horses managed to wallow their way through the snow, pulling the milk on sleds to the clear road where it was picked up.

Good roads had always been important to farmers because they had to transport their crops and products long distances to market. The dairy farmers in East Granby sometimes sued the town when milk spoiled because roads were impassable. However, according to most historians, the biggest incentive to improve the roads was the automobile.

In 1909 the state highway commissioner said that horse-drawn vehicles were disappearing from the main highways and that the sum total of automobiles manufactured and sold during the years 1906, 1907, and 1908 very nearly equaled the entire number of automobiles then in use. Roger H. Stowell says that Francis P. Granger owned the first car in town, a Stevens-Duryea bought about 1908. Painted black, with a buggy top, the car ran on one cylinder. It was started by means of a crank, like a Victrola crank, on its side.

Hazel Lampson remembers her grandfather's car, too: "It had one seat and a handle to steer with. In front where we now have motors was a pull-down seat where the children sat. We used to go on picnics to Forest Park in Springfield and up to Southwick to the Ponds for a picnic and fishing."

The first cars were reserved for pleasant weather and pleasure outings. They were

David A. Viets garage

put on blocks in barns during the winter "to save the tires," which frequently went flat under the best of circumstances. The early Stanley Steamers, Fords, Patersons, Oaklands, and Buicks were plagued by overheated radiators and a host of other mechanical miseries, which the owners generally had to tend themselves. Many townspeople stuck to their horses and buggies and a few, like Almon B. Phelps who owned Newgate Lodge (formerly Viets Tavern), owned cars but hired chauffeurs to handle them.

The local blacksmith shops did body work, and George E. Lincoln, Andrew Eagleson, and Frederick C. Dibble ran paint shops in the Center where they beautified either wagons or automobiles. David A. Viets opened the first true garage behind 11 South Main Street, and in 1917 he became an agent for Chevrolet.

In 1913 the *Journal* reported that many farmers in town had installed gasoline tanks on their properties which were filled periodically by a Standard Oil Company tank wagon. Joseph L. McKinnie remembers that Allen M. Barrett was the first to sell gasoline in town. He had a hand-operated pump in front of his store building, now gone, at 16 South Main Street.

McKinnie also recalls the cars and the men from the automobile factory in Hartford that used to stop at the hotel and bar at 28 School Street:

The Pope-Hartford had to be road tested before it was put together. I can remember three drivers who used to come out—and back in those days it was all dirt road. They had four wheels, an engine, a gas tank, a steering wheel, and a box. No fenders, nothing. They came out here and they used to go down there [to the hotel]. *They would jack the wheels up and let the thing run and they'd go in and play cards all day! They were supposed to be putting miles on, but they would just jack up the wheels. Especially if it was a rainy day. I would see them go by the house around four or five at night, heading for Hartford.*

As automobiles and trucks became more reliable, they began to compete with the rail lines and remaining stagecoaches. Harvey E. Dibble discontinued his stage route to Hartford in 1908 after the CNE went into operation. The trolley line extension from Rainbow to the Center which was proposed with much enthusiasm in 1912 never materialized. That was the year that Allen M. Barrett began an auto livery, or taxi service, from the Center, and most of his passengers went to the Rainbow trolley terminal. Almon B. Phelps began a similar service which brought trolley passengers to Newgate prison. About this time Tucker and Palmer updated their livery stable on Old Hartford Avenue and offered a jitney service between Granby and Hartford.

After the CNE cut back on its passenger service, some high-school students took a jitney to Simsbury and the rest went to Bloomfield in the town's first school bus, which was owned and operated by Warren E. Lampson. Florence Griffin Porter remembers that the bus was a made-over Model T Ford truck and many students from that time still mention the curtains at its side windows.

Better automobiles and roads also meant more varied recreation for townspeople. The Sunday drive became an event in its own right and automobile owners vied to see who could cover the most miles. The social news began to include stories of auto parties going into Springfield or Hartford for an evening of dinner and theater. The *Herald* concluded in 1912: "The auto makes it possible for the people living in country towns to enjoy the better part of city life as though they were residents of the same."

The Telephone and Wireless Telegraph

The Southern New England Telephone Company (SNET) ran a New York to Boston trunk line through East Granby in 1887 and soon after sold it to the American Telephone and Telegraph Company. The wires ran parallel to the main street and were part of the town scene for many years. In 1900 the poles were moved 75 feet east of the street in the Center to protect the elm trees along the road. The wires passed behind the Viets store and in front of the Congregational church. Roger H. Stowell remembered that when he was a boy the poles had six crossarms with ten lines on each.

This trunk line did not carry local calls, and not until 1905 did SNET announce that every town in Connecticut finally had local service. The first telephones in East Granby apparently were installed early in 1904, but it was not until long afterward that every house had one. Those who had phones shared their use with those who had none. Also, not every neighborhood was served by telephone lines until about 1913. Sometimes the crews setting poles around the town camped at their work sites. The CNE train station had a telephone installed in 1911.

East Granby was connected with the Simsbury division of SNET. Some residents would have preferred to be linked with the Enfield division, especially those who regularly called Windsor Locks and Suffield.

Older residents remember that they all listened to each other's calls on the earliest telephones. Hazel Lampson described how, as a child, she stood on a chair to reach the telephone, which hung on the wall. She had to crank the instrument, ringing its bell, before taking down the receiver. "We kept a jar by the phone and we paid each time we used it," she said. After the Simsbury exchange switched to the common battery system in 1918, the caller simply lifted the receiver and told the operator what number to connect.

Telephone trunk line along North Main Street

Although telephones were welcome, overhead wires were not. In 1917 the *Journal's* reporter wrote about legal disputes between the town and both telephone companies concerning the mutilation of trees along the public highways. Both a court and the public utilities commission decided in the town's, and the trees', favor.

While the officials argued about the lines, two residents began communicating by wireless telegraphy. This new invention only required an antenna. In 1913, while he was a student at Simsbury High School, P. Grohman Viets wired the belfry of the Congregational church to a telegraph set in his home that once stood in front of the church. George W. Tucker installed a one-fourth kilowatt wireless station in the Riverside Inn on Old Hartford Avenue in 1914. The *Journal* said, "He already has a government license [*and*] can transmit messages many miles out of state."

Electric Power

Electric lines first came into town west of the Mountain through Tariffville. Houses along Hartford Avenue had electric lights as early as 1910. Lines were run on poles along South Main Street and through the Center in 1915. Some residents had their houses wired in anticipation of the coming of the lines, often boarding the electricians while they worked. When power was turned on, many of the houses along the main street lit up together.

The town had its first lone electric street light installed near the railroad bridge across the south end of Old Hartford Avenue. In 1915 a special town committee contracted with the Hartford Electric Light Company for fifty to sixty lights along North and South Main streets and near the Congregational church and the CNE Railroad station. All sections of town had electric power by 1925. Joseph L. McKinnie, one of the several town men who became electricians, admired A. Robert Holcomb for stubbornly refusing to let the electric company run a high-tension line across his land at Copper Hill until it supplied power to that area.

Right behind the electric lines came electrical appliances. In 1919 the proprietor of the Viets store advertised a demonstration of an electric range; in 1920 the Congregational parsonage acquired an electric vacuum cleaner.

Indoor Plumbing and Furnace Heat

Townspeople began to have running water piped into their homes and barns at the beginning of the century, as soon as deep wells and pumps run by windmills made this possible. Indoor bathrooms did not come into general use until after the First World War, but there is a record of one being installed in 1914 in the home of Francis P. Granger, once the Granger Hotel in the Center. It had both hot and cold water.

The first furnace on record was installed in the home of Charles P. Viets at 81 North Main Street in 1907. The Congregational church used its furnace for the first time during the 1914 Christmas service, and the Falls District had a hot-air heating plant installed in its new schoolhouse in 1915.

22

The Business and Pleasure of Leisure

FOR AS LONG AS CITIES have existed, urbanites have been drawn to the healthful atmosphere of the countryside for vacations and pleasure outings. A gradually shortening workweek and improvements in transportation made the pastoral scenes, historic sites, and simple pastimes in East Granby more accessible to greater numbers of sightseers and sportsmen from among the citizens of Springfield, Hartford, and other congested communities. Several private businessmen in town grasped this new opportunity and developed recreation-oriented enterprises during the first quarter of the 20th century.

Among the influx of visitors, the most interesting to the townspeople were former residents and descendants of early settlers. Their stays were reported in the newspapers and they were cordially welcomed at church socials, holiday celebrations, and family reunions. On the other side of the coin, townspeople began to travel more often and longer distances, since they had bonds with residents in every corner of the United States, more leisure stemming from new labor-saving technology, and speedier transportation.

Newgate Becomes a Recreation Area

After Newgate ceased to be a state prison and whenever the site was free of sporadic mining activity,* various promoters conducted tours of the facility. In 1900, while Whitney D. Viets was proprietor, the *Journal* reported that the old mine and prison drew a growing number of tourists each year because of its historic interest and the beautiful scenery of the surrounding area. Newgate was a favorite destination for field trips from schools and colleges and a popular stop for the bicycle clubs that were the rage at the turn of the century. It was also the preferred place for the family reunions of the descendants of Dr. John Viets, which began in 1899 with a gathering of more than 200.

*The mine was reactivated in June 1907. H. Clifford Goslee remembered: "A spur track was inserted *[from the Copper Hill railroad crossing to Newgate]* and several carloads of copper ore were shipped to Wisconsin for smelting. The yield of copper was reported as less than 4 percent; about forty men were employed in the project. Copper Hill had a busy summer!" During a survey of the general area in 1971, the Atomic Energy Commission found evidence of uranium deposits in the mine, a common occurrence near copper.

Newgate Prison showing workhouse with cupola before fire of 1904

Almon B. Phelps of Copper Hill bought Newgate from Samuel D. Viets of Springfield in 1904, just after a fire had destroyed all the prison's wooden portions. The cupola, used as a lookout by visitors, was gone from the top of the large stone workhouse, as were the cells constructed of heavy planking in its basement, the treadmill, and many other relics on display. The interior woodwork of the warden and officers' quarters, also called the guardhouse, had been consumed by the fire along with more artifacts on display there and a tent and registry book for the Viets family reunions.

After making minor repairs, Phelps reopened the prison to the public with the idea that he would develop the property into a complete summer resort. He began by holding public dances in the guardhouse and they remained popular for three decades, even after the Phelps family sold the property. He customarily opened the tourist season with a Memorial Day dance and had others on the Fourth of July, Labor Day, and the closing day of the Suffield Agricultural Fair in October. Phelps hired orchestras and professional prompters, whose business it was to keep things lively and to see that everyone joined in the dancing.

Rebecca Phelps Holcomb came from Ohio in July 1912 when she was seventeen to work two years for Phelps, who was her uncle. This is what she had to say about the affairs almost seventy years later:

When you went to a dance, you danced with your partner, then you didn't dance with him again until [after] *intermission. You danced with everybody—that was the sociable way. This going to a dance and dancing with the same person—I could never see that. We had different things to make partners mix during the dances.*

Mrs. Holcomb added that although her grandmother wrote from Ohio opposing dancing on religious grounds, she went to all Phelps' socials and joined other young

Newgate Prison c. 1905, showing new tower and verandas

people from town who went to a dancing school in West Granby. Adelaide Millea also remembered that despite her strict upbringing, her parents allowed her to go to Newgate in 1915 for her first dance.

Renovating and improving the fire-damaged guardhouse was Phelps' second project. He added a broad veranda to three sides of the building and an observation tower to its west side. These additions so changed the aspect of the old guardhouse that it was soon being called "the new pavilion" by the merrymakers who strolled on the porches for a bit of air and an enchanting view of the valley below bathed in moonlight.

After renovation the guardhouse was suitable for very large private parties, as the Viets family discovered when all who came to the 1905 reunion were able to be seated indoors for dinner. Phelps also used the building to house his growing collection of relics and the souvenirs and postcards he sold.

Serious discussions about constructing a hotel near the prison began in 1905, but, although an option was taken, nobody ever built one. Meanwhile Newgate continued to be a favorite destination for day trips. The *Journal* reported that Labor Day 1909 set the first of many records at the prison: "Beginning early in the day teams bringing large crowds began to arrive at the prison and over one hundred persons registered during the day." In 1910 Phelps acquired a Buick touring car and a chauffeur to meet the trolley from Hartford at its terminus in the Rainbow section of Windsor. That year the prison had about 5000 visitors. As automobiles came into general use, the prison became a popular stop on Sunday drives.

Phelps revived the idea of a summer hotel in 1912. At first he talked about building a twenty-room inn and a large garage on the lawn south of the prison. Instead, he was able to buy the historic Captain John Viets farm across the road, then owned by Virgil E. Viets. After selling their farm opposite the Copper Hill Methodist church, the Phelpses moved to the old Viets homestead and began renovating and adding to the house. In September of that year the *Journal* commented on the results:

The house now has eighteen rooms, equipped with all modern conveniences. There are seven large fireplaces, the one in the dining room being particularly attractive. This is capable of taking in a six-foot-long log and is furnished with cooking utensils that would have delighted the heart of a housewife in the seventeenth century.
A unique feature of the small private dining room is a highboy, brought from England by Mr. Phelps' great-great grandmother, as part of her wedding outfit. Some handsome pieces of old china adorn the walls and in one room is an old-time buffet. Across the south side of the house is a wide veranda which will be a delight to all who can enjoy it.

The paper claimed that Phelps could fill his country inn many times over because it was a summer resort "unequaled by any place in Connecticut." Phelps named it the Newgate Lodge.

Phelps served both light refreshments and full dinners to tourists and to revelers on occasional hayrides and sleighing parties. He also began catering private dinners in the lodge for groups like the Masons, Knights of Pythias, Sons of the American Revolution, Alhambra Club of Hartford, and various business and hunting clubs. The Old Newgate Coon Club, of which Phelps was a charter member, had him serve dinners either at his lodge or its own, which at the time was in Hartland Hollow. Rebecca Holcomb remembered her uncle leaving for Hartland with a wagon loaded with food: "Everything in the wide world was on it, oysters and olives and everything like that, besides sweet cider. Probably some not so sweet, too."

The Phelpses and their hired hands made the cider and apple butter they served from apples that grew on the farm. They also kept their own cows and vegetable garden. Mrs. Phelps baked all the bread and pastry.

The main attraction, however, was still the old mine and prison. Rebecca Holcomb gave people tours for 25 cents apiece. The ladder down the mine shaft, which she maneuvered in an ankle-length skirt as many as twenty times on a busy day, was a trial for her modesty and an impassable deterrent for many tourists. Marie Hall, a writer, described her adventurous tour in the *Courant Sunday Magazine:*

Following our guide we descended [from a rooftop lookout] *and were shown fallen whipping posts, ruined cells, bars half filed through, and various other relics of tortured and despairing imprisonment.*
Then we were told that we must prepare ourselves for the descent into the chamber of horrors below: the Tory prison. The women of our party were attired in long linen dusters, the men in voluminous linen overalls. Our guide put several candles into her pocket and after leading us through a narrow stone opening, halted us at the top of a rung ladder, which led down apparently into the bottomless pit. At this point two of our party of six decided that "out-of-doors" was preferable to any descent into this terrifying blackness, and deserted us. As our leader slid from sight into the murky depths and called for followers, I confess to a certain amount of misgiving myself, as I very cautiously descended the steep and narrow ladder, having no idea where I was to land, and with total darkness enveloping me. When my foot struck solid rock, it was a welcome sensation, indeed.

The guide gave each of us a little oil lamp like the old Roman ones, but with long handles. We followed as best we could, slipping along on the smooth rocks. Above ground it was ninety in the shade, but here we shivered with cold. It seemed far from being an ideal health resort, especially as our guide told us of the clothing of the prisoners growing mouldy, and rotten, and falling away from bodies, while limbs grew stiff with rheumatism. The floor was wet with slime and full of holes.

We realize the barbarous punishments of those days, and grow anxious for the fair country above. Haste is impossible. Through one point there is a sort of "fat man's misery," where one is compelled to bend double, while the icy water trickling from the ceiling has a way of dropping down your spine, having entered at an unguarded point between your collar and you.

It took about fifteen minutes to make the circuit of the caverns, but it seemed much longer. The lowest point was the lake, a small body of water, with jagged walls at the sides. We were informed that sometimes it overran its border, and to substantiate this story, there was beside us a broken pump which the prisoners used when the waters rose so high as to threaten to flood the whole habitation. The lake emptied into a drain which led out to the hillsides beyond.

The sagging stones above us were propped up by slimy logs and in the midst of the general decay, seemed not unlikely to fall at any moment, and glad were we to turn here and begin our climb back toward the sunlight.

Care of the oil torches aptly described was Rebecca Holcomb's responsibility. Both the prison and the lodge were lighted with kerosene. "We had an awful lot of lamps I had to wash and polish," she said. Phelps put stoves in the prison buildings for heat.

One of the last things Phelps added to his list of attractions was a stagecoach which had belonged to Fredus Case of Windsor. It was reputed to be of pre-Revolutionary vintage and to have operated between Newgate and Windsor. Phelps continued the prison tours and ran Newgate Lodge until he died in 1925, after which his property was sold to members of the Seymour family, principally Clarence W. Seymour, and Kenneth M. Seymour became the proprietor.

Other Hotels and Inns

By the turn of the century, Fredrick W. Douglas had bought the old Cowles Manufacturing Company's boardinghouse, now gone, on the bank of the Farmington River east of Spoonville bridge. He was running what the *Herald* described as "a hotel," although his star guest, Captain George M. Lee, head of the power plant upriver, lived there fourteen years.

Douglas wanted to expand his business by adding a public bar, something Phelps' Newgate Lodge never had, but his application for a liquor license caused quite a bit of controversy, and it was turned down in 1900 by the county commissioners and by the Superior Court. Later at this location the Douglas family operated a restaurant called the Chop House where older townsmen remember being served legal 3.2 percent beer during national prohibition.

Early in 1906 Frederick C. Dibble decided to open a hotel in his house, which stands at 28 School Street (then called the Windsor Locks Road). He called his establishment the East Granby Hotel, a name which had been used before for at least two other

Riverside Inn

hotels in different parts of town. Joseph L. McKinnie, who grew up half a block from the hotel, remembered that it had four bedrooms on the second floor for overnight guests and a nice barroom on the first floor. Records show that the barroom had a pool table, as well as tables and chairs for playing cards and eating.

After Dibble applied for a liquor license the *Journal* commented: "There is one saloon in town at the East Granby end of the bridge that crosses the Farmington River at Tariffville. Many people are of the opinion that one saloon is enough." The reporter probably was referring to a bar run by Joseph H. Forsyth in the Riverside Inn, the former Holcomb and Merwin general store, since demolished to make an access road between Hartford and Old Hartford avenues. Although a number of townspeople filed a remonstrance against the license, the commission found in Dibble's favor.

By the beginning of 1909 Dibble had transferred title to his buildings and business to Ernest S. Palmer, who renamed the hotel the Palmer House. The *Herald* says his hotel had "a fine patronage from automobile parties and *[seemed]* to be a mecca for the men driving to try out cars of the manufacturing companies in Hartford."

It was long before Palmer decided to join his brother-in-law, Carl B. Tucker, who was operating the livery stable behind 24-26 Old Hartford Avenue. Palmer sold his interest in the hotel in December 1909 to Richard D. Cannon of Unionville. Cannon reinstated the hotel's original name, enlarged its dining facilities, and added a veranda. Under his proprietorship the bar became a popular gathering place for sportsmen, at least until the town voted to go dry in 1916. The *Herald* reported on a typical catered dinner at the hotel in 1912:

The business [of the Old Newgate Coon Club] *did not take long to dispose of and then at nine o'clock all sat down to a fine spread. There was scalloped oysters, scalloped potatoes, potato salad, steamed ham, Parker House rolls, pie, coffee, cheese, and cigars.*

Barrett's Hall

Allen M. Barrett built a small ice-cream parlor in 1909 near his house at the Center (22 South Main Street). The following winter he converted it into a pool and billiard parlor and a reading room where he sold candy and cigars. Before long men from all the towns around were competing for prizes in matched games of pool, and Barrett's Hall was on its way to being a recreation center.

The next winter (1911-12) Barrett hired an orchestra and began holding dances every other Friday night. These usually attracted about forty couples, while his masquerade balls, featuring a grand march, drew as many as seventy-five. Lest anyone worry about propriety, a news article promised "the exercises will be carried out with all the decorum that would attach to a drawing room." Barrett apparently did not hold dances during the summer when people went to those in the pavilions at Newgate and Rainbow Park. The latter is now submerged beneath Rainbow Reservoir in Windsor.

Roller-skating was next. The hall was open each evening for older skaters and for children on Saturday afternoons. Business was so good at this point that Barrett was able to enlarge and remodel his hall. The *Herald* described it thus:

The first floor is 86 feet long by a width varying from 20 to 30 feet and it has been covered recently with a first class maple dance floor. Upstairs he has a commodious room where soft drinks and cigars are sold and where he has three pool tables.

About this time Carl B. Tucker and Ernest S. Palmer furnished the Gaines building across the street from the Riverside Inn and in front of their livery stable with two mahogany pool tables. This created the third public poolroom in town counting the single table in the bar at the East Granby Hotel. Not to be outdone, Barrett went into the auto livery business, offering taxi service with a chauffeur-driven Paterson Model 37 touring car.

Barrett apparently never applied for a liquor license and never attempted to sell liquor in his hall. He did run afoul of the law in 1913 for possessing four gambling machines. The machines were confiscated in a raid by the state police and Barrett paid a fine.

In 1915 Barrett and his son-in-law Harlow T. Drew opened a small store in the lower floor of the hall, where they sold cigarettes, tobacco, candy, and ice cream. At the end of 1919 Charles C. Adams bought Barrett's house, farm, and business. Adams replaced Hiram C. Viets as postmaster and moved the location of the post office from the Viets store to his own newly acquired building. He hired school teacher Mazie Viets, daughter of RFD carrier J. Edward Viets, to run the post office for him. Soon after Adams sold his business to Warren A. and Ina Cushman Wilcox in 1922, the building which Barrett had built burned down. The Wilcoxes replaced it with the present structure standing at 16 South Main Street, continuing only the post office, poolroom, and an enlarged grocery store.

Church Sponsored Community Events

Organizations within the town's two churches sponsored a variety of social and cultural events throughout the year. Most of them were open to all. The more people who came the better, since each group usually raised money for special projects by charg-

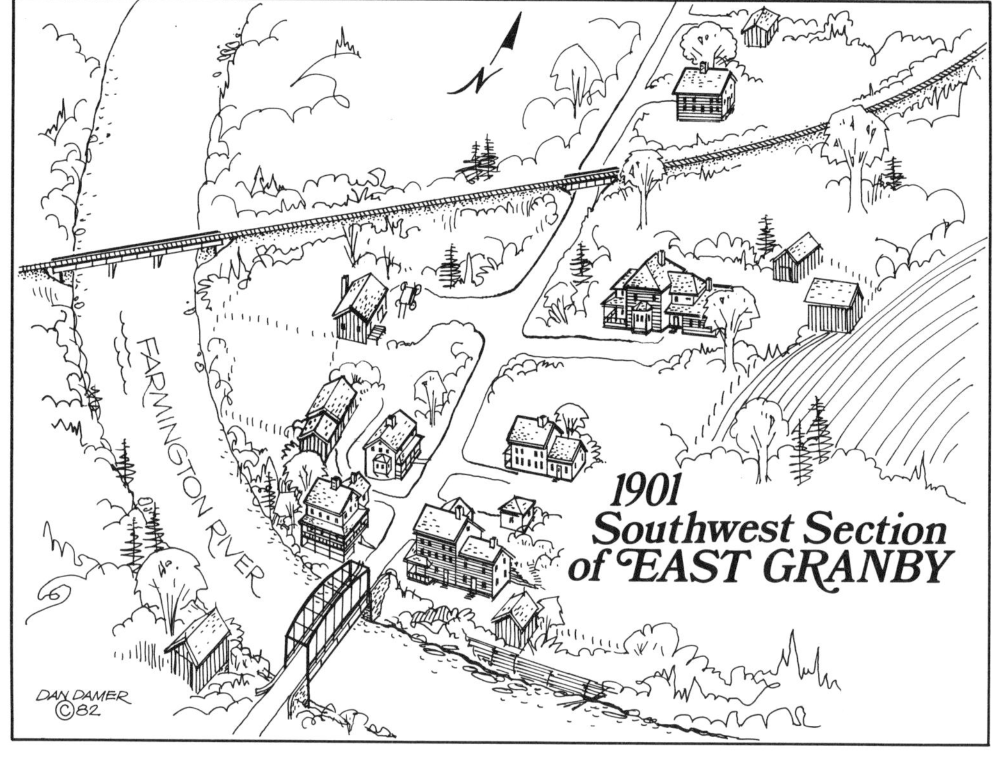

Artist's concept of Old Hartford Avenue. Note the Riverside Inn in the right foreground with the Gaines building opposite it and the Tucker & Palmer livery stable to the rear. The Central New England Railway Branch is in the background. This part of town was called Riverside, the Falls, and the Tariffville section of East Granby.

ing a small admission. Congregational church groups held most of their indoor events in the church basement. The Copper Hill Methodist church usually held socials in the church or in members' houses. Picnics and lawn parties took place on the church grounds, at nearby parks and lakes, and at Newgate Prison.

The women's groups in each church sponsored the greatest number of events during the year. Their regular program followed the seasons with socials featuring maple sugar in the early spring, strawberries and ice cream in the summer, and a harvest supper with chicken pie in the fall. The Congregational church's women also held a two-day chrysanthemum show in the fall for more than fifteen years. At some of the benefits the women sold aprons and other handmade articles.

The popular oyster supper, held each February, began as an event sponsored by the Congregational women, but was adopted by the East Granby Men's Club. In 1913 a record 300 people came to dine on oyster stew and an array of meats and cold dishes and to be entertained by the Tuxedo Mandolin and Guitar Club of Hartford.

Enthusiasm waxed and waned among the young people's groups connected with each church. When they were active they sponsored their own socials and enjoyed staging plays for the entertainment of the whole community. In 1914 the Reverend Charles

Warren A. Wilcox store

W. Hanna of the Congregational church organized the town's first Boy Scout troop. One of its first projects was to make a tennis court east of the church.

The churches welcomed anyone or anything novel with which they could vary their programs. Music, singing, recitations, and readings were current standards. Historical themes, like a "real old fashioned quilting bee" given in 1916, were also popular. Foreign students, travelers, and missionaries came to lecture on faraway places. Enthusiasts and educators, like the professor who gave a talk on the chemistry of the kerosene lamp, elucidated their special interests. The audio-visual aids they used followed the development of technology in that field from stereopticon slides in 1896, to the Edison phonograph used in 1903, to moving pictures in 1920.

The Turkey Hills Study Club

After several years of discussion, twelve townswomen were ready in 1913 to form a club which had an intellectual rather than a religious or social focus. The twelve organized the Turkey Hills Study Club in the home of Elizabeth Newberry (later Mrs. Gideon Parsons) at 27-29 North Main Street (once the infamous Montague farm). Their intention was to devote much of their free time to researching and writing papers on topics of interest to the club members and to meet regularly to listen to each other's reports.

They had with them at their first meeting genealogist Alice Maria Gay. Miss Gay, a native who had moved to Hartford, helped the women develop their first course of study around topics dealing with Connecticut history. According to club historian Ruth C. Gledhill, the group had moved into studies of English history and leading American women before World War I interrupted their progress. They devoted themselves to Red Cross work during the war, resuming their studies in October 1919. Later the club expanded its program to include book reviews, field trips, guest speakers, and any other avenue that might help its members become better informed citizens, then and now.

East Granby Drum Corps, c. 1900

Sports, Games, and Good Times

Baseball was the king of sports in the early 20th century, and East Granby had a uniformed amateur club that played teams from all the towns around each summer. Every so often men organized a rowing race on the Farmington River above the Tariffville bridge and the first mention of a power boat there came in 1909. That same year Joseph H. Forsyth of the Riverside Inn set up a public trap-shooting range behind Peter J. Burns' taxidermy shop and small grocery at 186 Hartford Avenue across from Seymour school. In 1913 the *Herald* mentions daily boxing matches "conducted in the scientific manner by the young men of East Granby" in the grain room back of the Viets store in the Center.

The Viets store itself was an unofficial men's club. Louise Johnson Sharp gave a woman's view of the evenings there:

I remember the men gathered around the stove at night. We did our shopping before they gathered around because they were smoking and spitting, you know. There were some that didn't do that. There were some that were a little more refined. They had their home life and they would drop in, maybe, at the store—for some little thing.
There used to be a class of men that were not really home folks. They would gather there. I don't think they were really allowed [to bring liquor] *but some of them brought it in the hip pocket. But that wasn't the drawing card. They didn't go there just to drink, just to talk, gossip—what they did all day and their busy side of life.* [They went home at] *a reasonable time, maybe nine o'clock.*

John G. Bazyk remembered that the Burns store was a gathering spot on the west side of the Mountain. The Bazyk brothers used to swap jokes with the Seymour brothers there, and children loved the store because of the candies Burns sold and the small animals he stuffed. Burns also had a small pool table there at one point, Bazyk said.

Children were also fascinated by the sights and sounds of the blacksmith's business. On hearing of the destruction of a blacksmith shop he remembered from his boyhood, a former Tariffville resident wrote the *Herald*:

As you read this can't you smell the burning hoofs as the shoes were being fitted? We were always told that the blacksmiths never had asthma—this suffocating smoke was a sure preventative. But the greatest excitement prevailed when a protesting ox was being shod. Do you remember how they placed a rope around his horns, passed it through the door and frame to the floor beyond where several men could pull while a braver man twisted the tail of the obstreperous creature and worked him into the frame where he was, by means of the great leather belts, soon suspended and his feet roped into place for the operation?

A happy child was one whom the blacksmith allowed to pump the bellows, he said.

Dr. Douglas M. Gay and his sister Helen Moody remembered that their mother read to them and that the stories they heard inspired their play. There were also picnics and clambakes and outings to Congamond Lakes, where you could ride on a steamboat. After Sunday Mass at St. Bernard's Catholic church in Tariffville members of Lithuanian-American clubs from surrounding towns gathered behind the May home at 249 Hartford Avenue to picnic in the meadow and dance in their pavilion.

In the winter there were sleigh rides and ice-skating in the moonlight. Olin Turner remembered that sledding on the roads was a lot of fun before all the hills were cut down to accommodate automobiles. People also gathered for sledding on the hill behind Newgate.

Whist was the most popular card game of the era, and more whist clubs, which rotated among members' homes for weekly games, were added to the list each year. Many homes had pianos and people were encouraged to play musical instruments and to join singing groups and church choirs. Newly married couples just back from their honeymoons might well be treated to an evening serenade.

Summering and Wintering

By the turn of the century people from urban areas had begun to view East Granby as a possible site for summer homes. A cottage on the Mountain behind 164 South Main Street was filled almost every weekend in fair weather. In 1910 the *Journal* said that it accommodated a chaperoned party of twenty-seven young people, mostly from Hartford. The S. E. Horton family of Windsor Locks maintained a hunting lodge in a field off North Main Street, and Arthur D. Coffin of the same town built a bungalow in 1914 nearby on Peak Mountain. The Reverend George E. Lincoln, who filled the pulpit of the Congregatonal church from 1904 until his retirement in 1912, occupied his home at 1 North Main Street as a summer house, going to Texas for the winter.

Winter was a popular time for local farmers to get away from town, if they could find a reliable hired hand to look after their stock. Every so often a couple of friends or a family set off for a trip to a warmer climate. In March 1903 Julius G. Dickinson, who preceded Hiram C. Viets as storekeeper in the Center, and Francis Granger made a six-week trip to Texas, Arizona, and the Pacific coast. "They will make an inspection of the oil region of the Southwest," the *Journal* said. The Charles P. Vietses and two Clark families traveled to California soon after, while Dora C. Griffin and Elizabeth Newberry sailed off to Europe.

23

World War I: Bringing Word from France

THE BATTLES of 1914 that began World War I were more than clashes in the distance to many East Granby people. Several residents recently had traveled in Europe and some who had emigrated from countries like Russian-controlled Poland and Lithuania on the war's eastern front had friends and relatives in jeopardy. Mary Victorine Rosier, wife of blacksmith E. Frank Rosier, received word early in 1915 that her hometown of Baccarat, France, on the western front, was more than half in ruins with most of its principal buildings destroyed.

As the fighting between the Allies and the Central Powers spread and intensified, it disrupted European agriculture, industry, and commerce. Americans noticed an increased demand for their products, while they also felt a shortage of materials usually imported from Europe. The lack of potash for fertilizer was probably the most immediate concern of local farmers and tobacco growers. Germany was the world's only commercial supplier of potash and trade with Germany ceased.

For three years the townspeople offered prayers for peace in their churches, but on April 6, 1917, they heard the dread news—the United States had declared war on Germany. On June 5, 110 men between the ages of twenty-one and thirty registered in the East Granby town hall for the draft.

Those Who Served in the Military

About fifty East Granby men, selected from among those who registered plus a few older and younger volunteers, eventually were inducted into the army or navy. Some men enlisted and were taken into the service immediately. The majority, however, waited to be drafted by lot. With so many men leaving and an army to feed, the farmers, their sons, and their hired hands were needed at their chores.

Two East Granby women did active war work. Rena Aherns, daughter of a German-born cigar manufacturer who lived on East Street, served with the Red Cross. Lily E. Watts, a nurse whose parents lived in the Floydville section of town, joined the Yale Mobile Unit, which went to England and France.

Approximately twenty men were sent overseas. Letters from them, beginning

"Somewhere in France," were highly prized and sometimes published in the newspapers. Upon his arrival abroad in April 1918 with the 4th Mortar Battery, Private Fred W. Viets wrote home:

France is surely one great country, as far as I have seen. The weather is about the same as it is at home, but there is a whole lot more daylight. It does not get dark until after ten o'clock, and it begins to get light about 3:30, so you see if a fellow wants to work from sun to sun he can put in a very good day.

We had a great trip over; the weather was fine and we had a good time. There was plenty of good books on board, so I spent most of my time up on deck reading and smoking. We didn't do any work so you can see how it suited me. I can see just now how busy you are at home, and suppose you have a lot of tobacco set out now. We had to push our watches along five hours on the way over, so when I think of what you are doing back on the old farm I have to figure back that much. When I go to bed it is only 5 o'clock over in dear old Connecticut. It does not seem like France, only the buildings are very funny and the trains are like our dinkeys.

We have got to get all our money changed into French money now. Some of the fellows have already, but I have not as yet, but expect to have a fine time counting it when I do. We can get smoking tobacco over here and as I have an old cob pipe I have a good time but miss my Connecticut cigars. I spent my first night in a pup tent last night. I felt fine this morning, but it sure was chilly. The fellows are playing tennis and baseball, so you see we are not out of the world. We also have a New York Herald *here and get some of the home news. Write to me and tell me all the home news and don't forget the little things as I will be very glad to hear about all the folks.*

There is a fellow cutting hair here now on a box out in the open and it does look a bit strange to see him. The French people have some fine gardens started now, but one does not see many men around. It looked funny to see an old woman driving a horse around hitched to a two-wheeled cart, but I expect to see a whole lot of strange sights before I get back to the United States.

In his next letter he wrote:

We met a lot of French people with their little two-wheeled carts. They have good horses but the wagons are like junk wagons. We passed through a town and saw the women down at a brook washing clothes which seemed to be the town washing place. The houses are all stone, and wine is sold at about every other one. This afternoon I cleaned my gun and lined up and waited for an hour to get into the canteen, only to have the door shut in my face. Perhaps I did not say a few things. The country around here is fine, but one can notice that the farms are not like those at home. It is remarkable how much the women and children of France are doing. They are doing all of the men's work on the farms, and take it from me, they are doing it well. The women look funny with their wooden shoes driving a horse.

We are now in some old buildings that I'll bet are hundreds of years old and by the way they are built are good for at least a thousand more. They are of stone, with heavy slate roofs and cement floors, and we are sleeping on beds which are no more than slats about two inches apart and a bit hard, but I slept fine last night. Went to see a show last night called "Baby Mine" at the Y.M.C.A. It was very good, considering that it was a stage like the one in the Town hall. We went on a hike to-day, starting at 8:30, walked three or four miles, pitched our pup tents, took them down again and hit the trail back, arriving here at 12:15. We had beans for dinner and they sure taste good to me.

You can tell the people one thing — that all the help they can give the Red Cross or Y.M.C.A. will be well spent, as they are doing all kinds of good work. It is nearly time for "chow" now, so I will ring off. I am feeling fine, so don't worry about me. Write soon.

Soon letters and reports from abroad were not so sanguine. Private First Class Wilbert W. Denslow, who was with the 307th Military Police Corps, wrote that he had been gassed and injured. From his pup tent he could see "air-ships flying like flocks of birds," he said. George W. Tucker, who was an ambulance driver at the front, also was wounded and gassed.

Two East Granby men were only eighteen when they enlisted. Owen E. Johnson of the Copper Hill section of town went overseas in June 1918 with the Quartermaster Corps. Mike Klecha, a Polish-born resident of the Spoonville section of town, enlisted in the National Guard and went to France with the 26th Division (the Yankees) made up of New England National Guard troops. He was wounded twice, once at Seicheprey in April 1918 during the first major engagement between the Americans and the Germans.

James R. Miller, who drove a supply wagon for the 20th Field Artillery, was twice cited for bravery, according to an account in the *Journal*. Saddler Myron S. Pease, Jr., of the 82nd Military Police Company and Private Richard M. Davis of Company B, 326th Infantry, were among those awarded victory medals. These three, along with Chester R. Seymour, John A. Eagleson, and possibly other East Granby men, took part in the American First Army's first large offensive action, St. Mihiel, and many other battles. None of the East Granby men fought shoulder-to-shoulder, but they tried to keep track of each other and the progress of their various companies. John Eagleson was in the service fourteen months, he wrote, before he again saw Jim Miller, with whom he had enlisted.

John Eagleson, who was with the 10th Field Artillery, 3rd Division, fought at Chateau-Thierry, Champagne-Marne, Aisne-Marne, and Meuse-Argonne, in addition to St. Mihiel. He was gassed and wounded twice, most severely in July 1918. After that he was promoted to corporal, transferred to the Signal Corps, and awarded the Silver Star for noteworthy gallantry. (After the war he also was given a Purple Heart.) He wrote home that he would rather be on the firing line again. Clarence W. Seymour expressed similar feelings when he wrote, "We love the soldiers life and we dread it, but until the war ends we would do nothing else."

Percy W. and Clarence Seymour, sons of the Moses E. Seymours of 192 Hartford Avenue, were among the few East Granby men who had had military experience before the war. Percy was called back into the army from civilian life and inducted as a second lieutenant. According to his published military record, he was never sent overseas. Clarence, who had a law practice in Hartford, had gone as a cavalryman in Troop B of the Governor's Independent Volunteer Troop of Horse Guards in 1916 to patrol the Mexican border against raids by Pancho Villa and his followers. After Clarence was inducted into the army, he served as an instructor of field artillery and then became judge advocate of his brigade. He attained the rank of first lieutenant and was overseas three months just as the war ended.

Chester R. Seymour, son of William A. Seymour, also had some military training, as a corporal in the Simsbury Home Guard. A graduate of Trinity College, Class of 1915, he worked for Ensign-Bickford of Simsbury before and after the war. He was an expert in high explosives; the company sent him to train engineers in laying mines using special fuse it made.

When Seymour enlisted, he was assigned to the 28th Regiment of Engineers where he again was in charge of explosives; he also taught French. He saw action as a sergeant, then went into officers' training and became a second lieutenant. After the Armistice his company remained in France for a time building roads.

Almost all the men and women who went into the service from East Granby survived the war. Frank Farrell is the only one listed as dead on the town's granite and bronze monument erected in 1949 to honor the veterans of two world wars. Private Zachary Kryvoy, twenty-four, who lived in East Granby, according to the published Connecticut service records, but whose mother lived in Russia, was killed in action June 15, 1918.

The military service of the foreign-born population heightened general awareness of their presence, and the nationally publicized activities of the new Bolshevik movement generated considerable uneasiness. "All have come to realize that after this war is all over, all efforts must be made to Americanize the people of diverse nations who have come here to make their homes," the *Herald* said in 1918. The East Granby School Committee reported the next year that it would sponsor evening classes, lectures, and entertainments to promote the study of the English language and to spread the "American ideals of living." The Turkey Hills Study Club, on the other hand, decided to try to come to a better understanding of the foreign-born population by doing studies of the native cultures of each ethnic group.

Most of the servicemen came home almost as soon as the armistice was signed. Owen E. Johnson stayed behind in France with a salvage squadron. John A. Eagleson and Fred W. Viets went into Germany with the Army of Occupation. Viets left Germany in January 1919 with thirty-six others in a railroad baggage car, and after a five-day trip to his port of embarkation, waited more than a month for a transport ship home.

A few men such as Percy W. Seymour, Jesse Farren, and Ralph Hemenway chose to remain in the army after the war, but most were glad to return to town and pick up their lives where they had left them. Douglas M. Gay recalled in a taped interview that his experience in the military significantly influenced his life. He said:

When I graduated from Bates College, World War I was on. Realizing that I was interested in biology more than anything else and thinking, perhaps, that I could be of most service in that field rather than going anywhere the Army wished to send me, I enrolled in MIT. I took all sorts of biology and chemistry courses for as long as I could. The day before enlistments were to close, I went to Camp Devens and enlisted in the medical department and there, of course, the contact with medical doctors in the Army interested me in medicine.

After almost two years of service, Gay was discharged as a sergeant. He accepted a position in the laboratory of tropical medicine at Harvard University and entered the medical school there. He became a doctor and specialized in pathology. After instructing for a time at Yale University, he operated a laboratory in Delaware until he retired in the 1970s.

Those Who Served at Home

Raising and conserving food were patriotic duties of every American during World War I, especially in farming communities like East Granby. Government representatives issued dire warnings in 1917 that the national stockpile of foodstuffs had dwindled from the normal supply of one and a half years to just six months. Everyone, the newspapers entreated, must help to feed the fighting men overseas. The *Herald* urged tobacco growers not to plow under their cover crops of rye, but to bring them to harvest. "Every bushel of rye grown in this valley and saved for food means a bushel of wheat released and sent across the water to help win the world's battle for us," it said.

In 1917 the *Herald's* agricultural columnist wrote: "I wish we could rename the biggest, mealiest, most prolific potato the Kaiser's Defeat. Every potato that grows in American soil this year is a steel-nosed bullet aimed point blank toward the heart of autocracy." The farmers in East Granby responded by devoting acreage to truck gardening, including potatoes, which army installations like Camp Devens in Massachusetts and Camp Dix in New Jersey were buying in million-bushel lots.

As food and animal feed became scarcer and more expensive, the farmers increased their grain production. The old mill in Simsbury known as the Ensign Grist Mill was reopened by the Woods Chandler Company. One day a reporter saw William A. Seymour transporting about 700 bushels of corncobs from his farm at 44 Hatchet Hill Road to be ground into feed at the mill. Seymour told the reporter that he planned to raise much more corn in 1918, as well as spring wheat and rye. He had a son "over there," he said, and he proposed to do his part and more toward feeding that son and a number of other boys as well.

To increase production local farmers reclaimed pastures and fields that had lain idle for years and cleared new land. Almost every able-bodied person was pressed into agricultural work to fill the void left by the young men in uniform and the laborers who had been lured away to the factories by "war wages." The principal of the Simsbury high school encouraged his students to do farm work during the summer rather than to go to Fisher's Island for a junior training camp in military tactics.

Farmers increased tobacco production, as well as food, to supply the boys in the trenches. In 1917 tobacco prices, at 26 to 30 cents a pound, were reportedly "beyond anything offered in recent years." By 1918 the average for a good crop of stalk tobacco was 45 cents and primed leaves brought more. A number of new tobacco barns were built in town during the war.

Thirty-seven percent of the Griffin-Neuberger Tobacco Company, whose plantation included some acreage in the southeastern part of East Granby, was held by H. Neuberger and Company, Inc. This was a large tobacco jobbing firm with an office in New York, but controlled by interests in Bremen, Germany. The principal shareholder was Captain Moritz Neuberger of the German army. In 1918 the United States government took over the German firm's holdings in this country and liquidated all its assets.

To deal with food shortages at home, the agricultural college at Storrs sent a force of a hundred women throughout Connecticut. Several of them gave cooking and canning demonstrations in the Congregational church and various homes in town. It was only German propaganda, the newspapers said, that the government intended to seize all canned goods put up by homemakers. Rowena Gardner Dibble, second wife of Town Clerk Frank H. Dibble, led the "canning canvass" that spurred the townspeople to exceed fourfold the government-set quota in 1918 of 3,600 quarts of canned fruits and vegetables. This feat was even more remarkable considering that sugar was being rationed, partly because of the lack of beet sugar from Europe.

While large quantities of red meat and flour were being sent to the doughboys overseas, East Granby women were learning about "war pastry," meat substitutes, preserving dandelion leaves and milkweed, and harvesting seeds from their vegetable gardens. Most families already knew how to raise chickens and fatten a hog or two to supplement their diets.

Coal for home heating was in short supply at times, but it never caused a great problem. Toward the end of the war, automobile owners were requested to limit pleasure driving to conserve gasoline. For two Sundays a State Guard unit from Granby patrolled Main Street, described as "a main throughfare for most people traveling between central Connecticut and the western part of the state to get to Springfield," to determine how much unnecessary driving was being done. Another government request reflected the new type of warfare originated in this war. Citizens were asked to save all nutshells and pits and stones from fruits like peaches and olives so that the carbon could be used in making gas masks.

Volunteers collected well over their assigned quota of money for the Soldiers' War Libraries on election day 1917, and Herbert C. Stowell offered his store in the Viets building at 9 South Main Street as a collection place for donated books and magazines. The members of the Turkey Hills Study Club began knitting for the Red Cross even before the town's branch formed at the end of that year. Most other civic groups also curtailed or discontinued their regular activities to do war work under Red Cross direction.

A call for clothing for Belgian and French refugees yielded two full truckloads. Women gathered in the Congregational church parsonage every Tuesday afternoon to make surgical dressings under the direction of Elizabeth Newberry. The Whatsoever Club specialized in making "comfort kits" with accessories for soldiers. Red Cross units in various parts of town met regularly to sew and knit. They made surgical gowns, caps, socks, and various types of duffle bags for servicemen and clothing of all kinds for refugees. Nellie St. John Seymour, wife of Lucius H. Seymour, raised money from out-of-town contributors for a knitting machine and Mary E. Briggs donated a sewing machine.

The town schoolchildren knitted sweaters, scarves, socks, and wristlets and made face cloths, towels, and pillows. Morgan J. Viets was reportedly the most prolific worker. The schools in the Falls, South, and Center districts and at Hazelwood opened half a day each week for most of the summer of 1918 so that children could continue their war work and "receive some instruction in agriculture, sewing, physical training and current events." The summer sessions ended in August because so many of the students were harvesting tobacco.

The Red Cross, along with relatives and friends, filled Christmas boxes for the men

World War I roll of honor

overseas. All packages going to and coming from the troops were inspected by a special committee.

Not all Red Cross activities were pure work, however. The Center Unit gave a benefit dance with entertainment at Newgate in April 1918, and the South Unit gave another in the home of Grace Perkins Cowles (118 Spoonville Road) in July. The reporter for the *Journal* noted that in the Cowles home "the large rooms and wide piazzas are particularly adapted for dancing."

Fund drives for the Red Cross under the direction of Henry Z. Thompson and Benjamin N. Alderman were unfailingly successful. In fact, there was not a single money-raising effort during the war in which the town did not exceed its quota. Most drives generated spirited rallies at the Center. After the third Liberty Bond drive, which yielded about $21,650 in subscriptions, the townspeople celebrated with songs and speeches, the booming of a cannon, and the raising of an honor flag on a pole in front of the Viets building. The fourth drive, which included liberal help from the American Sumatra Company, totalled $31,500. Not to be left out, the schoolchildren bought or sold more than $11,000 of War Savings Stamps. In comparison, the best single-family farms in town during this era sold for about $8,000.

Near the end of the war the Spanish influenza pandemic spread across the nation. The war claimed the lives of two of the town's soldiers and the flu carried off two townspeople, both in the Eno family, along with many friends and relatives in other towns. Between October 1918 and March 1919 local doctors reported 113 cases to Frank H. Dibble, the health officer and town clerk. Schools were closed for a time and most meetings were canceled while the illness raged.

The armistice went into effect Monday, November 11, 1918, and along with all the towns around, East Granby began a continuing fete that lasted a week. The *Journal* reported:

Tuesday evening the townspeople celebrated peace in a jovial but none too peaceful way. A large number of cars started from the Center and went as far north as West Suffield, then back to the Center and as far as Spoonville, returning to the Center where they disbanded. The town's two big milk trucks, loaded to their limit, were in the parade. All along the route houses were illuminated and decorated. Several from here also participated in the parade held in West Granby the same night. H. Clifford Goslee had a handsome float representing the Masonic order, of which he is master in this place.

In front of her house at 123 North Main Street, Clara Merrill Gay, Douglas M. Gay's mother, displayed a bullet-riddled and bloodstained flag with thirty-four stars. It had flown at Arlington and during the Northern soldiers' march home at the close of the Civil War.

One by one the surviving soldiers returned to their families and friends amid many joyous celebrations. At the Hazelwood Plantation, a reception with music and dancing honored James A. Sailor and James McCray, who had been in France with the all-black 92nd Division (the Buffalos). On November 15, 1919, the town officially welcomed all its servicemen home with a chicken pie supper in the Congregational church hall and a dance in Barrett's Hall, then owned by Charles C. Adams. All the men were given medals of appreciation.

The next year Mary Rosier, who had not seen her home town in France for twenty years, sailed from New York for a three-month visit.

24

Permanence and Progress

PROGRAMS and issues that had been overshadowed by World War I moved back into the limelight very quickly after the fighting stopped. Advocates of prohibition and woman suffrage brought about the passage of the 18th and 19th Amendments to the Constitution of the United States in barely a year of peace. These national reforms certainly affected the townspeople of East Granby, but at the time they were giving most of their attention to a more local issue. Less than two months after the armistice was signed, they found themselves embroiled in controversy over a new state prison for Connecticut.

The Defeat of the State Prison Proposal

The General Assembly had appointed a special commission in 1917 to secure a site for a new state prison to replace the one at Wethersfield, which in 1827 had replaced Newgate. During the first week of January 1919 the commission reported that it had found an eminently suitable site for a model penal institution that would incorporate many new ideas about handling inmates. It would have enough buildings to separate them into twenty-four classifications and a prison farm, woodlot, and shops to provide the able with jobs which would defray some of the prison's expenses. The architect's rendering that the commission presented showed a 28-acre walled prison yard between the CNE railroad tracks and North Main Street in East Granby.

The buildings within the yard were meant to accommodate 1149 prisoners and the commission's plans called for the purchase of up to 1000 acres of land. Before the end of the month the committee had purchased a total of 154 acres at 33 and 61 North Main Street in the area where Metacomet Homes and East Granby Estates are today.

The townspeople of East Granby had other ideas. At a special town meeting held in Newgate Lodge, about seventy-five voters unanimously opposed the state's plan. About fifty townspeople packed a 2½-hour hearing in the capitol in February, bringing State's Attorney Hugh M. Alcorn of Suffield as their spokesman and many distinguished government officials for support. As the *Journal* put it, the people did not feel that it was necessary for the state "to take the best part of an old, established town for a prison site" and they "wished to preserve the character of their community."

Attorney Alcorn repeatedly protested the expense of building the new facility, estimated at about $5 million, and he questioned whether the state really needed it. One of his arguments centered around the imminent passage of the Prohibition Amendment, which ideally would reduce crime. He also showed that East Granby would lose about $1500 annually from taxes on the farms the prison would displace. Selectman William A. Seymour testified that evicting families and replacing them with criminals would ruin the town, and Horace V. Griffin, whose 100-acre farm at 39 No. Main Street separated the two parcels the state had purchased, steadfastly refused to sell.

The townspeople's determined opposition apparently helped sway the commission, because it recommended in April that the state not build a new prison. The legislature approved spending about $50,000 to update the old one; then the state divested itself of the farms it had acquired, selling them to local families. When the government finally did replace Wethersfield Prison, it chose a site in the Town of Somers.

The Temperance Movement and National Prohibition

A state law passed in 1874 gave towns the right to decide whether or not to permit the sale of liquor within their boundaries. Both churches in town featured temperance speakers as a matter of course, and every so often the anti-alcohol contingent in East Granby was successful in petitioning to bring the matter to a vote at the annual town meeting. In 1898 and 1901 they achieved their aim of outlawing liquor licenses, only to have the townspeople reverse the decision the following years.

The temperance movement became more organized in 1903 when a group of women affiliated with the Women's Christian Temperance Union (WCTU) and embraced its goal: the protection of the home through the abolition of liquor traffic. The longtime president of East Granby's union was Anna Viets, who also served about twenty years as the town's correspondent to the *Journal*. Union members met every other week and sent delegates to regional and state conferences. The women in town seem to have followed a course of gentle persuasion coupled with good works, rather than saloon-smashing a la Carry Nation. They filled "comfort bags" with notions and sent them to sailors on the battleship *Connecticut,* took hundreds of bouquets to hospital patients, and distributed temperance literature.

The idea of legislating against all liquor consumption was controversial and generally unpopular both in the state and the town. In 1911 the *Herald* commented:

There does not seem to be any reason to expect that the people of East Granby will depart from their usual custom of voting license when they know that the county commissioners will grant but two licenses, one in the extreme southern part of the town within a few yards of a saloon in Simsbury [in the Tariffville section] *and the other to the East Granby Hotel, which is a carefully conducted place.*

Longtime residents readily admit that a few native-born individuals, members of their own families, drank to excess occasionally or became alcoholics. However, drunkenness among the labor hired by the large tobacco plantations seems to have been a much greater problem for the community as a whole. The paper was not subtle about laying blame:

With the large foreign population which East Granby has to deal with, the question is whether it is better to have them get intoxicants in well ordered places in town or to have it brought into town by the wagon load to be sold contrary to the law.

An article in 1912 pleaded the economics and difficulty of enforcement:

It is the testimony of the constable who makes all the arrests in town that he always had three times as much business to do when the town was no license as he does when license prevails. As practically all who are arrested for drunkenness under no license do not settle but go to jail it means a large bill of costs for the town to pay for each prosecution, and a loss of revenue from the licenses as well.

After a proposed state prohibition law failed to pass in 1915, temperance organizations concentrated on communities like East Granby, where there were at least three rallies and meetings in the month before the 1916 town meeting. The Reverend Duane N. Griffin of Granby, a well-known orator for the Prohibition Party and for a number of years an acting pastor at the Copper Hill Methodist church, preached against strong drink. Several well-known tobacco growers, including Marcus Floyd, lectured on the ill effects of saloons on workers in their employ. In general, prohibitionists regarded drinking as un-American and un-Christian and held that alcohol was an underlying cause of poverty, vice, and crime.

At their annual town meetings in October 1916, both East Granby and Simsbury went dry by a majority of one vote. A year later the *Herald* ran the headline: "License Vote a Surprise, Biggest No-License Majority in History of Town," after East Granby voted 103 to 83 against.

The Prohibition Amendment, the 18th Amendment to the United States Constitution, did not receive any support from the government of Connecticut. Both of the state's senators refused to vote for the amendment in Congress, and Connecticut's legislature, along with Rhode Island's, never ratified it. The primary reason given was that any such restrictive measure was an intolerable infringement on personal liberty.

The amendment was ratified by the necessary number of states in 1919 and went into effect January 16, 1920. The Christian Endeavor Society of the Congregational church marked the passage of the amendment with an evening service "in the memory of John Barleycorn." The first reported arrest in town was not made until 1926, when the state police seized three quarts of liquor and two gambling devices in a store near the Floydville Plantation. The *Journal* reported that one of the tobacco workers had turned black after drinking a beverage he bought there, but he had recovered. In 1930 the town health officer reported five cases of poisoning from drinking Jamaica Ginger.

Also in 1930 the *Journal* reported that the state police arrested a farmer in the Spoonville section, who lived in a house now gone, after finding in his barn a 250-gallon and a 500-gallon still with full equipment, three 1000-gallon vats of mash, and one upright 37-horsepower boiler. Marie Sheldon, who as a girl lived at 16 Tunxis Avenue, remembered that neighbors west of them had two faucets in their kitchen, one for water and one for rum. She said that one evening, unaware that the neighbors' house had been raided, her family went out on their front porch to enjoy the evening air only to discover that it was permeated with the smell of rum that had been dumped into the river.

A few more arrests were made for minor infractions before the 21st Amendment, which repealed the 18th, was ratified in 1933, this time with the support of the State of Connecticut. East Granby remained dry until 1936 when the townspeople voted to allow the sale of beer in taverns. Eventually the town issued licenses for the sale of all manner of liquor.

Woman Suffrage

The issue of women's right to vote and hold office in the United States grew along with the issue of freedom for blacks. After the Civil War women began to work for passage of an amendment to the federal constitution guaranteeing them equal rights with men. In Connecticut they won the right to vote on all school matters in 1893. East Granby had a woman on its board of education by 1912, when the *Herald* reported that Mildred Griffin was chairman.

In East Granby both the Congregational and Methodist churches invited guests in 1914 to speak on woman suffrage, and early the next year the Turkey Hills Study Club devoted a meeting to the subject. The *Journal* reported:

Each member had been supplied at previous meetings with literature obtained from the Connecticut Suffrage Association and from the anti-suffrage society and had come prepared to present arguments on both sides of the question. The tendency of the majority seemed to be toward the "antis" while there were possibly two or three suffragettes.

Afterward the club launched a study of seventeen leading American women, such as Lucretia Mott, Susan B. Anthony, and Elizabeth Cady Stanton.

Some older women remember suffrage parades in Hartford where a few went to march for and a few against enfranchisement. In town both factions joined to demonstrate the value of their citizenship by working hard to contribute toward winning World War I. When asked what happened when Congress passed the 19th Amendment in 1919 and three-fourths of the states ratified it the next year, H. Clifford Goslee responded, "Well, I think the men realized that the time had come when the women were going to vote, and I think the parties just simply went out and tried to have the women vote the way the husbands did." The Turkey Hills Ecclesiastical Society voted at its 1919 annual meeting that women were to have equal privileges with men at future meetings.

Town Government

Two first selectmen during the 20th century had tenures of twenty years or more: Republicans Willard W. Viets, who served from 1898 through 1922, and Richard Dudley Seymour, who served from 1934 through 1954. William A. Seymour, the Democrat with the longest term, served from 1925 through 1933. William Seymour, at seventy years of age, became the first townsman to be elected to public office outside the town when he won a hard-fought election for sheriff of Hartford County in 1934.

Town clerks have enjoyed even more permanence in office. Frank H. Dibble, a Republican, served thirty-one years, his last term ending in 1927. During his lifetime town officials, except for those on the school board, had to run for reelection each year and several times both parties nominated Dibble. The *Herald* offered an explanation for this in 1911: "He has a convenient office for keeping the records and can generally be found in the office when wanted. The people appreciate good service." His office was in the basement of his house, now rebuilt, at 12 School Street.

Effie Heaton Miller, a Republican, was elected town treasurer in 1927, making her the first woman ever to be elected to any office in East Granby except for a seat on the board of education. She held the post forty-four years. In 1929 she was elected town clerk and she remained in the post for forty-two years. During her long tenure she became respected by officials throughout the state for her thorough knowledge of the intricacies of government, and they often called on her for advice. She had an office in three successive East Granby town halls.

Millard C. Griffin, a Republican, held the office of judge of probate forty-four years. He conducted court in his home at 185 North Main Street from 1903 to 1947.*

Republicans usually won election to the office of representative to the General Assembly from East Granby, a two-year post eliminated in January 1967 after the new state constitution provided for forming house districts according to population. Charles G. Sandman, elected in 1922, was the first Democrat to hold that office in the 20th century. The Democrats' longest hold on the seat, eight consecutive years, began when Leon H. Viets won the 1930 election by just eleven votes. He ran only once, that being the usual practice for the town at that time.

Elections in general were rather cut-and-dried affairs, but every once in a while a contest was close enough to spark some campaign friction. This report ran in the *Herald* in 1910 after Republican George E. Bidwell, the eventual winner, and Democrat Harlow T. Drew polled 85 votes each:

Tuesday was the day when the tie on representatives in East Granby was voted off. Somebody must have furnished money by the quantity as seven automobiles were in use that day and one voter was sent for to come from Maine. It was a common report that votes in the town were worth all the way from $20 upwards. Of course the writer does not know of a single instance of vote buying, but rumors were current that a big day's pay was made by some of the needy in town.

Only one town official has ever resigned under duress. In 1916 Town Auditors Harlow T. Drew and Millard C. Griffin alleged that Town Treasurer Orrin Case, Jr., showed a $4000 shortage on his books. Case instituted slander proceedings, later withdrawn, against his fellow Republican, Griffin, before resigning. The town's financial predicament was aired in Superior Court and a special town committee reviewed the books. After a great deal of consternation the matter was settled in 1917 without a public trial, and a more modern method of bookkeeping was adopted.

Town Halls

The basement of the Congregational church was sometimes referred to as the "town hall" in early 20th century records and news articles. The town rented it annually for

*The federal government had a thirty-year employee in J. Edward Viets, who became the town's RFD carrier in 1917.

Town hall at 8 School Street after the fire in 1968

town meetings and elections, but town officials maintained offices in their own homes. The hall was reached by its own entrance and was not connected to the upstairs by a stairway until 1915.

As early as 1894 town meetings considered buying a site and building a town hall. While a new Center School was being built at 27 School Street in 1923, the town voted to spend $800 to refurbish the old schoolhouse across the street as a town hall. Town reports for the next couple of years show expenditures for renovations and equipment, incuding a telephone and a piano. Although no mention is made of a formal opening, the town probably began holding its meeting and elections there in 1924. The hall was also used for civic gatherings.

Most town officials continued to work in their own homes, but the town clerk eventually established an office with regular hours in this town hall. Later the first selectman furnished an office where he was available several hours a week.

The town built a new town hall at 8 School Street, west of the old one, in 1942. This brick building had a recreation room with a stage and kitchen on the second floor and town offices and a garage for two fire engines on the first. Until a new well was drilled, it was supplied with water from the same well that had served the Dibble blacksmith shop that had once stood on the property. The firemen dammed Sheldon Brook behind the building to make a pool from which they could supply their pumper truck with water, and the spot became a popular ice-skating place.

When this town hall burned in December 1968, only the town clerk's vault with the town records was saved. Townspeople remember Effie Miller holding office hours in her windowless vault until the present town hall at 9 Center Street was completed in 1971.

The East Granby Volunteer Fire Department

Fire has always been the principal destroyer of property in town. Each time a fire broke out, townspeople did all they could to extinguish it with whatever water was available while they waited for fire trucks to arrive from adjoining towns. When the Congregational church was threatened by a fire in its barn in 1925, the people talked, as they often did, about the need for a fire engine in town. In 1926 Town Clerk Frank H. Dibble's home burned to the ground. Luckily, the Simsbury fire department was

First town fire truck, acquired in 1930

able to control the blaze long enough for the safe in his basement office to be hoisted out, so most of the town records were saved.

Then in July 1929 at the Nicholson & Viets farm on Nicholson Road across from the Elmwood Cemetery, a charcoal fire being used to dry tobacco ignited a conflagration that spread from the barn over cloth-covered tobacco fields from building to building. According to the newspaper Nicholson & Viets lost their barn and all its contents, another shed full of tobacco, a hired hand's house, and tobacco cloth over seventeen acres, which either burned or had to be torn down. The fire spread to Herman Vogt's property and he lost his house and a large tobacco shed. The Simsbury, Windsor, and Suffield fire companies prevented even greater loss. The only good result of the fire was the immediate formation of the East Granby Volunteer Fire Department.

The town bought a 1929 Chevrolet pumper truck. The main chassis, purchased from the Adams & Woodworth (A&W) Motor Car Company of 26 South Main Street, traveled around the Northeast to have components added in various places. Norman I. Adams went to Tarrytown, New York, to get the completed fire engine and drove it to town, where it was housed in an addition to the A&W Company's garage. This building is now the town garage, and the ambulance used by the East Granby Volunteer Ambulance Association is kept in the same space.

The twenty-five volunteer firemen began their continual training under the leadership of their first chief, James R. Miller, and they responded to their first fire in March 1930, just over the town line in Windsor. It was probably a chimney fire, a common occurrence in those days when many people heated their homes with wood. The men also began the card parties, turkey shoots, dances, clambakes, carnivals, and other socials that still raise money for coats, boots, hoses, and other equipment. Before long they were invited to all the parades and firemen's carnivals in the area to show their new truck.

The fire department bought land for a firehouse in 1937 across from the cemetery in the Center, but did not build one. Instead, the town used the land for its town hall, which incorporated a garage for fire trucks. Development in the south of town spurred the building of a four-bay firehouse on the corner of South Main Street and Seymour Road in 1964. After the town hall on School Street burned, the town erected a free-standing firehouse at 6 Memorial Drive.

The East Granby Public Library

Since colonial times individuals had been good enough to keep the town's collection of circulating books in their homes. In 1914 the *Journal* announced that Gladys Griffin was distributing books from a state library agency. Reverend A. Avery Gates arranged in 1920 for a collection of eighty books from the Connecticut circulating library to be sent to the Congregational church where they were placed on shelves in the church balcony. The Falls School and others received similar collections from the state.

In 1922 a group of six townspeople met to form the East Granby Library Association. The Congregational minister, Reverend Burton F. Case, became the first president of the association, with Anna Viets as vice-president, Sadie Nicholson Viets, secretary, and Louis A. Bates, treasurer. Dora Griffin became the first librarian. This small group canvassed the town to enroll other members and by the end of the year they had almost 200. With the help of a 50-cent membership fee, donations, and seed grants from the state and town of $200 each, the association was able to accumulate about 1000 books and to send two members to a five-day course in library work at Yale.

In 1923 the association established a branch library in the home of the Falls schoolteacher Harriette "Hattie" Hayes near Granby Station, and in 1928 it placed a collection in the Watson Holcomb home at Copper Hill. In the summer of 1927 the main library collection was moved from the church to the parsonage. During the Great Depression the association proposed getting a Works Progress Administration appropriation to build a library, but contented itself with converting the vacated North School. Nearly 3500 books were moved from the parsonage to the school in May 1938. As usual, the library there opened for only two hours each week, on Saturday afternoons.

The library acquired a more central location in November 1942 when it moved into the vacated town hall on School Street, which had begun its existence as Center School. The library moved to its present location at 27 School Street, a newer Center School, in May 1967. The library has expanded its hours considerably and now has a permanent collection of about 15,000 books.

Moving Toward a Consolidated Elementary School

East Granby consolidated its school government in 1900 under a newly elected, six-member board of education. The board chose a local school visitor to supervise the schools until 1903 when they decided to employ a superintendent of schools from the state board of education.

The practice of having a school in each school district had already become impractical, because the population of school children had grown in some districts and

North schoolhouse

Hazelwood schoolhouse and pupils

South schoolhouse and pupils about 1913

Copper Hill schoolhouse

Falls schoolhouse and class of 1928 with teacher Doris Carruthers, later Mrs. Albert F. Cowles

diminished in others. By the turn of the century the Center District had enough students to warrant two rooms, one for the primary grades and another for the upper level. On the other hand, the Fourth District schoolhouse at 3 Old Road had been closed permanently in 1899, with the few students in its vicinity going either to the Copper Hill District schoolhouse at 23 Copper Hill Road or to the Center. The North District closed its schoolhouse and sent its students to the Center in 1900, but opened a newly constructed building at 139 North Main Street in 1909. The Falls District closed its school and sent its few children to a school in Tariffville in September 1900, only to reopen its building in 1903. The Copper Hill School also closed and reopened several times.

The development of the large shade tobacco plantations swelled the school population with workers' children. To alleviate crowding, the Falls District first sent some students to Tariffville again, then ran double sessions. Finally, in 1915, the district closed its one-room schoolhouse and opened a modern two-room building on the southeast corner of Hartford Avenue and Holcomb Street. A third room was added in 1924.

With funds raised by the students and the Falls District Neighborhood Club after World War I, the school added electric lights, a piano, and many other pieces of equipment. The board of education ran a night school in the building during the 1920s which taught English to foreign-born residents, general studies to students who had dropped out of school before completing the eighth grade, and dressmaking. People also used the building for community meetings and social events.

By the time the Hazelwood Plantation opened east of the Mountain, the townspeople had become concerned by the new expenses and problems that accompanied the growth of the plantations. The teamsters hauling fertilizer and tobacco to and from the fields played havoc with the surface of the roads, and the expense of extra classrooms and teachers needed to serve the fluctuating population of transient laborers' children raised the school budget. The people wanted the tobacco corporation to pay enough taxes to reimburse the town and to take some responsibility for educating their employees' children, so the company opened a classroom in one of its own buildings. In 1918 the company provided a parcel of land on the south side of Rainbow Road, east of Hazelwood Road, on which the town built the one-room Hazelwood School.

Like the Falls School, Hazelwood offered night classes for adults and they, in turn, raised money to equip the school with hanging oil lamps. They also held social and religious functions there. Since most of the children on the plantation at that time were black, the town hired its first black teacher, Margaret Scott Spence, a graduate of the normal school in Worcester, Massachusetts. Mrs. Spence left after the first year, but returned to teach for several years during the 1920s.

Some of the young women who taught in the other district schools had two-year degrees in education from a normal school, but many had only a six-week training course after high school. Very few East Granby women who became teachers took jobs in town, and teachers who came to town rarely remained more than a year or two. Hattie Hayes of the Falls School was an exception. She taught there a total of forty years, taking the upper grades when the school was enlarged. She retired in 1933. Older residents remember Miss Hayes as a devoted teacher who used methods well ahead of her time.

There were many reasons for the rapid turnover among teachers. Almost all women left teaching when they married; a few met their husbands in town. Those who wished to build a career usually left to go to more populous communities where they could teach one grade at a time, rather than all eight grades as in most of East Granby's small, remote schools. Also, after gaining work experience, they sometimes could command a higher salary than the town paid. Finding a suitable place to board was another problem for teachers, but maintaining a lively social life was not. Townspeople made them welcome by including them in activities, and if a young woman had any social aplomb and appreciation for their efforts, she was apt to become "the toast of the town."

The town's inability to hire and hold experienced teachers concerned some townspeople. They felt one answer to the problem would be having specialized teachers, each working with two or three grades. That would mean sending all the children to just two schools: the Center School east of the Mountain and the Falls School west of it. After roads and vehicles improved enough to make busing feasible, each successive supervisor of rural schools in the area and some school board members championed the idea. A few even proposed a single, centralized school with one teacher for each grade.

However, many families objected to sending their children out of their own sections of town for numerous reasons, not the least being the noon meal. It was the custom at that time, especially on farms, to have the main meal of the day at noon, and many children walked home from school to join their families for a little socializing and a big, hot dinner. Also, many taxpayers did not want to shoulder the costs of enlarging the two schools and hiring transportation for the children.

By the time the South School burned in Feburary 1923, its seventh and eighth grade students were being transported by the Prevo & Miller bus to the partially consolidated Center School, but South School was rebuilt to accommodate the primary grades. The town improved the new school by wiring it for electricity and buying additional playground space. When the town opened a new Center School at 27 School Street in 1924, it was better equipped than the old building across the street, but it still had only two rooms. This school was the first school to have its own well, but by the end of the year the Falls School also had a well and the North School had a piped water supply.

Early in the 20th century the town health officer had put an end to the practice of bringing drinking water from a neighboring home and letting it sit uncovered all day in the schoolhouse. In 1912 the board of education installed sanitary drinking tanks in the schools and required each child to bring his own cup. The town hired its first school nurse during the 1918-19 school year and she inspected the children for health problems like tooth decay, enlarged tonsils, and head lice. She brought individual problems to the attention of parents and reported to the town during the first year that three-fourths of the pupils had not been vaccinated.

Fortunately no case of smallpox occurred in town during the 20th century, but other infectious diseases like measles, mumps, whooping cough, scarlet fever, typhoid, and diphtheria closed individual schools for a week or two at a time. Several children died of diphtheria over the years, and when seven cases developed in the South School during the 1910-11 year, the school was fumigated and sprayed with disinfectant and all the textbooks were burned. The most dread scourge of the era was infantile paralysis and several children in town contracted the disease. Polio scares closed all schools and churches over a widespread area for about two weeks in 1916 and 1934. Quarantine was so strict and fear so great that people found it difficult to travel with children during these periods.

The role of the school nurse grew over the years to include instructing pupils about proper hygiene and nutrition and the schools became actively involved with promoting public health. During the 1930s chest X-rays for early diagnosis of tuberculosis were taken in the schools and clinics were held for dental exams, vaccinations, and well-child conferences. Many townspeople remember Dr. Owen L. Murphy of Simsbury, who was appointed medical examiner for East Granby in 1938 and remained active in public health and private practice into the 1970s. Among the many other doctors who made house calls in town, Dr. E. R. Pendleton is remembered for the small hospital he developed during the 1920s in Granby.

School consolidation slowly progressed, and in 1939 the school supervisor could report that, except for South School, all the one-room schools had been closed. By this time quite a few people liked the idea of building a single, centralized elementary school, which would have modern facilities, such as an auditorium-gymnasium, library, and cafeteria. They also wanted to hire a principal. These plans would wait, however, until after the Second World War.

During the years between the wars, the teachers, the board of education, and the inter-town supervisor worked together to expand the elementary school curriculum so that an education in the East Granby schools would compare favorably to that in any other school system; several girls proved them successful by becoming valedictorian or salutatorian of their high school classes. Through the years the schools added subjects like European history, commercial geography, business arithmetic, agricultural studies, art, music, and physical education to their basic programs. Students, sponsored by schools and civic groups, took part in local and statewide speaking and spelling contests. Toward the end of the Great Depression, the board of education initiated far-ranging field trips, sending classes to the Museum of Natural History and the aquarium in New York City and to historic sites in Boston.

The proportion of students who stayed in school to graduate from eighth grade increased steadily over the years, and the number who went on to secondary schools rose accordingly. Just as in the 19th century, a few went to private academies, but many more went to public high schools. With the opening of the Horace Belden Building in 1908, Simsbury High School could accommodate out-of-town students; the CNE railroad branch made commuting relatively easy for those from East Granby. However, a few chose to attend school in Windsor or Hartford. The town paid tuition and transportation costs for eleven public high school students that year, and an enumeration done the next year found that nine of those who had finished grammar school were not attending high school. Twenty years later sixty were attending.

About 1920 the town began to send some students to Bloomfield High School by bus. During this era it also paid tuition for a number of boys to go to trade schools in Meriden and in Hartford. Some parents sent their children through an agricultural course in Storrs.

The number of graduates who went on to higher education also increased and now included women. The young people had more colleges than ever to choose from, as well as teaching, nursing, and business schools throughout the Northeast, South, and Midwest. Unlike the townspeople who left for the fertile lands of the Midwest in the 1800s, some of those who went away to further their educations returned to settle in town.

25

Tobacco Loses Ground

THE CIGAR TOBACCO industry, which had boomed during World War I when importation of foreign tobacco virtually ceased, began to slump soon after the war. Tariffs, taxes, and production costs fluctuated, sometimes to the industry's benefit and sometimes to its detriment. Nature had a way of unleashing new plant diseases, like wildfire infection and blue mold, as fast as researchers and farmers learned to control old ones, and the weather was as unpredictable as ever. Worst of all, cigar smoking began to go out of fashion as cigarettes caught the public's fancy.

In 1925 the Tobacco Merchants Association announced that the production of cigarettes had increased over the previous ten years from 17 billion to 73 billion per year. The cigarette, a quicker smoke, seemed to suit the pace of the "Roaring Twenties" and its cheaper price suited the economics of the Depression era in the Thirties. To assist the public with discerning these facts, the cigarette manufacturers launched advertising campaigns on a scale never dreamed of in the heyday of the cigar.

The Slide into the Great Depression

By 1922 the prices for cigar tobacco were so poor that independent growers were willing to try a cooperative marketing venture, even though similar experiments had produced mixed results in the past. They formed the Connecticut Valley Tobacco Growers Association with members throughout New England. East Granby, where land records show a marked increase in tobacco land foreclosures that year, became part of the association's 13th district along with Granby and Bloomfield. Over 77 percent of the farmers in town joined the new cooperative and Charles P. Viets was elected chairman of the district's directors.

The new association helped its members to secure bank loans and arranged for insurance companies to cover hail and fire losses. It proved less successful at selling all its members' tobacco, primarily because it had no way to stop farmers from producing more than the dwindling market would bear. In 1925 the association warned that dealers and manufacturers already had a three-year supply of tobacco in their warehouses, when the customary supply covered only one year. According to one news account, Joseph W. Alsop of Avon, president of the association, concluded that farmers would be better off to go to the seashore than to raise tobacco that summer.

Shade tobacco syndicates were feeling the same pinch. The American Sumatra Tobacco Company was placed in equity receivership that year, but it recovered after being reorganized. This company was called the largest producer of shade-grown tobacco at the time with land in Georgia, Florida, Massachusetts, and Connecticut. It owned the Floydville and Hazelwood plantations in East Granby.

The independent growers' cooperative, which had the potential to set prices, made tobacco dealers and cigar manufacturers uncomfortable. So, according to a news account, they took advantage of the tobacco glut to undermine the growers' association by purchasing almost exclusively from farmers outside the membership or from renegade members who would sell to them directly. A study by Willis N. Baer notes that the association suffered from charges of exercising poor management, paying its officials salaries that were too high, and making too little use of publicity. Baer characterized the growers as being individualistic, self-sufficient, and unsuited for cooperative programs. The Connecticut Valley Tobacco Growers Association succumbed to internal dissension in 1928, leaving its former members carrying heavy debt.

The East Granby Farmers Exchange, a very much smaller cooperative that bought fertilizer, feed, coal, and other supplies for the farmers in town, had a longer life. It was formed in 1921 with Leon H. Viets as president, followed several years later by Jasper W. Bidwell. Benjamin A. Krick served as general manager, followed by Warren A. Wilcox. In 1926 the exchange transacted $65,912.65 worth of business, but by 1935 conditions were such that the members voted to discontinue the organization.

An even more significant development for the independent outdoor tobacco farmer began in 1920. The Fassler & Silberman company leased 300 acres of the Cowles land in Spoonville that year to grow shade tobacco, and by the end of the decade quite a bit of private land all over town was under tenting. Cullman Brothers, Inc., did most of the leasing west of the Mountain and the Gershel-Kaffenburgh company took land east of it. Company agents were put in control of the fields, or the farmers themselves worked for the companies as agents. Although the tobacco leases usually ran for only one year at a time and the rent might be less than the farmer could clear in a good year raising his own crop, many farmers chose to reduce their risk by leasing their land.

According to Edward A. Bartkus, the first tractors began to appear in town about this time. He said: "When somebody had some money he got an old iron horse, the Fordson, the 'man killer.' Just before the Second World War they started getting out smaller tractors; Ford and Ferguson got together and put out something that was halfway decent." By 1920 the Town of East Granby had ceased using oxen for road work and had bought a Fordson tractor.

Evidently the farmers who went into dairying either as a sideline or a major undertaking fared rather well during the 1920s. The *Journal* quoted a study by the Connecticut Agricultural College that said: "In 1926, when tobacco prices were high enough to permit the average farmer to pay the expenses of producing his tobacco, the addition of the dairy enterprise still added to his income. The farmer having no cows had an average income of $515 and those with 16 to 20 cows had an average income of $1,675." In 1930 East Granby had sixty-one accredited (tuberculin tested) dairy herds, according to a list published by the commissioner of domestic animals.

Tobacco grower, dairyman, and cattle breeder Charles P. Viets gained distinction for himself and the town when the college at Storrs awarded him a certificate of honorary recognition for his notable service in the advancement of agriculture and rural life in Connecticut. When making the award in 1927, the college recognized that he was the first in his area to grow alfalfa for cattle feed, that he had been instrumental in winning farmers' cooperation when tuberculin testing regulations went into effect, and that he had developed a cattle-buying business as a sideline to farming. His wife, Anna Viets, was a pioneer in the business of selling day-old chicks, one news account said.

Even though the farm economy was depressed in the 1920s, a number of East Granby farmers had accumulated enough net worth that their lives were not seriously affected in this decade or in the depression years to come. Quite a few still indulged in extended trips; Moses E. Seymour came back from a two-month, four-country trip to Europe in 1922, having seen the Passion Play in Oberammergau. Many townspeople, including the Charles Vietses, the Almon Phelpses, the Waldo Bateses, the Lucius Seymours, the Irving Griffins, and Hiram and Horace Viets, spent the winter months on the western coast of Florida. Also, some families bought hunting and fishing camps in Massachusetts.

In town, sports, especially baseball, and social events continued as usual. The Twenties were notable for the number of neighborhood groups formed: the Falls District Neighborhood Club, the Akita Club of Copper Hill, the Get Together Club of North Main Street, and more. The *Journal* mentions a Girl Reserve troop in the 1920s and Girl Scouts in the 1930s. The whole town usually had a picnic during the summer at Forest Park in Springfield, Mountain Park in Holyoke, or Keney Park in Hartford. In 1920 the tradition of a town Christmas tree was established.

City people continued to build summer homes around East Granby, some of which they later winterized for permanent homes. Granbrook Park was developed as a summer community by a Hartford realty corporation, which subdivided an area along Salmon Brook near the Granby Station. Many residents joined the summer people for dances at the pavilion there.

People also remember the Burns Amusement Park which Peter J. Burns developed behind his novelty store and taxidermy shop at 186 Hartford Avenue; he held many carnivals and baseball games there. Residents tell of going to the movies at the Tunxis House in Tariffville and the Casino in Simsbury, both of which are now gone.

People were so excited about the Chautauqua program held in Simsbury in 1919 that they decided to have the troupe come to East Granby the following year. That three-day program of music and entertainment was held in the hall below the sanctuary of the Congregational church.

In 1927 the Congregational church celebrated the finish of an extensive restoration project that renovated the interior of the building, adding a new heating plant, but preserving the style of decoration that had been adopted in 1865. Church members declared an Old Home Sunday in October and invited all past members and residents of the town to attend morning and afternoon services. Albert C. Bates, one of several speakers, read a paper on the history of the congregation. In 1930 the church held another Old Home Sunday with a morning service, a luncheon, and an afternoon social to celebrate the 100th anniversary of the erection of its stone building, which replaced the original wooden church. Bates gave another address, which he published as *Sketch of the Congregational Society and Church* . . . .

Another special event occured in 1937 when a party depicting the Ohio Pioneers

Leon H. Viets' show oxen in front of 81 North Main Street

left from the Eastern States Fair in Springfield, bound for Marietta, Ohio. They came through East Granby with their teams of oxen and had lunch at the Congregational church. The oxen were brought to Leon H. Viets' barn at 81 North Main Street to be shod. At the time, Viets himself had a number of yokes of prize show oxen, which he sometimes put to work around the farm to the delight of passersby.

The Depression Years

For a brief period after the stock market crash in October 1929 people were generally optimistic, not realizing that it was a symptom of conditions that would depress the national economy for almost a decade. By harvest time in 1930, though, Connecticut farmers had begun to worry about the sluggish flow of money into the marketplace. They appealed to the people of the state to help them and to keep cash in circulation locally by purchasing food grown in Connecticut. The *Journal* pointed out that the farmers were producing more than consumers could afford to buy. At the end of 1931 the *Herald* reported that the fruit crop was short, tobacco was not moving to market, and dairy and poultry products had fallen in price.

Since the town's economy was based on agriculture, everything else in town suffered when the farmers did. Merchants saw goods grow dusty on their shelves. The supervisor of schools reported to the town in 1931 that the reduction in farm revenues had kept the board of education from considering any enrichment of the educational program during the previous year. Those who depended on the farmers and tobacco syndicates for work took pay cuts or went jobless. This caused one potentially explosive incident among farm workers in the area.

One July morning in 1933 the truck from the Indian Head Plantation, then owned by the Cullman Brothers company, arrived in Tariffville as usual to pick up about eighty tobacco workers. Instead of boarding the truck, however, the workers began demonstrating against what they considered unfair wages, shouting, "A new deal for all." They demanded a raise of 50 cents a day for men and 25 cents for boys.

According to the *Herald*, Fred B. Griffin, vice-president of the company said: "We haven't made a dollar in five years and we just cannot pay any more. The pickers are paid $1.50, $2, and $2.25 a day for adults and $1 for boys." On hearing his statement workers at the Cullman Brothers plantation at Hoskins Station in Simsbury joined the strike, declaring that they had never been paid more than $1.50. Approximately 500 men, women, and children paraded the streets of Tariffville and the center of Simsbury in automobiles.

The company tried to break the strike by bringing in workers from their East Windsor Hill plantation; the state police were called in to keep the peace. Within a week, with the help of Simsbury's first selectman and the pastor of Trinity Episcopal Church in Tariffville, the workers' daily wage scale was increased to a $1.25 minimum and $2 maximum for pickers and an extra 25 cents per bundle for the women who strung the leaves onto the laths. This was still quite a bit lower than the $5 a day maximum that workers remembered from better days.

During the strike the police arrested two out-of-town agitators for breach of the peace. They allegedly urged the strikers to start a fight with the deputy sheriffs on duty, using the women workers as shields, and to join the International Labor Defense, called a Communist organization.

When asked about the Depression, the typical reply from older residents was: "No one ever went hungry in East Granby." Farm families used their land and skills to produce their own food when they needed to and they were quietly generous with any surplus. Gertrude McKinnie Fletcher remembered that even before the Depression her father gave milk left over from his milk route to children whose families could not afford it. She learned this during her father's final illness from his doctor, who had been one of the children.

During the Great Depression, however, human need far outstripped the capacity of private and institutionalized charity to cope with it. Under the heading "Paupers" the 1929 town report carried eleven entries naming one family and four individuals, three of whom were in institutions for the tubercular or the insane, as recipients of town aid totaling $538.29. The 1933 report carried 142 entries naming thirty individuals, including the same three in institutions, as recipients of town aid totaling $4,065.33. The payments for board, rent, electricity, wood, groceries, medical care, and transportation. The monies were not dispensed directly to the needy, but to the merchants and other people who provided the goods and services.

For the first few years the town carried much of its increasing relief burden by itself by instituting stringent economic measures. In 1932 the school supervisor reported that the board of education had reduced the teaching staff from eight to seven and cut their salaries 10 percent. At the depth of the Depression in 1933, voters at the annual town meeting held the tax rate to the 12 mills it had been the year before, reduced officials' salaries, and eliminated some street lights. By this time direct relief had started coming in from state and federal sources, particularly President Franklin D. Roosevelt's New Deal programs.

In 1933 First Selectman William A. Seymour made twenty trips into Hartford on business concerning the federal Civil Works Administration (CWA) program intended to provide jobs for the unemployed on relief. In 1935 the town received enough government cloth for local women to make five bed quilts for needy families under the direction of the Congregational minister's wife, Lillian Fletcher. The State of Connecticut began emergency relief payments of several thousand dollars a year, and in 1936 the federal Works Progress Admininstration (WPA) gave East Granby $13,405 under one of its programs.

Besides giving goods and services to those in want, the town tried to provide work for able-bodied men by hiring them to improve roads. Connecticut's rural towns had long hoped to divert some of the state money being spent on inter-town highways to local roads, so in 1931, despite many objections from the highway commissioner, the legislature passed a bill which gave town governments funds to use on secondary roads. Although the money was not specifically earmarked for relief and contracts were not awarded at the discretion of the selectmen, the governments of many towns, including East Granby, were able to secure many of the newly created jobs for their own citizens. The pay for road labor was generally $2 per day.

In 1931 town aid funds were used to put a layer of loose traprock on North, Hungary, and Russell roads and Newgate Road north of Copper Hill Road. In 1932 segments of Hatchet Hill Road and Holcomb and East streets and the road between Newgate Prison and the Copper Hill section of town were widened to 14 feet and improved with waterbound macadam, layers of crushed stone treated with a mud slurry. The remainder of Hatchet Hill Road and some of Rainbow Road were treated in 1933.

Town men had the opportunity in 1933 to work on a public works road project through West Granby and East Hartland and that year the state passed another "dirt roads bill," one clearly meant to provide jobs. In 1935 the town completed the road to Copper Hill and turned its attention to Miller and Hazelwood Roads.

In 1936 the *Courant* reported that East Granby had four young men in unspecified federal Civilian Conservation Corps (CCC) camps where they were most likely working on reforestation projects. Only men between the ages of seventeen and twenty-eight from families on relief were eligible for this program, and they were required to send home $25 of their $30 monthly wage.

Within a few years the dirt roads projects had run their course and inter-town highways began to receive more attention. Turkey Hills Road, from the Center westward 2 miles toward Granby, benefited from several sessions of roadwork in the late 1930s and early '40s. The state highway department filled enough of Griffin's Marsh, directly west of the Mountain, to straighten the road's course so that it no longer had to run by way of what is now Old Road to skirt the swampy area. Hartford Avenue also was straightened somewhat in 1939.

East Granby farmers who owned their land free and clear were secure enough to ride out the Depression without much trouble, although their yearly income dropped considerably. Those with mortgages had more difficulty. A few lost their farms in the economic crunch, but some others were saved from foreclosure or bankruptcy by New Deal programs that provided low-interest, guaranteed loans and mortgage relief.

The Agricultural Adjustment Act of 1933 created the AAA program that paid farmers a stipend for leaving a certain percentage of their acreage fallow. Along with the fact that the price of tobacco had dropped to a ruinous level with Havana leaf bringing only 5 cents a pound in 1932, this act provided the impetus needed to stop some of the growers from overproducing. At least thirty East Granby farmers took advantage of the offer. The AAA program was invalidated by the United States Supreme Court in 1936, but quickly replaced, in effect, by the Soil Conservation and Domestic Allotment Act, which emphasized soil enrichment and reforestation.

The rise in taxes that accompanied all the new government programs cut into farmers' incomes, however, and local tobacco growers were hurt by a New Deal trade treaty that lowered the tariff on imported Sumatra leaf. Because the public had cut its consumption of cigars, manufacturers sought cheaper and, sometimes, inferior quality tobacco from other areas to produce the fabled 5 cent cigar. At the same time trade associations in the state tried to bolster the market for Connecticut leaf by advertising its superior quality.

During two decades of economic struggle, it became apparent that fewer and fewer families were going to be able to support themselves on small farms. The number of farms and amount of farm acreage throughout the country decreased while the size of farms increased. In East Granby one child in each family usually took over the farm, while the rest of the children trained for work other than farming. A great many of the latter moved to towns and cities where they had found work, but for the first time moving was not always necessary. Improvements in transportation, such as the bus which ran along Tunxis Avenue and another which ran for a while through the Center, made it relatively easy to travel to Hartford every day. A small number of young townspeople of this era became the town's first wave of commuters.

The Connecticut Tercentenary Celebration

Still beset by the problems of the Depression in 1935, the townspeople put their hearts and energies into celebrating the 300th anniversary of the founding of Connecticut. Many went to Simsbury's celebration in June, where Millard C. Griffin, a direct descendant of first settler John Griffin, officially represented East Granby as a guest of honor. East Granby had its own day on September 22, which also was designated an Old Home Sunday when all those who had moved from town were invited back for a reunion.

Flags flew in front of homes and many townspeople donned colonial costumes. Morning services at the Congregational church, attended by more than 350 persons, included a speech on the history of the town by Colonel Clarence W. Seymour, followed by a luncheon. An early afternoon program at Old Newgate Prison featured another speech and old-time songs rendered by a male quartet. Later four venerable homes were open for tours. The statewide celebration ended in October with a grand tercentenary parade through the streets of Hartford.

The Floods of 1936 and 1938

The 1930s brought numerous quirks of nature, from a fine display of the aurora borealis reported in 1931, to a couple of earth tremors, to a dust storm in May 1934, which Anna Viets said in her diary came from the west and obscured the sun nearly all day. Nothing seemed likely to match the calamity of the flood in March 1936 caused by melting snow and rain. Then came the flood and hurricane winds of September 1938.

East Granby suffered much less damage in 1936 than the towns and cities along the Connecticut River, which crested at a record high of 37.5 feet. Almost all the summer

Center schoolhouse at 27 School Street after the 1938 hurricane

homes in the Granbrook Park community were inundated by the rising waters of Salmon Brook made even higher near its confluence with the Farmington River by a dam break upstream on the river. Many of the lots where the houses had stood were sold for back taxes in the following years, as much the result of prevailing economic conditions as the flooding. More houses were built in the community during the 1940s and some of them were winterized before they were flooded again in 1955.

The 1938 storm wreaked far more damage on the town because of its high winds, which gusted up to 100 miles per hour in some parts of the state. A number of houses in town were damaged by falling trees and an estimated $100,000 worth of potential lumber was lost. The Congregational church lost its chimney, and both ends of the Center School (now the East Granby Public Library) and part of its roof were blown off. Classes were held in the old school across the street (then being used as the town hall) until repairs were made.

Most streets and highways were quickly cleared of fallen trees, but parts of Hartford Avenue remained flooded for days. Anna Viets recorded that mail service did not resume for three days, electric service for ten, and telephone service for nineteen. Farmers lost many tobacco sheds full of crops and the entire potato crop was destroyed.

By the beginning of 1939 the storm damage had been repaired and the cigar industry seemed to be turning around. The surplus of tobacco in warehouses had dropped to normal levels and cigar consumption was on the rise again. Local storekeepers and others businesses were doing an increasing amount of trade and it truly looked as if prosperity were just around the corner. In nearby cities and industrial towns, factories suddenly had an influx of orders from European buyers; the products: war materials.

26

World War II: Prelude to Growth and Change

THE INVASION of Poland by Germany on September 1, 1939, evoked memories of World War I and electrified the atmosphere throughout the United States. Prices rocketed overnight as housewives, fearing wartime shortages, cleared market shelves of sugar, flour, and canned goods. Headlines blared declarations of war against Germany by France and the United Kingdom. Americans followed every move of Nazi Germany and its ally, Fascist Italy, as fighting spread in Europe and North Africa. On the other side of the world, Japan invaded French Indo-China.

During 1940 all aliens in the United States were fingerprinted and registered with the government. In East Granby, Eunice Miller Prevo organized a drive for the Finnish Relief Fund after Russia invaded that country. Under the direction of the American Legion post in Windsor Locks, a group of East Granby men established an aircraft observation post in the lookout tower at Newgate Prison and started their training.

Early in 1941 town men began to report for induction into the armed forces, either as draftees or enlistees. James H. Burns was the first to enlist from East Granby, according to the *Journal.* Townspeople formed a Defense Council to organize war-related activities within the town and to see that they conformed to the requirements set by the state and federal governments. Selectman Richard D. Seymour was chosen to head the council. The town had several drives that year; Sadie Viets headed one for the British Relief Fund, Georgianna Feley Quick (later Mrs. Chester Rebillard) and her volunteers collected 400 pounds of scrap aluminum needed for manufacturing weapons and military equipment, and Selectman Seymour led the first of eight campaigns to sell United States Defense Bonds.

Men began to train as air raid wardens with World War I veteran John A. Eagleson as their first chief, followed by John W. Sheldon and Selectman Seymour. The air observation post, under Chief Observer Kenneth M. Seymour, had a seven-day daylight test and reported 365 airplanes to their command post at Mitchell Field in New York. Along East Granby's southwest border, flyers began testing army parachutes by dropping them onto the Simsbury Flying Services airport on Wolcott Road with 165-pound dummies attached.

The Construction of Bradley Field

During the first months of 1941 the State of Connecticut bought about 1600 acres of land, principally in Windsor Locks but stretching across East Granby's eastern border, and leased the tract to the federal government for an Army Air Corps base. Much of the land was open field owned by the American Sumatra Tobacco Corporation; it also included about forty houses, most of which were moved. At Miller Road, several miles southwest of the planned airport, the state bought 20 acres in East Granby that the army needed for a radio control station to guide airplanes safely to the runway with a signal beam in darkness or foul weather.

As soon as preliminary work started at the base site in February, the state highway department announced that it would relocate Route 20 to the south over Rainbow Road, closing sections of Nicholson and Russell roads that were now on the air base. Workmen laid a spur line from the New Haven Railroad track, formerly the NYNH&H, in Suffield into the base. Construction began under the direction of Army engineers: thirty-six barracks, eight mess halls, five officers quarters, a commisary and an exchange, seventeen hospital buildings and an infirmary, a recreation building and a movie theater, a guardhouse, six operations buildings, ten supply buildings, four magazines, a hangar shop, motor repair shop, utility shop, parachute building, and radio station, along with a water system, roads, sidewalks, fences, and three camouflaged runways.

Anticipating the arrival of base personnel numbering several thousand, town officials decided that it was time to draft zoning regulations. Windsor Locks also undertook this task. East Granby's first zoning code went into effect in March 1941, and the five men who wrote it became what is now the planning and zoning commission.

Germany invaded the Soviet Union in June; all of Europe was locked in conflict. The first plane, a B-19 bomber, touched down at the new airfield in July and several hundred people went to see it. Soon all forty aircraft attached to the 57th Pursuit Group arrived and that force of 400 men assumed responsibility for protecting the base from hostile planes. The *Journal* reported that the regular work of the base would be organizational and tactical training. Base personnel would include about 400 men from the 30th Air Base Group, plus engineering, materiel, and medical staff.

The main fighting force of servicemen, including trainees, arrived by troop train and truck convoy during August. Before the end of the month, a P-40 fighter on a routine flight crashed on the field, instantly killing Second Lieutenant Eugene M. Bradley, twenty-four, of Antlers, Oklahoma. The army honored him by naming the base Bradley Field.*

The Town of Windsor Locks provided a United Services Organization (USO) recreation center for the service personnel, and East Granby joined the other towns surrounding the base in raising money and donating books and magazines. A few service couples rented apartments in private homes around East Granby, and the North District schoolhouse became a temporary home for a group of civilians employed at Bradley Field. Some men and women found work on the base, and a few young women from East Granby married soldiers stationed there.

*After the end of the war, the State of Connecticut developed a commercial airport on the air base. In 1966 the name was changed to Bradley International Airport.

The War Years

The Japanese bombing of Pearl Harbor on December 7, 1941, seared a memory in the minds of Americans that they would share with their children and grandchildren in private and in countless editorials, books, and films. The scenario for that day in East Granby began the day before when a convoy of army trucks returning soldiers to Camp Edwards, Massachusetts, from maneuvers in the South passed through the town. One truck broke down and seventeen soldiers were left stranded near the general store at 16 South Main Street.

They arranged to sleep on cots in the basement of the Congregational church Saturday night, and they were being royally entertained by families around town at Sunday dinner when the news of the bombing flashed over the radio. Report after report followed. The soldiers' comrades in arms were being fired on; the United States was under attack. Before the townspeople could feed the men breakfast the next morning, they were picked up and transported back to their base. Franklin D. Roosevelt's declaration that day only confirmed what they all knew: the United States was again at war.

The air defense observation post at Newgate went on immediate 24-hour duty, and the town soon decided to erect a new tower on the Mountain slightly south of Route 20, so the observers would have an unobstructed view and a few more comforts. The staff increased to 112 people, who worked two at a time in shifts around the clock, and a call went out for more women to free men for plowing and planting in the spring.

In the first week of 1942, word reached Mr. and Mrs. Anthony Bartkus of 5 North Main Street that their son Private Ferdinand Bartkus had been wounded in action in Manila. Eight months later he was listed as missing in action in Bataan; he never returned.

While families waited anxiously for reports from their servicemen overseas and in training camps, work went on in town. Dora Griffin and Helen Root reorganized the East Granby Red Cross chapter which had ceased functioning shortly after World War I. Before the end of January town women had turned in 122 knit articles, and they continued to answer calls for clothing, supplies, and money just as generously throughout the war. Lillian Fletcher turned the library in the parsonage into a Red Cross sewing room.

Mildred Hamilton Viets, who was Defense Council chairman for emergency evacuation housing, had her group canvass all households to determine the number of evacuees the town could accommodate. Houses were prepared for the first of many trial blackouts.

A twin-engine plane out of Bradley Field crashed in a pasture behind the Petraitis house at 161 South Main Street in February. According to an account in the *Journal,* members of the family were working in a woodlot when they heard the plane's engines sputter and saw it zigzag to the ground. All six men aboard died, including one who tried to parachute to safety.

Hazel M. Rollins received permission from the building committee to set up a casualty center in the nearly completed new town hall. Red Cross first aid courses began and countless people took them during the war. Ida Ludwig Cannon, R.N., held a series of home nursing courses, as did school nurse Gladys Tipple Jones.

Her husband, Welcome N. Jones, Defense Council salvage chairman, asked for donations of machinery, metal scrap, paper, rubber, and rags. Townspeople flattened their empty tin cans and searched their cellars and barns for every bit of usable material they could contribute to the war effort. The first scrap drive yielded twenty-eight tons.

Later that year Alice Phelps James of Springfield gave the East Granby salvage committee the iron fence that surrounded the Phelps family burial plot in the Center cemetery.

Shortages of vital goods developed immediately. Sugar rationing began before the rationing board had a chance to set up headquarters in the new town hall. People went to the schools to be fingerprinted and to register with Chairman Maida Griffin Seymour for their sugar ration books. Over 1200 books were issued the first week; most of the allowance was for home canning.

The fire department hired entertainers and threw a big party to officially open the town hall. Afterward the rationing board moved in and began taking applications for certificates to purchase tires and for gasoline ration cards. The government allotted an ample supply of gas for farm machinery, but curtailed almost all forms of travel. Roger H. Stowell remembered that gasoline rationing put an end to grocery store delivery routes, a service which both his father and grandfather had maintained from their stores in the days of horse-drawn wagons.

Rubber for tires was in particularly short supply, as Japan's advances in the Far East gave that country control of 95 percent of the world's supply. Government attempts to formulate synthetic rubber met with only limited success.

Cars and tires had to be registered and dealers could not sell any without the approval of the ration board. Bicycles and home appliances fell in this category, too. Nonessential manufacturing was stopped and many factories were converted to make war machines. Copper was not available for new telephone wires, so people were asked not to jam the circuits with unnecessary calls.

In July Edward M. Sanford was appointed to promote the use of wood for fuel and to make arrangements between woodlot owners and those wishing to cut their wood. Anna Viets noted in her diary that her husband had put five tons of coal in the cellar in case they could not get oil that winter.

People were asked to collect and turn in all used cooking fat, meat drippings, and grease. Fat was needed to make glycerine, used in some explosives. Citizens were asked to limit their consumption of meat and other foods voluntarily so that the country could feed its soldiers. Imported foods like coffee and tea became particularly scarce. When shortages resulted in hoarding, rising prices, and a black market, the government resorted to rationing food.

The school supervisor reported that rationing had led to the study of the geographical sources of many materials. Letters from relatives and friends stationed in various parts of the globe and news accounts of the war had given new meaning to the world geography course. In addition, pupils had begun to collect scrap and buy war stamps. The Falls School was unable to hire a janitor because of the manpower shortage, so the teachers and children cleaned the schoolrooms.

It would not have bothered farmers that tobacco shipments from the East Indies ceased, except for the shortage of farm labor. Many of their sons had gone off to fight and the usual hired men were also in the service or working for high wages in defense plants. Millard C. Griffin announced in November that he was going to sell his herd of cows because he was unable to find hired hands and to stay in the dairy business. Mildred Viets began to enlist a "land army" of women and teenagers to do farm work.

With the bombing of Pearl Harbor fresh in their minds, Americans worried about possible attack and internal disruption by the enemy. In East Granby the townspeople raised money to outfit air wardens and the town installed ten sirens, in addition to the fire siren, in strategic locations. The aircraft spotters in the observation post kept a lookout for forest fires and each area of town had a forest fire warden. Many constables trained to become auxiliary state police. Over at Bradley Field, where Flying Fortresses and other bombers were awaiting orders to proceed to North Africa, parachute troops simulated an attack on the base and engaged in a two-hour "battle." Townspeople gathered in the town hall to see movies of the bombing of Pearl Harbor and the war in the Pacific.

The year 1943 brought more departures of men to the armed forces and news, good and bad. In March, Air Cadet William E. Bates, Jr., of 116 North Main Street died during training, the first known death of a serviceman from East Granby. In August, when Mary Ronan Lipinski was preparing to report to the women's unit of the U. S. Naval Reserve, the WAVES, she received word that her husband, Private First Class Joseph W. Lipinski, twenty-eight, had been killed in action in the South Pacific. She became a naval storekeeper and relieved a sailor for duty at sea. Her cousin Hilda F. Eames (later Mrs. William Wendell) also enlisted and was assigned to the Coast Guard's SPARS. Jane Fox (later Mrs. Raymond Lennell) joined the WAC.

Throughout 1942 newspaper accounts placed Bernard W. Fearon, Edward Liss, Kenneth W. Viets, and Albert Misiak, Jr., in the South Pacific and James Burns in North Africa. Of the McGuire brothers, John J. was in the Pacific, Martin B. was in Alaska, and Joseph E. was in Panama. They were just a few of the East Granby men overseas.

When a fourth McGuire son, Francis M., enlisted, he joined other East Granby men who were in training or in support positions around the United States. Albert W. Lampson was in Officers Candidate School in Texas. Alfred J. LeMire, an OCS graduate, was an air cadet in Colorado. Edward D. Millea, a veteran World War I army pilot, was in Washington, D.C.

At home the USO group continued to raise money for recreation and provide transportation to events. The firemen held dances in the town hall every other Friday night and the air base had public band concerts.

Shortages grew worse. Governor Raymond E. Baldwin requested businesses to conserve heating fuel, so the Granby Supply Company on Hartford Avenue and the Wilcox store at the Center closed one extra day a week. The proprietors of the old Viets store at 9 South Main Street announced that they were closing for the duration to take jobs in a defense plant.

In February 1943 the federal government began limiting people to three pairs of shoes a year. The Office of War Information announced continuing shortages of canned vegetables, meat products, butter, cheese, canned fish, and shellfish. Anna Viets recorded in her diary that over 200 items of food were being rationed. Those who could went hunting and fishing and planted victory gardens.

The government announced that it would have to ship abroad at least 25 percent of all food produced in the United States to feed military personnel and to give stamina and courage to the hungry citizens of Italy and other war-torn countries as our troops liberated them. The cost of food rose so alarmingly in the United States that the government established price ceilings on some farm commodities. Farm incomes went up, as did the price of land. People who remembered conditions after the last war worried that farmers would overextend themselves again, buying land at high prices that might drop as soon as the war ended. Selectman Seymour recommended that the town raise taxes and put aside money for relief for the period of depression that might follow the boom.

Meanwhile, the town's Food for Freedom chairman, John H. Viets, tried to help farmers solve their labor problem. Women manned tractors, as the Selective Service reclassified potential draftees and tried to spare essential farm labor. Some town farmers resorted to bringing in jail labor. Yet Anna Viets noted in September: "Acres of tobacco in the fields and more acres of hay that won't be cut for lack of help."

With margarine encroaching on the sale of butter, feed prices up, and no one to cut hay for the winter, dairy farmers became discouraged. Warren E. Lampson, whose only son was in the service, gave up his dairy herd, as Millard C. Griffin had the year before. Frustrating gluts developed in other commodities. Potato farmers found that they had produced too many for existing storage facilities, and people with victory gardens wondered what to do with all their tomatoes and beans when the stores ran out of canning supplies.

It was a year of unrest in industry, too, with lengthened work weeks and strict controls on hiring and wage increases. Strikes broke out in vital industries like railroads, rubber manufacturing, and coal mining. Fuel Administrator Harold L. Ickes threatened the head of the United Mine Workers union, John L. Lewis, that he would have striking coal miners drafted.

Men in East Granby formed a State Guard unit in April with Captain Chauncey T. Mitchell as its head. They called it the Turkey Hills Pioneer Reserve and encouraged men from North Bloomfield, Simsbury, and Granby to join. The men received military training, drilled, and took part in a number of military exercises. State Guard units from Hartford, Wethersfield, Bloomfield, Bristol, and Meriden joined them for a maneuver near Hatchet Hill Road on a Sunday in September. Many of the guard members were fathers of servicemen.

Avis Sackett Stowell called for donors for the Red Cross blood bank as the auxiliary policemen added more names of service people to their wooden roll of honor in the Center. At the Congregational church the Ladies Social Union collected clothing for Greek Relief, and church members filled Christmas packages for East Granby's servicemen and -women.

Although some of the worst fighting was yet to come, war materiel stockpiles had grown to the point that in 1944 some factories were allowed to revert to making consumer goods. Some shortages eased a bit. The Selective Service reached deeper into the supply of potential fighting men, and a call went out for women to join the WAC at Bradley Field to release soldiers for the front. Toward the end of the war 40 percent of the airplane mechanics at the field were women.

On D-Day, June 9, 1944, Allied troops under General Dwight D. Eisenhower crossed the English Channel into France and began pushing the Axis forces from their strongholds in Western Europe. A number of East Granby men went into France. Alex G. Oksys was wounded in action in July. Later that year Thomas H. Leathem, who had been captured in Italy, was sent to a prisoner of war camp near Eggengelden, Germany, where he was liberated after nine months by General George S. Patton, Jr.'s Third Army. Before Christmas the Congregational church sent fifty-one packages to

East Granby's townspeople in the military overseas and about seventy-five to those stationed around the United States.

In January 1945 Private First Class Donald Tobin, twenty-five, was killed in action in Luxembourg, leaving a wife and four small sons. Private First Class Russell A. Wheeler was killed in action in France in March and Westley J. DeGray was dead before the fighting stopped.

At home, townspeople collected more clothes for European Relief and entertained convalescents from the hospital at Bradley Field. German prisoners of war, all enlisted men, were being held at the air base. They were repatriated late in the year. President Roosevelt died in April and President Harry S. Truman took office.

On V-E Day, May 9, 1945, Truman proclaimed, in part:

The Allied Armies, through sacrifice and devotion and with God's help, have won from Germany a final and unconditional surrender. The western world has been freed of the evil forces which for five years and longer have imprisoned the bodies and broken the lives of millions upon millions of freeborn men.

Later in the month heavy bombers began arriving from Europe bringing fighting men to Bradley Field and waiting troop trains, so they could go home on furlough before proceeding to the war in the Pacific. On V-J Day, September 2, 1945, after the United States' atomic bombs had destroyed their cities of Hiroshima and Nagasaki, the Japanese surrendered. People all over the world celebrated, dizzy with the prospect of peace.

More than 125 townspeople served in the armed forces during World War II, including the five who died. The survivors returned with many medals, ribbons, and stories to tell elated families and friends. Warren A. Viets had fought in the battles of Burma and China and traversed the Burma and Stilwell roads. Walter H. Sosneski could tell of North Africa, Sicily, and Italy. When the excitement and celebration of their return had passed, the veterans who settled in East Granby found the town much the same as they had left it.

Farming Declines and Suburbia Arrives

The tobacco market adjusted to resumed competition from foreign leaf after the war, and the number of dairy cows, which had dropped to the 915 shown on the 1948 Grand List, began to climb above 1000. The rapid growth in population that some townspeople felt would accompany the openings of Bradley Field did not materialize. In the late 1940s, when nearby towns boomed with postwar construction, East Granby only added about thirty homes, and its townspeople went on with tobacco and dairy farming as usual.

The town government changed slightly with the addition of a board of finance in 1948 to take the responsibility of writing the budget and setting the tax rate off the shoulders of the board of selectmen. Town coffers had funds to spare, so Selectman Seymour started rebuilding and blacktopping the roads. His goal was a mile a year and he eventually covered all the 10 miles or so then maintained by the town. In an interview he remembered that it took his whole time in office to get the upper end of Holcomb Street paved, because as long as they lived Chloe, Elizabeth, and Virginia Holcomb,

Hartford Electric Light Co. hydroelectric plant on the Farmington River during the 1955 flood

sisters who resided at 38 Holcomb Street, steadfastly refused to give up any of their land so that he could straighten and widen that section.

After hostilities began in Korea in 1950, young men and women left town again to serve in the military. By the time they returned, the town had its first small housing development: eleven houses on the south side of Miller Road built by Bidwell & Pescatello, Inc., of Hartford. During the late 1950s and the early 1960s, the town would see the beginning of much larger subdivisions, such as Melody Acres, Wynding Hills, and Nutmeg Hills as well as a number of houses built on single sites. In 1955, however, one community of homes would be decimated.

On August 18, 1955, showers began during the day and grew steadier toward nightfall. Most people knew the rain came from Hurricane Diane, but few gave this much thought as they went to bed, because the hurricane had already blown itself out and was proceeding up the eastern seaboard as a tropical storm with little or no wind. The rain, however, continued to pour, inundating Connecticut with almost 15 inches of water in a thirty-six-hour period.

According to an account in the *Courant*, Salmon Brook overflowed its banks sometime during the night and began rising at the rate of 8 feet an hour until it crested at 30 feet. Along its bank in Granbrook Park, where about a hundred houses were occupied either as summer homes or permanent residences, people awoke in the dark of night and found themselves engulfed by a raging flood. The only escape for some was to their rooftops.

Walter E. Miller, his wife, and their three young children clung to a portion of their roof after a house carried by the torrent smashed their house beneath them. They were swept downstream until their bit of roof wedged against a stand of tall pine trees, and there they remained through the night.

Canoeing in the Tariffville Gorge

In the morning two military helicopters were unable to save them. When Leon H. Viets, Jr., and Adolph W. Viets, Jr., attempted a rescue, their boat swamped as they drew near the Millers. Leon managed to reach the trees, but his companion was swept under the piece of roof by the swift current. Hearing pounding coming from under the debris, Viets and Miller tore shingles away and pulled Adolph out of the water, unconscious. About twelve hours after the Miller's ordeal began, they were all picked up by boat. Two residents of Granbrook Park died in the flood.

Volunteers from the fire department, civil defense corps, Salvation Army, and Red Cross worked around the clock to rescue flood victims and relieve their suffering. About seventy-five people were brought to the town hall where they were dried, fed, and given medical attention. Some were taken into private homes. In September the elementary school opened with about forty fewer pupils than expected, as their homes had been destroyed. The East Granby Redevelopment Agency, with the help of the federal government, purchased the lots and remaining buildings in Granbrook Park. A $7200 grant from the George Dudley Seymour Trust Fund enabled the Granbrook Park Commission to turn the property into the town's first public recreation area.

On the Farmington River the flood waters of 1955 tore 8 feet off the top of the concrete dam that served the Hartford Electric Light Company's hydroelectric plant and buffeted the powerhouse. The company decided to demolish the plant rather than rebuild. Part of the dam is still in place today at the foot of the Tariffville Gorge, where kayakers and canoists now hold annual white water competitions.

The Middle bridge, which spanned the gorge, washed away, never to be rebuilt. Spoonville bridge went out and eventually was replaced by a much larger, more solid structure slightly west of its original site. More than $18,000 was needed to repair washed-out roads.

World War II

Something else occurred in 1955 that would work a great change on the town once its result was felt. It was the introduction of "homogenized tobacco." When cigar manufacturers discovered that they could cut costs by binding cigars with manufactured sheets made of powdered tobacco mixed with adhesive, demand for the outdoor tobacco produced by the independent growers plummeted. One by one, they stopped planting.

Of course, a cigar made with a homogenized-tobacco binder was not of the same fine quality as one made with a piece of whole leaf, but the general public did not know or care about the interior of the cigars they smoked. Edward Bartkus listed a number of popular brands of cigars made with attractive shade-grown wrappers over homogenized binders, and he declared with disgust that he had not smoked a cigar in over twenty years.

With the Grand List showing the addition of ninety-seven houses in 1957, East Granby was definitely in the midst of a building boom when it was time to mark the 100th anniversary of the town's incorporation. Old and new townspeople alike decked the Center with red, white, and blue banners and celebrated for three days in June 1958. Governor Abraham A. Ribicoff crowned a centennial queen at a ball on Friday night, and the next afternoon 7000 people lined Route 20 to watch a two-hour parade with eighty units, including twenty floats and many old vehicles and marching bands.

During the three days townspeople participated in athletic events, round and square dancing, a community pizza party, and an old-fashioned New England dinner. The International Silver Company of Meriden sent a display of spoons to commemorate the town's part in the development of silverplating. The festivities closed Sunday afternoon with thirty crack teams participating in a horse drawing contest, which attracted 3000 spectators.

Since residential development was on the rise and farming was in a decline, townspeople realized that they would have to attract more business and industry. They needed it to increase and diversify the town's tax base so that they could have adequate schools and other services without spiraling property taxes. The centennial year of 1958 saw the formation of the East Granby Chamber of Commerce and the industrial development commission. The latter, which became an official town body in January 1959, was the forerunner of the present economic development commission. Over the years its many members have worked to bring business and light industry to town, especially to the Bradley Industrial Park near the airport.

The influx of young families during the 1950s meant many more children for the town's already overburdened schools. Back in December 1944 the Center School was crowded enough to be sending some of its students to the South School when the Falls School burned to the ground. The elementary school in Tariffville immediately provided two rooms for East Granby's use, but within a few years Tariffville's own school population had grown so much that it could no longer accept outside classes. North and Hazelwood schools were reopened for the 1946-47 school year while a new consolidated school was being built.

East Granby Center School at 33 Turkey Hills Road, now called Carl Allgrove Elementary School, opened on January 26, 1948, with six classrooms; a combined auditorium, gymnasium, and cafeteria; and the town's first school principal. The building had enough classroom space to accommodate all the elementary pupils in town. Their parents formed a Parent-Teacher Association which ran a lunch program and donated educational materials.

By September 1949 the school population of over 250 was too large for the new school, so the old Center School was reopened. For the first time the town had a separate classroom for each of its eight grades. By 1952 part of the Center School cafeteria had been temporarily partitioned into a classroom, and the town had enough postwar baby boom children to fill two classrooms with first graders.

The town opened a new wing of the Center School on January 4, 1954. This contained four new classrooms and a cafeteria with a kitchen. The old Center School was closed, only to be reopened again in 1958.

The town opened West School at 185 Hartford Avenue, now the R. D. Seymour School, in September 1959. It served part of grades one through six with eight classrooms and a cafeteria. The total elementary school population that September was 380 and the old Center School was closed once again.

Meanwhile the number of high school students was growing rapidly, too. Simsbury High School became so full that it could no longer accept out-of-town students. In September 1955 East Granby began phasing its students out of Simsbury by sending its ninth graders to Granby High School. That year East Granby, Hartland, and Granby held referendums to decide whether or not to construct a regional high school. Granby's voters defeated the measure.

In September 1957 East Granby began to phase its students out of Granby by sending its ninth graders to Suffield High School. By that time plans were underway to build a junior-senior high school, and in 1960 the school system opened a junior high school of seventh, eighth, and ninth graders in the one-year-old West School. The old Center School was pressed into service again for elementary school classrooms, as was the Center School cafeteria.

East Granby Junior-Senior High School at 95 South Main Street opened in September 1962 with fourteen rooms and a gymnasium housing grades seven through eleven. When the school reached its full complement of six grades the following year, the town became ineligible for a supervisor from the Rural Services of the State Department of Education, so East Granby became an independent school district with its own superintendent of schools. West School reverted to being an elementary school and crowding was eased for a time, but the board of education warned in its annual report that the number of pre-school children living in town exceeded the total number of students enrolled in the twelve grades.

Center School gained ten more classrooms when a second wing opened in 1966. It housed the town's first public kindergarten that year, too. The name of the school was changed in 1978 on the retirement of Carl G. Allgrove, who had served as principal there for twenty-eight years.

In 1971 the West School was remodeled to accommodate a modified open classroom concept of education. Its name had been changed to honor Richard D. Seymour in 1965 when he resigned after forty-one years of service on the board of education.

The Junior-Senior High School was enlarged by eleven classrooms, a library, a stage, and a cafeteria in 1967. It assumed its present form when it was enlarged and modified in 1974 and it is now the East Granby Middle & High Schools. Only in recent years has the town's school population again begun to decline.

The Center also changed in the 1970s with the building of a new town hall, firehouse, and United States Post Office and the opening of several businesses. A portion of Route 20 was relocated in 1974 so that the highway now bypasses School Street and runs along an extension of Rainbow Road. The traditional Memorial Day parade down School Street, which Colonel Edward D. Millea had revitalized and enlarged after World War II, added more veterans and Gold Star Mothers in the 1960s and '70s, this time from the Vietnam War.

Newgate Prison, which the State of Connecticut bought in 1968, underwent extensive renovations to preserve the ruins and to provide better access to the old copper mine below them. The state also acquired the Viets Tavern across the street. The United States government declared Newgate Prison a National Historic Landmark in 1973 and a record number of 36,000 visitors toured the buildings and caverns in the national bicentennial year of 1976.

With time the growing of shade tobacco in town fell victim to competition and rising production costs, just as outdoor tobacco had. The Culbro Tobacco Corporation recently opened an industrial park on part of the Hazelwood Plantation. Other shade and outdoor tobacco land that has not been subdivided for homes either lies fallow or grows nursery shrubs and a small amount of produce for market. A few farms have been converted into recreational facilities like the Copper Hill Country Club and the Hartford Gun Club.

Cattle, mostly dairy rather than beef, still have a place in town, along with a few other farm animals and fields of hay and corn for feed. About eleven farms operate full or part time in East Granby today; all but one are west of the Mountain or north of the Center. Six of them ship milk to pasteurizing plants, and on one, the Charles P. Viets cattle dealership is being carried on by two of his grandsons.

Since the census of 1950, which listed 1327 residents, the population of East Granby has more than tripled and the style of life has changed. With farming no longer a major occupation, most workers now commute elsewhere to a variety of jobs in engineering firms, government offices, insurance companies, industrial plants, health facilities, schools, and other enterprises.

Over the years town boards and commissions, as well as civic and social organizations, have increased in number to accommodate the growth and diversity of the population. Members of families old and new have worked together in government affairs and community activities to preserve and enrich the quality of life for all. The townspeople enjoy a legacy of old homes, historic sites, open fields, and wooded acres from the country town of the past as they go about the business of shaping the suburban town of today and adding a new chapter to East Granby's centuries-old story.

East Granby Center, 1982

APPENDICES

FIRST SELECTMEN AND TOWN CLERKS

Source: Minutes of town meetings

First Selectmen

Henry L. Holcomb	June 1858 - October 1859
Isaac W. Thompson	October 1859 - October 1860
Issac P. Owen	October 1860 - October 1864
Charles H. Clark	October 1864 - October 1866
Ebenezer Talbot	October 1866 - October 1867
Charles P. Clark	October 1867 - October 1871
Ebenezer Talbot	October 1871 - September 1873
Charles P. Clark	September 1873 - October 1876
Morton Cornish	October 1876 - January 1878
Samuel A. Clark	January 1878 - October 1882
William A. Viets	October 1882 - October 1886
Frederic F. Stevens	October 1886 - October 1887
William A. Viets	October 1887 - January 1892
Wilbur E. Northway	January 1892 - January 1893
William A. Viets	January 1893 - October 1895
George E. Bidwell	October 1895 - October 1898
Willard W. Viets	October 1898 - October 1923
Amos R. Holcomb	October 1923 - October 1925
William A. Seymour	October 1925 - October 1934
Richard D. Seymour	October 1934 - October 1955
Edward F. Killian, Jr.	October 1955 - October 1956
Norman I. Adams	October 1956 - November 1969
William S. Mayer	November 1969 - January 1974
Frank R. Rothammer	January 1974 -

Town Clerks

Elmore Clark	June 1858 - January 1887
B. Ellsworth Smith	January 1887 - January 1888
Charles A. Tudor	January 1888 - January 1892
Albert C. Bates	January 1892 - January 1893
Benjamin N. Alderman	January 1893 - January 1896
Frank H. Dibble	January 1896 - October 1927
Maurice W. Condon	October 1927 - October 1929
Effie H. Miller	October 1929 - January 1972
Miriam W. Viets	January 1972 -

POPULATION STATISTICS

(From the Federal Census)

	1790	1800	1810	1820	1830	1840	1850	1860	1870	1880
Granby	2595	2735	2696	3012	2733	2611	2498	1720		
East Granby								833	853	754

	1890	1900	1910	1920	1930	1940	1950	1960	1970	1980
East Granby	661	684	797	1056	1003	1225	1327	2434	3532	4102

BIBLIOGRAPHY

THE INFORMATION in this book has been drawn as much as possible from primary sources. They include many private records of which the diaries, letters, and account books mentioned in the text are typical. Some of these documents were lent or donated to the East Granby Historical Committee, and some were found in the archives of the Connecticut Historical Society, the Connecticut State Library, and the historical societies or public libraries in Suffield, Windsor, Simsbury, Granby, and East Granby. The state archives also yielded petitions and reports to the Connecticut General Assembly.

Researchers have consulted land and probate records at the Connecticut State Library and at the town halls in Windsor, Simsbury, Granby, and East Granby, as well as the minutes of town meetings in these towns and East Granby's town reports. They also have referred to the Colonial Records to 1776, Records of the State of Connecticut from 1776 through 1803, and General Statutes, Public Acts, Private Acts, and Special Laws of the State of Connecticut. Additional information has come from the Journals of the Senate and House of Representatives of the General Assembly and from federal census records from 1790 through 1880.

Newspapers have been another important resource. The most helpful were: *The Connecticut Courant, The Hartford Courant, The Farmington Valley Herald,* and *The Windsor Locks Journal.* Interviews with present and former residents of East Granby have provided insight about the town as it was during the first half of the 20th century.

The following books, articles, and papers also have been most useful:

"Albert Carlos Bates." *Connecticut Historical Society Bulletin 19.* April 1954.

Alcorn, Robert Hayden. *Biography of a Town: Suffield, Connecticut, 1670-1970.* The Three Hundredth Anniversary Committee of the Town of Suffield, 1970.

American Battle Monuments Commission. *American Armies and Battlefields in Europe.* Washington, D.C.: U. S. Government Printing Office, 1938.

Ashman, Robert. *The Central New England Railroad.* Salisbury, Ct.: The Salisbury Association, 1972.

Austin, Ethel Lindstrom. *The Story of the Churches of Granby.* [Granby, Ct.]

Baer, Willis Nissley. *The Economic Development of the Cigar Industry in the United States.* Lancaster, Pa.: [The Art Printing Co.], 1933.

Baker & Tilden. *Atlas of Hartford City and County, with a Map of Connecticut from Actual Surveys.* Hartford, 1869.

Baker, George Pierce. *The Formation of the New England Railroad Systems.* Cambridge: Harvard University Press, 1937.

Barber, Daniel. *The History of My Own Times.* Washington City, 1827.

Barber, Lucius I. *A Record and Documentary History of Simsbury.* Simsbury, Ct.: The Abigail Phelps Chapter, Daughters of the American Revolution, 1931.

Bates, Albert Carlos. *Ancestral Line for Eight Generations of Capt. Lemuel Bates 1729-1820.* Hartford, 1943.

Captain Enoch Powers and His Wife Sophia Teresa Collins with Notes of Their Descendants. Hartford, 1945.

An Early Connecticut Engraver and His Work. Hartford: The Case, Lockwood & Brainard Co., 1906.

Historical Sketch of Turkey Hills and East Granby, Connecticut. Hartford, 1949.

Sketch of the Congregational Society and Church of East Granby, Connecticut. Hartford, 1930.

Bates, Albert Carlos, comp. *Records of the Congregational Church in Turkey Hills, Now the Town of East Granby, Connecticut, 1776-1858.* Hartford, 1907.

Records of the Reverend Roger Viets, Rector of St. Andrews, Simsbury, Conn., 1763-1800. Hartford, 1893.

Records of the Second School Society in Granby, Now the Town of East Granby, Connecticut, 1796-1855. Hartford, 1903.

Records of the Society or Parish of Turkey Hills, Now the Town of East Granby, Connecticut, 1737-1791. Hartford, 1901.

Simsbury, Connecticut, Births, Marriages, and Deaths. Hartford, 1898.

Sundry Vital Records of and Pertaining to the Present Town of East Granby, Connecticut, 1737-1886. Hartford, 1947.

Bates, Walter. *The Mysterious Stranger; or Memoirs of Henry More Smith; Alias Henry Frederick Moor; Alias William Newman.* New Haven: Maltby, Goldsmith & Co., 1817.

Bidwell, Percy W. *Rural Economy in New England at the Beginning of the 19th Century.* New Haven, 1916.

Black, Mary. "The Voice of the Folk Artist." In *The Artist in America,* compiled by the editors of *Art in America.* New York: W. W. Norton & Co., 1967.
Black, Robert C., III. *The Younger John Winthrop.* New York: Columbia University Press, 1966.
Browne, G. Waldo. *Real Legends of New England.* Chicago: Albert Whitman & Co., 1930.
Burpee, Charles W. *History of Hartford County, Connecticut, 1633-1928.* 3 vols. Hartford: The S. J. Clarke Publishing Co., 1928.
Capitol Region Council of Governments. *Survey of Architectural and Historic Resources for the Town of East Granby.* Hartford, 1979.
Carrington, George H. "Trio and Tripod." *Connecticut Quarterly.* January-December 1895.
Center for Connecticut Studies of Eastern Connecticut State College. *Series in Connecticut History.* Chester, Ct.: The Pequot Press, 1975.
Chamberlain, Charles. A Sermon given at the East Granby Congregational church July 9, 1876, on the history of the church with a sketch of the settlement of Simsbury. (Unpublished)
Clark, Delphina L. H. "Iron in the Woods of Suffield." *The Connecticut Antiquarian 21.* June 1969.
Connecticut, a Guide to Its Roads, Lore and People. Written by Workers of the Federal Writers' Project of the Works Progress Administration for the State of Connecticut. Boston: Houghton Mifflin Co., 1938.
Connecticut, Adjutant-General. *Connecticut Service Records, Men and Women in the Armed Forces of the United States During World War 1917-1920.* New Haven: United Printing Services, Inc.
Record of Service of Connecticut Men in the Army and Navy of the United States During the War of the Rebellion. Hartford: The Case, Lockwood & Brainard Co., 1889.
Record of Service of Connecticut Men in the Army, Navy and Marine Corps of the United States in the Spanish-American War, Philippine Insurrection and China Relief Expedition from April 21, 1898, to July 4, 1904. Hartford: The Case, Lockwood & Brainard Co., 1919.
Record of the Service of Connecticut Men in the I. — War of the Revolution. II. — War of 1812. III. — Mexican War. Hartford, 1889.
Roster of Connecticut Volunteers Who Served in the War Between the United States and Spain 1898-1899. Hartford: The Case, Lockwood & Brainard Co., 1899.
Connecticut. American Revolution Bicentennial Commission. *Connecticut Bicentennial Series.* 1973-78.
Connecticut. Board of Commissioners of Common Schools. *First Annual Report of the Board of Commissioners of Common Schools in Connecticut together with the First Annual Report of the Secretary of the Board.* Hartford, 1839.
Connecticut Evangelical Magazine and Religious Intelligencer. Hartford: Hudson and Goodwin, 1800-15.
Connecticut. General Assembly. *Report of the Committee Appointed by the Legislature of Connecticut to Inspect the Condition of New-Gate Prison.* Hartford: Charles Babcock, 1825.
Report of the Committee Appointed by the Legislature of Connecticut to Inspect the Condition of New-Gate Prison. New Haven: J. Barber, 1826.
The Connecticut Granges. Edited under the supervision of a committee of the State Grange. New Haven: Industrial Publishing Co., 1900.
Connecticut Historical Society. *Collections.* Vols. 8, 9 & 10. Hartford, 1901-05.
Connecticut Register. New London, Hartford, etc., 1785-1886.
Connecticut. Secretary of the State. *Register and Manual.* Hartford, 1887-1982.
Connecticut. State Board of Education, *Annual Report to the General Assembly, 1866-1900.*
Connecticut. Superintendent of Common Schools. *Annual Report to the General Assembly,* 1846-65.
Connecticut. Tercentenary Commission. Committee on Historical Publications. *Tercentenary Pamphlet Series.* New Haven: Yale University Press, 1933-36.
Conrat, Maisie and Richard. "How U. S. Farmers Became Specialists — in Cash and Debts." *Smithsonian.* March 1977.
Continental Congress. *Papers of the Continental Congress 1774-89.* National Archives Microfilm Publications 6398 Microcopy 247 Roll 72.
Contributions to the Ecclesiastical History of Connecticut, prepared under the direction of the General Association. New Haven: William L. Kingsley, 1861.
Contributions to the Ecclesiastical History of Connecticut, Volume II, prepared under the direction of the Connecticut Conference of the United Church of Christ. 1967.
Cornish, Joseph E. *History and Genealogy of the Cornish Families in America.* Boston: Geo. H. Ellis Co., 1907.
Cowles, Calvin Duvall. *The Genealogy of the Cowles Families in America.* New Haven: Tuttle, Morehouse & Taylor Co., 1929.
Coxe, Tench. *Statement of the Arts and Manufactures of the United States for the Year 1810.* Philadelphia: A. Cornman, Jr., 1814.

D'Amato, Archangelo Anthony. "Newgate to Wethersfield: The Development of Prison Reform in Early Nineteenth-Century Connecticut." Master's thesis, Trinity College (Hartford, Ct.), 1972.

DeForest, John W. *History of the Indians of Connecticut from the Earliest Known Period to 1850.* Hartford: W. J. Hamersley, 1851.

Dickens, Charles. *American Notes for General Circulation.* New York: Appleton & Co., 1869.

Domler, William. "Old Newgate Prison and Copper Mine, East Granby, Connecticut." *The Lure of the Litchfield Hills.* 1970-72.

Duggan, Thomas S. *The Catholic Church in Connecticut.* New York: States History Co., 1930.

Dwight, Timothy. *Travels in New England and New York.* New Haven, 1822.

Egleston, N.H. "The Newgate of Connecticut." *Magazine of American History.* April 1886.

Ellsworth, John E. *100 Years: The Ensign-Bickford Company and the Safety Fuse Industry in America.* Chicago: The Lakeside Press, 1936.

Simsbury: Being a Brief Historical Sketch of Ancient and Modern Simsbury, 1642-1935. Simsbury Committee for the Connecticut Tercentenary, 1935.

Encyclopedia of Connecticut Biography. Vols. 6 & 7. New York: The American Historical Society, Inc., 1917-23.

Fisher, Douglas Alan. *The Epic of Steel.* New York: Harper & Row, 1963.

Fite, Emerson David. *Social and Industrial Conditions in the North During the Civil War.* New York: Peter Smith, 1930.

Francfort, E. *The Simsbury Copper Mine.* Hartford: Case, Tiffany & Co., 1857.

Gay, Frederick Lewis. *John Gay of Dedham, Mass., and Some of His Descendants.* Boston: David Clapp & Son, 1879.

Genealogy of the Clark and Forward Families from 1668.

Granger, James N. *Launcelot Granger of Newbury, Mass., and Suffield, Conn.* Hartford: The Case, Lockwood & Brainard Co., 1893.

Greene, M. Louise. *The Development of Religious Liberty in Connecticut.* New York: Houghton Mifflin & Co., 1905.

Griffin, Duane N. *Genealogy of the Descendants of Sergeant John Griffin.* [1971].

Griffin, Fred. "Tobacco Valley." *The Connecticut Magazine.* June 1935.

Griswold, Glenn E., comp. *The Griswold Family England-America.* Rutland, Vt.: Tuttle Publishing Co., 1935.

Handlin, Oscar. *The Americans, a New History of the People of the United States.* Boston: Little, Brown & Co., 1963.

Harte, Charles Rufus. *Connecticut's Canals.* [New Haven, 1938.]

Connecticut's Iron and Copper. 1944.

Some Engineering Features of the Old Northampton Canal. [New Haven: Quinnipiack Press, Inc., 1933?]

Harte, Charles Rufus and Keith, Herbert. *The Early Iron Industry of Connecticut.* [New Haven: Mack & Noel, 1935.]

Hayden, Jabez Haskell. *Historical Sketches.* Windsor Locks, Ct.: The Windsor Locks Journal, 1915.

Records of the Connecticut Line of the Hayden Family. Hartford: The Case, Lockwood & Brainard Co., 1888.

Hayward, John. *New England Gazetteer.* Boston: John Hayward, 1839.

Hinman, Royal R. *A Historical Collection from Official Records, Files, Etc. of the Part Sustained by Connecticut During the War of the Revolution.* Hartford: E. Gleason, 1842.

History of Battle-Flag Day, September 17, 1879. Hartford: Lockwood & Merritt, 1879.

"Hitchcock's Geology of the Region Contiguous to the Connecticut River." *American Journal of Science.* 1823.

Holland, Josiah Gilbert. *History of Western Massachusetts.* Springfield: S. Bowles & Co., 1855.

Howard, Daniel. *Glimpses of Ancient Windsor from 1633 to 1933.* Windsor, Ct.: The Herald Press, 1933.

Howard, James L., ed. *The Origins and Fortunes of Troop B 1788; Governor's Independent Volunteer Troop of Horse Guards 1911; Troop B Cavalry, Connecticut National Guard 1917.* Hartford: The Case, Lockwood & Brainard Co., 1921.

Isham, Norman M. and Brown, Albert F. *Early Connecticut Houses.* Providence, R.I.: The Preston & Rounds Co., 1900.

Johnson, Mary Coffin. *The Higleys and Their Ancestry.* New York: D. Appleton & Co., 1896.

Kelly, J. Frederick. *The Early Domestic Architecture of Connecticut.* New Haven: Yale University Press, 1924.

Kendall, Edward Augustus. *Travels Through the Northern Parts of the United States in the Years 1807 and 1808.* New York: I. Riley, 1809.

Kirkland, Edward C. *Men, Cities and Transportation.* Cambridge: Harvard University Press, 1948.
Lang, Lawrence W. *Newgate Prison and Copper Mine.* 1979. (Unpublished)
Latham, Esther Gillett, ed. *Genealogical Data Concerning the Families of Gillet–Gillett–Gillette.* Appleton, Wis., 1953.
Lathrop, Samuel. "High Street Since the Civil War." In *It Happened in Our Town,* edited by Paul G. Sanderson, Jr. [Suffield, Ct.]: Suffield American Bicentennial Commission, 1978.
Leach, Douglas Edward. *Flintlock and Tomahawk.* New York: Macmillan, 1958.
The Northern Colonial Frontier, 1607-1763. New York: Holt, Rinehart & Winston, 1966.
Lee, W. Storrs. *The Yankees of Connecticut.* New York: Henry Holt & Co. , 1957.
List of Congregational Ecclesiastical Societies Established in Connecticut Before October 1818 and Their Changes. Hartford: Connecticut Historical Society, 1913.
Mallmann, Jacob. *Historical Papers on Shelter Island and Its Presbyterian Church.* New York: A. M. Bustard Co., 1899.
Mather, Frederic Gregory. *Refugees of 1776 from Long Island to Ct.* Albany, N.Y.: J. B. Lyon Co., 1913.
Mather, Increase. *A Relation of the Troubles Which Have Happened in New England by Reason of the Indians There From the Year 1614 to the Year 1675.* Boston, 1677.
May, Earl Chapin. *A Century of Silver 1847-1947.* New York: Robert M. McBridge & Co., 1947.
McPherson, Hannah Elizabeth Weir. *The Holcombs, Nation Builders.* Washington, 1947.
Merrill, David Oliver. "Isaac Damon and the Architecture of the Federal Period in New England." Doctoral dissertation, Yale University, 1965.
Milmine, Charles. *The History of the C. N. E.* Salisbury, Ct.: The Salisbury Association, 1972.
Mitchell, Edwin Valentine. *It's an Old New England Custom.* New York: Vanguard Press, Inc., 1946.
Moore, Horace L. *Andrew Moore of Poquonock and Windsor, Conn., and His Descendants.* Laurence, Kans.: Journal Publishing Co., 1903.
Morse, Jarvis Means. *A Neglected Period of Connecticut's History 1818-1850.* New Haven: Yale University Press, 1933.
National Society of United States Daughters of 1812. *An Index of Veterans of Connecticut During the Years 1812, 1813, 1814, 1815, 1816, War of 1812,* by Mrs. Charles William Crankshaw. [1964].
Osborn, Norris Galpin, ed. *History of Connecticut in Monographic Form.* 5 vols. New York: The States History Co., 1925.
Owen, Ralph Dornfeld, ed. *Descendants of John Owen of Windsor, Connecticut, 1622-1699.* Philadelphia, 1941.
Parker, William Alderman. *Aldermans in America.* Raleigh, N. C., 1957.
Parsons, Elizabeth Newberry. *A Brief History of East Granby 1688-1866.* (Unpublished)
Paulsen, Garry. *Farm: A History and Celebration of the American Farmer.* Englewood Cliffs, N. J.: Prentice-Hall, Inc., 1977.
Pease, John C., and Niles, John M. *A Gazetteer of the States of Connecticut & Rhode Island.* Hartford: William S. Marsh, 1819.
Perrin, John D. "Geology of the Newgate Prison-Mine of East Granby, Connecticut." Master's thesis, University of Connecticut, 1976.
Peters, Samuel. *General History of Connecticut.* New York: D. Appleton & Co., 1877.
Pettengill, Samuel B. *The Yankee Pioneers.* Rutland, Vt.: C. E. Tuttle Co., [1971].
Phelps, Noah A. *History of Simsbury, Granby and Canton from 1642 to 1845.* Hartford: Case, Tiffany & Burnham, 1845.
Phelps, Oliver Seymour and Servin, Andrew T., comps. *The Phelps Family of America and their English Ancestors, with Copies of Wills, Deeds, Letters, and Other Interesting Papers, Coats of Arms and Valuable Records.* Pittsfield, Mass.: Eagle Publishing Co., 1899.
Phelps, Richard H. *Newgate of Connecticut.* Hartford: American Publishing Co., 1876.
Phenix Mining Co. *Proposals of the Phenix Mining Co. with a Statement of the History and Character of Their Mines, Property, and Leases, Course of Investigation and Its Results.* New York: J. Seymour, 1831.
"The Phoenix Mining Company 1830-1836." *Connecticut Historical Society Bulletin 21.* July 1956.
Pierce, Neal R. *The New England States.* New York: W. W. Norton & Co., Inc., 1976.
Pinkham, Harold A. "The Division of Granby, Connecticut." Master's thesis, University of Connecticut, 1966.
Pinney, Laura Young. *Genealogy of the Pinney Family in America.* San Francisco: Harr Wagner Pub. Co., 1922.
Potter, David M. *The Impending Crisis 1848-1861.* New York: Harper & Row, 1976.
Purcell, Richard J. *Connecticut in Transition: 1775-1818.* Middletown, Ct.: Wesleyan University Press, 1963.

Rainey, Froelich G. "A Compilation of Historical Data Contributing to the Ethnography of Connecticut & Southern New England Indians." *Bulletin of the Archeological Society of Connecticut.* April 1936.

Records of Plymouth Colony, Acts of the Commissioners of the United Colonies of New England, vol. 1, 1643-1651. Boston: William White, 1859.

Richardson, Creel. "History of the Simsbury Copper Mines." Master's thesis, Trinity College (Hartford, Ct.), 1928.

Richardson, Douglas C. *The Eno and Enos Family in America.* [Sacramento, Calif.], 1973.

Robbins, Thomas. *Diary of Thomas Robbins.* Edited by Increase N. Tarbox. Boston: T. Todd, 1886-87.

Salmon Brook Historical Society. *The Heritage of Granby 1786-1965.* Springfield, Mass.: Burt Printing Co., 1967.

Scanlon, Lawrence. "A New Look at an Old Map." *The Lure of the Litchfield Hills.* Fall-Winter 1974-75.

Seaver, Jesse. *The Holcomb(e) Genealogy.* Philadelphia: The American Historical-Genealogical Society, 1925.

Seymour, Clarence. "Historical Background of East Granby." Address at tercentenary observance. (Unpublished)

Shade Tobacco Growers Agricultural Association, Inc. *The Story of Tobacco Valley.* Windsor, Ct.

Shannahan, John W. "Old New-Gate Prison and Copper Mine." *The Connecticut Antiquarian 25.* June 1973.

Sheldon, Hezekiah Spencer, comp. *Documentary History of Suffield 1660-1749.* Springfield, Mass.: The Clark W. Bryan Co., 1879.

Shepard, Charles Upham. *Report on the Geological Survey of Connecticut.* New Haven: B. L. Hamlen, 1837.

Shepard, Odell. *Connecticut Past and Present.* New York: Alfred A. Knopf. 1939.

Shurtleff, Harold Robert. *The Log Cabin Myth.* Cambridge: Harvard University Press, 1939.

Siebert, Wilbur H. *The Underground Railroad from Slavery to Freedom.* New York: Russell & Russell, 1967.

Sinnot, Edmund W. *Meetinghouse & Church in Early New England.* New York: McGraw-Hill Book Co., Inc., 1963.

Smith, Samuel. *Inside Out, or Roguery Exposed.* Hartford: Norton & Russell, 1827.

Southwick Congregational Church History 1773-1973. [Southwick, Mass.] Church History Committee.

Stallings, Laurence. *The Story of the Doughboys, the AEF in World War I.* Condensed and adapted by M. S. Wyeth, Jr., from *The Doughboys.* New York: Harper & Row, 1966.

Start, Edwin A. "The New England Newgate." *New England Magazine.* November 1890.

Steiner, Bernard C. *History of Education in Connecticut.* Washington, D. C.: U. S. Government Printing Office, 1893.

History of Slavery in Connecticut. Baltimore: John Hopkins Press, 1893.

Stevens, Mary K. "The Convention Troops in Connecticut." *Connecticut Quarterly.* January-December 1897.

Stiles, Henry R. *The History and Genealogies of Ancient Windsor, Connecticut.* 2 vols. Hartford: The Case, Lockwood & Brainard Co., 1892.

Stone, Frank Andrews. "Connecticut's Kilmarnock Scots." *Connecticut Historical Society Bulletin 44.* October 1979.

Strother, Horatio T. *The Underground Railroad in Connecticut.* Middletown, Ct.: Wesleyan University Press, 1962.

Stuart, William. *Sketches of the Life of William Stuart.* Bridgeport, Ct., 1854.

Sweet, William Warren. *The Methodist Episcopal Church and the Civil War.* Cincinnati: Methodist Book Concern Press, [1912].

Terrill, John Upton. *American Indian Almanac.* New York: World Pub. Co., [1971].

Terry, James. *Allyn Hyde of Ellington, Connecticut, Together with a Review of "An Early Connecticut Engraver and His Work."* Hartford, 1906.

Thomas, Edmund B., Jr. "Politics in the Land of Steady Habits." Doctoral dissertation, Clark University, 1972.

Timlow, Heman R. *Ecclesiastical and Other Sketches of Southington, Connecticut.* Hartford: The Case, Lockwood & Brainard Co., 1875.

Tobacco Institute. *Connecticut and Tobacco.* Washington, D. C., 1972.

Trumbull, J. Hammond. *Historical Notes on the Constitutions of Connecticut and on the Constitutional Convention of 1818.* Hartford: Brown & Gross, 1873.

Trumbull, J. Hammond, ed. *The Memorial History of Hartford County, Connecticut, 1633-1884.* 2 vols. Boston: Edward L. Osgood, 1886.

Tyler, Bennet. *Memoir of the Life and Character of Rev. Asahel Nettleton, D. D.* Hartford: Robins & Smith, 1844.

Tyler, Daniel P. *Statistics of the Condition and Products of Certain Branches of Industry in Connecticut, for the Year Ending October 1, 1845.* Hartford: John L. Boswell, 1846.

Van Dusen, Albert E. *Connecticut.* New York: Random House, 1961.

Vaughan, Alden T. *New England Frontier, Puritans and Indians, 1620-1675.* Boston: Little Brown & Co., 1965.

Vibert, William M. *Three Centuries of Simsbury 1670-1970.* Simsbury Tercentenary Committee, Inc., 1970.

Viets, Francis Hubbard. *A Genealogy of the Viets Family with Biographical Sketches.* Hartford: The Case, Lockwood & Brainard Co., 1902.

Viets, S. D., *Newgate of Connecticut and Other Antiquities of America.* Meriden, Ct.: Meriden Gravure Co., 1895.

Walton, Emma Lee, comp. *The Clark Genealogy: Some Descendants of Daniel Clark of Windsor, Connecticut, 1639-1913.* New York: Frank Allaben Genealogical Co., 1913.

Warmsley, Arthur J. *Connecticut Post Offices and Postmarks.* Hartford: Connecticut Printers, Inc., 1977.

Weaver, Glenn. *The Hartford Electric Light Company.* Hartford, 1969.

Weller, John L. *The New Haven Railroad: Its Rise and Fall.* New York: Hastings House, 1969.

Williams, Frederick H. "Prehistoric Remains of the Tunxis Valley." *Connecticut Quarterly.* January-December 1897.

Williams, Henry Lionel and Williams, Otalie K. *A Guide to Old American Houses 1700-1900.* New York: A. S. Barnes & Co., 1962.

Winchell, Alexander. *Genealogy of the Family of Winchell in America.* Ann Arbor: Dr. Chase's Steam Printing House, 1869.

Winthrop, John, Jr. *The Art of Making Pitch and Tar in New England.* [1662], (Unpublished) *Correspondence of Some of the Founders of the Royal Society of England with Governor Winthrop of Connecticut 1661-1672.* Reprinted from the proceedings of the Massachusetts Historical Society, 1878.

Yeoman, R. S. *A Guide Book of United States Coins.* Racine, Wis.: Western Publishing Co., Inc., 1982.

ILLUSTRATIONS AND CREDITS

THE ILLUSTRATIONS in *East Granby, the evolution of a Connecticut town* came from many sources. Both local residents and the archives of historical institutions within the state proved to be invaluable sources, and the Committee and authors are deeply grateful to all who helped provide such a broad range of subject matter for selection. Of the many illustrations developed specifically for this volume, Edward Phillips' photographs, Daniel Damer's artistic drawings based on research by Betty Guinan, and Barbara Marks' maps are worthy of special note.

In the following, all illustrations are listed chronologically as they appear in the book. The abbreviated title of each is followed by the photographer's or the delineator's name or the source where known and the page number on which the illustration appears.

INDEX

Personal Name Index

Street Name and House Number Index

General Index

IN APPRECIATION

FUNDING for this book has come from many sources, including some annual appropriations from the town and money left over from the town's centennial celebration in 1958.

In 1973 Stuart Higley of New Canaan, Connecticut, paid to have a handwriting expert verify that his ancestor Samuel Higley was the cartographer who prepared the 1732 map of Simsbury, a very important document in East Granby's history.

The East Granby Historical Committee received a grant from the American Revolution Bicentennial Commission of Connecticut in 1976 and one from the George Dudley Seymour Trust in 1982. A specific purpose of this latter fund is the preservation of the history of Connecticut's towns, and the committee has agreed to send a copy of the book to principal public libraries and selected institutions of higher learning in the state.

Contributions were made in memory of Albert P. Cowles by Mr. & Mrs. Laroy Brown, Mr. & Mrs. George L. Guinan, and Mr. & Mrs. Robert R. Patterson.

Contributions were made in memory of Effie H. Miller by Mr. & Mrs. Laroy Brown, Mr. & Mrs. Richard H. Butler, Mr. & Mrs. Howell D. Freeman, Mr. & Mrs. George E. Fryer, Dr. & Mrs. Douglas M. Gay, Mr. & Mrs. George L. Guinan, Astrid T. Hanzalek, Mr. & Mrs. Welcome Jones, Sr., Mr. & Mrs. William S. Mayer, Kathlyn M. Parrick, Mr. & Mrs. John J. Prevo, Mr. & Mrs. Edward R. Thompson, Mrs. Adolph W. Viets, Sr., and the Turkey Hills Study Club.

Many individuals, civic organizations, and businesses assisted with generous contributions in an effort to keep the price of this book in a moderate range. Their assistance is hereby gratefully acknowledged on this and the following page.

Patrons

Norman I. & Alice T. Adams
David R. and Anne D. Barnes
Mr. & Mrs. Laroy Brown
Steven A. & Evelyn S. Caranchini
Charles & Patricia Chatey
Kathleen Guinan Connelly
Dr. Steven R. & Christina Dieterich
Douglas M. Gay
H. Clifford Goslee
Fred G. & Elsie S. Granger
Mr. & Mrs. Gordon F. Granger
Mr. & Mrs. Norman R. Granger
George L. Guinan
Janice L. Guinan
John C. Guinan
John L. Guinan
Stuart Higley
Mr. & Mrs. Walter D. Hill
Hubert C. & Hope W. Holden
Thomas F. & Virginia Howard
Amy & Charles Hunderlach
Mr. & Mrs. Arthur J. Ide
Dr. & Mrs. Alfred Lederman
William S. & Florence S. Mayer
Mr. & Mrs. Anthony L. Mei
Rufus I. & Ruth Viets Munsell
William Newman
William J. & Beulah Nicholson
Edward L. O'Neill
Mr. & Mrs. Edward F. Phillips
Charles S. & Wyima M. Root
Mr. & Mrs. E.A. Root
Frank R. & Dorothy Rothammer
Elizabeth & Richard Rumohr
Marion N. Seymour
Joseph W. Springman
Mr. & Mrs. Roger Stowell
John Harries Viets
Mildred H. Viets
Mrs. Miriam W. Viets
Ralph H. & Sally P. Viets
Mr. & Mrs. William J. Viets
Walter & Virginia Wileikis
Mr. & Mrs. G. Winthrop Wilson
Mr. & Mrs. William H. Wilson

Civic Organizations

Copper Hill United Methodist Church
East Granby Chamber of Commerce
East Granby Congregational Church
East Granby Democratic Town Committee
The East Granby Garden Club
East Granby Historical Society
East Granby Jaycees
East Granby Lions Club
East Granby Senior Citizens Club
The Women's Club of East Granby

Commercial Sponsors

Atty. Bruce E. Bergman
Colabella Construction Company
Fitzie's Market, Inc.
Gas Turbine Corporation
Robert L. Gordon, D.D.S., P.C.
Homestead Executive Center
Juliar Precision Ball
MAGNATECH - The DSD Company
Mark V Laboratory
Mark's Auto Parts, Inc.
Wm. S. Mayer Agency, Inc.
Northern Connecticut National Bank
Pease, Main & Berger, Attorneys-at-law
Pioneer Pharmacy, Inc.
Roncari Industries, Inc.
The Simsbury Bank & Trust Company
Turbine Engine Services Corp.
United Metal Products Corporation
Winsted Savings Bank

East Granby

the evolution of a Connecticut town

---

has been published in a first edition
of fifteen hundred copies
of which two hundred and fifty
have been numbered and signed
by the authors.
This is copy number

and is here signed.

North Branch of Salmon Brook
Granby
West Branch of Salmon Brook
Monatuk Mountain